WOMEN IN MANAGEMENT WORLDWIDE

We would like to dedicate this book to Dafna Izraeli who died shortly after completing the final draft of her chapter.
She is greatly missed.

Women in Management Worldwide
Facts, Figures and Analysis

Edited by

MARILYN J. DAVIDSON
University of Manchester Institute of Science and Technology, UK

RONALD J. BURKE
York University, Canada

ASHGATE

Published by
Ashgate Publishing Limited
Gower House
Croft Road
Aldershot
Hants GU11 3HR
England

Ashgate Publishing Company
Suite 420
101 Cherry Street
Burlington, VT 05401-4405
USA

Ashgate website: http://www.ashgate.com

British Library Cataloguing in Publication Data
Women in management worldwide : facts, figures and analysis
    1.Women executives - Case studies 2. Women - Social
    conditions - Case studies
    I.Davidson, Marilyn J. II.Burke, Ronald J.
    658.4'0082

Library of Congress Cataloging-in-Publication Data
Women in management worldwide : facts, figures and analysis / edited by Marilyn J.
  Davidson and Ronald J. Burke.
      p. cm.
    Includes bibliographical references and index.
    ISBN 0-7546-0837-9
      1. Women executives--Cross-cultural studies. I. Davidson, Marilyn. I. Burke, Ronald J.

    HD6054.3.W66 2004
    331.4--dc22

                                                                    2003058297

ISBN 0 7546 0837 9

Reprinted 2005

Printed and bound in Great Britain by MPG Books Ltd, Bodmin, Cornwall

Contents

SECTION VII: WOMEN IN MANAGEMENT – AFRICA

List of Figures

List of Tables

List of Contributors

Zeynep Aycan is Associate Professor of Cross-Cultural Industrial and Organizational Psychology, Koç University, Istanbul, Turkey.

Ronald J. Burke is Professor of Organizational Behavior, School of Business, York University, Toronto, Canada.

Carlos J. Cabral-Cardoso is Associate Professor of Management, School of Economics and Management, University of Minho, Braga, Portugal.

Fang Lee Cooke is Lecturer in Employment Studies, Manchester School of Management, UMIST, Manchester, UK.

Marilyn J. Davidson is Professor of Managerial Psychology, Co-Director of the Centre For Diversity and Work Psychology, Manchester School of Management, UMIST, Manchester, UK.

Andrew Gale is Senior Lecturer in the Division of Project Management, Manchester Centre for Civil and Construction Engineering, UMIST, Manchester, UK.

Dafna N. Izraeli was a Professor in the Department of Sociology, Bar Ilan University, Ramat Gan, Israel.

Hayat Kabasakal is Professor of Organizational Behaviour, Boğaziçi University, Istanbul, Turkey.

Fahri Karakaş is currently a Ph.D. candidate at McGill University, and usually based at Boğaziçi University, Istanbul, Turkey.

Rekha Karambayya is Associate Professor in Organizational Behaviour and Industrial Relations, Schulich School of Business, York University, Toronto, Canada.

Roberto Kertész is Founder, Argentine Institute of Family Businesses and Rector, University of Flores, Buenos Aires, Argentina.

Ana Kessler is Economical and Financial Consultant specializing in Small and Medium Enterprise and Former Director of the Board of Buenos Aires Warranty Fund, Buenos Aires, Argentina.

Athena Petraki Kottis is Professor of Economics, Athens University of Economics and Business, Department of Business Administration, Athens, Greece.

Haydée Kravetz is Dean of the School of Administration, University of Flores, Buenos Aires, Argentina.

Babita Mathur-Helm is Senior Lecturer of Business Administration in Organizational Development and Transformation and Gender Development, University of Stellenbosch Business School, University of Stellenbosch, Cape Town, South Africa.

Eunice McCarthy is Director, Social and Organisational Psychology Research Centre, University College Dublin, Dublin, Ireland.

Judy McGregor is Equal Employment Opportunity Commissioner of the Human Rights Commission, Wellington, New Zealand.

Susan Michie is currently a Ph.D. candidate in the Department of Management, Oklahama State University, Stillwater, Oklahoma, USA.

Debra L. Nelson is the CBA Associates Professor of Management, Department of Management, Oklahoma State University, Stillwater, Oklahoma, USA.

Zoe Ventoura Neokosmidi is Lecturer in Economics, Athens University of Economics and Business, Department of Business Administration, Athens, Greece.

Azura Omar is currently a Ph.D. candidate at Manchester School of Management, UMIST, Manchester, UK.

Larissa Polnareva is General Director of St Petersburg Construction Partnership, St Petersburg, Russia.

Astrid M. Richardsen is Associate Professor, Department of Leadership and Organizational Management, Norwegian School of Management, Sandvika, Norway.

Renata Siemieńska is Professor of Sociology, Institute of Sociology, Institute for Social Studies, Warsaw University, Warsaw, Poland.

Leonie V. Still is Director, Centre for Women and Business, Graduate School of Management, The University of Western Australia, Perth, Australia.

Kea G. Tijdens is Research Coordinator, Amsterdam Institute for Advanced Labour Studies (AIAS), University of Amsterdam, Amsterdam, The Netherlands.

Laura E. Mercer Traavik is Associate Professor, Department of Leadership and Organizational Management, Norwegian School of Management, Sandvika, Norway.

Fiona M. Wilson is Professor of Organizational Behaviour, Department of Business and Management, University of Glasgow, Glasgow, UK.

Alison E. Woodward is Professor of Sociology and Political Science and Professor of International Affairs and Politics, Vesalius College, Vrije, University of Brussels, Brussels, Belgium.

Gina Zabludovsky is Professor and Researcher of Sociology, Facultat de Ciencias Políticas y Sociales, Universidad Nacional Autónoma de México, UNAM, México.

Acknowledgements

We would like to acknowledge the assistance of Cath Hearne for her dedication and expertise in the co-ordination of the chapters and managing of correspondence. Her enthusiasm and initiative have proved invaluable.

Chapter 1

Women in Management Worldwide: Facts, Figures and Analysis – An Overview

Marilyn J. Davidson and Ronald J. Burke

Introduction

Women have entered the workplace in increasing numbers during the past two decades, in all developed countries. Furthermore, a number of broad forces worldwide, have resulted in more women entering managerial and professional careers. More economies have become industrialized; the expansion of financial services and the service sector more generally, has opened up positions for women. The growth in the public sector in some countries, has also created new opportunities for women. Changes in societal attitudes towards working women (particularly those married/partnered with children), along with political and legal changes (of varying degrees), have also taken place providing additional impetuses for this trend.

Nevertheless, the pace of change in relation to women professionals and managers, has often been slow and progress has generally been uneven in different countries and cultures (Wirth, 2001). Many of these women have prepared themselves for careers by undertaking higher and university education. In the USA for example, women now comprise almost half of the graduates of professional schools such as accounting, business and law (Catalyst, 1999; 2000). Research evidence suggests that these graduates enter the workforce at levels comparable to their male colleagues and with similar credentials and expectations, but it seems that women's and men's corporate experience and career paths begin to diverge soon after that point (Davidson and Burke, 2000).

It is evident that although managerial and professional women are at least as well educated and trained as their male counterparts and are (in many countries) being hired by organizations in approximately equal numbers, they are not entering the ranks of senior management at comparable rates. The supply of qualified women for these management jobs has increased steadily as more women accumulate experience and education. Women are more likely to occupy managerial jobs in fields in which more women are employed in non-management jobs (Catalyst, 1999a; 2000).

Women are gaining the necessary experience and paying their dues but still encounter a 'glass ceiling' (Powell, 1999). The relative failure of these women to move into the ranks of senior management, in both private- and public-sector organizations in all developed countries has been well documented (Adler and Izraeli, 1988; Davidson and Cooper, 1993). According to Wirth (2001):

> Women's interest in professional and managerial work and the predicted shortages of highly qualified managers have not, however, resulted in women obtaining senior executive positions in significant numbers. The glass ceiling continues to limit women's access to senior management and to management positions in those sectors and areas which involve more responsibilities and higher pay (p.26).

Why should organizations be interested in developing and utilizing the talents of women? Schwartz (1992) summarizes reasons why supporting the career aspirations of talented and successful managerial women makes good business sense. These include:

- Obtaining the best people for leadership positions, giving the chief executive officer (CEO) experience in working with capable women;
- Providing female role models for younger high-potential women, ensuring that companies' opportunities for women will be noticed by both women graduates in recruiting and women customers; and
- Guaranteeing that all ranks of management will be filled with strong executives.

The recruitment, hiring and development of managerial women is increasingly seen as a bottom-line issue related to corporate success.

Research on women in management has reflected these changes in organizations. The first women in management researchers asked 'Why are there so few women in management?', and their work had an impact on the practice of management. Early writers (e.g. Riger and Galligan, 1980; Hennig and Jardim, 1977) considered both person-centred (personality traits, skills, education) and situation-centred factors (different rewards and training opportunities, men's attitudes, token status). It was concluded that person-centred variables were less important than situation-centred variables in explaining the small numbers of women in management.

The appearance of the American Publication *Breaking the Glass Ceiling* (Morrison et al., 1987) gave renewed energy to women in management research. This book, with its attendant publicity, captured the attention of women managers and professionals, researchers interested in women in management issues, and organizations interested in furthering the careers of managerial and professional women. Later reviews predominantly from North America and the UK (Burke and

McKeen, 1992; Davidson and Cooper, 1992; 1993; Morrison and Von Glinow, 1990) showed that women had made considerable progress in some areas (entering the workforce, occupying managerial and professional jobs) but limited progress in other areas (senior management jobs, top wage earners, clout positions, corporate directorships).

This interest, coupled with increased research attention, highlighted the importance to business leaders and educators of understanding the impact of large numbers of managerial and professional women entering the workplace. These demographic changes are some of the most significant organizational changes taking place in the industrialized world. During the 1980s and 1990s the numbers of women in management (broadly defined) in many countries worldwide, increased substantially. Yet, the numbers of women holding top management positions has held fairly constant. This leads to a second, and more contemporary, question: 'Why are there so few women in top management?'.

Catalyst (1998) has identified the following as the most powerful barriers to female career advancement:

- Negative assumptions in executive ranks about women, their abilities and their commitment to careers;
- Perceptions that women don't fit with the corporate culture;
- Lack of career planning and the range of job experiences commensurate with the future needs of the organization;
- Lack of core opportunities for female employees who have management potential;
- Assumption that women will not relocate for career advancement;
- Failure to make managers accountable for advancing women;
- Management reluctance to giving women line (that is, revenue-generating) experience;
- Absence of, or too limited, succession planning;
- 'Negative mentoring' and self-selection where women move into staff areas instead of line positions;
- Lack of mentoring and exclusion from informal career networks, where men have typically learned the unwritten rules of success;
- Appraisal and compensation systems that are not uniform for men and women;
- Corporate systems designed prior to women's large-scale infusion into the workplace, such as benefits systems and productivity measures that don't take into account new policies such as flexible work arrangements;
- Other forms of 'cultural discouragement', like a work environment that values long hours over actual performance or that offers limited support for work-family initiatives and limited commitment to diversity programmes in general;
- Discrimination and sexual harassment.

Powell (1999) addressed more specifically the issue of why the proportion of women in top management has remained relatively small. He noted that there are many interested and qualified male candidates for senior jobs. It is difficult to prevent bias and discrimination at these levels, because objective credentials (e.g. more education) are less important at these levels, and male decision makers at the top are more likely to use gender-based models and criteria in selection. Men may be more comfortable with other men, and may view women as less competent. Decision processes at top levels of the organization are often unstructured and unscrutinized. Women at lower organizational levels may not be developed or groomed as often or as well, and may have more trouble getting mentors. In addition, women themselves may select out of top jobs because of family responsibilities, and the desire to make fewer personal sacrifices (Powell and Graves, 2003). Frustrated by the glass ceiling, they may quit, often to start their own businesses (Fielden and Davidson, in press).

As business becomes increasingly global, competitive pressures increase accordingly, and demographic arguments still persist. In Europe for example, only Finland does not have a negative birth rate and according to the Commission of the European Communities, Directorate General for Employment, Industrial Relations and Social Affairs, recruitment in Europe beyond 2010 will continue to be difficult (Bank, 1999). Firms are searching for the best talent available to respond to these forces. Unfortunately, too many firms unnecessarily limit the pool of managerial talent on which they draw. Although women represent almost half the workforce worldwide, females continue to represent a low percentage of senior management (Wirth, 2001).

Aims of book

Women in management research is now increasingly being conducted in a greater number of countries, reflecting both the globalization of business and the international competition for talent and the increasing numbers of women pursuing professional and managerial careers (Davidson and Burke, 2000; Burke and Nelson, 2001). Cross-cultural research on women in management issues however, still remains an under-researched and underdeveloped area of study (Cahoon and Rowney, 2001). Interestingly, as more countries enter the free trade arrangements (WAFTA, EEU) it becomes easier for managers (and workers in general), to move across countries. Nevertheless, it is too soon to determine how this potential increase in labour mobility will impact on women's careers.

We had several objectives in mind for this book which included:

- Understanding more about the status of women at work and women in management in a number of countries throughout the world;
- Begin a process for collecting common information in a variety of countries to capture both trend over time and support comparisons across countries;
- Collect baseline information to provide benchmark data indicating the current status of women in management;

- Facilitate more cross-cultural research in this area;
- Encourage the exchange of research findings as well as company 'best practice' efforts;
- Shed light on the role of country culture on women's career advancement and international career assignments;
- Encourage more research in this area, and more collaborative research across countries;
- Raise the issues in utilizing the best talents available.

We attempted to solicit chapter contributions from countries in all major regions of the world, including both developed and developing economies. We invited authors from our target countries based on their previous research and publications in the women and management areas, those that were known to the editors and individuals that were nominated by others in a particular country. (Interestingly, one of our potential contributors indicated that her country did not systematically collect information of the kind we wanted to include, and consequently declined our invitation.) Some chapters in this collection, e.g. Malaysia, are the first description of women in management in that specific country.

The book is divided into seven sections evaluating women in management in: European Union countries i.e. Greece, Belgium, Ireland, the Netherlands, Portugal and the United Kingdom; Europe i.e. Norway, Poland and Russia; North and Central America i.e. Canada, Mexico and the USA; Australasia i.e. New Zealand and Australia; Asia i.e. China, Malaysia, Turkey and Israel; South America i.e. Argentina; and finally Africa i.e. South Africa.

The contributors representing different countries in each chapter, not only detail more fully the most recent available employment statistics, but also help to unravel some of the reasons for similarities and differences between the countries. Here, discrepancies based on such issues as different traditions, cultures, historical events and political history, ethnicity, religion, education, training, legislation, management, entrepreneurs, attitudes and behaviours, employment conditions, employment rights and benefits (including home/life balance issues), equal opportunity policies, practices and initiatives, as well as positive action and diversity programmes, are discussed. In order to facilitate cross-cultural comparisons of facts, figures and analysis of the position of women in management in each of the different countries, contributing authors have adhered to common topic subheadings throughout their respective chapters.

Obviously, the availability of relevant employment statistics broken down by gender and ethnicity varies from country to country, as well as the differing volumes of relevant published research. Nevertheless, the authors highlight specific problems and barriers being experienced by women in management and business in their countries and examine the effects on these women and organizations. In addition, they examine ways of reducing these problems, highlighting examples of good practice and positive initiatives for present and future practice, so that the opportunities to enter management, and climb the corporate ladder, are as accessible to women as they are to men.

Throughout this book it will be evident that of the issues raised by the authors in each of the chapters, some are specific to their own country and a number are common across many of the countries. Let us explore, therefore, what are some of the commonalities and differences between countries with regard to the plight of women in management and business and the ways in which particular countries are dealing with it.

Similarities and differences between countries

Labour force characteristics

Throughout almost all the countries, the common trend has been that over the past twenty years, the proportion of women in the paid workforce (particularly married women with children and part-time workers) has increased and today ranges from 30 per cent (in Turkey) to 53 per cent (in the Netherlands). These two countries have very different female demographic work profiles. In Turkey, the majority of working women are concentrated in the rural, rather than urban areas, often in unpaid family work, including agriculture and home-based production. In the Netherlands, on the other hand, they have the highest percentage of female part-time workers in the E.U. with two-thirds of all working women being part-timers and few distinctions between rural versus urban locations. It should also be noted that some countries also have significant ethnic and national differences in the demographics of their female workforce. In Israel for instance, 53 per cent of Jewish women are in paid employment, compared to only 17.5 per cent of Muslim women. Similarly, due to the stricter religious codes of conduct for Muslim women, in Malaysia, the employment of Malay women is lower than that of Chinese women.

Certainly, there is still great concern about the provision of childcare facilities in many countries, which are felt to be prerequisite to encouraging women to enter the world of business and management. Interestingly, however, supported by the provision of adequate childcare and the 'one child policy', unlike most other countries, the majority of Chinese women work full-time and have uninterrupted work profiles. Nevertheless, despite constituting 47 per cent of the total workforce, fewer Chinese women occupy managerial or professional positions compared to their British, American or Japanese counterparts. Although China and Russia have been found to have the least occupational gender segregation compared to the other countries featured in this book, women are still concentrated in clerical and lower-level manual work. Interestingly, in Russia where unlike many other countries, women dominate certain occupations such as economists, doctors and engineers – these occupations are assigned less status than in countries where they are categorized as 'male occupations'. What is evident, is that occupational segregation by gender (both horizontally and vertically/hierarchically) has tended to persist in all the countries, with the occupations women hold and the areas of work they manage, having remained fairly constant over the past few decades. This has been the case even in countries such as the USA and Australia who have introduced legislative Affirmative Action Policies. In Australia for example, 56 per cent of all employed women are concentrated in two occupations – clerks and sales, and personnel services. Furthermore, in every single country, the pay gap between women and men's earning persists. In Poland and Canada, for instance, the income for women is now 80 per cent of men's and this has not changed in Poland since the transformation of the political and economic system. In Norway, men and women's difference in earnings is the same as in Russia, and has remained the constant over the past 25 years, i.e. 65 per cent of men's despite some of the strongest legislation in the EU! Moreover, in Ireland where the pay differential gap is smaller at 15.5 per cent, it has been estimated it will take another 40 years to close.

Women pursuing education

Linked to some extent to the increasing numbers of women in the workplace, has been the increasing numbers of women entering higher education. With the exceptions of China (35 per cent) and Mexico (49 per cent), over 50 per cent of higher education students in all the countries represented in this book, were female. As well, in numerous countries, the proportion of women taking management and business degrees has not only increased over the past twenty years, but is now greater than that of men (see Table 1.1). Furthermore, the percentage of women taking postgraduate business qualifications has also increased and in countries such as Canada for example, they now constitute 30 per cent of all Master of Business Administration (MBA) students.

Table 1.1 Women enrolled in higher education/university and those studying management and business degrees

Women as a percentage of all students

Country	In Higher Education/ University*	Taking Management/ Business Degrees*
Greece	50	53
Belgium	50	38
Ireland	50	-
Netherlands	50	-
Portugal	57	-
UK	55	50
Norway	61	30**
Poland	57	60

Russia	55	81***
Canada	56	49
Mexico	49	56
USA	57	-
New Zealand	-	50
Australia	58	-
China	42	-
Malaysia	55	64
Turkey	41	35
Israel	57	48
Argentina	52	40
South Africa	-	-

*   Latest available data – category definitions vary between countries
**   Elite Business Degree
***   Economics and Management

However, most of the authors in the differing chapters acknowledge that the majority of university subjects have kept constant in their sex typing over time, with women still concentrated in the arts and men dominating subjects such as physical sciences, engineering, information technology (I.T.) and construction. Nevertheless, in several countries such as Belgium and the Netherlands, certain faculties such as medicine, law and psychology have faced a feminization with over half of the students now being female. Not surprisingly, the least gender segregated universities by subject, are to be found in Poland, Russia and China. Interestingly, political and governmental changes in the new Russia has meant a dramatic decrease in women engineering students for example, which has dropped from 58 per cent in 1995 to 30 per cent in 2002.

Women in management

It can be seen from Table 1.2 that the percentage of women as managers in the various countries ranges from a low 2 per cent in Malaysia to 45 per cent in the USA. Interestingly, a country such as Russia which has less occupational segregation in the workplace or in its student population, has one of the lowest percentages (i.e. 11 per cent) of women managers. Similarly, China with the highest percentage of full-time workers who are female, has very few female managers (only 8 per cent of all managers in large firms).

Table 1.2 Women in management and business worldwide

Working females as a percentage of all

Country*	Managers	Entrepreneurs/ Self-employed
Greece	11**	27
Belgium	31	29
Ireland	34	-
Netherlands	33	32
Portugal	27	-
UK	24	26
Norway	26	29
Poland	30	50
Russia	32	36
Canada	35	35
Mexico	17	31
USA	45	25
New Zealand	27	-
Australia	23	33
China	8***	-
Malaysia	2	25
Turkey	8	11
Israel	26	6
Argentina	28	39
South Africa	28	25

*   Category definitions vary between countries
**   Largest firms only
*** Government organizations only

While it is important to note that the category definitions of 'manager' vary between countries, undoubtedly the proportion of women as managers has tended to gradually increase in many countries over the past few decades; however, advances have often been slow. Indeed, in Canada, the percentage of women has dropped from 37 per cent in 1996 to 35 per cent in 2001. In all the countries represented in this book, women managers are still concentrated in lower level management jobs in sectors associated with people and services rather than the higher paid energy, IT and transport industries. They continue to earn less than their male counterparts at every level of the managerial hierarchy (including Board level), and find it difficult to break the glass ceiling into senior executive positions. This is even the case in the USA where 45 per cent of management positions are occupied by women and yet they constitute only 5 per cent of senior management (a percentage which has hardly changed in the past quarter century).

There are also country differences in the socio-economic class, ethnic and religious composition of women managers and professionals. In the USA for example, black women are the largest group of minority women and Bell and Nkomo (2001) found dramatic differences in black and white women's career progress in American corporations. Although the women in their study shared some common work experiences, race and class often created tensions between white and black women. Interestingly, white women often aligned themselves more often with white men than black women. The profile of the managerial hierarchy in the USA still consists of white men at the top, then white women, then black women, then black men. Gender, race and social class are all connected.

In contrast in Canada, Asian women (Chinese) are the largest female minority management group. On the other hand, in South Africa despite white people only constituting 13 per cent of the total workforce, 41 per cent of all managers are white males and 28 per cent are females (12 per cent of these being black, coloured or Asian).

Clearly, all these groups of minority women enter the workplace and more specifically, management positions; with dramatically different histories, expectations and experiences. To date, many groups of minority women in various countries and cultures, have remained largely invisible in the women in management literature (Davidson, 1997). From the evidence presented in this book, even the demographic breakdown of these women is still unavailable in some countries and many questions still often remain unanswered - what are the career needs of minority women managers?; how do minority women understand and experience their racial, cultural, religious and gender identities?; how can companies deal with cross-race and cross-gender dynamics? Clearly, minority women managers do not have access to the same power and privilege and are likely to have different work experiences, identities and paths to advancement.

Finally, in many countries it would appear that more women are now undertaking international job assignments. As business becomes more global, firms are becoming more transnational. Transnational firms not only employ women expatriates; these firms are also more likely to hire women managers than ever supported by the local culture of a particular country. Moreover, by hiring women managers and professionals, transnational firms often serve as role models for other companies that would not have considered promoting women into managerial jobs.

Women entrepreneurs

Many of the difficulties women experience in corporate environments (including home/work conflicts) in the different countries, have been highlighted in this book, and although some progress is being made in many countries to develop strategies to help women managers, these barriers have also encouraged many to consider setting up their own businesses. As can be noted in Table 1.2, between 6 per cent and 50 per cent of enterpreneurs/self-employed are women. What is clear from the data presented throughout this collection, is that this trend seems to be increasing worldwide and indeed, official statistics may well be an underestimation. Allen (1999) for example, pointed out that a survey in the EC found that the numbers of women who worked independently or ran their own business, or work unsalaried in their partner's business, was higher by some 10 million women than those recorded by official Eurostat figures. Certainly a dominant type of self-employment for women still continues to be unincorporated business without paid help and in Canada alone, this category of women constitutes 61 per cent of all self-employed women. Similarly, in Turkey official statistics indicate that only 7 per cent of entrepreneurs are female and excludes the many Turkish women who are restricted to working in the home (e.g. weaving). Due in part to the patriarchal relationships in Turkish society and families, it is only the men who deal with outside relationships and receive financial payment from customers and clients.

While the majority of female-owned businesses are small and often stereotypically female in the services-producing sector, there are indications that in some countries at least, female entrepreneurs are beginning to diversify into different types of businesses. In the USA for example, the 'new generation' of female business owners are better educated and moving into non-traditional industries such as agricultural services, transportation and communication, and construction. Moreover, one in five of female-owned firms are now headed by a minority and female business owners are focusing more on growth and expansion compared to their female predecessors. However, compared to their male counterparts, on the whole, women business owners worldwide, are still earning less and are more likely to encounter problems regarding access to financial support and sexual stereotyping and discrimination from others (including banks, clients and customers) (Fielden and Davidson, in press).

Legislation and initiatives supporting women in the workforce

Another issue that seems to emerge throughout this book, is the mechanism by which women obtain management jobs in the first place. In a number of countries the issue of either voluntary or legislated affirmative action is now on the agenda following Pay and Gender Equality Acts, as well as family friendly policies such as maternity and paternity leave etc. The failure of Equal Pay legislation to completely close the pay differentials between men and women is evident in every single country. What is also clear, is that gender equality legislation alone, without sufficient clout or sanctions (as well as a lack of changes in societal attitudes), has limited effect on change to the status quo. Norway, for instance is an example of social welfare policies and political initiatives that promote equality, and yet have failed to achieve the desired results. Parental leave is still predominantly taken by mothers and it has been suggested that some legislation has had unintentioned effects. For example, financial incentives to encourage parents (particularly fathers) to spend more time at home with their children has been taken up predominantly by mothers and reduced the number of employed mothers in the Norwegian workforce by 18 per cent.

Undoubtedly, Affirmative Action Legislation with strong punitive incentives in countries such as the USA and Canada, has substantially increased the proportion of women in management positions. Nevertheless, glass ceilings still exist at senior executive and board levels and partly due to 'backlashes' against affirmative action policy, there has been a shift towards making equal opportunities attractive to employers via the business case of diversity management. According to Davidson and Fielden (2003, p.xxii):

> Managing Diversity initiatives seek to fully develop the potential of each employee and turn the different sets of skills that each employee brings into a business advantage. Through the fostering of difference, team creativity, innovation and problem-solving can often be enhanced. The focus is therefore, much more on the individual rather than the group. Having a diverse workforce not only enables organizations to understand and meet customer demand better, but also helps attract investors and clients, as well as reduce the costs associated with discrimination.

Certainly, changes in corporate cultures to ones in which diversity was valued, managed and embraced, was rarely reported in the countries included in this book. Organizational life was too often imbued with 'male values' of dominance, aggression, competition and 'transmitting' rather than 'receiving' information. Corporate cultures need to change to encourage listening skills, problem resolution, support co-operation, participation and negotiation. Interestingly, previous leadership research has reported cultural universality from some leadership behaviours (supportive, charismatic, contingent reward) and cultural specificity for others (directive, participative, contingent punishment). Moreover, Den Hertog and his colleagues (1999) found that attributes associated with charismatic/transformational leadership were universally endorsed cross-culturally in 62 cultures, as contributing to outstanding leadership.

Most importantly, individualism needs to be valued regardless of their ethnic origin, religion, age or disability. These changes in the workplace will benefit all individuals, males and females. Increasingly, the evidence is mounting that confrontation, competition and the 'macho' management style are producing more workplace stress and less productivity (Sutherland and Cooper, 2000). In many countries, organizations are demanding long hours, at a time when both partners are working. Certainly problems, stresses and dilemmas related to home/work conflicts are still very real issues in relation to career development and aspirations of women managers throughout the world. A recent study in the UK for example, has found that in families where both the mother and father have jobs, one in five mothers and twice as many fathers were at work between 6.30 am and 8.30 am. In the evening, a quarter of mothers and 45 per cent of fathers regularly worked between 5.30 pm and 8.30 pm (Greenhill, 2002).

The future

Overall, the facts, figures and analysis of the position of women in management in the 21 countries represented in this book, have revealed some positive aspects in many of the countries: more women in management, more supportive government policies and organizational practices, changing family roles and responsibilities, the availability of more widespread support systems, improved economic and labour market conditions and changes in demographic characteristics of the populations offering more opportunities to women.

However, some aspects of the picture are proving slow to change, even in those countries with higher percentages of women as managers. Men still dominate senior executive positions, CEO positions and board directorships. Women still face discrimination and gender stereotyping (in addition to ethnic, cultural and religious stereotyping).

Concerning the factors that continue to limit women's advancement in management careers, these are widespread: discrimination and prejudices, organizational culture/policies and practices that hinder women's progress and ineffectual discriminatory legislation. It follows then, that change efforts should be directed toward these obstacles. This is particularly important taking into account we have entered a new millennium to find some countries (e.g. Australia, Canada and Norway) are reporting a situation in which the proportion of women as managers seems to have plateaued with little dramatic change expected in either opportunities or numbers under present circumstances. In Norway, the Centre for Gender Equality has estimated that at the current rate of overall increase, it will take another 62 years to achieve gender equality in senior management and 115 years before equality is reached on corporate boards.

Clearly, efforts to increase the proportion of women into management (at all levels) at a faster rate worldwide, should not diminish. The review and arguments presented from the country contributors throughout this book, reinforce Powell and Grave's (2003) assertion that there are a number of complex factors that affect the number and various sub-groups of women in management, including societal norms regarding women's roles and women's educational attainment. Other factors relate to the demand for labour, the participation rates of women relative to men, and the structure of the economy. In addition to legislative factors, there are organizational factors cited by Powell (1999): enforcement of equal opportunity/affirmative action, organizational attitudes toward equality and diversity, and organizational work/family initiatives. These factors should be the target of ongoing efforts to ensure women's participation in management positions.

Understanding the experiences of this large and growing segment of the workforce, in whom education, effort and hopes have been invested, is critical for economic survival. Organizations cannot afford to under-utilize or lose this talent. There is a need for both changes in societal attitudes (including the media) and individual behaviour. Educators need to understand the barriers encountered by women, both in organizations employing them and in their own educational institutions, and managerial and professional women need to understand why they are experiencing particular work situations.

We hope this book will serve to interest more organizational researchers to consider women-in-management issues; to develop projects in areas that are just now emerging, and to envision projects that will have value to the individuals whose work and life experiences we are trying to better understand, women and men in managerial and professional jobs, and organizations that are currently struggling with developing a level playing field. These demographic changes and the questions they raise have the potential for creating new ways of thinking about work, careers and organizational purposes and policies, as well as family and leisure. Governments and worldwide organizations must grasp the significance of these issues, adjust to them, and focus on the positive opportunities these forces offer. The economic success of business hinges on their efforts.

References

Adler, N.J. and Izraeli, D.N. (1988), *Women in Management Worldwide*, Armonk, NY: M.E. Sharpe.

Allen, S. (1999), 'Gender inequality and divisions of labour', in H. Beynoon and P. Glavanis (eds), *Patterns of Social Inequality*, Longman: London.

Bank, J. (1999), 'Dividends of diversity', *Management Focus Issue*, **12**, Summer (Cranfield School of Management), 1-10.

Burke, R.J. and McKeen, C.A. (1992), 'Women in Management', in Cooper, C.L. and Robertson, I.T. (eds), *International Review of Industrial and Organizational Psychology*, New York: Wiley, pp. 245-284.

Burke, R.J. and Nelson, D.L. (2001), *Advancing Women's Careers: Research and Practice*, London: Blackwell.

Cahoon, A.R. and Rowney, J. (2001), 'Valuing diversity in a global economy: The sad state of organizations and gender', in Golembiewski, R.T. (ed.), *Handbook of Organizational Behavior*, New York: Marcel Dekker, pp. 457-490.

Catalyst (1996), *Women Corporate Leadership: Progress and Prospects*, New York: Catalyst.

Catalyst (1998), *Advancing Women in Business: The Catalyst Guide*, San Francisco, CA: Jossey-Bass.

Catalyst (1999), *The 1999 Catalyst Census of Women Corporate Officers and Top Earners*, New York: Catalyst.

Catalyst (2000), *The 1999 Catalyst Census of Women Corporate Officers of Canada*, New York: Catalyst.

Davidson, M.J. (1997), *The Black and Ethnic Minority Woman Manager: Cracking the Concrete Ceiling*, London: Chapman/Sage.

Davidson, M.J. and Burke, R.J. (eds) (2000), *Women in Management: Current Research Issues Volume II*, Thousand Oaks, CA: Sage Publications.

Davidson, M.J. and Cooper, C.L. (1992), *Shattering The Glass Ceiling: The Woman Manager*, London: Paul Chapman.

Davidson, M.J. and Cooper, C.L. (eds) (1993), *European Women in Business and Management*, London: Paul Chapman.

Davidson, M.J. and Fielden, S.L. (eds) (2003), *Individual Diversity and Psychology in Organizations: Wiley Handbooks in the Psychology of Management in Organizations*, Chichester: Wiley.

Den Hertog, D.N., House, R.J., Hanges, P.J., Ruiz-Quintanilla, S.A. and Dorfman, P.W. (1999), 'Culture specific and cross culturally generalizable implicit leadership theories: Are attributes of charismatic/transformational leadership universally endorsed?', *Leadership Quarterly*, **10**, 219-256.

Fielden, S.L. and Davidson, M.J. (eds), *International Handbook of Women and Small Business Entrepreneurship*, in press.

Greenhill, S. (2002), *Long-Hours Culture Hits Family Life-Studies*, Press Release, P.A. News based on Joseph Rowntree Foundation Study, York: UK.

Morrison, A.M. and Von Glinow, M.A. (1990), 'Women and Minorities in Management', *American Psychologist*, **45**, 200-208.

Morrison, A.M., White, R.P. and Van Velsor, E. (1987), *Breaking the Glass Ceiling*, Reading, MA: Addison-Wesley.

Powell, G.N. (1999), *Handbook of Gender and Work*, Thousand Oaks, CA: Sage Publications.

Powell, G.N. and Graves, L.M. (2003), *Women and Men in Management (3rd Edition)*, London: Sage.

Riger, P. and Galligan, S. (1980), 'Women in management: An exploration of competing paradigms', *American Psychologist*, **35**, 902-910.

Schwartz, F.N. (1992), *Breaking with Tradition: Women and Work, The New Facts of Life*, New York: Warner.

Sutherland, V. and Cooper, C.L. (2000), *Strategic Stress Management – An Organizational Approach*, London: Macmillan.

Wirth, L. (2001), *Breaking Through The Glass Ceiling – Women in Management*, Geneva: International Labour Office.

SECTION I
WOMEN IN MANAGEMENT –
EUROPEAN UNION COUNTRIES

Chapter 2

Women in Management in Greece

Athena Petraki Kottis and Zoe Ventoura Neokosmidi[*]

Introduction

Women's relative position in Greece has improved in many respects in recent decades. However, existing evidence shows that gender inequality is highly prevalent. Women continue to be in a rather disadvantageous position in the workplace, in decision-making mechanisms and at home. In almost all areas of activity their possibilities and prospects for professional advancement are much inferior compared to men. Greece has a long way to go to achieve gender equality.

In this chapter we present information concerning women's relative position in employment and in higher-level managerial and other activity in the country and discuss issues related to gender inequality. Despite the importance of this subject, and contrary to what has happened in many other developed countries, there has been very little research and bibliography in this area in Greece. The lack of required statistical data prevents an in-depth analysis. As a result, we will limit our exposition to what the available information allows.

Labour force characteristics

Evidence relating to women's situation in the labour market indicates that during the last two decades there has been considerable improvement in many areas. However, this is not to the extent that one would expect on the basis of the experience in other developed countries (Petraki Kottis, 1990). Moreover, there have been certain negative developments, such as a steep rise in women's unemployment rates, creating new problems for them.

In the year 2000, women in Greece constituted 52 per cent of the population of 15 years and over, and only 37.7 per cent of employed persons. The majority of women were clustered in traditional industries and occupations. Their unemployment rate was more than double of that for men. The unemployment rate for women below 25 years was 37.7 per cent. A considerable part of employed women were unpaid assistants in family businesses. This type of employment is particularly disadvantageous because it makes women dependent upon other family members, usually men.

Looking at the educational background of the labour force we observe that women have higher educational qualifications compared to men, and are constantly improving in this regard. In the year 2000, about one-third of women in the labour force had a post-secondary education degree while only one-quarter of men had such a degree.

Table 2.1 presents statistical information concerning women's position in the labour market within the last two decades. In brief, the following observations can be made about the changes that have been observed:

- A substantial increase in women's participation in the labour force and in employment. However, the relevant rates are considerably lower compared to those in other developed countries.
- A striking rise in women's share in employment growth. In the period 1980-1990 the absolute increase in women's employment was larger than the increase in total employment, while in the period 1990-2000, 80 per cent of the new job creation went to women.
- A decrease in the proportion of women employed in the primary and secondary sectors, and a parallel increase in their proportion in the tertiary sector.
- A considerable fall in the proportion of employed women working as unpaid assistants in family businesses.
- A steep rise in women's unemployment rates and in their share in unemployment. Women's share in long term unemployment was relatively high and showed an increase.
- A constant growth in the percentage of employed women having more than secondary education.

Table 2.1 Women's labour market situation, 1981-2000

	1981 %	1990 %	2000 %
Women's labour force participation rate	29.8	34.9	38.7
Women's share in the labour force	31.9	37.1	40.3
Women's employment rate	28.1	30.8	32.3
Women's share in employment	31.3	35.2	37.7
Women's unemployment rate	5.7	11.7	16.7
Women's share in unemployment	44.9	61.8	60.6
Women's share in long-term unemployment	61.5	68.9	65.1
Ratio of women's to men's unemployment rate	1.7	2.7	2.3
% of employed women working as unpaid assistants	36.2	27.7	16.8
% of women in the labour force with more than secondary education	29.9	44.1	61.4

Source: Unpublished data, National Statistical Service of Greece, Labour Force Survey, 2000

The data for the occupational structure of women's employment (Table 2.2) indicate that their participation in the group of legislators, senior officials and managers is relatively small. However, their share in scientific and artistic occupations is larger than their share in employment. On the other hand, more than half of non-specialized workers were women.

Table 2.2 Women in one-digit occupational groups

One-digit occupational groups	% of women
Legislators, senior officials and managers	25.4
Scientific and artistic occupations	46.7
Specialized personnel	47.5
Office clerks	57.8
Service workers and sale workers	51.4
Agricultural and fishery workers	42.9
Craft and related trade workers	13.8
Plant and machine operators and assemblers	9.5
Non-specialized workers	52.3
Unclassified workers	7.7
Total labour force	37.7

Source: Unpublished data, National Statistical Service of Greece, Labour Force Survey, 2000

Women's participation in employment in the public sector has increased in recent decades more than that of men and is higher than that in the private sector. In 1998, 40.7 per cent of all tenured employees in the civil service administration were women. Despite women's concentration in the lower ranks, their relative position in the public sector is better than in the private sector.

There has been a rapid increase in the number of women employed in positions related to new technology in both the public and the private sectors. However, women cluster in lower-level tasks such as key punching and have low participation in higher-level positions. In a recent survey covering the public sector it was found that women constituted 99.5 per cent of key-punching staff and only 10 per cent of computer engineers and scientists (General Secretariat for Equality, 2000).

Women's presence in engineering professions has increased in recent years but remains small. In the year 2000, women constituted only 18.6 per cent of all engineers while close to 40 per cent of women engineers were architects (Greek Women's Engineering Association, 2000).

Finally, turning our attention to pay, women's average earnings have always been considerably lower compared to those of men (Petraki Kottis, 1988). According to 1998 data, the average monthly earnings of women in various sectors ranged between 65 and 80 per cent of those of men. The average hourly earnings of women workers were around 80 per cent of those of men, while in the primary sector they were substantially lower.

Women pursuing education

Girls' participation at all levels of education does not deviate significantly from that of boys. However, there are differences in the subjects they choose to study. Women's enrolment at higher education institutions comes close to 50 per cent of total enrolment. In certain subjects such as literature and social sciences, the proportion of women enrolled is larger than that of men. However, women's enrolment in areas such as physical sciences, engineering, information technology and medicine is substantially lower.

Women's participation in business studies has shown a spectacular increase. In the academic year 1997-98, women's new enrolments in business studies represented 53.3 per cent of enrolments in this area at universities and 63.2 per cent of enrolments at higher technical schools. This constitutes a big change compared to the past. To a smaller extent, there have been positive changes through time in other subjects, such as engineering, in which women were under-represented.

In connection to education, mention should be made of women's participation in teaching. Their percentage among the teaching staff starts from 98.7 in preschool education and decreases dramatically as one moves from lower to higher levels of education. At universities only 24.8 per cent of lecturers are women and most of them are at the lower ranks.

Women in management

Despite the large number of women taking up business studies, relatively few end up in managerial positions. Due to an oversupply of university graduates, many women business graduates are obliged to accept jobs below their qualifications. The majority of those who get managerial positions usually enter and remain at the lower to middle ranks of the hierarchy. Only few women succeed in breaking the glass ceiling and reaching the top of the managerial ladder.

Data concerning women's position in management in Greece is scanty. However, whatever evidence exists shows that the top positions are held mostly by men. Few women can be found at the higher levels of the managerial ladder and in the majority of cases they are daughters or wives of owners of the firms. Prejudices and traditional attitudes concerning gender roles, formal and informal power structures and the unequal division of family responsibilities at home, prevent women from reaching top managerial positions.

Recent information concerning 336 firms listed in the Athens Stock Exchange indicates that only eleven of them had a woman president and only fifteen had a woman general director. In most cases these women were associated with the ownership of the firm.

More revealing, are the results of an in-depth survey conducted in the mid-1990s among 107 of the largest firms in the country (Petraki Kottis, 1996). In 94 per cent of them the president, and in 96 per cent of them the general director was a man. In 43 per cent of those firms, there was no woman on the board of directors and in 36 per cent there was only one woman. In most cases where a woman was at the top of the firm or on the board, she was associated with the ownership of the firm. In 98 per cent of subsidiaries of multinational firms, the person at the top was a man and in none of them was there a woman on the board.

In the firms surveyed by Petraki Kottis (1996), among the persons holding managerial positions at any level, 89 per cent were men. In 31 per cent of the firms there were no women at all holding managerial positions, in 28 per cent there was only one woman among the managerial staff and in 12 per cent there were two. In sum, more than two-thirds of the rather large firms participating in the survey had two or fewer women among their managerial staff. This means that even when women participated in management, in most cases they were a tiny minority.

The most interesting part of the above survey were the answers given by the male top executives to a question concerning the reasons for the relatively small participation of women in management. Almost half of them considered that women did not show the commitment needed for a managerial position because of family responsibilities or their nature and upbringing. Close to half of the respondents acknowledged that there were unjustifiable prejudices against women, preventing them from reaching top positions. Forty one of the respondents held the opinion that there was an insufficient supply of women with the required level of education. This view seems inexplicable, since a large number of women business graduates entered the labour market during the last two decades. It may be that due to conscious or unconscious biases on the part of the respondents, these women did not become visible to them, or that women business graduates refrained from applying to firms employing few or no women. About one-third of the respondents believed that women would quit their careers early because of family responsibilities and it would not be profitable for firms to invest in them. One-quarter of the respondents held the view that women were not interested in greater participation in management and more than one-fifth of the respondents considered that women had abilities for certain types of work, but men were more suitable for managerial positions. Fourteen per cent of the respondents considered that women lacked the characteristics required to undertake positions of high responsibility and ten per cent that the appointment of women to positions with male subordinates would create problems.

It is worth noting that 88 out of the 107 heads of firms, that is 82 per cent of the total, gave as an explanation for the small participation of women in management at least one reason revealing prejudices and biases which undoubtedly created attitudinal and perceptual barriers to women and an environment inimical to their advancement. The striking features of those responses were the importance attributed to women's traditional role in raising children and taking care of household responsibilities, the belief that it was impossible for women to harmonize this role with a managerial career and the view that women lacked certain important characteristics that managers should have.

The views expressed by the few women who held top managerial positions were entirely different. They pointed to the preconceptions and stereotypes that women had to face, the problems from the unequal division of household responsibilities and the vicious circle that discouraged women from participating in training programmes and trying harder. As one woman put it:

> women usually do not advance to leading positions and as a result many of them do not see any purpose in exerting the required effort and in participating in training programmes (Petraki Kottis, 1996).

At present the attitudes of male heads of firms towards women may be less negative because the business world has undergone considerable transformation in recent years. However, as far as the presence of women in top managerial positions is concerned, the situation has not changed much.

A mixed picture is presented by the results of a survey conducted in 1990 of 309 employees, holding various positions in the private and public sectors, about the performance of female managers and the need for equal opportunities for men and women. The views expressed in this survey about women in management were positive, but at the same time doubts were expressed about women's ability to respond to the heavy demands of managerial jobs (Papalexandris and Bourantas, 1991).

The results of a more recent survey conducted by the Granet Network refer to women's presence in top positions in human resource departments. From a sample of 136 firms, each with more than 200 employees, it was found that in the year 2000, 29 per cent of them had a woman in charge of their Human Resource Departments. This represented a significant improvement compared to 1993 when a similar survey was run for the first time (Papalexandris and Nikandrou, 2002). With regard to job performance, the recent survey showed that on the basis of various indicators, women heads of human resource departments exhibited a more dynamic profile and greater professionalism than their male counterparts. The results of an earlier study concerning subordinate satisfaction and leadership styles of men and women managers had not shown any significant gender differences (Bourantas and Papalexandris, 1990). These findings were also recently replicated in another study concerning public relations managers (Panigyrakis and Veloutsou, 1998).

Women in other decision-making positions

Women's participation in higher positions in other areas also has been very small. In the national elections for members of parliament of the year 2000 only 14.3 per cent of the candidates and 10.3 per cent of those elected were women. This was an improvement compared to 1996 when only 6.3 per cent of the elected members of parliament were women. Indeed, the participation of women in the national and local governments and in the European parliament has always been token.

There has been extensive concern and debate, particularly on the part of feminist organizations, about the very limited presence of women in higher political positions. The most frequently mentioned reasons are women's lack of financial resources and political connections and their inability to devote sufficient time to political matters because of the unequal division of family responsibilities at home.

Women are under-represented also in the higher echelons of the public administration services but they are doing better there compared to the private sector. In 1998 about 30 per cent of public employees in charge of directorships were women.

During the last decade women have made significant steps in taking positions at various levels in the judiciary system. About 75 per cent of those entering the judiciary system are women. However, there are no women among the presidents or vice-presidents of the supreme court and the state council while the number of women among the judges of the highest level is less than 10 per cent of the total.

Furthermore, women's participation in the diplomatic corps is constantly increasing but their presence at the higher echelons is minimal. In the year 2000, 23.7 per cent of those serving at various levels of the diplomatic services were women but among the 99 diplomats at the highest levels of the hierarchy only two were female.

Women are also under-represented at the top positions of the labour unions. In the year 2001 there was only one woman among the 45 members of the Governing Board and there were no women in the Executive Committee of the National Confederation of the Greek Labour Unions (GSEE). Women constituted only 9.6 per cent of the members of the boards of labour centres and 9.8 per cent of the members of the boards of labour federations. Although a relatively large proportion of civil servants are women, there were no women among the 17 members of the Executive Committee of the National Confederation of the Unions of Civil Servants (ADEDY).

Women entrepreneurs

Given women's high unemployment rates and their problems in entering and moving up the managerial ladder, entrepreneurial activity seems an attractive alternative for them. Such activity has the advantage of greater work schedule flexibility, enabling these women to reconcile better work with family responsibilities. Nevertheless, there are many obstacles facing female entrepreneurs. For example, finding the capital to start and operate a business has been found to be commonly problematic. In a survey of newly self-employed in the early 1990s, a relatively high percentage of women considered the financial problems as the most serious factor limiting the survival and growth prospects of their enterprises (Haratsis et al., 1993). The lack of experience and business connections is another impediment. In addition, negative male preconceptions and attitudes towards female entrepreneurs has also been found to often create additional problems for these women (Haratis et al., 1993).

Undoubtedly, there is significant diversity among women entrepreneurs. A relatively large number of them have become self-employed because of their inability to find dependent employment and have low levels of education and low incomes (Petraki Kottis, 1998). Female entrepreneurship is concentrated mainly in the so-called feminized sectors such as retailing, hairdressing, handicrafts, making of clothes, etc.

In a recent survey concerning entrepreneurship in Greece, it was found that among 500 firms, only 15 per cent of them belonged to women (Hassid, 2000), and a larger proportion of women was found among younger groups of entrepreneurs. This can be attributed to the relatively high unemployment rates of younger women and the gradual change in prevailing mentalities and attitudes regarding female entrepreneurship. It is natural that this change will be reflected more in younger women's aspirations and activities. As a result, the firms created by women increased from around 15 per cent of all new start-ups in the 1970s, to around 18 per cent in the 1980s and to around 27 per cent in the 1990s.

Hassid's (2000) survey showed that women's new entrepreneurial activity concentrated mostly in the service sector and particularly in personal services and retail trade. Another interesting finding was that in almost all cases, the firms that belonged to women were created by them or were inherited. Due to women's limited financial resources they did not become entrepreneurs by buying a firm. Women entrepreneurs came mostly from larger cities and created small firms in the service sector, while men developed entrepreneurial activities more in the industrial sector and established larger firms (Hassid, 2000).

Despite the importance of entrepreneurial activity for women's employment, very little research has been done in this regard. There are many areas that have to be investigated. There is very little known about the problems that women entrepreneurs face, the survival and failure rates of their firms, the sectoral and industrial concentration of these firms, their growth prospects, etc. Also, it will be useful to know more about the relation between the characteristics of female entrepreneurs and how these characteristics relate to the survival and growth rates of the enterprises.

Country legislation supporting women in the workforce

The existing legislative framework for promoting gender equality is founded on the State Constitution of 1975. Since then, a large number of important pieces of legislation has been introduced. In 1975 the country passed a law ratifying the

International Labour Treaty entitled 'Equal pay between men and women for work of equal value'. The 1979 UN Treaty for the elimination of all types of discrimination against women became law in 1983. The country has also signed several other international treaties aiming to promote gender equality. After the accession of Greece to the European Community in 1981, all Community rules and regulations for the promotion of gender equality became part of the Greek Law. The Community Guidelines for equal opportunities led to various types of legislative and other action. The modernization of the Family Law in 1983 introduced significant changes in women's position. With a recent revision of the State Constitution, it became possible for the Government to use positive measures to correct existing inequalities. Of special importance is legislation passed in the years 1999 and 2000 for compulsory participation of both sexes in at least one-third in candidate's lists for municipal and prefectural elections and also in public administration decision-making councils.

In general terms, the Greek legislation for gender equality can be characterized as advanced and progressive. The obstacles to women's advancement and the persistence of the glass ceiling cannot be wholly attributed to inadequate legislation or defective application of the legislation. Problems arise because many cases of unfair treatment cannot be taken to the courts due to their indirect or covert character and women's inability to assemble the required legal evidence. Moreover, in a large number of cases women cannot seek legal help because they do not have sufficient information about their rights, lack financial resources or are afraid of social disapproval or punitive action on the part of their employers.

Initiatives supporting women in the workforce

During the last two decades several institutions and mechanisms have been established and various types of action have been taken to promote equal opportunities for women. In 1985 the Government founded the General Secretariat for Equality with the task of disseminating information, proposing corrective measures and intervening at all levels for the promotion of gender equality. It also established Committees for Equality in all prefecture offices for disseminating information, sensitizing local communities about gender issues, formulating proposals for new measures and ensuring that women in local communities receive the same treatment as men. Furthermore, Offices for Equality have been founded in all ministries and public organizations. In 1994 the Research Centre for Gender Equality was created, under the auspices of the General Secretariat for Equality, with the task of undertaking research and other activities for improving the position of women.

Women's organizations have undertaken various initiatives and have played an important role for the promotion of gender equality. Most of these organizations are members of the European Women's Lobby and participate in its initiatives.

An institution that could play an important role is the Inter-Ministerial Committee for Gender Equality established in the year 2000, its main tasks were to a) coordinate and supervise existing policies and measures for promoting mainstreaming which involves the incorporation of an equal opportunities dimension in all policies, b) prepare annual action plans for improving the position of women and c) disseminate information and sensitize society about issues related to equal opportunities.

In the context of the European Union Employment Strategy, Greece prepares an annual National Action Plan (NAP) for Employment, which includes a special chapter on measures and policies for promoting equal opportunities for women. Mainstreaming strategies have included the creation or strengthening of institutions and mechanisms to deal with problems related to gender equality, the establishment of facilities that would enable individuals to reconcile work with family responsibilities and special actions to facilitate women's entrance to the labour market. All these issues receive special attention in the annual NAP.

To promote women's entrepreneurship, the Government provides assistance in the form of subsidies and technical expertise to those interested in starting a new enterprise. Efforts have been made to take care of weaknesses highlighted by an evaluation study of similar public programmes applied in the past (Haratsis and Petraki Kottis, 1993). Of particular interest is a programme introduced recently by the Research Centre for Gender Equality, under which individualized support in the form of mentoring and technical assistance is provided to women aspiring to become entrepreneurs.

An important role for the support of women managers and entrepreneurs could be played by the Institute for the Development of Women Managers and Entrepreneurs, established in 1995 by the Greek Association for Business Management. The purpose of this institute is to undertake action for promoting the status and image of women managers and entrepreneurs and expanding their numbers.

To improve women's position, the national confederation of labour unions representing workers in the private sector has established a General Secretariat for Women and a Network of Women Syndicalists in the labour centres and federations. In addition, a General Secretariat for Women has also been established at the confederation of unions representing public sector employees. However, it should be pointed out that the major employers' organizations have not yet undertaken any substantial initiatives for promoting the position of women.

To sensitize teachers about gender equality, the Ministry of Education in collaboration with the General Secretariat for Equality, have organized special training programmes for primary and secondary school teachers. However, up to now, only a small number of teachers have participated in them.

During the last few years, various initiatives have been undertaken by the General Secretariat for Equality in collaboration with women's organizations, to assist women candidates during political elections. A special organization was formed by them in 1998 to undertake such activities, prior to elections, with the aim of supporting women candidates of all political parties.

The future

To assess future prospects it is useful to start with a summary of the situation at present. As outlined in this chapter, women's participation in the higher levels of the managerial ladder and in all top positions in Greece is very small. Women can reach the lower and middle hierarchical levels, but very few of them can break the glass ceiling. Their advancement is inhibited by preconceptions, outdated stereotypes and institutional and social structures inherited from the past. Unfortunately, some of these factors are indirectly re-enforced by advertising and the mass media. The previously mentioned survey of male top executives carried out by Petraki Kottis (1996), revealed perceptual and attitudinal barriers that would require a titanic effort on the part of women to be overcome. The response of a woman top executive gives a vivid picture of the problem:

> The Greek society is run by men who dominate in all aspects of life – family, politics, public administration and firms. The difference between men and women within an organization lies in that it is considered natural for a man to reach higher positions, while a woman's abilities are constantly doubted by those at the top. Women can move up the hierarchical ladder only after a very hard struggle, but for many the struggle often proves to be fruitless.

To date, there is no other published literature about corporate views and attitudes concerning women in management. Although there is general concern and the issues involved are of great importance, there is a lack of in-depth research in this regard. However, the important point is that the glass ceiling continues to exist in all areas of economic, social and political life in Greece. Despite positive developments, women's participation in top management and in decision-making positions continues to be very small. Greek society is still under-utilizing the talents and abilities of women, that is of half its population. This is wasteful and absurd, particularly in a period when the country and the firms have to perform in a highly competitive world.

It is worth pointing out that one of the main causes of the existing gender inequality in the country is the unequal division of household responsibilities between women and men. Due to tradition, such responsibilities fall almost entirely on women. The situation is aggravated because of the inadequacy of public and enterprise arrangements for supporting the work/family reconciliation (Evans, 2001). As a result, working women with families carry a heavy load and this limits the time and energy they can devote to advancing their careers. Some men's opposition to women in higher positions may have its root in their subconscious fear that a disturbance in the *status quo* could lead to a change in their privileged position at home.

Moreover, because of various obstacles to their advancement, many women retire earlier than men. In the past, women's early retirement was encouraged by special provisions in social security legislation. While such arrangements were viewed to be favouring women, in essence they often worked against them. The mere knowledge that women may retire early discouraged employers from assigning them to jobs of higher responsibility.

Looking at future prospects, there are several reasons for optimism. First of all mentalities and attitudes in relation to women's roles and possibilities are slowly changing, particularly among younger people. The institutional and legislative framework established in recent decades, the increasing sensitization about issues related to gender equality and the gradual strengthening of women's presence in decision-making centres are bound to create an environment more favourable to the advancement or women. Furthermore, the constant increase in women's participation in all areas of higher education is expected to add a new impetus to their advancement.

We believe that women's future depends to a large extent upon themselves. It is important that they strengthen their determination to fight for what they deserve and that they discard any remains of old mentalities and attitudes and any feelings of victimization and despair. The notion that in a male-dominated environment women do not advance to top positions may become a self-fulfilling prophesy. Furthermore, although views and attitudes creating obstacles to women's advancement are unfounded, they should not be entirely written off by them. Women aspiring to higher positions must undertake a careful examination of their priorities and attitudes to ensure that nothing feeds or sustains existing biases or stereotypes. Special attention should be paid by women to changes in the arrangements at home to reduce their burden of household responsibilities.

The Government, the universities and all interested organizations can play a key role in speeding up change. Among other actions, more attention should be paid to encouraging and supporting research concerning the relative position of women and the obstacles that impede their advancement, the consequences for private and public organizations and society in general from the under-utilization of women's talents and the policies and measures that must be used to rectify the situation. It is important to produce evidence showing society the absurdness of devoting large amounts of valuable resources to educate women and then letting a large part of this investment be wasted.

In the final analysis, we propose that family responsibilities seem to be at the root of many obstacles restricting women's advancement in Greece. The dissemination of information about the need for a more equal division of household responsibilities between men and women and the establishment of institutions that would enable people to reconcile better work and family can have a big impact on women's future prospects for advancement.

References

Bourantas D. and Papalexandris, N. (1990), 'Sex Differences in Leadership: Leadership Styles and Subordinate Satisfaction', *Journal of Managerial Psychology*, **5** (5), 7-10.

Evans, J.M. (2001), *Firms Contribution to the Reconciliation Between Work and Family Life*, OECD Labour Market and Social Policy Occasional Papers, No 48.

General Secretariat for Equality (2000), *Greek Report to the United Nations.*

Greek Women's Engineering Association (2000), *Special Report.*

Haratsis, E. and Petraki Kottis, A. et al. (1993), *Self-employment in Greece*, Manpower Employment Organisation of Greece.

Hassid, I. (2000), 'Greek women entrepreneurs', *The Greek Economy*, EPILOGI, 202-206.

Panigyrakis, G. and Veloutsou C. (1995), 'The brand management of consumer products in Greece: A comparison study of gender differences', 24th European Marketing Academy Conference (EMAC), 1931-1940.

Panigyrakis, G. and Veloutsou C. (1998), 'Sex related differences of public relations managers', *Women in Management Review*, **13** (2), 72-82.

Papalexandris, N. and Bourantas, D. (1991), 'Attitudes towards women as managers: the case of Greece', *The International Journal of Human Resources*, **2** (2), 133-148.

Papalexandris, N. and Nikandrou, I. (2002), *Profile of Women Managers in Human Resources Departments in Greece*, Research Centre, AUEB.

Petraki Kottis, A. (1998), 'Self-employment in Greece', *TRENDS*, **31**, European Employment Observatory, European Commission, 22-26.

Petraki Kottis, A. (1996), 'Women in management and the glass ceiling in Greece', *Women in Management*, **11** (2), 30-38.

Petraki Kottis, A. (1991), 'Single European labour market: Equality between women and men', *International Journal of Manpower*, **12** (3), 3-8.

Petraki Kottis, A. (1990), 'Shifts over time and regional variation in women's labour force participation rates in a developing economy', *Journal of Development Economics*, **33**, 117-132.

Petraki Kottis, A. (1988), 'Sources of growth of female employment in Greece: A shift-share analysis', *International Journal of Manpower*, **9** (1), 18-20.

Petraki Kottis, A. (1987), 'Earnings differentials in manufacturing in Greece', *International Journal of Manpower*, **8** (4), 26-32.

Chapter 3

Women in Management in Belgium

Alison E. Woodward

Introduction

Education and increasing European integration are the two factors most responsible for the changed position of women in the Belgian economy since 1990. Women are now the majority of students at university and achieve better results than men. The increasing integration of European business and the infiltration of American human resource management practices has also meant that diversity is no longer a dirty word. The first woman has been spotted in positions ranging from university rector to a top post at the national TV channel. The houses of parliament are almost one-fourth female, and the governments have visible and important women Ministers. While Belgian women are good students, they consistently fall behind in salary and career progression once they enter the world of business. Isolated women are spotted at the top, and women passed over now openly expose discrimination, but the world of top management in large organizations remains a 'man's world' in Belgium. No Belgian woman was named as one of the top-30 women in European management by the Wall Street Journal (*De Standard*, 3 March 2001). Many indications are that while the increasing globalization of business and the restructuring of the world of work in developed countries will create good opportunities for women, the penthouse at the top has moved one storey further up, with an even more recalcitrant version of the glass ceiling for European business women. Finally, the entrepreneurial spirit, that key motor for the economy, does not seem to be growing among Belgian women. The future is sure to be mixed.

Labour force characteristics

Paid work is not new to women in Belgium. Women have been in the workforce throughout the last hundred years, and since the second world war, women in Belgium have been somewhere in the middle in terms of labour force integration in Western Europe, showing a pattern more typical of France than of either Sweden (citizen worker) or Germany/Netherlands (breadwinner) or Spain (family/agricultural). This has to do both with the pattern of industrialization in Belgium and with the welfare provisions for child-care, which have been among the most generous in Europe. In fact, given the pattern of enrolling children older than 2.5 years in pre-school publicly funded care, which has a take up rate of over 90 per cent, it is perhaps a wonder that more Belgian women have not entered the work force. However, the percentage of women with a paid job has been growing with each generation. While the percentage of all men who are in the employed population has shrunk slightly in the last 30 years from 54 per cent of all men to 49 per cent, the percentage of all women on the labour market has increased from 25 per cent of all women in 1970 to 37 per cent in 1998 (Van Haegendoren et al., 2001). At present women make up 42 per cent of those active on the labour market (employed at least one hour a week or looking for work, Van Haegendoren et al., 2001). This is slightly below the average for the European Union (European Commission, 2001).

The increase in jobs in the public sector since the seventies has primarily benefited women. Around 28 per cent of women are working for the public sector while the figure is around 20 per cent for men. The percentage of public sector employment held by men has been steadily declining since the 1970s. As can be seen in Table 3.1, the public sector employs men and women virtually at parity. As women make up only 40 per cent of the workers, they are over-represented in the public sector. Private sector employment is still 60 per cent masculine. This has remained stable since 1990 (Van Haegendoren et al., 2001).

Table 3.1 Employment in public and private sectors and full- and part-time work by sex

	1985		1998	
	M	**F**	**M**	**F**
Employed				
Private	62	38	60	40
Public	60	40	50	50
Part-time work	n.a.	n.a.	13	87
Hours per week	40	34	40	32

Source: Van Haegendoren et al., 2001

The employment figures are higher for women compared to men – (14.9 per cent versus 9.0 per cent in 1998 - Van Haegendoren et al., 2001). They are more likely to be in part-time work (see Table 3.1) and more likely to be out of the work force once they reach middle age than men. This is related to the fact that until 1996 the legal pension age for women was 60 while men worked until 65. (It will change to 65 for women in 2009, thanks to the Royal Decree (KB) of 23/12/96 - cited in Buyck, 2000.)

In comparison to other countries such as Ireland and the United Kingdom, Belgium has little ideological commitment to mothers staying at home (Brannen et al., 2001). There is little discussion about whether mothers of small children should work. The issue is rather how family and job responsibilities can be combined. Most women have worked because they have to, and increasingly the two-earner model has become the standard for maintaining an acceptable life style (Cantillon, 1990). However, it is still rather unusual for women to have their career as their central identity. Part-time work is a valued option for women with children. It is only recently that a growing number of educated women have appeared with a vision of a life cycle including a long-term full-time commitment to the labour force in a well paid job. Today almost 85 per cent of women between 25-35 years of age are employed in Belgium, but very few women over 55 hold a job. When they work, Belgian women are increasingly paid in an egalitarian way, although the gender pay gap still exists. The longer the career, the greater the pay gap between men and women. Belgium follows Finland, Sweden, Denmark and Germany with a pay ratio to men of 85.7 per cent for full-time workers (the 1995 data shows Sweden at 88 per cent, see Plasman, 2001).

The higher the education, the more likely that a Belgian woman will have fewer children and a continuous career without breaks. However, studies of time use in Flanders indicate that even highly educated women are working fewer hours a week in paid labour than men, and spending more time on housework than men (Glorieux and Vanderweyer, 2001; Glorieux et al., 2002). Table 3.1 gives the impression that women are working fewer hours than men, but this is a reflection of the fact that more women are working but in part-time work. If one considers the total volume of hours worked per week by each sex, the ratio of hours between men and women was 70:30 in 1985, while today it is 60:40 thanks to the increased contribution of women.

The transformation of employment felt across Europe has also been important in Belgium. Between 1980-1998 masculine type jobs decreased by around 6 per cent, while female employment opportunities have increased by 25 per cent (Ministerie van Tewerkstelling en Arbeid cited in Buyck, 2000). This is due to the decrease in heavy industry and agriculture and the increase in the service sector. There is also a general increase in jobs for highly skilled employees. One might assume that women would also take a disproportional share of these highly skilled positions, but in fact women have only taken about half of the new jobs in management, while more than 80 per cent of the jobs in sales and service have gone to female employees (Buyck, 2000).

In terms of types of employment as revealed in Table 3.2, there is an evolution that is very gradual and difficult to compare over time. There seems to be a very slight increase in the number of women entrepreneurs, and a stronger representation of women as salaried administrative personnel, while proportionally fewer women are manual workers now as compared to 15 years ago. However, these evolutions have also been paralleled by a redistribution of male activities in a similar manner.

Table 3.2 Types of employment for men and women in 1985 and 1998

	1985			1998		
	M	F	Total	M	F	Total
Employer	2.3	.5	1.7	2.5	.8	1.8
Independent	16.3	10.4	14.3	16.0	10.1	13.6
Worker	36.7	21.2	31.2	35.8	19.3	29.0
Salaried	23.2	34.5	27.2	27.6	42.6	33.8
Civil servant	20.4	23.7	21.6	17.6	23.1	19.9
Helper	1.0	9.6	4.0	.5	4.1	2.0
Total	100	100	100	100	100	100

Source: Van Haegendoren et al., 2001
Based on National Institute for Statistics Survey of the Employed Population, 1998.

Women pursuing education

In comparison with the U.S. or Canada, Belgian women were relatively late in taking up seats in higher education (several universities prohibited female students until the 1930's or required them to sit at the back of the room). It was first in 1998 that women in Flanders passed the 50 per cent mark in university registration. The human capital argument to explain the low proportion of women in management gets some fuel here. Not only has there been a relative lack of highly educated women on the labour market, but further, female fields of study seldom led to leading jobs in business. Hard science remains heavily male dominated (21 per cent in Flanders), although business studies in Flemish universities have become increasingly feminized (37.8 per cent), as have law (50.8 per cent) and medicine (57.3 per cent) (figures for Flanders, Vercoutere, 2002). Professional top management in Belgium, as in much of Europe, still shows a predilection for those with engineering degrees. One of the most prestigious degrees is 'Business Engineer', a five year programme which attracts relatively few female students.

An encouraging, although controversial breakthrough, has been the increasing observation that women throughout their studies are more likely to complete their studies on time, and furthermore tend to achieve slightly better results on average than men (Janssens and DeMetsenaere, 2000; Meulders and Plasman, 2001). This should bode well for their placement on the labour market. However, a number of depressing findings in studies of alumni of business schools have indicated that women are hired at less favourable salaries and conditions than their male class mates and that the gap grows throughout their career (Buyck, 2000, Vandenhove and Hiltrop, 1991 cited in Buyck, 2000). Women end up working in the so-called soft sectors (insurance, sales, distribution) where the salaries are lower. Wyns and Van Meensel (1990 cited in Buyck, 2000) found that three fourths of women in private business are located in only three of the 9 service sectors (banking and finance, hotel and shops, and other services).

Women in management

Women managers are found in sectors associated with people and services, rather than in the more lucrative sectors such as energy, industry and transport which often require technical training. Women are still to be found in the niches where there is a lower salary generally. There has been no dramatic change in the representation of women senior management in either the private or the public sector in the last 20 years, although there does seem to be some slow progress in middle management and in smaller firms. Data using the International Standard Classification of Occupations of 1988 collected by the minister for Equal Opportunities and Employment in 1997 nonetheless showed that a relatively surprising one-third of positions in the top range of policy making and leadership functions belong to women. The National Institute of Statistics figures show 30.7 per cent of the positions in policy making and higher management, directors and company managers, to be female. This is level one of the ISCO code representing about 11 per cent of all employees. Thus among the top 11 per cent of the jobs, women seem to hold about one third. Unfortunately there is no directly comparable data showing the evolution over time, as the codes were changed in 1988 (National Institute of Statistics Survey of Employed 1999 cited in Van Haegendoren et al., 2001). Some nuance is provided when one examines the finer two-digit code. Women make up around 38 per cent of the managers of small companies, 31 per cent of top administration in the public sector, and 26 per cent of the top management in larger firms (Van Haegendoren et al., 2001, based on NIS 1999-2001).

This does not correspond with studies of top public administration in Flanders and in the Federal Government which show that the highest functions are 10 per cent female (Hondeghem et al., 1999). In the universities around 7 per cent of the full professors are female (European Technology Assessment Network Report:10 cited in Van Haegendoren et al., 2000; Meulders and Plasman, 2001). Reliable figures on the private sector are much harder to obtain. The only well-known study looks at the top 30,000 firms in Belgium as ranked by the top business magazine *Trends* using data from the beginning of the 1990s. This data takes into account the formal, publicly listed functions of each company, such as CEO and member of the board of directors, and finds that overall among the top positions 17 per cent are held by women (cited in Buyck, 2000 from Tack et al., 1993). The larger the number of employees, the smaller the number of women in management positions. For example, the 307 companies with more than 500 employees had only 7 per cent women of top positions, while for the 8,472 companies with 2-10 employees, there were 19 per cent female managers. These figures provide a more realistic picture of the situation in top management in Belgium than the above mentioned official study. Further, the large majority of the 'managerial' women in this study served as Secretary to the Board. In 84 per cent of the companies, this is a female role. However it is not a managerial position.

Valgaeren's preliminary analysis of the 2001 *Trends* Top 30,000 company data, including the top positions in firms, concluded that women held 17.8 per cent of all top positions, but only 7.93 of the managerial functions of CEO, owner or delegated top manager, showing virtually no increase since 1990. The study also observed the same pattern of fewer women the larger the size of the firm (Valgaeren, 2001). Barring dramatic evidence to the contrary, it is still safe to conclude that the top of the hierarchy in Belgian business is no more feminized than that in Belgian universities, that is to say far less than 10 per cent female.

Civil service and public employees

Women are also underrepresented in the senior executive positions of public bodies in Belgium, although the situation has improved. At the beginning of 1990 not a single female was to be found at the top of the big public services of rail, telephone and mail services (Buyck, 2000). Given that more than half of public personnel is female, the situation is even more dramatic. Van Haegendoren (2001) relates that if you had had a meeting of all the top officials of the ministries in 1980 you would have had 12 women and 466 men. In 1999 that would have been 69 women and 500 men, a progression from 3 per cent to 12 per cent. In the very highest position in the hierarchy of the civil service of the ministries there is only one woman. On a more optimistic note, there are more women represented at the top of the scientific institutions such as museums and research labs, where 16 per cent of the personnel in the highest ranks are female.

Politics

Politics is the only sector that has shown dramatic changes in female leadership since 1993. Although Belgium stood still both in terms of elected parliamentarians and certainly in terms of ministers throughout the 1970s and 1980s, the 1990s brought gradual and convincing progress at all levels of politics. In 1995 the proportion of women in the Lower House went above 10 per cent for the first time. This progress will almost surely continue thanks to some significant changes in legislation such as the 1994 Smet-Tobback (quota) law which required that electoral lists may be maximally two-thirds from one sex. This law began to take effect in 1999. The constitutional amendment of 2002 mandating equality between men and women is expected to have further effects. Initiatives to strengthen the quota law are being taken in the present legislature, as the government now aims for parity in parliament.

The Belgian government is very complicated, and has numerous parliamentary bodies. Table 3.3 illustrates that in 2002, with 23 per cent in the federal Lower House and 28 per cent in the Senate, it ranks 23rd in the world in terms of women representatives in national parliaments, and around the middle in terms of the European Union. (Inter-Parliamentary Union Women in National Parliaments, 10 April 2002), a dramatic increase from the 9 per cent in 1991 (http://www.db-decision-de/English/Parl consulted April 30 2002). As a federal state, it not only has a central government, but also several powerful regional governments. Since 1995, there are 5 directly elected regional parliaments. In many policy areas these bodies are more powerful than the central government. Two of the five regional parliaments score better than the federal chambers in terms of female representation. In 2002, only the German-speakers and Brussels regional executive governments had no women ministers. The Flemish and French community governments both had one-third female ministers, while the Federal government had 17 per cent (3 women of 18 ministers in total). The Walloon regional parliament and German region seem to be making slower progress in reaching gender balance than the Flemish and Brussels regions. In the cities, female representation improved from 13.8 of city council seats in 1988 to 26.1 per cent after the election in 2000 (Van Haegendoren et al., 2001).

Table 3.3 Percentage of female representatives in government and parliaments in Belgium in 2002

Body	Government	Parliament
Federal House/Senate	16.6	23.2/28.2
Flemish Parliament	33.3	20.2
French community parliament	28.6	18.1
Walloon regional parliament	11.1	12.0
Brussels regional parliament	0.0	34.7
German community parliament	0.0	32.0

Source: International Parliamentary Union (http://www.ipu.int.org), Belgian Federal Government http://www.fgov.be/nl_index.htm consulted September 2002

Women entrepreneurs

Although female entrepreneurship is seen as the hope of the European economy, Belgian women seem to be among the slowest in joining the entrepreneurial parade. Manigart et al. (2000) concluded that 'if considered as a major independent variable, the relative participation of women in entrepreneurship would account for as much as two thirds of the variation in entrepreneurial activity between countries...[yet] Belgian men are more than five times more likely to be involved in entrepreneurial activities as Belgian women'. If it is difficult to find data on women in management, it is almost impossible to find good studies on women entrepreneurs. This is a Europe wide problem, recognized by the OECD and the European Commission. The organizations of entrepreneurs in Belgium do not cover all entrepreneurs and are divided by political persuasion, complicating data collection. Certain features of the Belgian fiscal system may lead women entrepreneurs to disguise their activities, while male entrepreneurs may use female fronts. Thus a reliable count of entrepreneurial women is not forthcoming (Woodward, 2001). Nevertheless, based on statistics of registration as independents, there seems to be a slow but constant growth, with women rising from 26 per cent of those claiming entrepreneurship as their main source of income in 1986 to 29 per cent in 1999 (Entreprises: Où sont les femmes?, 2001).

Women in Belgium do not seem to be queuing up to start firms. 1.92 per cent of Belgian men were the owners of a new company compared to 0.4 per cent of the women, one of the lowest percentages in the developed world (Mangiart et al., 2000). Although there have been training programmes for women starters, generally the interest has been low (Vermeylen, 2000). An organizer of such training courses at one of the business schools commented that the American literature seemed to indicate that all sorts of women were leaving the corporate world because they were dissatisfied. They were reacting to the so-called 'push factors', 'but in Belgium I don't see that trend. Actually I don't know a single woman starter who got her motivation from a push factor. There are women who migrate from corporate life to entrepreneurship, but that is much more of a 'pull' factor, of being able to work part-time or combine work and family' (Woodward, 2001).

The sectors where women start businesses in Belgium are also still stereotypically female. They include hairdressing, restaurants, and personal care, although more and more older women seem to be starting personnel, employment and public relations businesses, judging from portraits in the popular press. This is not to say that Belgian women entrepreneurs are not also becoming more public figures—in fact, the top business woman in Holland in 2001 was a Belgian transport firm owner. Further, surveys carried out by entrepreneurial organizations also indicate a high degree of self-confidence among present Belgian women business owners and suggest that they have specific competitive advantages in doing business.

Country legislation supporting women in the workforce

The Ministry responsible for Equality of Opportunity (established in 1985 and combined with the Ministry of Employment and Labour) has pursued a continuous policy of stimulating equal opportunities in the labour market and developed a significant equality policy machinery. Belgium is ranked near the top by many in terms of its welfare provisions to ease the combination of work and the family (Singh, 1998; Korpi, 2000; UNDP, 2002 (http://www.undp.org/hdr2002/presskit/HDR%20PR_GEM.pdf)). Although its maternal and paternal leave policies at childbirth are near the middle of the European standard, provisions for child care after birth are generous. The combination of family and work is supported by relatively good family-friendly policies in Belgium. Every mother has a right to 15 weeks of paid maternity leave and fathers may take 10 days of paid paternal leave. A further possibility is the provision for career breaks which since 1985 allow people to break their career while maintaining a small allowance, and permitting them to return to their employer at the end. These career breaks were almost entirely used by women, for care of the elderly and child care. The present career break system is known as the time-credit system (since January 2002) and it is a right for all employees to take a break of up to one year without harming their seniority and other rights. The take-up is now much more gender balanced, although men seem to be using it for early retirement.

Publicly supported child care is readily available, even for small infants, although the majority of parents handle the first two years of the child's life through combinations of family, part-time work, and day-care mothers. Costs for childcare for children under three years of age are tax deductible. Children may commence publicly funded school from the age of 2.5 years, although compulsory schooling begins at age 6. The overwhelming majority of parents place their young children in school programmes which begin at 8.30 am and end at 3.30 pm. There is no stigma involved with sending the child to school at this early age. Both working and non-working parents enrol their children in these programmes. Furthermore, most schools provide lunch-time supervision. As there is free school choice, schools compete with each other on the basis of pre- and post-school programmes, so that parents also have a chance to find a school that provides a full-working day of educational and recreational activities, especially in urban communities. School vacations are also well covered by initiatives from both schools and civil society for excursions, courses, and neighbourhood supervised play camps.

Initiatives supporting women in the workforce

Over a decade ago, legislation was passed to encourage private firms to pursue equal opportunity and affirmative action programmes (1987) and to require public bodies to file affirmative action plans (1990). The Ministry of Labour and Equality of Opportunities developed an affirmative action methodology for firms based on Total Quality management, and provided individualized consultancy and courses for firms working on improving their equality record. Networks of equality officers at the provincial level were started to advise public authorities in preparing their affirmative action plans.

In the 1980s, the federal government encouraged private business to register their ambitions to promote equal opportunities with free advice—the take up rate was so low that a research project was initiated to discover why firms did not jump on the equal opportunity wagon (Woodward, 1990; Frank et al., 1990). The ones that did respond tended to be disproportionately American. Although this trend still holds, and American multi-nations are probably the ones using the most aggressive aspects of affirmative action, some indications are that increasingly Belgian-based firms at least aim to have an equal opportunities policy. Buyck found in her study of firms employing economics alumna that 84 per cent of 103 companies had an equal opportunities policy, although less than a third included family friendly policies and only 7 per cent would give jobs to the under represented sex in the case of equal qualifications (Buyck, 2000) meaning that only a very weak form of policy is in place, which had little chance of breaking any glass ceilings. Both this study and the Belgian data from the Comparative Leadership Study, indicated that men and to a greater extent women, generally believed that their firm preferred men to women for management functions (Buyck, 2000; Siemienska, 2000).

Informal, primarily anecdotal evidence is that the attitude of the popular business press has been increasingly making the case for the 'added value' of women's leadership, at least in the Flemish press. While in the 1980s almost no mention was made of women/and or gender in management, this theme, as well as the combination of work and family and examples from enterprises now are a regular feature. The theme of 'woman' was included almost 400 times in the leading employment supplement in Flanders, *Vacature*, in the two years 2000-2001 (http:www.vacature.com). This general publication regularly summarizes recent international publications about gender and management issues. Successes of women in management are also given attention in the daily press, which helps raise awareness. For example, anecdotes such as the fact that the Antwerp Chamber of Commerce went from 2 women out of 100 to 30 women out of 100 in twenty years were given coverage, thus raising awareness (*De Standard*, 3 March 2001).

Both the government and women's organizations have tried to sensitize the business world to the importance of women in management, using both legislative tools, and sensitization and training initiatives directed at potential women managers and innovative firms. Award programmes have been sponsored by federal and regional governments to recognize firms with good equality policies or with family friendly work organization. Women's magazines such as *Marie-Claire* have also sponsored awards for the Woman Manager of the Year. The Vlerick school of the University of Gent sponsored training programmes for women managers and entrepreneurs, although these have recently been dropped. European money stimulated a start-up-enterprise site for new women entrepreneurs, offering services such as an on-site secretarial arrangement and child-care, although this too has since ceased functioning. One of the more interesting recent initiatives has been a European co-operative project to stimulate young women to try a management career – '*Preparing Women to Lead*'. Senior women managers are shadowed by a young potential manager selected in competition, and also act as mentors. There are also efforts to maintain and stimulate networks of female managers through both voluntary organizations of women in management and those stimulated by programmes such as Sofia. Sofia, a mentoring and networking programme has spread from its original target region in Limburg, and has also been adapted by a major Belgian pharmaceutical firm as an in-house programme

(Jellema, 2000; Blommaert, 2001). However, this sort of project and its development indicates that the most useful programmes are the ones coming from organizations themselves. Unfortunately information about the spread of gender-sensitive training programmes in companies is still very limited.

The future

The future for women in management and senior executive positions in Belgium generally seems optimistic. This is certainly the case where public sector management is concerned. The stringent measures being applied to the world of politics should surely lead in the next ten years to a dramatic improvement in women's presence at all levels of elected government. This is the most easily predicted change for the future. A second front where optimistic news is to be expected concerns the gender wage gap between men and women in management functions in the same sector. Again, firm legislation coupled with the increasingly good education of women and high public support for child care have all contributed to a gradual lessening of this gap, especially among the youngest cohorts.

The future of the glass ceiling in relation to those at the very top in business and in public life in both administration and elected government is much less clear. The glass ceiling shows little danger of cracking. The progress in reaching balance around the tables of the Board of Directors and in the top management teams of major organizations has been minimal. Many observations seem to indicate that the increasing number of mergers in continental Europe will lead to ever larger organizations and more powerful pan-European top positions in management. Given that women are underrepresented in large businesses, and less likely to be offered positions requiring mobility, the signs that power is shifting upward are not positive for gender balance at the top.

But there is increasing pressure on the glass ceiling in Belgium stemming from several factors. The influence of the continuing integration of the European market on personnel practices could be ultimately be positive for increasing gender balance. Many of the firms who were awarded prizes for excellence in Belgium have been multi-nationals with a strong American-style management, and therefore an eye for diversity issues. This is often a code word for gender. Their practices in human resource management have become models in Belgian MBA programmes, and thus can be expected to have positive spin-offs for women. Certain skills are in short supply on the labour market, and so there are examples of top firms in consultancy, making strong recruitment efforts and policy changes to attract women. The increasing number of women in fields such as law and business administration and their excellent study results, are also factors which could encourage optimism, although the progress in the field of information technology which should offer new opportunities for women is not brilliant (Valgaeren, 2001). The glass ceiling itself seems to be as cloudy as the Belgian weather as far as the future is concerned. Globalization may hold mixed news for ambitious women if businesses do not begin to make more allowances for dual career families and the balance of work and home life.

References

Blommaert, J. (2001), 'Meester van de macht', *Weekend Knack*, **20** (16-20 May), 78-84.

Brannen, J., Lewis, S. and Nilsen, A. (eds) (2001), *Young Europeans and the Future,* London, Routledge.

Buyck, C.R. (2000), Een onderzoek naar de positie van vrouwelijke kaderleden in KMO's en Grote Ondernemingen Licence Thesis, *Faculteit Economische en Toegepaste Economische Wetenschappen*, Katholieke Universiteit Leuven, Leuven.

Cantillon, B. (1990), *Nieuwe behoeften naar zekerheid: Vrouw, gezin en inkomensverdeling*, Leuven: Acco.

De Standaard (2001), 'België ontbreekt in top-30 van Europese leidinggevende vrouwen'.

Dupont, A.S. (1997), 'Zelfstandig Ondernemende Vrouwen', *Vrouwenraad*, 29-32.

European Commission (1996), *The European Observatory for SMEs: Fourth Annual Report*, Office for Official Publications of the European Communities/ Enterprise Policy/European Network for SME Research, Luxembourg.

European Commission (2000), *The European Observatory for SMEs: Sixth Report*, Luxembourg: Office for Official Publications of the European Communities/Enterprise Policy.

European Commission (2000), 'Promoting Excellence through mainstreaming gender equality' Report of the European Technology Assessment Network (ETAN) Women and Science Working Group, Brussels.

Federale ministerie van tewerkstelling en arbeid (2001), *Gelijke kansen voor mannen en vrouwen*, Brussels: Federaal Ministerie van Tewerkstelling en Arbeid.

Franck, P., Van Put, A. and Vermeulen, L. (1990), *Personeelsbeleid en bedrijfscultuur. Carrièremogelijkheid voor vrouwen in ondernemingen*, Antwerp: Universitaire Instelling Antwerpen.

Gerloof, J., Grotenhuis, H.T. and Kamstra, E. (1994), *Vrouwen als ondernemers: een kwestie van beleid*, Den Haag: B&A Groep Beleidsonderzoek 1 -Advies BV.

Glorieux, I., Copens, K. and Koelet, S. (2002), *Vlaanderen in uren en minuten: de tijdsbesteding van de Vlamingen in 480 tabellen* [CD-ROM], Brussels: VUB Press.

Glorieux, I. and Vanderweyer, J. (2001), 'Belgian Men and Women, a world of difference', in Federal Ministry of Employment and Labour, Equal Opportunities Unit (ed.), *Women and Men in Belgium. Towards an Equal Society*, Brussels: Federal Ministry of Employment and Labour, Equal Opportunities Unit, pp.67-73.

Janssens, R. and De Metsenaere, M. (2000), *Een maat voor niets? Zin en onzin in een universitaire preselectie*, Brussels: VUB Press.

Jellema, J. (2000), 'Best Practices van Mentorprogramma's in België: Een methodologie voor de empowerment van vrouwen', *Sophia Nieuwsbrief*, **23** (September), 21-24.

Hondeghem, A. and Nelen, S. (1999), *Ken- en stuurgetallen- Instrument voor een evenredige vertegenwoordiging van mannen en vrouwen in de federale ministeries*, Leuven: Instituut van de Overheid, Katholieke Universiteit Leuven.

Korpi, W. (2000), 'Faces of Inequality: Gender, Class and patterns of inequalities in different types of welfare states', *Social Politics* (Summer), 127-192.

Manigart, S., Clarysse, B., Crijns, H. and Goosens, H. (2000), *General Entrepreneurship Monitor: Executive Report Belgium and Flanders*, Gent: Vlerick Leuven Gent Management School.

Meulders, D. and Plasman, R. (2001), 'Women's Place in the Working World', in Federal Ministry of Employment and Labour, Equal Opportunities Unit (ed.), *Women and Men in Belgium. Towards an Equal Society*, Brussels: Federal Ministry of Employment and Labour, Equal Opportunities Unit, 59-66.

Plantenga, J. and Rubery, J. (1997), *State of the Art Review on Women and the Labour Market*, Utrecht: Institute of Economics University of Utrecht, Employment and Social Affairs and European Commission.

Plasman, R. (2001), 'Indicators on gender pay equality: The Belgian presidency initiative' Paper at Launch of Programme relating to the Community Framework strategy on gender equality (2001-2005), 13 September, Brussels: European Parliament.

Sels, Luc and B. Overlaet (1999), *Vacature Salarisenquête:Lonen in Vlaanderen:Wat verdient U en wie verdient meer?* Leuven: Acco.

Siemieńska, R. (2000), 'Elites' value orientations', in M. Vianello and G. Moore (eds), *Gendering Elites: Economic and Political Leadership in 27 Industrialised Societies*, London: Macmillan, 247-267.

Singh, R. (1998), *Gender Autonomy in Western Europe*. London: Macmillan Press.

Tack, T., Dries, H. and Berings, D. (1993), *Vrouwen in beleidsfuncties in Trends Top 30,000*, Brussels: EHSAL.

Union Syndicale des Classes Moyennes (2001), *Entreprises: Où sont les femmes?*, Brussels: Union Syndicale des Classes Moyennes Brussels.

Valgaeren, E. (2001), *Loopbanen van vrouwen in management en ICT* Dilbeek: Sociaal Economisch Instituut, Limburgs Universitair Centrum.

Vandenhoeve, J. and Hiltrop, J.M. (1991), Carrièreontwikkeling van mannelijke en vrouwelijke economen Onderzoeksrapport no. 9105, Leuven: Katholieke Universiteit Leuven.

Van Haegendoren, M., Valgaeren, E. and Noelanders, S. (2000), *Gezocht: Professor (V) Een onderzoek naar vrouwen in academia* Wetenschappelijke monografie 4, Brussels: Ministerie van de Vlaamse Gemeenschap, Gelijke Kansen in Vlaanderen.

Van Haegendoren, M., Steegmans, N. and Valgaeren, E. (2001), *Mannen en vrouwen op de drempel van de 21ste eeuw. Een gebruikershandboek genderstatistieken*, Brussels: Ministerie voor Tewerkstelling en Arbeid.

Van Hellemont, C. (1999), Vrouwelijke zelfstandige ondernemers anno 1999 Master's Thesis, *Interunivesitair programma GAS-Vrouwenstudies*, Antwerp: Universiteit Antwerpen.

Vermeylen, S. (2000), De case van het vrouwelijke ondernemerschap *KMO magazine*, October 25-26.

Vercoutere, K. (2002), *Wetenschappelijk Onderzoek en de Genderproblematiek*, Studiereeks 4, Brussels: Vlaamse Raad voor Wetenschapsbeleid.

Woodward, A.E. (1990), 'Why Don't Firms Jump on the Equal Opportunity Wagon? The Belgian Case', *European Network for Women's Studies Newsletter*, February, **2**, 7-8.

Woodward, A.E. (1993), 'Women in Management in Belgium', in C.L. Cooper and M.J. Davidson (eds), *Women and European Management*, London: Paul Chapman Publishing, 133-145.

Woodward, A.E. (2001), 'Vrouwen als leidsters van eigen bedrijven: wat weten wij over de Vlaamse en Belgische onderneemsters vandaag?', in L. Van Molle and P. Heyrman (eds), *Vrouwenzakenvrouwen: Facetten van zelfstandig ondernemerschap in Vlaanderen, 1800-2000*, Bijdragen Museum van de Vlaamse Sociale Strijd no. 18, Provinciebestuur Oost-Vlaanderen, Gent, 211-226.

Wyns, M. and Van Meensel, R. (1990), *De beroepensegregatie in België (1970-1988)* Leuven: Hoger Instituut voor de Arbeid.

Chapter 4

Women in Management in Ireland

Eunice McCarthy

Introduction

In Ireland, as in other countries, an upsurge of interest in the leadership and work roles of women has been spearheaded by a convergence of forces. This chapter traces patterns of change and transformation to equal opportunity and advancement to management and leadership roles for women in Ireland from the early 1970s to the present. Major developments and transitions will be mapped from the perspective of labour force participation of women workers; educational trends and gender diversity; women in management and paths to opportunity and decision-making; women in local government and local development; women's access to boardrooms and gender equality in the Civil Service. Barriers to women's advancement will further be highlighted followed by an assessment of change initiatives which are needed to impact on and significantly enhance the role for women in management and leadership in Ireland into the future.

Casting an eye back to the early 1970s, a landmark document – *Report of the First Commission on the Status of Women in Ireland (1972)* – identified societal institutions and work organizations as being locked into old, rigid, patriarchal and fearful ways of organizing, structuring, developing and thinking about female potential and resources. More specifically, it identified patterns of gross inequality and discrimination in relation to pay, opportunity, recruitment/selection, marriage bar and work, training, appraisal, women in decision-making and promotion of women at work. Women's story in this old era (pre-1972) was one of gross discrimination in all major spheres of life. This mapping provided the first comprehensive platform for change and legislative action in the field of gender equality. During the 1970s and 1980s the first tranch of equality laws was introduced and opened up the debate on the *prevention of inequality* (1970s) and later on the *promotion of equality* (1980s) (McCarthy, 1988). Spurred on by developments in the European Union throughout the 1990s, Ireland's awareness of barriers to positive action and the need for strategic positive action was becoming grounded. Windows to the vulnerabilities and fallacies of the past were opened, while at the same time generating a new awareness which reinforced a sense of hope about implementing effective change. By 1993, the Second Commission on the Status of Women (established by the Government) published a challenging analysis of the entrenched inequalities still in place, with strong recommendations for new legislation to drive equality change into the third millennium. This deeper awareness is characterized by mainstreaming gender equality in organizations, monitoring equality change and the development and promotion of gender equality cultures. A key equality indicator now being recognized and accepted at national and organizational levels, is a significant increase in the numbers of women in senior and decision-making roles. Currently gender mainstreaming is a required strategy for the National Development Plan 2000-2006 (NDP, 1999) and the National Employment-Action Plan (NEAD, 1999).

Labour force characteristics

The Irish economy since the mid-1990s is illustrative of how rapidly Ireland has advanced from 'famine to feast'. President Mary Robinson in her inaugural address as President of Ireland (1990) estimated the legacy of the Irish diaspora to be 70 million people world-wide claiming Irish descent. After the failure of the potato crop some 150 years ago, the Great Famine blighted the landscape. Since then, waves of involuntary emigration characterized Ireland, and the high level of emigration was seen as a measure of national economic failure. Since the foundation of the Irish State in 1922, women's restricted economic role has been inextricably linked to an economy where emigration appeared a self-perpetuating phenomenon and a depressed economy almost a natural way of life. While entry to the EC in 1973 opened up avenues of gender equality, the backdrop of uncertain economic growth still played a dominant role in the slow achievement of gender equality goals. In 1988, Ireland was labelled the 'poorest of the rich' among EU countries, but by the late 1990s, it was considered that its new *Celtic Tiger* status was well deserved to describe Ireland's economic miracle. The OECD's report in 1999 was further impressed by sustained growth performance – in its view Ireland had notched up five straight years of 'stunning economic performance'. This remarkable economic turnaround out of the Celtic twilight zone has been attributed to many factors as follows: the role of education, fiscal adjustment, foreign direct investment, social partnership, EU support, population changes (Sweeney, 1998; McSharry and White, 2000; Partnership, 2000; Kennedy, 2002).

The country's changing democratic structure has meant an expanding labour force, which has, in turn, facilitated the increased participation of women in general and of married women and mothers in particular into the labour force.

A massive growth in women's involvement in the workforce in Ireland has occurred over the two decades 1980s-2000s (Table 4.1). Up until the 1980s, however, women's participation in the labour force in Ireland, compared with that of other industrialized countries was significantly different as follows: the participation of women was low; and the demographic structure of the female workforce was primarily young single women.

The corollary to this pattern was that a substantial number of women between the ages of 25-65 were fulltime homeworkers engaged in non-paid work in the home. During the economically depressed years 1951-1981, women's participation in the workforce was low and relatively unchanged (an average of 26.7 per cent). From the 1980s onwards, however, driven by the high performance economy, heightened awareness of gender inequality issues, equality laws, and the Celtic Tiger economy, women's participation rate increased dramatically to 41.0 per cent in 2000 – reflecting a doubling of the numbers of women employed during the 1990s alone (see Table 4.1).

Table 4.1 Labour force participation of out of work women and men in Ireland, 1981-2000 (aged 15 years and over)

Year	Men	Women	Total	Women as % of Total
1981	912,495	358,627	1,217,122	28.2
1991	748,100	377,000	1,125,100	33.5
2000	1,007,400	702,600	1,710,300	41.0

Source: Central Statistics Office, 2001

Another key milestone is the increased participation of married women in the labour force. Married women, as a percentage of women workers, grew from a low of 3.6 per cent in 1971 to 48.2 per cent in 2000, matching that of other EU countries (CSO, 2001). This increase can be accounted for by the removal of legal restrictions to women staying on at work after marriage (the marriage bar), the introduction of equality laws, as well as the erosion of restrictions based on custom and cultural issues during the intervening years. Callan and Farrell (1991), observed that married women's participation is highly responsive to higher real wages, to changes in potential earnings, especially after tax, a decline in fertility and higher levels of educational attainment. The increase in women's participation in the work force also embraces a significant number of working mothers. In 1991, a quarter of all mothers were gainfully employed which grew to 36.6 per cent in 1996 (CSO, 1997). The participation rate was higher for mothers with one and two children (42.9 per cent average), but was lowest for mothers with three or more children to care for (33.2 per cent).

The change towards a dual role in women's involvement in both work and home arenas, has taken place within a psycho-cultural context in which the attitude that 'women's role in the home is paramount' is still strong. The increase in working mothers over this period provides new additional models of dual-role involvement across a wide spectrum of work settings, thus paving the way for the evolution of a critical mass that is gaining momentum in the threshold years of the third millennium. Between the years 1986-1996, the number of couples in which only the man worked had fallen steeply, while the number in which both partners work had more than doubled (CSO, 1997). These changes are also reflected in the number of women and men who are engaged solely in 'home duties'. In 2000, a significant downward shift for women is evident i.e. from 54.6 per cent in 1979 to 36.3 per cent in 2000. Over the same period men's involvement displayed a small upward swing from 0 per cent (1979) to 0.5 per cent (CSO, 2001).

High unemployment and high emigration were the constant of the Irish economy. In 1992, the overall Irish unemployment rate well exceeded the EC average rate (15.4 per cent v. 9.3 per cent). Ambiguities in labour force aggregates for females have been identified and there has been calls for cultural evaluation. In recognition of these problems, the Second Irish Commission on the Status of Women (1993) recommended that labour force statistics should provide detailed breakdown of women's employment by occupation showing full-time, part-time, atypical work, home-working rates and patterns of participation. It was accepted that until appropriate distinctions are applied to women workers, that our understanding of women's employment, unemployment and home-working status would be poorly understood and policies for improvement weakly based. By 2000, with the growing economy, the overall unemployment rate for both women and men fell dramatically to 3.9 per cent (CSO, 2001). This further reflects the new waves of opportunity sweeping Ireland for both sexes. Women are well represented in the 'high growth' sectors/occupations (e.g. Insurance, Finance and Business Services; Professional Services; Personal Services (CSO, 2001)).

Earnings gap between women and men workers

The magnitude and persistence of an earnings gap between women and men is familiar and an important issue among working women. The analysis of occupational structure as shown below demonstrates a concentration of women in certain job categories and in particular in manufacturing jobs. *An Economy-Wide Investigation of Sex Differences* by Callan and Wren (1992) showed that in the international context over the previous three decades female relative earnings had increased in most OECD countries causing wage gaps to fall 10-15 per cent. In Ireland, however, the changes were less dramatic. In 2000, women's industrial weekly wage was 67.96 per cent of men's yielding a gap of 32.04 per cent (CSO, 2001). Between 1975 and 2000 the pay gap narrowed at a rate of 0.4 per year and it is estimated at 15.5 per cent throughout all work areas (Irish Congress of Trade Unions (ICTU, 2002). The ICTU has estimated that at this rate it would take another 40 years to close this gap. They further observe that:

> it is evident therefore that the legislation alone is not sufficient to eliminate the difference in pay between men and women. In addition men are more likely to have jobs that include a range of benefits, such as pension and health insurance, thus making the real gap even greater (ICTU, 2002; The Pay Gap, p.2).

Three main causes of unequal pay have been isolated:

- Discrimination in pay systems. The slow progress in change can be attributed to the

  current system of determination operated by employers such as grading structure, performance related pay or appraisal systems, incremented pay systems and competency pay (ICTU, 2002: p.3).

- Reduced Labour Market Attachment: Working women tend, more than men, to have breaks in their working lives due to children or elder care responsibilities. Further, the cost of childcare and the need for flexibility alone contributes to the number of women working part-time. The ICTU makes a strong call for efforts to make work places more family friendly. In Ireland, women represent 73 per cent of part-time workers and on average earn 30 per cent per hour less than full-time workers.
- Occupational Segregation: Both horizontal and vertical segregation are in place.

To reduce the gender pay gap the ICTU has launched a new *Gender and Pay Project* (April 2002), which will run until March 2004. A second objective is to develop, test and diffuse gender-neutral guidelines for job evaluation and for gender proofing and gender impact assessment. Thirdly, this project is designed to develop tool kits for managers and for workers in order to increase their awareness raising skills, job evaluation skills, gender impact assessment skills and training needs analyses skills. Fourthly, this project is designed to develop the capacity to strengthen equality in policy development and service delivery within Trade Unions and to develop guidelines for upskilling and training women. The project is an ambitious initiative to improve the gender learning cultures of organizations, drawing on the expertise of the business sector and research from academics.

Strategies for integrating women into the labour market – childcare

There is a growing acceptance that *'families and companies'* must move in new mutually satisfying and beneficial ways in order to develop *family-friendly* organizations and further to create a satisfactory balance between working and living (Maternity and Protection of Employees Act, 1981; 1994). While new forms of structures and processes began to evolve particularly in the 1980s, this development was slow. By the late 1990s however a deeper recognition of the issues involved and the gains and benefits that can be achieved at individual organization family and community levels. The *National Childcare Strategy* (1999) noted that the lack of provision of quality childcare had reached a crisis level. This crisis in childcare received strong publicity in this report which recommended a wide range of measures including tax relief for working parents, and for employers, as well as the need for the State to support the provision of national childcare facilities. A later report by the Chambers of Commerce of Ireland (2001) – *Labour Force 2001 – Childcare* which tapped employers' views in 503 companies, revealed the growing impact that the lack of childcare places is having on labour market participation in 2001. In particular it revealed that 57 per cent of companies (whose staff have children under 12 years) are concerned about childcare, and that 72 per cent provided at least one form of family-friendly arrangement (e.g. part-time employment; flexitime; unpaid maternity leave in excess of the statutory entitlement). A mere 9 per cent considered assisting employees with the provision of childcare (e.g. financial assistance/subsidy; company crèche). It is of further interest that these companies view the onus for change to be primarily that of employees, and the government, and a combination including employers. More recently, national research on women returning to employment, education and training by the Economic and Social Research Institute ('Getting Out of the House' Russell, Smyth, Lyons and O'Connell, 2002), highlighted the need for a significant improvement in family-friendly policies offered by employers. It also emerged that women with children under the age of 5 are less likely than those with either older children, or no children at all, to make the transition to work.

It was further observed that while the National Development Plan (1999) had money earmarked for childcare, the allocation made had been significantly low. These findings clearly indicate that the crisis in Ireland's childcare requires a critical review of funding coupled with a long term strategy for the development and maintenance of the childcare sector, and a proactive approach in work organizations to enable women to develop and progress their careers and participation in senior roles.

Women pursuing education

The Irish educational system has a long and complex tradition that goes back many centuries and according to recent reviews modern Ireland has one of the most highly developed educational systems in the world (OECD, 1991). For the period 1985-1998 there were some one million people within the educational system at all levels (approximately 28 per cent of the overall population). During the period 1991-1997 there has been intense debate on the most appropriate framework for the future development of education in Ireland. The resulting *Government White Paper on Education 1995* mapped out the fundamental principle of equality as it related to gender equality and education as follows:

> The education system for the future should have a philosophy that embraces all students, male and female, on a basis of equality (1995:687).

Department of Education statistics from 1980-2000 reveal a relative balance of female and male students at each age level from 3 years to 20 years and over. These data also reflect the growing significance of higher level education for all school leavers. Over this period, the overall percentage of female access to third level education has exceeded 50 per cent by the late 1990s. The high increase in female students participating in third level education, over the past two decades is not however reflected in women's access to academic roles and in particular, to senior roles.

Since its inception in 1971 the Higher Education Authority (HEA) observed that the issues of equity and equality of opportunity have been of central importance and draw attention to the provision in the Higher Education Act (1971) to promote the *attainment of equality of opportunity in higher education* (Lindsay, 1994). It is of interest however that the first published report by the HEA – *Women Academics in Ireland* – had to wait until 1987. This report noted with concern the marked concentration of female academics in the junior lecturing grades, with women constituting a mere 5.5 per cent of the staff in senior grades in Irish universities. It further noted the concentration of women in certain fields of study, mainly Arts and Social Science, and low levels of representation in areas such as Engineering.

In recognition of the slow advancement of women in the third level sector, the Second Commission on the Status of Women (1993) recommended that all third level colleges should be required to develop and implement equal opportunities policies and action programmes and a policy on sexual harassment for students and employees.

A review of Women in Academia in Ireland (McCarthy and Kelly, 2001) stressed the need to accelerate women's progress into academic roles (which now stands at 28.9 per cent) and in particular to increase the number of women who are professors (6.5 per cent in 2001), and associate professors (8.7 per cent in 2001).

Other developments which have occurred in the third level sector across Ireland have acted as catalysts for change. In particular, universities and colleges have issued Equal Opportunities Policies over the period 1986-2001. Further, several colleges have established Gender Equality Committees to advise on the formulation, implementation, and monitoring of action programmes to implement equality policies.

Women in management

Irish Census of Population data over the period 1981-1991 demonstrates a steady increase in the number of women who attained *Directors, Managers and Company Secretaries* work status i.e. from 9.1 per cent in 1981 to 21.7 per cent in 1991. Later Labour Force Survey statistics in 1997, show a further increase of women in managerial roles to 27.9 per cent (refers to *Proprietors and Managers*), while the profile for 2000 which refers to *Managers and Administrators*, reveals a stabilization at 27.7 per cent (CSO, 2001) (see also Table 4.2).

Table 4.2 Persons employed as directors, managers and company secretaries in Ireland, 1981-2000

Year	Male	Female	Total	Females as % of Total
1981	26,672	2,679	29,351	9.1
1991	35,201	9,792	44,993	21.7
1997	34,800	13,500	48,300	27.9
2000	217,200	83,400	306,600	27.7

* *Source*: Census of Population 1981, 1991 and 2000 (Vol. 4)
Labour Force Survey 1997 (Proprietors and Managers), CSO, Statistical Bulletin, 2001.
These figures include retired persons.

These national patterns exhibit clear progress in women's access to senior and prestigious jobs up to the early 1990s. Yet it is also evident that the pace of access has flattened out into the 2000s.

Reasons for the low involvement of women in managerial roles, which applied in the early 1970s, still carry a strong resonance in the decades that follow. By the late 1980s male managers in 44 companies (McCarthy, 1988) identified four core factors which they perceived as inhibiting women's promotional prospects as follows:

- women are less ambitious in their jobs than men,
- women's work is less varied and more limited than men's,
- women are not assertive enough,
- women are geographically less mobile than men.

This longitudinal research demonstrated that the organizations examined did not exhibit any evidence of having initiated change, over a twelve year period, which encouraged female employees to seek training and development and opportunities to higher level jobs. The barriers identified by male managers to women's progress were predominantly intrapsyhic, attributing to women personality traits that are deemed to be negative.

Later attitudinal research in the 1990s, which once more explored male managers' perceptions of barriers to women's promotion, yielded a profile similar to that of the earlier study in which three core factors, lack of experience, lack of assertiveness and low ambition received the highest response. It is significant that these managers attributed little or no responsibility to their own organizational structures, policies and the dominant organizational cultures as sources of sex discrimination (direct or indirect) (see McCarthy and Drew, 1993). Further, it emerged that existing negative organizational self-fulfilling prophecies regarding women's leadership potential and competencies had not been dissolved during the intervening years.

Paralleling these attitudinal studies the Council for the Status of Women (CSW) initiated a programme of monitoring women's participation at organizational Board level (in Irish State-sponsored Bodies). In 1981, the total number of members of the Boards of 90 State-sponsored bodies was 1,098, 8.8 per cent (N=94) of whom were women. Government ministerial women appointees constituted a mere 7.9 per cent (N=79). The CSW (later called National Women's Council of Ireland: NWCI), concluded that:

> Women throughout the country must be formally involved in the decision making process...ultimately this question is the responsibility of the Government (1986:16 and 17).

A later follow-up report by the NWCI (1990) demonstrated that limited progress was achieved during the 1980s. In recognition of women's slow progress to membership of State Boards the NWCI put forward the proposal that a 40 per cent gender balance policy for State Boards should be introduced. On the recommendation of the Second Irish Commission on the Status of Women (1991, 1993) this policy was adopted by the Government in 1991. In 1997, a comprehensive report by the NWCI – *Getting the Balance Right: Who Makes Decisions in 1997*, which reviewed this policy over the six years since first adopted, found a welcome increase to 29 per cent Board membership for women (i.e. 812 women out of total of 2,814, ranging from 67 per cent in Equality and Law Reform to 9 per cent in Marine).

The NWCI (1997) reported that this change was significant and concluded:

> Today there are many more women sharing the Government responsibilities on Boards of our State companies, bringing their insights and experience to the boardrooms and adding to their own knowledge (1997:11).

Women in local government and local development

Over the three decades from 1967 to 1999 the percentage of women elected to local government has been very slow to rise despite significant changes in women's formal labour market activity. A first statistical profile of women's participation in elected local government roles conducted in 2000 (Áit ag an mBórd, 2000), showed an increase from a low of 3 per cent in 1967 to 15 per cent in 1999. This national research had a dual focus: firstly to detail the *representation of women in decision-making structures for Local Development in Ireland*, and secondly to explore through focus groups women's experience of the existing structures and processes. It was concluded that barriers to women's involvement in local decision-making structures (e.g. County Councils; City Councils/Corporations; Borough Corporations, Urban District Councils) are *strong and persistent and include a lack of provision for flexible child and elder care services, transport, lack of money, training and experience and the inflexibility of the times at which meetings are organized or training and other initiatives are provided* (2000:80). It was further observed that the culture and practices of traditional local administration structures, together with the workings of the electoral system at local level discourage women's involvement. In addition, local government continues to be dominated by the political party system within which women have traditionally been under represented – under these conditions independent women candidates could experience great difficulty in accessing funding and support.

Following the adoption of the National Development Plan, new *Gender Impact Assessment Guidelines* were developed by the Irish Government in March 2000. In the future these guidelines will be applied to every measure financed by the National Development Plan. Two departments of Government (Department of Justice, Equality and Law Reform, and Department of Education and Science) have established Monitoring Units to monitor gender mainstreaming generally and to advise on the development of appropriate indicators in this regard. These initiatives go beyond aspirational statements to the development of grounded mechanisms that can monitor and measure the degree of gender equality change that is occurring.

Entering the boardrooms

Within the private sector (public quoted companies) data on women's access to Boards is limited. A first study undertaken by O'Higgins (1992) on *Non-Executive Directors in the Irish Board Rooms*, noted that a mere 2 per cent of directors were women (10 females: 427 males). She further observes that female representation on Irish PLCs

> is even worse when one takes into account that this includes executive as well as non-executive directors (1992:54).

The directors interviewed (24 males: 2 females) agreed that the mode of selecting the Irish directors was a traditional one which did not tap into potential women directors and they further conceded that more ways needed to be found to recruit women into decision-making roles as non-executive directors and to provide opportunities for organizations to utilize the talents of women for competitive advantage.

By 1997, a survey of 60 leading companies in Ireland (plcs) conducted by the *Sunday Tribune* established that there were some 14 non-executive female directors on boards compared with 290 men – yielding a mere 4.8 per cent representation of women. More disturbing, some 48 per cent of these large companies had no women at non-executive director level (Coleman, 1997).

Women in management in Irish business

Coming from a perspective that in today's competitive environment a quality employee is a major asset to any business, IBEC (Irish Business and Employers Confederation) conducted a recent comprehensive survey on *Women in Management in Irish Business* (Coughlan, 2002). In this study of some 6,012 managers and executives in 297 companies covering a total of 51,505 employees, it was established that women occupy only 8 per cent of chief executives (level I), 21 per cent of heads of functions/managers (level II), 31 per cent of middle managers (level III), and 45 per cent of junior managers (level IV) (see Table 4.3).

Table 4.3 Women's participation in management in business in Ireland: Levels of management in 297 companies (N=6012 managers in 2002)

Levels I-IV	Males N	Females N	Total N	Female as % of Total
I: Chief Executives/Managing Directors	260	23	283	8
II: Heads of Functions and Senior Managers	984	271	1255	22
III: Middle Managers	1245	551	1796	31
IV: Junior Managers/Professional	1464	1214	2678	45
TOTALS	3953	2059	6012	34

Source: Coughlan (2002)

While this research did not include a specific attitudinal analysis, the 'glass ceiling' phenomenon as developed by Mattis (1995) and Wirth (2001), is presented by Coughlan (2002) as a significant barrier to the promotion of highly educated Irish women. In particular, the following dilemmas are isolated as core barriers maintaining the 'glass ceiling' in place in Irish business

- *Structural/institutional factors* which include occupational segregation by gender, unclear criteria for promotion, work/family responsibilities, long hours culture, overall general corporate culture.

- *Attitudinal and psycho-social factors* which embrace perceptions of traditional male/female roles, women's self-selection out of senior roles, women leading men etc.
- *Networking* both formal and informal, in particular exclusion from informal management networks.
- *Women and pay* – the traditional pay gap between women and men, still permeates decisions relating to rewards at higher levels.
- *Women and self-employment* refers to a tendency for women who reach senior management positions to have higher drop-out rates than men.

When middle and senior management and chief executives are combined, women comprise a quarter of all managers, which closely matches the national data presented in Table 4.3. When all four levels are combined, female employment constitutes just over a third (34 per cent) of all managers/executives. Further analyses showed that more female chief executives are likely to be found in service sector companies; in small companies and in Irish owned companies. Given the increased achievements of Irish women in higher education, the question arises as to why these have not translated into greater/equal participation by women in middle and senior management?

Equality of opportunity in the Irish Civil Service

The Irish Civil Service is one of the largest employment areas in Ireland, and thus developments relating to equality and opportunity in this arena set a powerful marker for other fields. Since the mid-1980s, the Civil Service has initiated a policy and strategy to promote positive action and equal opportunity.

A report *Equality of Opportunity in the Civil Service 1993* (Department of Finance, 1995), details statistical information relating to gender equality and revealed that there was no woman at the highest grades of Secretary (of a Government department).

A later profile of women and men in the top Civil Service grades for the years 1995-2000, clearly shows that the proportion of female staff diminishes sharply according to ascending grades from *higher executive officer* to *Secretary General/Deputy Secretary* (see Table 4.4).

**Table 4.4   Women and men in the top service grades in the Civil Service for
the years 1995-2000**

Grade	1995		1997		2000	
	Women %	(n)	Women %	(n)	Women %	(n)
Secretary General	4	(1)	4	(1)	9.1	(2)
Deputy Secretary	6	(5)	10.2	(10)	12.2	(13)
Principal	13	(43)	11.9	(41)	16.1	(82)
Assistant Principal	23	(227)	24.5	(251)	26.5	(372)
Higher Executive Officer	37	(697)	39	(760)	39.3	(1035)
Executive Officer	51	(1200)	54	(1403)	56.7	(2114)
Total					64.3	(13,209)

Source: Report: Equality of Opportunity in the Civil Service – 1993 (Department of
Finance, 1995) and Second Report to Government of the Co-ordinating Group of
Secretaries: A Programme of Change for the Irish Civil Service (1996). Civil Service Data
(1997, 1998), CSO Database 2000

A relatively static picture depicts this period – two women (9 per cent) occupy the
top role of Secretary in 2000 compared with one woman (1 per cent in 1995).
Given that female employment in the Civil Service is increasing (64.3 per cent in
2000, out of a total of 20,000), the rate of change is minimal. To explore and
explicate the reasons for the considerable under-representation of women in higher
grades in the Civil Service, research was commissioned by the Civil Service
(conducted by Humphreys, Drew and Murphy, 1999). Three main categories of
factors were identified as contributing to the gender imbalance at higher grades in
the Civil service. These include:

• Organizational cultural barriers: women excluded from the core; long hours
  culture; work/family conflict; negative perception of job sharing; lack of female
  role models.
• Personnel policies and practices: negative historical legacy; lack of gender
  balance in interview boards; ageism etc.
• Societal factors: sex-role stereotypes, expectations and outcomes which were
  seen as still alive in the Civil Service.

The core areas suggested for changing the gender imbalance in the Civil Service
targeted:

• Training/development initiatives.
• Family/development initiatives.
• Promotion policy review.

Overall, it was proposed that a 50:50 gender balance by grade, over a time frame that is both realistic and demanding, should be aimed for. A new milestone for the achievement of gender equality in the Irish Civil Service, was reached in 2001, with the launch of a five year plan by the Government in consultation with the Civil Service union – *Equality Policy in the Civil Service 2001.*

The new policy consists of two main targets:

- Equality objectives – heads of departments will be responsible for the setting of equality objectives. A department policy on equality of opportunity will be reviewed by management, ministers of State and the Government. In the future, statements of strategy of Government Departments must include new equality objectives.
- Guidelines on best practice in relation to recruitment, placement and mobility, training and staff developments, promotion, work and family responsibilities in areas such as bullying and harassment, constitute the core of the implemented policy.

Barriers to women's advancement – Some perceptions from woman managers

The research outlined in this chapter, as well as international studies during the past decade or so confirm that corporate barriers to women's advancement are deep and entrenched (see Adler, 1993; Davidson and Burke, 2000).

To clarify the organizational and personal work-family hurdles, that women in active management roles experience, the perceptions of some 124 women managers in major Irish organizations were asked to compare their *present position as women managers, with that of male managers* (see McCarthy and McGinn, 1996).

Results from this study revealed that 57 per cent women managers perceived factors relating to *job opportunities, opportunities for overall organizational learning,* and *comprehensive work experience* as equivalent for both women and men managers.

The findings also indicate that a majority of women managers in modern day Irish organizations clearly perceived themselves to be receiving extrinsic rewards (working conditions, flexibility, job security, opportunities for job training, financial, mobility etc.), comparable with those of their male counterparts. Thus, those visible components of equal opportunity (rewards etc.) have been put in place to a large degree in those organizations. The area where the greatest gap is evident is in those aspects of organizational leadership and culture which support the progress of women into senior management roles. For example, support from senior management, opportunities for advancement, involvement in decision making, and availability of a mentor were viewed as worse for women managers to a large degree.

When these women managers were further invited to rank the most salient barriers to women's advancement in organizations, the top ranks (1-7, in a 14 item scale), once more highlight the entrenched problems of child-care support and exclusion dynamics. The two factors which receive the highest rank scores:

- *Lack of recognition by Irish companies and management of the need to provide support systems for women with young children* (rank 1.5), and
- *A pattern of business and professional relationships that have not included women* (rank 1.5), clearly documents that Irish women managers are very conscious of the extent to which exclusion dynamics have operated against women in that:

Limited support systems in terms of crèche facilities, parental leave, flexible work hours, work sharing have existed for women workers with young children.

The dominant business culture has traditionally excluded women – this culture pervades not only formal business/professional settings but also the political/social domains (politics, sports clubs, golf, football; men's clubs etc.) These powerful business and social arenas embody gendered cultures – structures and processes – which typically have nurtured and supported men while on the other hand they have excluded women. The patriarchal gender legacy inherited from the past can influence and reinforce gendered cultures either consciously or unconsciously.

Traditional attitudes of men at work towards women which received third rank reinforces the strength of entrenched gender stereotypes and the complexity and stability of inter-group sex orientations. Despite change relating to women's access to a broader range of organizational roles, the lack of female role models in senior roles comes through in the concerns which received rank 4 *the difficulty for the organization in visualizing women in leadership and management roles.* The dominance of work places designed to support men's traditional life styles (rank 5) and the *conflicting pressure/demands between the work place and the home environment* (rank 6.5), further highlighted the need for creative innovative family-friendly workplaces, and supportive childcare facilities. Positive changes for women managers were also identified by this sample of women managers. In particular, a large majority noted that women were not less professionally competent than men, were not less committed to their jobs than men, and did not display less leadership ability than men. Thus, a very strong profile of affirmation of women's competence, leadership and commitment is evident (McCarthy and McGinn, 1996).

Women entrepreneurs

According to a recent European Commission Survey of women entrepreneurs (conducted by the OECD, 2001), women make up just 15 per cent of self-employed people in Ireland – a figure well below the European average (35 per cent) as well as the US (35 per cent) and Canada (37 per cent). It is observed that the low share of female entrepreneurs in Ireland may reflect cultural attitudes and other gender-specific constraints which limit occupational options of women, according to the study (e.g. many older women came from a generation when they would not have worked outside the home). Another explanation proffered by Bowler (2001), President of the Institute of Directors, is that with the rise of the Celtic Tiger in Ireland, the level of entrepreneurship has declined, due to the increase in the availability of jobs at good salary levels (graduates could earn Euros 31,743 at entry levels).

While the Commission's survey measured the share of female entrepreneurs during the 1980s and 1990s, Ireland however did not have any figures available for the 1980s. It is evident that Ireland is not yet exploiting the full entrepreneurial potential of its adult female population.

Country legislation

As discussed earlier, the *First Report on the Status of Women in Ireland* (1972) delineated the position of women in the world of work as a significant arena where gross discrimination was dominant. Highly gender-differentiated work environments and unequal pay were the norm, with women viewed as a poor investment for future training and development.

- **The Anti-Discrimination (Pay) Act 1974** introduced equal pay for work in the same place of work. Due to the poor economic situation the Government delayed the enforcement of the Act until 1976. Ireland joined the EEC in 1973 and the European Directive on Equal Pay was the catalyst for enforcement.
- **The Employment Equality Act 1977** was introduced in 1977 to tackle non-pay matters relating to employment discrimination on the grounds of sex and/or marital status. It further introduced the concept of equal opportunity relating to promotion, training and development, selection and appraisal etc. This Act also led to the establishment of the Employment Equality Agency in 1977, whose primary task was to drive the implementation of the Equality Acts and to promote gender equality in all work setting (see McCarthy, 1988).
- **Employment Equality Act (1998).** The intent of this Act is to force employers to take preventative measures by putting in place policies and procedures that prevent discrimination and harassment occurring – to engender a culture of zero tolerance. The Act identifies nine categories of discrimination as follows: sex, marital status, family status, gender orientation, religious belief, age (between 18 and 65), disability, race and membership of the travelling community. Employers must ensure that their practices do not discriminate in relation to recruitment, conditions of employment, grading, training or promotion. Managers will have to be on the alert for instances of harassment and bullying and take immediate corrective action. The penalties in sexual harassment and discrimination cases can be very substantial. This Act further established a new infrastructure to promote and enforce equality – it provides a statutory office of

Director of Equality Investigations to hear claims for redress in the event of discrimination. An Equality Authority was also established under the Act to promote equality on each of the nine grounds and to make available advice and to support the drive towards equal opportunities. This Authority replaced the Employment Equality Agency and the Employment Equality Act (1998) supersedes the earlier Acts (1974, 1977).

- **The Equality Status Act (2000)** was introduced to transform the old paradigm of inequality at a societal level. These Acts constitute another significant step forward in the evolution of equal opportunity in Ireland.

Initiatives supporting women in the workforce

National plan for women 2001-2006

The National Development Plan is acting as a catalyst for change driving gender equality. Its operationalization embodies gender mainstreaming and the construction of gender indicators to measure the effectiveness of a policy in delivering gender equality. To date, deficiencies identified in implementing gender equality include the absence of agreed indicators, lack of a comprehensive bank of gender disaggregated data and the low level of women's input into the Government's gender equality strategy (see also Gilligan, 2000).

Building on the UN General Assembly meeting (June 2000) which called on Governments to develop national plans to implement the Beijing Platform for Action, the Irish Government (Department of Justice, Equality and Law Reform) has introduced a National Plan For Women, 2001-2006.

This plan, which embraces an extensive consultation process with women's groups in particular, is a positive development in the pursuit of substantive equality. Government departments are the first target and given their visibility and centrality in Irish society, it is expected that other public bodies, private companies and small and medium sized enterprises will also be driven to gender mainstreaming so as to have a tangible impact on policy outcomes and women's representation in senior and decision-making roles.

Mentoring as a change strategy

There is agreement that the mentor/mentee relationship has considerable positive and negative potential (Kram, 1985). It can serve to include or exclude, to promote opportunities or to oppress, to encourage creative expansion in to maintain the *status quo*. Field research conducted by Foley and McCarthy (1995) with female mentees in a large commercial Irish organization on their experience of a mentoring programme that had been introduced, highlighted the following beneficial outcomes of the mentoring experiences.

- Female mentees were attracted to the mentoring process primarily to develop relationships with senior managers and to benefit from their experience.
- Mentees further felt that the mentoring relationship, helped women develop more and feel more confident; and opened up channels of communication in the company for them. Mentees obtained an opportunity to observe senior managers working – thereby losing *the mystique*, and to get to know more about organizational management.
- Mentees also observed that mentors learned about the mentee's department and work and gained a better understanding of gender issues in the organization and got to know younger female managers in the company.

Given that mentoring relationships do not occur in a vacuum, and that mentoring can have a profound impact on the gender culture of an organization, this research recommended that the mentoring strategy studied, should be viewed by other Irish companies as a major tool for change in organizational gender equality and that cultivating female mentors in turn could have a synergistic effect on dissolving the dominant *glass ceilings*, and creating gender equality cultures.

Communal empowerment

It is recognized that election to local authorities remains a crucial entry point for national politics. However, the persistent low percentage (15 per cent) of women elected as local councillors during the 1990s is a cause for concern. Given this dominant pattern, significant change is unlikely to occur over the next three decades without conscious political party and government interventions.

Communal empowerment for women is however emerging in the form of community women participating in Partnerships Groups. Conscious of the powerful exclusion dynamics embedded in societal culture, they have invested considerable effort in carving out representation in the new local/regional Partnership Developments aided by EU funding (NOW programmes).

The leadership and decision-making learning generated in these community settings provides new models of participation and involvement for community women and further may prove to be the creative pool from which future women politicians (at local and national levels) will develop and evolve.

Visions of leadership and decision-making

Women in Ireland have for some time now become more aware of their invisibility in leadership roles in work places, communities, home and school systems, sport and recreation. When it comes to female representation in politics, Irish women lag behind seven EU countries (Sweden, Denmark, Finland, Holland, Germany, Spain and the UK) (NCWI, 2002).

In May 2002, a General Election saw the termination of a Government in which female representation was a mere 12 per cent (N=21 women v. 145 men). During the election campaign, issues of gender equality did not rate high and the final outcome was a minimal increase to 13.8 per cent (N=23 women v. 143 men). The adversarial nature of Dáil (Parliament) politics is viewed as off-putting for women members and the re-drawing of constituencies did not favour leading women politicians who lost their seats. A respected feminist columnist, McCafferty (2002), argues that the election of two women in succession as Presidents of Ireland, since 1990 (i.e. President Mary Robinson, 1991-1998; President Mary McAlesse, 1998-2005) may have satisfied the electorate's appetite for gender politics. This is a phenomenon that the broad spectrum of women voters will have to be alerted to; and the need to channel resources into areas of great need for women e.g. health, education, family-friendly work places, community support, requires gender-focussed policies and decision-making.

The future

There is a new angst that involvement in decision-making and leadership is not something that happens easily. Mary Robinson, President of Ireland (1991-1998), articulated very clearly an understanding of women and leadership which resonates with the newly emergent ideas on women and transformational leadership:

> As women lead, they are changing leadership, as they organize they are changing organizations...as women are adding to the product of leadership they are also changing the process. It will be one of the finest gifts we can give to coming generations a more open, flexible and compassionate style of administration and a new relation between the individual leader and the community leadership... (Robinson, 1992:2).

These words provide a narrative which talks of the need for leaders to shape culture in such a way as to provide meaning to people's lives. The challenge for women leadership which flows from these words is that of embodying the practice of leadership and the expression of power with an ethical dimension – a truly transformational process.

References

Adler, N.J. (1993), 'An International Perspective on the Barriers to the Advancement of Women Managers', *Journal of Applied Psychology: An International Review*, **42** (4), 289-300.

Áit ag an mBórd (2000), *Representation of Women in Decision-Making Structures for Local Development in Ireland*, Dublin: Partnership Organisations.

Anti-Discrimination Pay Act (1974), Dublin: Stationery Office.

Callan, T. and Farrell, A. (1992), *Women's Participation in the Irish Labour Market*, Dublin, National Economic and Social Council Report No. 91.

Callan, T. and Wren, A. (1992), *An Economy under Investigation of Sex Differences in Wage Roles*, Dublin: The Economic and Social Research Institute, Working Paper, No. 34.

Central Statistics Office (1997, 2001), *Census of Population Statistics, 1971, 1981, 1991, 1996, Statistical Bulletin*, Dublin: Stationery Office.

Chamber of Commerce of Ireland (2001), *Labour Force 2001 – Childcare*, Dublin: Chambers of Commerce of Ireland.

Coleman, S. (1997), 'Severe shortage of women on Irish boards', *Sunday Tribune*, 17th August; 3.

Coughlan, A. (2002), *Women in Management in Irish Business*, Dublin: Report of Irish Business and Employers Confederation.

Council for the Status of Women (1981), Who Makes the decisions? Dublin: CSW.

Davidson, M.I. and Burke, R.J. (2000), *Women in Management: Current Research Issues Volume II*, London: Sage Publications.

Department of Education Statistics (1980-2000), Dublin: Stationery Office.

Department of Finance (1995), *Equality of Opportunity in the Civil Service*, Dublin: Department of Finance.

Department of Finance (2001), *Gender Equality Policy for the Civil Service*, Dublin: Department of Finance.

Employment Equality Act (1977), Dublin: Stationery Office.

Employment Equality Act (1998), Dublin: Stationery Office.

ETAN (2000), *Science Policies in the European Union: Promoting excellence through mainstreaming gender equality*, Brussels: European Commission.

European Social Fund, Programme Evaluation Unit (1999), *Evaluation Report: ESF and the Local Urban and Rural Development Operational Programme*, Dublin: ESF Programme Evaluation Unit.

Foley, T. and McCarthy, E. (1995), 'An evaluation of a formal mentoring programme report', research report, Social and Organisational Psychology Research Centre, University College Dublin-NUI.

Galligan, Y. (2000), *The Development of Mechanisms to Monitor Progress in Achieving Gender Equality in Ireland*, Dublin: Stationery Office.

Higher Education Act (1971), Dublin: Stationery Office.

Higher Education Authority (1987), *Women Academics in Ireland*, Dublin: Higher Education Authority.

Humpreys, P.C., Drew, E. and Murphy, C. (1999), *Gender Equality in the Civil Service in Dublin*, Institute of Public Administration.

Irish Congress of Trade Unions (ICTU) (2002), *Gender and pay project – Information*, Dublin: ICTU.

Kennedy, K.A. (2002), 'Economic Growth in Ireland: Where has it come from, where is it going? In *Journal of the Statistical and Social Inquiry Society of Ireland* (One hundred and fifty-fourth session, 2000/2001) Vol. **XXX**: 123-139.

Kram, K.E. (1986), 'Mentoring in the Workplace', in Douglas T. Hall and Associates (ed.), *Career Development in Organisations*, Jossey-Bass Publishers, 160-201.

Lindsay, N. (1994), 'Equality of Opportunity in third level education in Ireland', in Egan, O. (ed.), *Proceedings Forum*, Cork: National Unit of Equal Opportunities in third level.

MacSharry, R. and White, P. (2000), *The Making of the Celtic Tiger – the inside story of Ireland's Boom Economy*, Dublin: Mercier Press.

McCarthy, E. (1988), *Transitions to equal opportunities at work in Ireland: Problems and Possibilities*, Dublin: Employment Equality Agency.

McCarthy, E. (1990), *Innovation and Women and Work in Ireland*, Research report, Social and Organisational Psychology Research Centre, University College Dublin, NUI.

McCarthy, E. and Drew, E. (1993), 'Training and Development: A Survey of Irish Companies', in Kennedy, M. (ed.), *Athena Report – Ireland*, European Commission and Dublin Technology Partnership Ltd.

McCarthy, E. and Kelly, A. (2001), *Women in Academia Research Report*, Dublin: Social and Organisational Psychology Research Centre, University College Dublin, NUI.

McCarthy, E. and McGinn, A. (1996), *The participation of women in management*, research report, Fourth Government Joint Oireachtas Committee, in Association with Social and Organisational Psychology Research Centre, University College Dublin, NUI.

McCafferty, N. (2002), Here's women for you: Just 12% of the Dáil', Dublin: *Sunday Tribune*, 6th May 2002.

Maternity Protection of Employees Act (1981), – Dublin Government Publications.

Maternity Protection of Employees Act (1994), – Dublin Government Publications.

Mattis, M. (1995), 'Corporate Initiatives for advancing Women', *Women in Management Review*, **10** (7), 5-14.

National Childcare Strategy (1999), *Report of the Partnership 2000 Expert Working Group on Childcare*. Dublin: Stationery Office.

National Development Plan (1999) (NDP2000-2006), Dublin: Stationery Office.

National Employment-Action Plan (NEAD) (1999), Dublin: Stationery Office.

National Women's Council of Ireland (1990), 'The Participation of Women on the Boards of Six State-Sponsored Bodies', *Annual Journal,* Winter: **8**, Dublin.

National Women's Council of Ireland (2002), *Politics Need More Women: What the Irish Political System must do*, Dublin: NCWI.

National Women's Council of Ireland (1997), *Getting the balance right: Who makes the Decisions in 1997*, Dublin: NWCI.

O'Higgins, E. (1992), *Non Executive Directors in the Irish Boardroom: Selection and Characteristics,* Dublin: Network.

OECD, *Economic Surveys: Ireland 1974-1999*, Paris: OECD.

OECD (2001), Survey of Women Entrepreneurs, European Commission/OECD.

Partnership 2000 for inclusion, employment and competitiveness (1996), Dublin: Stationery Office.

Programme for Prosperity and Fairness (2000), Dublin: Department of the Taoiseach.

Report of the First Commission on the Status of Women (1972), Dublin: Stationery Office.

Report of the Second Commission on the Status of Women (1993), Dublin: Stationery Office.

Robinson, Mary (1990), *President of Ireland Inaugural Address*, Dublin.

Robinson, Mary (1992), *President of Ireland Opening Address – Visions of Leadership*, Global Forum of Women Conference, July 1992, Dublin.

Russell, H., Smyth, E., Lyons, M. and O'Connell, P.J. (2002), *Getting Out of the House*, Dublin: Economic and Social Research Institute.

Sweeney, P. (1997), *The Celtic Tiger: Ireland's economic miracle explained*, Dublin: Oaktree Press.

The Equal Status Act (2000), Dublin: Stationery Office.

White Paper on Education (1995), Dublin: Stationery Office.

Wirth, L. (2001), *Breaking Through the Glass Ceiling: Women in Management*. Geneva: International Labour Office (ILO).

Chapter 5

Women in Management in the Netherlands

Kea G. Tijdens

Introduction

This chapter highlights the current labour force characteristics in the Netherlands, including an overview of the changes over the past 10 to 20 years. It extends the conclusions of a similar chapter for the 1970s and 1980s (Tijdens, 1993). First, this chapter details women pursuing education, and the focus then changes to women in management. This broad category is subdivided into women in managerial occupations, women in supervisory jobs, women on corporate boards of directors, and women holding elected offices in local and national government. The following section draws attention to women entrepreneurs, notably the self-employed women, the assisting members of the family, and the professional women. The final sections highlight the legislation in the Netherlands, the initiatives to support the advancement of women, and predictions about the future.

Labour force characteristics [1]

During the post-war period Dutch women were supposed to contribute to the rebuilding of society by setting up a family. Many of them did, as the baby boom in the late 1940s and early 1950s shows. Women overwhelmingly left the labour market on the day of their marriage to become full-time, permanent housewives. More than 98 per cent of the married women aged 15-65 were housewives. The breadwinner system was firmly established in industrial relations, in wage policies as well as in general attitudes towards gender roles. Male workers were supposed to earn a family wage in a 48-hour working week, and nearly all men were able to do so, thanks to a non-dispersed wage distribution. Women spent on average far more than a 48-hours week on their household chores.

From the 1960s onwards, this breadwinner/housewife model came under pressure, initially because of labour market shortages. Married women with grown-up children re-entered the labour market in part-time, temporary jobs. Most of them wanted to earn additional money for their children's education. In the 1970s, when fast increasing numbers of young women were better educated than ever before, this group dismissed the idea of becoming a full-time housewife after marriage. Nevertheless, because of the absence of day care and part-time jobs most of them quit the labour market when giving birth, but they definitely had the desire to re-enter. By then, average household time had dropped under 40 hours a week.

During the 1960s and 1970s, the Dutch female participation rate in the labour market remained stable, notably 24 per cent in 1960, 25 per cent in 1971, and 28 per cent in 1981 for the population aged 14-64. From the 1980s onwards, female participation rates increased steadily. A break down by age group provides a clear picture of the dynamics. The participation rate of girls aged 14-19 dropped from 55 per cent in 1960 to 20 per cent in 1997, and in the 20-24 age group it grew little, but in both the 25-39 age group and the 40-49 age group the rates showed a sharp increase from 17 per cent and 19 per cent respectively in 1960, to 68 per cent and 59 per cent respectively almost forty years later. In the post-war period, women's work changed from girls' labour to labour of prime age women.

During the recession period in the early 1980s, women who gave birth increasingly tried to prevent a career break, because the high unemployment levels reduced the chances of re-entering the workforce with a comparable job, while it increased the likelihood of an unemployed husband. Secondly, an increasing share of the female work force performed skilled jobs and thus the opportunity costs of a homemaker career increased. Thirdly, periods away from the labour force would cause loss of skills and thus depreciation of human capital, which would depress women's wage levels at re-entry.

Finally, during the 1990s women's participation rate increased to the average levels of the European Union. Regarding the supply side of the labour market, the major factors here have been women's fast increasing educational levels, decreasing family size, and fall in household time, caused by better housing, domestic equipment, heating with gas instead of coal, etc. By the mid 1990s, the average household time of a married or cohabiting woman aged 16 to 64 had fallen below 25 hours a week. Regarding the demand side of the labour market, major factors were the increasing demand for labour in female-dominated jobs as well as an increasing demand for part-time labour. Since 1993, as a consequence of favourable economic development, employment continuously increased, particularly for women. In 2001, unemployment had fallen to a level that was low by European standards.

By 1992, more than 2.1 million women had a job of at least 12 hours a week, and nearly 0.5 million had a job up to 12 hours. By 2000, the female labour force totalled 2.7 million working 12 hours or over and nearly 0.6 million with a part-time job. The definition of the net participation rate includes the population aged 15-64 with a job of at least 12 hours, not including the unemployed. From 1990 to 2001, the net female participation rate grew from 39 to 53 per cent. A break down by age reveals that the rates increased in all age groups, except for the 15-24 years.

The Netherlands is well known for the highest part-time rate of female workers in the European Union. Figure 5.1 shows the figures. In 1992, nearly 31 per cent or

814,000 women had a 20-34 hour job. Eight years later, this had increased to 37 per cent or 1.232 million women. Similarly, the share of women in 12-29 hour jobs had grown from 12 to 14 per cent, whereas the share of women in jobs of 35 hours and over had declined from 38 to 31 per cent, and the share of women in a job less than 12 hours had dropped from 19 to 17 per cent. When taking also into account the women with a 1-12 hour job, more than two-thirds of the working women in the Netherlands were not employed full-time.

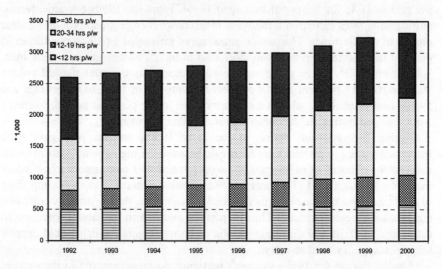

Figure 5.1   The female workforce (x 1000), breakdown by working hours, 1992-2000

Source: CBS, Website, March 2002

Since the early 1980s, women increasingly prefer to continue their job when having a baby, but only under the condition that they can reduce the working hours in their job. There are several reasons for this behaviour. The absence of extended families and thus insufficient informal day care, insufficient formal day-care, the absence of domestic help, and a highly cultivated motherhood culture influenced women's preferences to work part-time instead of full-time. In the early 1980s, when the unions demanded a collective working time reduction to fight unemployment and the female workers preferred an individual working time reduction, the negotiations resulted in an increasing number of collective bargaining agreements with both general working time reduction, mostly without loss of pay, and the right for workers to reduce their working hours individually at their own costs (Tijdens, 1998a, 1998b). In growing numbers, female workers succeeded in requesting that their employers reduce working hours in the job. It was not until 1989, that political pressure led to a governmental decision to subsidize day-care centres. In the 2000s, most women with young children have both a part-time job and a part-time arrangement for day-care. In comparison to other EU member states, the presence of children under the age of 15 in the household is the best predictor for Dutch female workers to be in part-time employment (Tijdens, 2002). Women who once reduced their working hours, are likely to request an extension of working hours when their children have grown up.

Increasingly, employers have adapted to the part-time requests (Tijdens, 1998a; Visser, 2000). In the early 1980s, some employers did so as their main strategy against union demands for a shorter working week. Then, increasingly, employers preferred skilled female employees to remain working part-time rather than not working at all because of their investments in women's training and qualifications. Since the late 1980s, employers were pressed by the unions, who in turn came under pressure from their growing female membership. Moreover, in the early 1990s, some employers were eager to bring staffing levels in line with the varying supply of work, and part-time jobs fitted this strategy perfectly. Yet nowadays, particularly in health care and education, the number of part-timers has grown so much that the organizational span of control limits further growth in part-time work, but given the tight labour market, these organizations continue to support part-time employment.

The acceptance of the reduction of working hours did not happen simultaneously in all industries and occupations. Part-time work was accepted in health care and education at a very early stage, whereas in the manufacturing industry and in secretarial work it was accepted later. The latter is perhaps best explained by managers' strong preferences for their secretary to be present full-time. In the 1960s and 1970s, part-time employment used to be low-skilled, but this has changed completely. In the banking sector for example, part-time work predominantly was found in the area of data-entry, whereas nowadays it can be found in nearly all jobs. In the 2000s, discussions about the acceptance of part-time work concentrate on the male-dominated professional occupations, particularly in case of a growing percentage of women, such as the legal and medical professions (for the latter, see Heiligers and Hingstman, 2000).

In many countries, part-time jobs are still marginal and low-paid jobs. In the Netherlands, however, with the rise of part-time employment, awareness grew regarding discriminatory clauses in Labour Law based on working hours. For example, part-time jobs up to 13 hours a week used to be excluded from regulations regarding the minimum guarantees for wages and holiday allowance. In the early 1990s, substantial attention was paid to equalizing pay and working conditions with regard to working hours in collective agreements and in legislation[2]. A 1996 Act prohibits discrimination between full-time and part-time employees. Today, part-time work enables women to have continuous employment without withdrawing from the labour market, a situation which makes it more likely that they enjoy tenure benefits.

Women pursuing education

During the 20th century, participation rates in education grew steadily, the boys mostly a step ahead of the girls (Pott-Buter and Tijdens, 1999). In 1950, almost 70 per cent of the boys aged 14 and 15 were in full-time education, as opposed to 60 per cent of the girls. It was not until 1975 that girls closed this gap. At that time, almost 100 per cent of the boys and girls in this age group were in full-time education. Similar patterns can be seen for older girls and boys. By 1985, 17 year old girls had closed the gap with participation rates of nearly 90 per cent. By 1995, the gap for the 20 year olds was closed at a participation level of 45 per cent. Now girls' education attainments are generally better that those of boys. Girls more frequently complete their education with a diploma, and – in some forms of education – also more quickly.

In the 1960s, the last separated educational systems for boys and girls were integrated into co-education. Although women nowadays more frequently opt for subjects and disciplines, which have traditionally been a male preserve, gender-based differences in subject choices still remain (Keuzenkamp and Oudhof, 2000a). A major reason is that there has hardly been any increase in the number of males opting for traditionally female courses in education. In secondary education, boys in contrast to girls choose far more often subjects in science, chemistry and advanced maths, whereas girls are still more likely to choose French language, German language, and biology. With regard to subjects such as economics or introductory maths, the gender gap is small (CBS, 1999). In universities, most studies have kept constant their sex typing over time, but some faculties have not. In particular, medicine, law and psychology have faced a feminization.

In the 25-44 years age-group men and women have virtually the same level of education (Keuzenkamp and Oudhof, 2000a). The female workforce in employment is on average a little higher educated than the male workforce in employment. Compared to higher-educated women, lower-educated women far more often choose a homemaker career. Non-western ethnic minorities are clearly less educated than indigenous persons, and this gap rises with age. Among those aged under 35, Moroccan women in particular and to a somewhat lesser extent Turkish women, are comparatively educated. Generally speaking the labour market prospects for training courses predominantly taken by girls are good, although many of these courses offer few career opportunities and are generally not as well paid. More men than women take part in education at a later age. Furthermore, the men are more often concerned with obtaining professional qualifications.

Women in management

In this section, the focus is firstly on women in managerial positions. Figure 5.2 reveals that both the number of men and the number of women in managerial positions has increased from 1992 to 2000. Here, managerial positions are defined as occupational groups at higher vocational training level and at university level[3]. Expressed in a percentage of the male and female work force employed 12 hours and more, the share in managerial positions has increased from 2.0 per cent to 2.8 per cent for the males and 0.6 per cent to 1.4 per cent for the females. Although the percentage of women in managerial positions is still far behind that of men, the gap is slowly diminishing.

During the 1990s, women's share in managerial positions steadily increased from 16 per cent in 1992 to 33 per cent in 2000. The managerial positions include both women in wage employment and the self-employed women. Figure 5.2 shows that this growth must primarily be attributed to women's substantial increase in managerial positions in wage employment and only slightly to a the minor growth of women's share in self-employment.

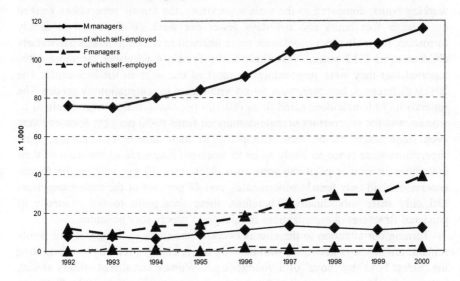

Figure 5.2   The male and female workforce in managerial positions (x 1000), breakdown by employment status, 1992-2000

Source: CBS, Website, March 2002

Taking a closer look at the characteristics of women in supervisory positions compared to men, the data of the Wage Indicator Survey 2001/2002 can be used[4]. At the Internet pages of the Wage Indicator, visitors were asked to enter data about their occupation, working time, industry, education, age and tenure. They then received information on the average hourly and monthly wages in their occupation, mostly specified for age group or other relevant factors. Visitors were also asked to complete a questionnaire to keep the wage indicator up-to-date. From May 2001 till July 2002, 18,229 employees did so, slightly more than 40 per cent were complete a questionnaire to keep the wage indicator up-to-date. From May 2001 till July 2002, 18,229 employees did so, slightly more than 40 per cent were women, and 43 per cent of the females and 29 per cent of the males held a supervisory job. The data allowed for a detailed comparison of male and female supervisors. Regarding job characteristics, the two groups hardly differed. Compared to the male supervisors, the female supervisors perceived slightly less career opportunities, and they had slightly less often been promoted. Equally, the male and female supervisors did not have a job below their educational level, and did not fear a job loss. Furthermore, to an equal extent as their male counterparts, the women reported conflicts in their department, insufficient staffing, or reorganizations. Female supervisors were a few years younger, and had served fewer years with their current employer in their current position. When it came to working hours, compared to the male supervisors, the female supervisors worked on average five hours and 0.4 days fewer per week. With regard to family formation, the male supervisors were more likely to have children, and particularly children aged 0-12 years. Nevertheless, the female supervisors far more often reported that they were responsible for most of the tasks in the household. The largest differences, however, were found with regard to segregation by gender. The supervisors in female-dominated firms (80-100 per cent females) were likely to be women, and the supervisors in male-dominated firms (0-20 per cent females) were even more likely to be men. Compared to their female counterparts, male supervisors were twice as likely to be in work environments where most of their colleagues in similar positions were men. Moreover, 39 per cent of the female supervisors had only female subordinates, and 44 per cent of the male supervisors had only male subordinates. Therefore, these data point to the existence of gendered structures in organizations in relation to supervisory positions.

Turning our attention to the elite network of the stock exchange, it still firmly remains an 'old boys network', with the only major changes relating to substituting the 'oldest boys' by 'boys' of a younger age[5]. Women are almost wholly absent, but there has been some small progress over the past ten years. In 1992, there was no single woman on the Board of Executive Directors of the hundred largest Dutch companies quoted on the stock exchange, and this had increased to one in 1999 (Keuzenkamp and Oudhof, 2000b). However, the gender composition of the Board of Governors of these hundred companies has changed slightly between 1992 and 1999, with the percentage of women Board Governors increasing from 3.1 per cent to 6.7 per cent. Weighted for firm size, the 1998 list of the 25 most influential persons on the Boards of Governors includes only one female, who is also the youngest individual. In 2001, she had entered the top 10[6].

When it comes to women holding elected offices in national government, their share has increased steadily since World War II, but particularly between the mid-1970s and the mid-1980s (Keuzenkamp and Oudhof, 2000b). During the 1990s, women held approximately one quarter of all positions in municipalities, and almost three out of ten elected positions in regional bodies. Their share in Parliament grew steadily over the 1990s up to 36 per cent in 1998. However, in the

Dutch delegation in the European Parliament the women's share peaked at 32 per cent in the mid-1990s, but subsequently declined to 29 per cent in 1998. The percentage of female Mayors shows an upward movement since the 1980s, rising steadily from 4 per cent in 1984 to 17 per cent fifteen years later. The percentage of aldermen has shown a similar increase up to 17 per cent (Keuzenkamp and Oudhof, 2000b).

Although the Netherlands has no legislation on quotas, and contract compliance is rarely included in equal opportunities programmes, during the 1990s there was definitely increasing government pressure and policies towards stimulating women's participation in decision-making bodies. Also, there appears to be a growing awareness in the electorate for supporting female candidates. Furthermore, the majority of the political parties are also aware of the importance of having women on their list of candidates. Nevertheless, the 2002 elections have shown a heavy backlash as the percentage of female Ministers went down from 31 to 8 per cent.

Women entrepreneurs

When examining the position of female entrepreneurs in the Netherlands, we need firstly to focus on the self-employed. This category ranges from freelancers, who have no employees, to managers or owners of large companies, employing tens of thousands of employees. To study this group, we use data from the website of Statistics Netherlands[7]. In 1992, the self-employed working at least 12 hours a week in their business, totalled 627,000 persons, of which 28 per cent were female. In 2000, the number had increased to 800,000, and the share of women amounted to 32 per cent. This percentage of women is lowest in the manufacturing industry and building and highest in non-commercial services (16 per cent and 53 per cent respectively). Over time, women's share among self-employed has particularly grown in agriculture and in non-commercial services. In the labour force aged 45-64 years, self-employment is more often present than is the case for the group aged 25-44. Self-employment in the labour force to 24 years of age is extremely low. The rise in female self-employment may reflect the often-heard statement that it is better for the women themselves to become self-employed in case they meet problems in their career development.

In 2000, 24 per cent of entrepreneurs, be it owners or managers, in small and medium-sized companies were females[8]. The 122,000 female-headed firms have an estimated turnover of nearly €25 billion, employing totally 305,000 workers (on average, 2.5 employees per firm). Since 1992, the number of female entrepreneurs in small and medium-sized companies more than doubled, the average number of employees in their firms tripled, and their turnover quadrupled. A 2001 study revealed that most entrepreneurial women can combine work and family life, though it requires substantial planning and organizing (Mandos, Kuiper and Bouwmeester, 2001).

Increasingly, women are considered good successors in family-owned businesses. For example, in a family-based publishing and printing company, established in 1836, it was not until the fourth generation that daughters were considered to be possible successors[9]. The current director has four daughters, and the oldest is working in the company. The director considers her to be a successor. This example is illustrative of many family-owned companies in the last decades of the 20th century.

When it comes to the female assisting members of the family, their numbers have shown a sharp decline over the 1990s (data from Labour Force Survey, see CBS, 1993; CBS, 2000). By 1992, altogether 118,000 women were counted as assisting members of the family. Over one third of them were found in agriculture and nearly half of this group were in commercial services. Women make up nearly 90 per cent of all assisting family members. By 1999, the number of female assisting members of the family had dropped to 41,000. Now, one-quarter is found in agricultural businesses and one half-in commercial services. This decline partly reflects the decreasing number of farms in the Netherlands. Yet, it reflects primarily that women can now, both for tax reasons and for legal reasons, be registered as co-entrepreneurs with their husband instead of an assisting family member. Presumably most of all, it reflects the growing self-confidence of women.

Considering the professional occupations, the percentages of women are quickly rising. These are lawyers and other legal professions, and doctors and other medical professions. In both, the pressure for part-time jobs is increasing, as said before. A 2002 study concerning the possibilities of medical specialists having part-time jobs, recommended how to organize the work[10].

Country legislation supporting women in the work force

The feminist and women's movement in the late 1960s and early 1970s made it very clear that government needed to respond to changes in society, particularly women's demands not to spend their whole adult life as housewives. Among others, they aimed for equal rights. In 1974, an Equal Opportunities Commission was set up as an advisory body and since 1978 government made funds available to stimulate equal rights policy throughout society. Subsequently other measures were to follow, which increasingly aimed at women in paid employment. In legislation, the issue of reconciling work and family life has received substantial attention throughout the 1980s, 1990s and 2000s. These acts will be summarized here.

For many years, maternity leave used to be 12 weeks. It was not until 1990 that this leave was extended to 16 weeks, being still one of the shortest in the European Union. Except for EU-directives, research had shown that women were likely to extend their short maternity leave by using sickness leave or vacation days. Maternity leave is applicable to women in wage employment. A 100 per cent replacement rate applies, paid according to the Sickness Benefits Act. In 1998, the self-employed women and assisting members of the family, in particular in the agricultural sector, demanded successfully for paid maternity leave. In 1991, the Parental Leave Act became effective. It entitles both women and men in wage employment to half-time, unpaid parental leave for 520 hours in total. Parents with children aged 4-8 are entitled to flexible leave arrangements. The leave arrangements are not transferable between parents.

In February 1999, the secretary of state for women's affairs announced the Work and Care Framework Act[11]. Among others, employees will be entitled to 10 days of paid leave when they have to care for a sick relative. In case a long-term leave period is desired, the employer is obliged to meet this request, but is not obliged to pay the absent hours. These proposals reflect more or less the beneficial leave regulations for the public sector as agreed upon between employers and unions in this sector. Initially, the major employers' association declared to be fully against the paid ten-day leave arrangement, because this would increase the firm's labour costs[12]. In 2001, the Act was passed through parliament with some changes. Altogether these acts enable women to remain in employment when they have young children.

Women's rising participation rates in paid employment, particularly those women with young children, caused a fast growing demand for day-care. This is particularly the case in countries, such as the Netherlands, where maternity and parental leave are short. The state used to finance playgrounds for children from 2-4 years, where they could play for a few hours a day. During the 1980s, regardless of the severe pressure from women's organizations, trade unions, tripartite bodies and others, the government maintained its view that the care for children was solely the parents' responsibility. It was expected that private day care centres would come into being, because the demand for childcare was estimated to be high. This did not happen, because only a small minority of women could afford this. Thus, the mothers' mothers, mothers-in-law or other relatives predominantly arranged the care for children informally. It was not until 1989, that the government changed views and decided to subsidize childcare, under the condition that both employers and parents took part in the costs. A substantial increase in day-care facilities followed. In 1990, more than 46,000 children made use of day care centres, the vast majority for two or three days a week. Three years later, their number had grown to 76,000 children, and again three years later, it was 104,000. In 1996, the government took measures to enlighten the taxation burden for business. Firms were entitled to subtract 20 per cent of their total childcare costs from social security payments and 80 per cent of total costs from taxation for profit. In 1998, the government agreed on expanding day care. Within a year, a plan was ready to finance an additional 71,000 places, of which 60 per cent were aimed at primary school children. This policy aimed at subsidizing places for social assistance mothers, for extra possibilities for firms to subtract day care costs from taxation, and for extra possibilities for families to subtract day care costs from income taxation. So far, the growth in day-care has not been sufficient to meet the demand, predominantly because of the fast increasing participation rates of mothers with young children. As it was in the 1980s, most of the childcare is still provided by family and neighbours (see Keuzenkamp, 2001).

For decades, working hours were regulated according to the 1918 Working Hours Act. According to this Act, working days should be eight hours. In 1996, the increasing demand for working-time flexibility from both employers and employees led to a total revision of this Act[13]. The new Act aims to protect the 'safety, health and well-being of employees in relation to their work' and to promote the 'reconciliation of work and family life, as well as other responsibilities outside the workplace'. In 1992, the Green Party proposed to entitle employees to reduce their working hours, but this proposal did not get passed and was opposed by employers. However, the social partners agreed on equal treatment of part-timers and full-timers[14]. Many years of debates and seeking support resulted in a revised proposal that was send to parliament in 1998[15]. It waspassed more than a year later[16]. A major change was that employees were not only entitled to reduce working hours, but also to extend hours. These requests have to be rewarded, unless the employer has serious objections, such as a limited budget. The law follows a long lasting tradition found in many in collective bargaining agreements, that employees are entitled to request for a reduction of working hours.

As far back as 1951, the International Labour Organisation (ILO) agreed on equal pay for equal work for male and female employees. Typical of the Netherlands, the government did not take action until the social partners had agreed upon the principle, which took more than two decades. Minimum wages were introduced in 1966, but for men only. It was not until 1969 that the principle was also applied to women. By doing so, this was the first act incorporating the principle of equal wages for men and women (Pott-Buter, 1993). In 1971, when all wage inequality had been removed from collective agreements, government ratified the ILO convention. Yet, it was not until 1975 that parliament passed the Equal Pay Act. In 1976 and 1980, the Equal Pay Act was followed by two acts prescribing equal treatment at work in the public and private sector. According to these laws, women, be it individually or as a group, could submit complaints to the Equal Treatment Commission when feeling that they have been treated unfairly at work or paid unequally. The 1975 legislation on equal pay and the 1980 legislation on equality were integrated into the 1994 legislation on equal treatment[17]. In the early 2000s, it became clear that equal pay legislation would not solve the gender wage gap. This inequality had to be solved by the social partners in collective bargaining, not through legislation.

Initiatives supporting women in the workforce

In this section, attention is drawn to initiatives to support the advancement of women in the workplace in relation to positive action plans, and to a government lead initiative known as *Opportunity in Business*[18]. In 1984, the concept of positive action was first mentioned in parliamentary documents, partly because of an EU-directive on positive action plans. Soon after, central government implemented a positive action programme for its own staff, aiming at preferential treatment for job openings and at career counselling for women, but most of all aiming at a representative share of women at all levels of the organizational hierarchy. By 1995, 30 per cent of all employees in central government had to be female. The Ministry of Home Affairs established a national information centre on positive action to consult the municipalities, provinces and water control boards for advice. It was not until 1988, that the Positive Action Programme was passed by parliament. Among others, special attention was paid to positive action at work, to women as entrepreneurs, and to women in men's jobs. The four-year programme introduced a grants scheme for organizations that wished to carry out positive action programmes. These grants amounted to tens of thousands of Euros per organization. In 1992, the programme was continued for another two years.

More than a hundred organizations received a grant. The evaluation showed that public sector organizations were heavily over-represented (Van Amstel and Van den Berg, 1991). One out of three applications came from a municipality, and one out of three from other sectors in the public sector, such as universities and Higher Vocational Schools, health care, and welfare. The remaining applications came from organizations in the private sector. The positive action programmes made very clear that it was rather easy to meet goals such as the 30 per cent of women in the central government work force, but that it was very difficult to reach a proportional share of women at all hierarchical levels. The higher the grade, the lower the proportion of women, and the more difficultly there was in setting targets. Moreover, once targets were set, it was even more difficult to meet the goals.

In order to increase women's entrance into higher grades, it became clear that other measures had to be taken. In the mid-1990s, tight co-operation with companies was assumed to be crucial. As a consequence, positive action plans came to an end as a government policy goal. At the same time, interest in equal opportunities policies at the workplace declined slightly, though in some organizations these policies were continued. Time was ready for an initiative focussing primarily on women's advancement into higher-level jobs.

In 1996 *Opportunity in Business* was established. It was shaped after the UK's *Opportunity 2000* that in 1991 was launched by a business association and backed by the Prime Minister. Signatories to *Opportunity 2000* were predominantly large companies who were publicly committed to improving the proportion of women in middle and higher managerial levels through various forms of positive action. Its goalwas to ensure that, for economic reasons, employers make better use of women's potential by encouraging their recruitment and discouraging their departure. Although originally initiated by the Ministry of Social Affairs and Employment, from the very beginning *Opportunity in Business* was meant to become an independent consultancy, predominantly financed by the members' fees. Its consultants support members in analysing the workforce with regard to the gender characteristics, setting goals and targets for the proportion of women in higher grades, and introducing a plan of action. Furthermore, the consultancy maintains a relationship with recruitment agencies for women, with management consultants, and others. The signatories agree upon the goals they want to reach with regard to the recruitment, turnover and career steps in their female workforce. Both reducing recruitment and training costs, and improved customers service are said to be goals. According to the personnel director of the largest bank, companies have to support these goals, because otherwise they will face problems related to their image, in particular problems regarding the labour market[19].

The future

This chapter on women in management in the Netherlands has shown the dynamics in the female work force over the past 10 to 20 years. Striking findings include the fast increasing participation rate, the decrease of homemaker careers among young women, the increase and acceptance of part-time employment, and the rising share of women in managerial and entrepreneurial positions. Yet, the chapter also shows that when it comes to the highest hierarchical levels and to the decision-making positions, women have made some progress, albeit very little. There is still a world to be won.

In the Netherlands, women's participation rates have increased rapidly over the last two decades. Yet, women's increased participation has not been spread proportionally over all organizations, as male-dominated organizations seem to remain male-dominated, and female-dominated organizations seem to feminize. Both, self-selection by potential employees and selection by the organization play a role in continuation of a masculine organization culture. A recent study of five organizations in the private and public sector revealed, however, that even when organizations superficially adopt 'feminine' values, the top levels of the organization are likely to maintain the masculine *status quo* (Fisher et al., 2000). By doing so, glass ceilings are created that hinder women from having a career into the top levels. Not surprisingly, according to Fisher et al. (2000), female managers perceive masculine attitudes as a major asset for being a successful manager. Future developments with regard to women's entrance to higher hierarchical levels will depend upon changes in the gender balance in organizations. As regards to future developments, women's increased participation in the labour force and women's increasing purchasing power will force male-dominated organizational levels with predominantly masculine organizational culture to adopt feminine values.

In general, segregation by gender is assumed to have a large impact on women's careers. Particularly, the hierarchical gender balance will be of extreme importance to women. Though female-dominated organizations still more often employ male managers, the likelihood to meet a female manager is far greater in female-dominated companies compared to male-dominated ones. Most female supervisors themselves are supervised by males. In the near future it is more likely that this hierarchical gender balance will be changed in female-dominated organizations than in male-dominated organizations. This may lead to better career possibilities for women in these female-dominated organizations. Breaking through the thick walls in male-dominated organizations will definitely require more time, and more effort.

To conclude, gendered organizational structures and career structures are quite likely, mutually interlocked. However, relationships between gender segregation, and power and authority in organizations, and how these relate to women's subordinate positions, have not been studied to a large extent. Further research is necessary on how gendered organizational structures coincide with unequal attribution of power, including for example the allocation of budgets, internal career opportunities, managerial commitment, authority, and contacts within and outside the organization.

References

CBS (1993), *Enquête beroepsbevolking 1992*, The Hague: Centraal Bureau voor de Statistiek.

CBS (1999), *Werken en leren*, Alphen aan de Rijn: Samsom.

CBS (2000), *Enquête beroepsbevolking 1999*, The Hague: Centraal Bureau voor de Statistiek.

Fischer, A., Rodriguez Masquerade, P.M. and Rojahn, K. (2000), *Masculiniteit met een feminien gezicht*, The Hague: Ministry of Social Affairs and Employment.

Heiligers, Ph. and Hingstman, L. (2000), 'Career preferences and the work-family balance in medicine: gender differences among medical specialists'. *Social Science & Medicine*, **50**, 1235-46.

Keuzenkamp, S. and Oudhof, K. (2000a), *Emancipatiemonitor 2000*, The Hague: Centraal Bureau voor de Statistiek and Sociaal en Cultureel Planbureau.

Keuzenkamp, S. and Oudhof, K. (2000b), 'Op naar de top? Actuele gegevens uit de Emancipatiemonitor 2000', in Gort, A. (ed.), *Jaarboek Emancipatie '00: Door het glazen plafond?*, The Hague: Elsevier Bedrijfsinformatie.

Keuzenkamp, S. (2001), 'Kinderopvang in cijfers', *Tijdschrift voor de sociale sector*, **55** (7/8), 22-27.

Mandos, E., Kuiper, C. and Bouwmeester, J. (2001), *Vrouwelijke zelfstandigen en de combinatie van arbeid en zorg. Eindrapport.* Onderzoek door Research voor Beleid in opdracht van het ministerie van Sociale Zaken en Werkgelegenheid. Doetichem, Elsevier Bedrijfsinformatie.

Pott-Buter, H.A. and Tijdens, K.G. (1998), *Vrouwen, leven en werk in de twintigste eeuw*. Amsterdam: Amsterdam University Press.

Pott-Buter, H.A. (1993), *Facts and Fairy Tales about Female Labour, Family and Fertility*. Amsterdam: Amsterdam University Press.

Tijdens, K.G. (1993), 'Women in Business and Management - The Netherlands', in Davidson, M.J. and Cooper, C.L. (eds), *European Women in Business and Management*, London: Paul Chapman Publishing, pp. 79–92.

Tijdens, K.G. (1998a), *Zeggenschap over arbeidstijden: De samenhang tussen bedrijfstijden, arbeidstijden en flexibilisering van de personeelsbezetting*, Den Haag: Uitgeverij Welboom.

Tijdens, K.G. (1998b), 'Gender and labour market flexibility: the Case of Working Hours', in Wilthagen, T. (ed.), *Advancing theory in labour law and industrial relations in a global context*, Amsterdam/Oxford/Tokyo: North Holland, pp. 131-141.

Tijdens, K.G. (2002), 'Gender Roles and Labor Use Strategies: Women's Part-time Work in the European Union'. *Feminist Economics*, **8** (1), 71-99.

Van Amstel, R.J. and van den Berg, T. (1991), *Evaluatie stimuleringsregeling positieve actie voor vrouwen, Interrimrapportage 1990*, The Hague: Ministerie van Sociale Zaken en Werkgelegenheid.

Visser, J. (2000), *The first part-time economy in the world. Does it work?* Amsterdam: AIAS working paper - WP00-01 www.uva-aias.net/files/aias/WP1.pdf.

Notes

1   The first part of this section is based on the historic overview in Pott-Buter and Tijdes (1998).
2   See Emancipatieraad (1992), *Deeltijdwerk: Het volle pond.* Emancipatieraad (1993), *Wettelijk Recht op volwaardig deeltijdwerk.* The Hague.
3   These are codes 788 respectively 988 in the occupational classification scheme of Statistics Netherlands.
4   See www1.uva-aias.net/wage-indicator/ (English) or www.loonwijzer.nl (Dutch).
5   'Nieuwe 'oude jongens' zijn in opmars' en 'Nederlandse commissarissen zitten stevig op het pluche', in *de Volkskrant*, March 29, 2002.
6   See endnote 5.
7   See www.cbs.nl.
8   The figures in this paragraph are based on a study by MKB-Nederland in 2000, see www.mkb.nl/mkbnederland/berichten/3796.shtml.
9   'Waanders Uitgevers, Drukkers en Boekverkopers (1836)', in *Forum*, March 7, 2002.
10 'Genezen in deeltijd', in *de Volkskrant*, March 6, 2002.
11 See www.eiro.eurofound.eu.int/1999/02/inbrief/NL9902126N.html.
12 See www.eiro.eurofound.eu.int/1999/03/feature/NL9903128F.html.
13 See www.eiro.eurofound.eu.int/2000/02/feature/NL0002182F.html.
14 See Stichting van de Arbeid (1993), Overwegingen en aanbevelingen ter bevordering van deeltijdarbeid en differentiatie in arbeidsduurpatronen. Publicatienr. 7/93.
15 See www.eiro.eurofound.eu.int/1998/03/feature/NL9803164F.html.
16 See www.eiro.eurofound.eu.int/2000/02/feature/NL0002182F.html.
17 See www.eiro.eurofound.eu.int/2002/01/word/NL0110103s.doc.
18 See www.opportunity.nl/index.html.
19 See their brochure *Opportunity in Business. Give Equality a Chance.* Amsterdam, 1996.

Chapter 6

Women in Management in Portugal

Carlos J. Cabral-Cardoso

Introduction

As in most other countries in the industrialized world, women in Portugal represent an increasing proportion of the labour force. Women are also pursuing higher education, and business education in particular, at levels comparable to their male colleagues. Furthermore, they are occupying managerial jobs in increasing numbers. And yet, women are still less likely to hold top management positions, and like many of their female counterparts in other countries represented in this book, face glass ceilings. This chapter reflects on the situation of women managers in Portugal, their characteristics and recent developments. Moreover, particular emphasis is put on women holding top management positions.

Labour force characteristics

Official statistics show that the proportion of women in the labour force has increased steadily since the mid-1980s, rising from 32.5 per cent in 1985 to almost 40 per cent ten years later, and reaching 41.8 per cent in 1999, the latest data available from the Ministry of Employment. In public administration, women already make 55.2 per cent of the civil servants. The participation rate of women in this sector has been growing, slowly but steadily, since the 1930s (DGAP, 2001).

When the participation rate of women in the labour force is desegregated by age group (see Table 6.1) it is observed that in the new generation that is now 'under 30', women already constitute 46.5 per cent of the labour force. In the period 1995-1999, the overall number of women in the labour force rose by 20.9 per cent, but such an increase in women's representation in the labour force cannot be exclusively attributed to the arrival of a new generation of women wanting to pursue a career. New entrants in the labour market were detected in all age groups with percentage raises higher, the older the age group. In fact, while the number of women in the 'under 30s' group has 'only' rose 11.4 per cent, a dramatic rise of 41.5 per cent iwa reported in the number of women in the 'over 50s' group. Such an increase occurred in the older age groups is remarkable on any account. While still constituting only 30.9 per cent of the labour force, the increase in the frequency of women over 50 means that a considerable number of women have joined the labour market at an older age.

Table 6.1 Labour force percentage participation rate of women by age group, 1995-1999

	1995	1999
Women in the labour force	39.8	41.8
Age groups:		
Under 30	45.5	46.5
31 to 40	41.5	43.7
41 to 50	35.3	39.4
Over 50	26.5	30.9

Source: Computations based on DETEFT, Ministry of Employment, Quadros de Pessoal, 2002

Official statistics from the Ministry of Employment were used to analyse the characteristics of the Portuguese labour force. It is worth pointing out that self-employment is not considered in the data set, though it is generally assumed that the proportion of self-employed workers has risen since the early 1990s, implying that labour force statistics such as the ones reported here do not give a full picture of what goes on in the economy. Employment statistics do not consider diversity dimensions such as the ethnic group or religion and it is difficult to find any reliable statistics on minority groups.

Taking into account the educational level of the labour force, it becomes evident that the proportion of women in the workforce holding a university degree is progressing at a higher rate than women overall (see Table 6.2). While increasing in all educational groups, the number of women holding a university diploma almost doubled in four years accounting, in 1999, for 48.4 per cent of the labour force in that educational group. In other words, women constitute the better-educated segment of the workforce.

The percentage of female graduates in the labour force has risen across disciplines. Female holders of an engineering degree, although starting from a very low figure, have increased by about 48 per cent in just four years. Even more remarkable is the percentage of women with a degree in Management or Economics which has risen by an incredible 94.5 per cent in the same period constituting more than 41 per cent of all professionals in this field in the labour force. Among holders of university degrees in fields such as Social Sciences, Psychology, and Law, Maths and Sciences, and Arts and Education, women already constitute the majority of the workforce.

Table 6.2 Labour force percentage participation rate of women by educational level and field of studies, 1995-1999

	1995	1999
Up to 9 years education	38.7	40.1
9 to 12 years education	47.0	48.4
Higher education, of which	38.6	43.8
Business and Economics	33.9	41.1
Social Sciences, Psychology, and Law	43.9	54.8
Engineering	13.3	15.7
Arts and Education	67.4	68.6
Maths and Sciences	53.1	53.3

Source: Computations based on DETEFT, Ministry of Employment, Quadros de Pessoal, 2002

Table 6.3 indicates the participation rate of women in the 1995-1999 period in sectors with an overall labour force of at least eighty thousand individuals. The two major conclusions can be drawn from the table are that the proportion of women in the labour force has increased in most sectors but occupational segregation remains largely unchallenged. Women tend to be concentrated in a few sectors, particularly in health and social services, and in the clothing industry. Women are also the majority of the workforce in the tourist sector, in business services, and in the textile industry. In contrast, the car repair and petrol services, and the building industry remain highly male-dominated sectors, despite the considerable increase in the number of women in the latter (a 75 per cent rise).

In this period, the number of women has increased in virtually all sectors, and particularly in the three fastest-growing labour sectors: the retail sector (the number of women increased by 70 per cent), the already mentioned building industry, and the business services sector in which the number of women almost doubled (rise of 95 per cent).

Table 6.3 Labour force percentage participation rate of women by industrial sector, 1995-1999

	1995	1999
Retail	54.2	58.7
Trade and Commerce	31.4	34.0
Tourism	52.4	56.6
Business services	52.4	53.2
Food processing	43.5	45.4
Building	7.0	7.8
Clothing	88.1	88.5
Textile	51.8	52.4
Car repair and petrol	19.1	19.1
Health and social services	84.9	85.2

Source: Computations based on DETEFT, Ministry of Employment, Quadros de Pessoal, 2002

When employers are desegregated by size, it becomes clear that women's participation in the labour force is very similar in all groups, ranging from 40 to 44 per cent. In other words, women are just as likely to find a job in a small or in a large company.

Women pursuing education

The majority of students in higher education have been female for a number of years. In 1999, women represented 56 per cent of all undergraduate students, rising to 57.2 per cent the following year. Official statistics of student enrolment in public universities indicate that the proportion of women in higher education has been above 55 per cent for over a decade. The participation rate of women in higher education has risen steadily since the 1960s, but it is possible to identify the 1980s (during which the criteria for accessing higher education was changed to take into account the students' marks during secondary education) as the time when women's numbers in higher education started to climb. Furthermore, the gender gap widens when it comes to actual graduates, suggesting a higher rate of male students underperforming or dropping out of the system. Women represent about 63 per cent of all graduates.

With the exception of some engineering fields that remain male-dominated, women now represent the majority of the students in virtually all other academic disciplines. Even in traditionally male-dominated areas such as maths, law and business, women have consolidated their lead as the demographically dominant student group in most university departments. In 1990, women represented 56 per cent of the graduates in law (up from just 22 per cent ten years before), 68 per cent of the graduates in medicine (up from 55 per cent ten years before), 80 per cent in arts (up from 68 per cent ten years before and only 20 per cent in 1960), 30 per cent in engineering (up from only 10 per cent in 1970), and 64 per cent in the social sciences (up from 46 per cent ten years before).

Women have also made progress at postgraduate level. In the early 1990s, women represented about 45 per cent of the overall number of master's students and about 42 per cent of doctoral students (Cabral-Cardoso, 1999). But in 1997, women were awarded 50.1 per cent of master's degrees and 44.4 per cent of doctoral degrees. And in 1998, women represented 51.8 per cent of master's students and 40.7 per cent of doctoral students (DESUP, 2002). Technological subjects, broadly speaking, remain male-dominated doctoral programmes, but women have reached at least parity in all other fields.

Such a persistent trend for more than a decade means that the labour market has been fuelled with highly qualified women in most fields, competing for jobs with their male colleagues. As a consequence, in most sectors employers could not avoid hiring women to overcome the shortage of male graduates. It may be just a matter of time before the considerable supply of highly qualified women makes an impact on the labour market statistics. Whether, or not, Portuguese women will find their way to the top positions or get stuck in the lower and middle management levels remains to be seen.

Women in management

Official statistics from the Ministry of Employment show that almost sixty-three thousand full-time executive and managerial jobs in 1999, that is 26.7 per cent of all managerial positions, were occupied by women. More recent data from Dun & Bradstreet (Ramos, 2002) estimate the proportion of women in management at about 28 per cent.

While far from reaching parity, women are closing the gap in management positions. According to the official statistics, in four years alone (1995 to 1999), the number of women in management has risen by more than thirteen thousand individuals, which represents an increase of about 27 per cent since 1995, thus exceeding the increase in the proportion of women in the overall labour force (nearly 21 per cent). Table 6.4 shows the percentage participation rate of women in management for all age groups. The proportion of women in management decreases with age reaching 32.6 per cent in the generation that is now 'under 30', suggesting a sustained advancement of women and a progress towards parity in management positions.

Two years were taken into consideration in the analysis: 1995 and 1999. The latter is the latest data available. The former was the first year to use the coding that is now adopted, thus making the comparison meaningful.

Table 6.4   Percentage participation rates of women in management, by age group, 1995-1999

	1995	1999
Women in management	24.5	26.7
Age groups:		
Under 30	30.4	32.6
31 to 40	27.1	28.9
41 to 50	23.8	26.2
Over 50	20.1	22.5

Source: Computations based on DETEFT, Ministry of Employment, Quadros de Pessoal, 2002

Table 6.5 illustrates the progress in the proportion of women managers holding a higher education degree. Their number has risen by almost 54 per cent between 1995 and 1999, therefore exceeding the increase in the number of women managers overall. By desegregating the data taking into consideration the academic field, it becomes clear that considerable growth has taken place in the proportion of female graduates in business related fields – management or economics – that now hold management positions. Among the managers with a business related degree, women account now for 27.6 per cent. It is also worth noting the considerable proportion of women managers holding degrees in the 'unlikely' fields of Arts and Education, or even Maths and Sciences.

Table 6.5   Percentage participation rates of women in management, by field of studies in higher education, 1995-1999

	1995	1999
Higher education, of which	22.7	26.6
Business and Economics	23.1	27.6
Social Sciences, Psychology and Law	28.3	34.8
Engineering	8.7	10.4
Arts and Education	55.5	56.3
Maths and Sciences	42.2	38.6

Source: Computations based on DETEFT, Ministry of Employment, Quadros de Pessoal, 2002

Table 6.6 indicates the proportion of women managers in the 1995-1999 period in sectors with an overall labour force of at least eighty thousand individuals. A considerable increase in the proportion of women in management has taken place across sectors in this period. Burke and Nelson (2002) admit, 'women are more likely to occupy managerial jobs in fields in which more women are employed in non-management jobs' (p.3). The Portuguese data confirms this assumption. The three sectors with the highest percentage of female managers (health and social services, clothing, and the retail sector) are also the ones with the highest proportion of women in the labour force (see Table 6.3). However, the proportion of women in management positions is generally below non-managerial jobs in nearly all sectors. In other words, despite the considerable progress that women have made at all levels and economic sectors, they are still more likely to stay in the lower organizational ranks than their male counterparts.

Table 6.6 Percentage participation rates of women in management, by industrial sector, 1995-1999

	1995	1999
Retail	32.6	36.8
Trade and Commerce	21.2	23.0
Tourism	25.2	30.0
Business services	28.5	31.0
Food processing	20.6	24.7
Building	14.1	14.3
Clothing	44.0	48.5
Textile	26.7	31.0
Car repair and petrol	16.9	16.8
Health and social services	49.8	51.2

Source: Computations based on DETEFT, Ministry of Employment, Quadros de Pessoal, 2002

In terms of organizational size, women appear to have a better chance of reaching a management position in smaller firms. In fact, 28.7 per cent of the micro business (less than 10 employees) managers are women. In medium (between 101 and 500 employees) and large companies (more than 500 employees), that rate is only 21.7 per cent and 23.2 per cent, respectively. Unlike the labour force, in which the participation rate of women was found not to depend on firm size, access to management positions appears to be easier for women in smaller firms, a trend that persists during the 1995-1999 period.

While the overall number of women in management is on the rise, it is interesting to note that such an increase has basically taken place in Portuguese owned firms. In the 1995-1999 period, the number of women managers in Portuguese owned firms has risen by 40 per cent, accounting now today 27 per cent of managers. In firms with foreign capital the number of women managers has actually declined in this period, and their participation rate is now only 19.2 per cent.

Figures for the public sector are closer to parity. In public administration, by the early 1990s, women occupied almost 40 per cent of A4-A8 level positions (middle management) and about 20 per cent of A1-A3 level positions, that is, of the very top management jobs. These figures were then nearly twice as high as the European average (Cunha and Marques, 1995). Private companies are lagging behind, but the pace of convergence that was detected during the nineties portrays a relatively optimistic picture for women in management in Portugal.

Women senior managers

Using a variety of sources, further information was collected on the directorships of Portuguese largest companies. Although lacking the reliability of official statistics, the directories of managers of the largest companies give additional information about some individual characteristics of their senior people which is worth looking at.

In a list of the top 2500 corporate directors and top managers in 1999 (Exame, 1999), it is observed that only 172, that is 6.9 per cent of this sample, were women. Therefore, the gap between the proportions of women in management overall (26.7 per cent) and in top management remains wide. It is difficult to compare these figures to what has been found elsewhere due to differences in how top management is defined, but they appear to resemble other countries. For instance, Powell (1999), and Burke and Nelson (2002), report figures from the US and other countries about or below 5 per cent. In other words, while the proportion of women managers has made considerable progress during the nineties, access to the very top remains problematic. And Portugal appears to be no exception to this general picture.

But who are the lucky few Portuguese women who have succeeded in shattering the glass ceiling? According to the directory referred to above (Exame, 1999), 11 of them, or 6.4 per cent, held the high-ranking positions of chairman, president, and vice-president. 46 others were board members ('administradoras'), and 39 (or 22.7 per cent) were CEOs. In sum, 96, or 56 per cent of the female top managers actually held the most influential positions in their companies. Perhaps more interesting only a minority among them (29 per cent) were also shareholders. In other words, only in a limited number of cases, women's presence in the higher ranks can be attributed to capital ownership.

The composition of the management teams gives additional information, thus helping to draw a clearer picture of these very senior women. Unlike other countries where women appear to get stuck into the 'stereotypical female management function', to use Thomas's words (Thomas, 2001) referring to the personnel function or other caring roles, Portuguese top women managers appear to have accessed positions where they can play a more influential role. In fact, among the women listed in this *Who's Who* (Exame, 1999) 15.1 per cent appear to show a preference for the more traditionally masculine finance directorship, which compares to only 7.6 per cent holding the position of human resource director. More recent data from Dun and Bradstreet (Ramos, 2002) indicates that overall there are twice as many women finance directors than there are human resource directors. Finance directors are said to play a very influential role in companies with dispersed ownership, standing as 'first among equals'. The profile of Portuguese senior women managers seems to suggest that the glass on the walls is not as thick as the glass in the ceiling.

Merit and high qualifications rather than capital ownership appears to explain women's presence in senior positions. According to the 1999 directory (Exame, 1999) in terms of academic background, only 25 out of 172 senior managers do not hold a university degree. In other words, 85 per cent of women in senior positions were graduates, and 10 per cent were awarded degrees at master's level. In terms of field of studies chosen for their first degree, these women show a preference for business-related subjects, such as management (25 graduates), economics (25), and finance/accounting (17) degrees. Law graduates (22) are also well represented. It is also worth noting the considerable number of graduates in fields unrelated to business such as maths and sciences (9), pharmaceutical sciences (6), arts (6), psychology and sociology (7), or even education (2).

Perhaps unexpectedly, none of the women at the very top (chair, vice-chair) hold a degree in management or business. They, in fact, come from quite diverse backgrounds, such as economics (2), law (2), finance/accounting (1), but also from fields unrelated to business such as psychology and sociology (1), maths and sciences (1), education (1), and arts (1). CEOs are more likely to have a management background (9), but they can also hold a degree in pharmaceutical sciences (5), maths and sciences (4), or arts (3). In sum, all academic fields appear to give almost equal opportunity of getting access to the very top.

In terms of the industrial sector, a wide variety of industries are represented in this sample, and in this case, with no apparent relationship with the fields in which more women are employed in non-managerial jobs. Yet again, Portuguese women appear to show a preference for the traditionally masculine financial sector (40 out of this sample of 172). Other sectors well represented in this group are retail and commerce (28), manufacturing (26), the chemical industry (15), media and publishing (13), and the transport sector (11).

Other demographic characteristics also help to draw a more detailed picture of Portuguese senior women managers. They are, in general, relatively young. Twenty-eight women, or 38 per cent, at the very senior level of chair/administrator/CEO are under 40 years of age. Access to the very senior positions is also a relatively recent event. Among those who disclosed this information, only one woman at that level had held that position for more than four years. Overall, fifty-nine senior managers were married, two others were single, five were divorced and one was a widow. Quite significantly, 105 others did not disclose their family status. Fifty-five managers also declared having children with an average of 1.8 children per mother. But again, 107 did not disclose this information.

Non-work activities also say a lot about people. For the women in this group of senior managers reading appeared to be the preferred way of spending their free time. A majority of 79 indicated reading as one of their favourites hobbies, 35 showed a preference for travelling, 24 for music listening, and 20 for going to the pictures. Swimming came out as their favourite sport, indicated by 20. More traditionally feminine hobbies did not seem a popular pursuit to this group of women. Decoration was enjoyed by just three senior managers, handcraft by two, and tapestry and embroidering by just one each. Even cooking was enjoyed by only one senior manager. Very active sports and outdoor activities also did not appear to be very appealing. Squash, sailing, water-skiing, and mountain biking were their favourite way of spending free time by just one senior manager each. Horse riding was enjoyed by five, golf by six, and tennis by eight. Moreover, only three senior women managers, as the favourite way of spending their free time, mentioned voluntary work and other activities in the community.

In sum, the picture that comes out of this *Who's Who* directory illustrates that some Portuguese women managers succeeded in shattering the glass ceiling and the glass walls. These are a young and highly educated group of women who have reached the very top in the recent past, presumably by their own merit. Furthermore, academic background in nonrelated business fields was no barrier to access senior positions. Bearing in mind their favourite free time hobbies, they do not fit into the traditional feminine stereotype but the image of women executives enjoying outdoor activities and sports that is often portrayed in advertising seem not to match them either.

Comparing these figures to the data provided by the directorship and board composition of Portuguese companies six years earlier (DN, 1993) some progress is suggested in the access of women to top management positions. In 1993, only 141 out of the largest 451 firms did have at least one woman as a senior manager (board member or director). In other words, 310 firms, or 69 per cent, had no women among the directors, and in 85 cases, or 19 per cent, only one woman was present. Only 56 companies, or 12 per cent, had more than one woman in senior positions. Among the women in senior positions 68, or 34 per cent, were at the very senior ranks of chair/administrator/CEO.

But already in 1993, Portuguese women had established a preference for the more influential financial matters: 33 were finance directors, as opposed to only 26 in marketing/sales/PR, or 23 in human resources. Unlike other countries, women's involvement in financial matters appears to have some tradition in Portugal. How far back this goes could not be uncovered.

Bearing in mind that these figures are not fully comparable due to their different nature, it is nonetheless clear that some progress was made during the nineties. With all due caution derived from the use of secondary and non-official data, there is little doubt that an increasing number of women senior managers appear to have made their way to the very top during the 1990s.

Women entrepreneurs

In a recent survey of 29 countries from all continents, Portugal ranked 21st in entrepreneurial activity, 'slightly better than Germany and slightly worse than France' (GEM, 2001, p.14). Market openness and easy access to physical infrastructure were rated in this study as the main drivers of entrepreneurship in Portugal. The main problems hindering its development included 'a lack of entrepreneurship-oriented education, too much employment regulation, limited funding/accessibility mechanisms and a lack of awareness of government programmes' (p.45). It is worth pointing out that the cultural background may not be adequate for entrepreneurship to flourish. The Portuguese ranked very high on risk aversion in the Hofstede's study (1991), and seem to 'deem business failure inexcusable' (GEM, 2001).

According to GEM (2001), entrepreneurs in Portugal are evenly distributed in terms of age, with a slight prevalence of entrepreneurs over 35 years old. Their findings also show that 'Portuguese men are more than twice as likely to be involved in entrepreneurial activity than Portuguese women' (p.15), following a pattern that is not uncommon among European nations. In another study, it was found that women entrepreneurs tend to start their business at an older age than men (Pereira, 2001).

Pereira (2001) found that women are more likely to start a small business in retail and the service sector. But significant differences between men and women entrepreneurs were also found by this author in their motivational factors to start a business. Women appear to have a higher need for achievement than men. While personal achievement was found in that study to be the women's driving force for starting a business, among men, family stability and wealth has emerged as a primary motive to become an entrepreneur. In their decision to start a business, women were mainly concerned with the identification of a market opportunity and the availability and support of public funds. Men, on the other hand, gave major importance to macroeconomic and financial factors. Women, more so than men, rate marketing as a critical factor for the success of their companies, according to Pereira (2001).

Country legislation supporting women in the workforce

Since the mid seventies, substantial changes in legislation have granted equal rights for men and women. If some inequality persist in Portuguese work settings legislation cannot be to blame. However, the country has a reputation of weakness in law enforcement, and the judicial system is often accused of being too slow and ineffective.

Written in a period of particularly high political awareness and social concern, the Constitution of the Republic of Portugal of 1976 is very progressive in social matters and civil liberties. In art. 9°, it includes 'the promotion of equality between men and women' among the primary duties of the State. In another article (13°) it prohibits any citizen to be discriminated against on account of family origin, sex, race, language, national origin, religion, political convictions, education, and social and economic status. Art. 58° adds that the State should promote equal opportunities in the access to any profession or job, and prevent any measure that could hinder equal access on the grounds of sex. Art. 59° requires that everyone be paid equal wages for equal work. It also grants special protection for women during pregnancy and other maternity rights. Further legislation has been passed intended to grant equality and improve the condition of men and women.

The *Equal opportunities between men and women Act of 1979 (Lei nº 392/79)* is intended to prevent discrimination of men or women on the grounds of sex. It details the principles employers should follow to prevent discrimination of women in hiring, pay, access to training, and career opportunities. Women who consider they were discriminated against must justify their allegation while employers have to prove that payment differentials are not due to sex. It also established the Commission for Equality in Work and Employment, later relabelled as Commission for Equality and Women's Rights. These principles were later extended to public administration (*Lei nº 462/88*).

The *Equal treatment in work and employment Act of 1997 (Lei nº 105/97)* further regulates equality in employment relations. The concept of indirect discrimination is introduced, and it states that sex imbalance in an organization is sufficient condition to allege discrimination, leaving it to the employer to prove otherwise.

Other legislation is also available intended to prevent racial discrimination, and to protect maternity and regulate maternity and paternity leave. The sole affirmative action programme applies to the access of handicapped people to jobs in the public sector. As pointed out above, in spite of the legislation in place, few legal actions against sex discrimination have reached the courts.

Initiatives supporting women in the workforce

The Commission for Equality in Work and in Employment (CITE) was established in 1979 and since then it has played a considerable role in promoting equal opportunities for men and women in the work context. The Commission set up a system for handling complains of unfair discrimination at work in co-operation with other public institutions, and provides legal recommendations and interpretations of the legislation. It also publishes a number of brochures and leaflets on workers' rights in different aspects of the employment relationship such as work-family relations, maternity leave, equal pay legislation, among others, intended to translate legal principles into common language. Specific programmes have also been designed by the Commission to promote training sessions in equal opportunities to workers in general.

By the mid-nineties, a programme called 'Equality is quality' was set up to give public recognition of private companies implementing equal opportunities initiatives (CITE, 2002). A number of companies have been awarded public recognition by their equality initiatives. No data is yet available on the actual impact of these initiatives in other companies, but they undoubtedly helped raising awareness and increase social and political visibility to these matters.

During the nineties, Portuguese society was confronted with proposals to set up quotas for women in Parliament, and the focus of the discussion inevitably moved to the labour market. But with the good progress women have been making in all sectors of Portuguese society, these social engineering initiatives were rejected by public opinion. Arguing the case against such initiatives, some women sectors were particularly active and outspoken in the press about what they called an unnecessary paternalistic initiative. And in a recent survey of HR managers (Cabral-Cardoso, 2002), very few, both men and women, appeared receptive to affirmative policies intended to increase the representation of women in top management positions.

The future

The data collected from a variety of sources show that management is still a male dominated activity, particularly at the very top. At the senior level, business in Portugal is still overwhelmingly male. Yet, women are reaching management positions in increasing numbers. Even in senior positions, it is clear that a young and highly educated small group of women have already succeeded in shattering the glass ceiling and secured key positions among senior management. Slowly but steadily, their number will undoubtedly increase, or at least these are the indications that are evident from the increasing number of women graduating from higher education and from the rising number of women in management positions in general.

And yet, some barriers seem to remain hindering women's access to top positions. In the human capital framework, differences in the management profession are attributed to the reduced investment in education and job training. But Portugal is a particularly good example of the effort made by women to increase their skills and knowledge, and to increase their human capital through the enhancement of their academic credentials. Human capital seems, therefore, unable to account for women's low status in management.

Different theoretical perspectives have offered explanations for the scarcity of women in the higher management ranks (Morrison and Von Glinow, 1990; Powell, 1999; Burke and Nelson, 2002), and in recent years, a number of studies were carried out in Portugal aiming to shed some light on the gender gap in management. It is worth noting that comparative studies such as Hofstede's (1991) seem to portray a cultural context rather distinct from the one in the US and the UK where most studies on women in management reported in the literature have been conducted. One dimension is particularly relevant for this problem - femininity - which 'pertains to societies in which social gender roles overlap', explains Hofstede (1991, p.82). According to his findings, the Portuguese population scores among the highest on femininity, which may be influential in shaping the individual's behaviour and attitudes towards gender and the role of men and women in the organization. Can one expect less job segregation in such a context and, therefore, fewer barriers in the access to management positions?

A study conducted among Portuguese management students of both sexes found that even in a gender-balanced environment such as the business school these days, the image of 'the manager' remains closer to the masculine stereotype than to the feminine stereotype (Fernandes and Cabral-Cardoso, 2002). This will obviously disadvantage women in their management careers. Gender stereotypes that men make better managers and that better managers are masculine are still entrenched in society, helping masculinity to remain prevalent in the ranks of management and ultimately leading to differential treatment of women in management, argued Powell (1988). The findings of that Portuguese study in the same vein sugges that women are held back by the nature of the work environment, namely the group norms and organizational culture.

Another theoretical perspective uses structural discrimination as revealed in organizational policies and practices to explain the differential treatment of women in management and account for their limited number in the higher ranks. Such a view has led to research into the identification of barriers to female career advancement. The women's exclusion from informal networks (O'Leary and Ickovics, 1992; Ibarra, 1993) and their greater difficulties in establishing mentoring relationships (Ragins and Scandura, 1994) have been identified as powerful barriers to women's career advancement. Similar barriers were identified in a study conducted in Portugal among bank managers (Loureiro, 2002). But according to this study, other social and family constraints also play a significant role in their career progress. The expected role of women in the family that appears to prevail in Portuguese society was found to hinder women's mobility, and reduced mobility came out in this study as the major factor preventing women from competing with men to the higher positions (Loureiro, 2002). Similar impact of social and family constraints has been identified in another study as the major barrier to the career advancement of Portuguese women academics (Santos and Cabral-Cardoso, 2002).

Gender roles in the family appear, therefore, to be falling behind and hindering the general progress that has taken place in work settings in terms of gender equality. There is an obvious role waiting to be played by work-family policies. So far, these matters tended to be dealt with informally (Cabral-Cardoso, 2002). The lack of policies to accommodate work-family arrangements is, therefore, an important structural barrier and one that appears to partially account for the relatively small number of women in the higher ranks. In sum, in spite of considerable changes in the role played by women in most areas of Portuguese society, important barriers remain hindering women participation and access to top positions. Achieving gender equality is still a challenge to Portuguese managers.

References

Burke, R.J. and Nelson, D.L. (2002), 'Advancing women in management: progress and prospects', in Burke, R.J. and Nelson, D.L. (eds), *Advancing women's careers: research and practice*, Oxford: Blackwell, pp. 3-14.

Cabral-Cardoso, C. (1999), '*A integração nas empresas de pós-graduados nas áreas das ciências e das tecnologias*', Relatório Final do Projecto PCSH/OGE/1023/1995, Fundação para a Ciência e a Tecnologia, Lisboa.

Cabral-Cardoso, C. (2002), 'Perspectives on diversity in a feminine culture: HR managers and the political game', paper presented at the International Conference on Perspectives in diversity research and diversity practices, Göteborg, 29th-31st August 2002.

CITE (2002), '*O prémio Igualdade é Qualidade*', Comissão para a Igualdade no Trabalho e no Emprego, Lisboa, http://www.igualdade-qualidade.org/

Cunha, R.C. and Marques, C.A. (1995), 'Portugal', in Brunstein, I. (ed.), *Human resource management in Western Europe*, Berlin: Walter de Gruyter, pp. 211-229.

DESUP (2002), '*Pós-graduação: Algumas estatísticas*', Ministério da Ciência e do Ensino Superior, Lisboa, http://www.desup.min-edu.pt/pgstats.htm

DGAP (2001), '*Caracterização dos recursos humanos*', Direcção-Geral da Administração Pública, Lisboa, http://www.dgap.gov.pt/2pap/rhs_adm/rec_hum.htm

DN (1993), 'Top managers of the largest 550 companies', *Diário de Notícias*, May.

Exame (1999), 'Who's Who: The 2500 executives that lead Portugal', *Exame*, July/August.

Fernandes, E. and Cabral-Cardoso, C. (2002), 'Gender Stereotypes in management: a study of Portuguese management students', paper presented at the EIASM Workshop 'Crossing Issues in Gender & Management in Organisations', Brussels, 15-16 March 2002.

GEM (2001), '*2001 Portugal Executive Report*', The Global Entrepreneurship Monitor.

Hofstede, G. (1991), *Cultures and organizations: software of the mind*, London: McGraw-Hill.

Ibarra, H. (1993), 'Personal networks of women and minorities in management: A conceptual framework', *Academy of Management Review*, **18**, 56-87.

Loureiro, M.P. (2002), As carreiras de gestão no feminino: o efeito 'tecto de vidro' no sector bancário, unpublished dissertation, M.Sc. Degree in Human Resource Management, University of Minho, Braga.

Morrison, A.M. and Von Glinow, M.A. (1990), 'Women and minorities in management', *American Psychologist*, **45**, 200-208.

O'Leary, V.E. and Ickovics, J.R. (1992), 'Cracking the glass ceiling: overcoming isolation and alienation', in Sekaran, U. and Leong, F.T. (eds), *Womenpower: Managing in times of demographic turbulence*, Newbury Park: Sage, pp. 7-30.

Pereira, F.C. (2001), *Representação social do empresário*, Lisboa: Edições Sílabo.

Powell, G.N. (1988), *Women and men in management*, Newbury Park: Sage.

Powell, G.N. (1999), 'Reflections on the glass ceiling: recent trends and future prospects', in Powell, G.N. (ed.), *Handbook of Gender and Work*, Thousand Oaks: Sage, pp. 325-345.

Ragins, B. and Scandura, T. (1994), 'Gender differences in expected outcomes of mentoring relationships', *Academy of Management Journal*, **37**, 957-971.

Ramos, S. (2002). 'Classe: executiva', *Fortunas & Negócios*, **15**, 28-41.

Santos, G.G. and Cabral-Cardoso, C. (2002), 'Academic careers and work-family linkage: a case study', paper presented at the European Academy of Management Conference, Stockholm, 9-11 May 2002.

Thomas, A.B. (2001), 'Women at the top in British retailing: a longitudinal analysis', *The Service Industries Journal*, **21**, 1-12.

Chapter 7

Women in Management in the United Kingdom

Fiona M. Wilson

Introduction

'The typical UK manager is male, married and earns between £31,000 and £40,000 a year' (Institute of Management, 2001a).

This quote resulted from a survey of managers in the UK in 2001. The lack of equality of women in management in Britain is quite striking and begs the question why are so few female managers to be found at senior levels? But before we look at women in management, let us look at women's employment more generally in the UK.

Labour force characteristics

One of the more important social and economic changes in the last thirty years has been the increase in women's employment, particularly that of mothers. More women in the UK are either seeking work or in work than was the case in the past. While only a half of women were in or areseeking any sort of work in 1971, this proportion had grown to two thirds by 1983 and almost three quarters by 1999 (British Social Attitudes, 2000). However women in the labour force face inequality. Women still lag behind men in terms of income (Rake, 2000). While the average gross annual earnings for men in Britain is £24,298, females only earn £11,811 (48.6 per cent of men's earnings). In management women fare better. The average gross weekly earnings for male managers and administrators are £668.9, while for females it is £468.8 (70 per cent) (New Earnings Survey, 2000).

There is a strong relationship between occupational sex segregation and lower pay for women. Millward and Woodland (1995) refer to this as the 'wage penalty' associated with working in organizations and occupations dominated by women. Women's employment tends to be concentrated in certain occupations and industries. They form the majority of workers in three occupational groups (EOR, 1998). These are clerical and secretarial work where women make up 75 per cent of employees, personal and protective services (66 per cent female) and sales (62 per cent female). They also predominate in health and social work (81 per cent), education (69 per cent), hotels and restaurants (59 per cent), the retail trade (60 per cent), and clothing manufacture (71 per cent) (EOR, 1998).

The expansion of women's employment has been mainly in part time jobs, predominately in the service industry. The growth in part-time work has been most concentrated among women with dependent children underscoring the point that women's labour market participation is closely bound to childcare. Women who switch to part time hours usually find they have jobs of lower pay, lower status, poorer conditions of employment, skills atrophy and other disadvantages (Blackwell, 2001). One of the contributory factors to inequality is undoubtedly the unequal sharing of childcare responsibilities (La Valle et al., 2000).

Higher educated skilled women can command higher wages which makes it more profitable for them to enter and stay in the labour market, even if they have children. This is borne out in the statistics. Of those women with children under five, 77 per cent of highly qualified women are in employment compared with 26 per cent of women without higher level qualifications (EOR, 1998). When work is more extrinsically and intrinsically satisfying, the motivation to continue work throughout the child rearing years is likely to be stronger. Employment commitment is also highest for those in the higher status jobs, where both the financial and intrinsic rewards are generally high compared to other occupations (Gallie et al., 1998). Certainly there are good reasons to pursue higher education.

Women pursuing education

Participation in higher education is expanding. Participation by full-time, home-domiciled students in Great Britain is targeted to reach 35 per cent of all 18-to 21-year-olds by 2002, with a longer-term aim of 50 per cent for those aged 18 to 30 who are domiciled in England (DFEE, 2001). There are now four times as many women enrolled in higher education than there were in the early 1970s (ONS, 2000). Women now outnumber men as registered students in the UK. There were 906,620 female and 725,060 males students registered in 1999/2000 (HESA 2001), and 55 per cent of students were female in 2000/2001 compared with 52 per cent in 1996/7. In 1999/2000 exactly one half of all students studying Business and Administration in the UK were female (HESA, 2001). The proportion of women taking MBA courses has also risen from around 10 per cent a decade ago to nearly 40 per cent today (*The Guardian*, 5th November 2001).

Women in management

As Table 7.1 shows, the percentage of women managers has risen in the last 3 decades. However women in the UK hold just 24 per cent of all management positions and 9.9 per cent of directorships (Institute of Management and

Remuneration Economics, 2001). Only one woman made it to CEO in the FTSE 100 list and she was the only female in that list paid more than £1m in 1999 (Singh et al., 2001). While there are signs of positive trends in increasing numbers of women in managerial and administrative posts, the jobs taken by women are mostly in low paid service sector jobs, for example in the hotel sector (Wilson, 1994; Rubery and Fagan, 1994); in this sector women earn below the average of all women's earnings.

Table 7.1 Percentage of female executives by responsibility level

Responsibility level	1974	1990	1995	2000	2001
Director	0.6%	1.6%	3.0%	9.6%	9.9%
Function head	0.4%	4.2%	5.8%	15%	15.8%
Department head	2.1%	7.2%	9.7%	19%	25.5%
Section leader	2.4%	11.8%	14.2%	26.5%	28.9%
Whole sample	1.8%	7.9%	10.7%	22.1%	24.1%

Source: Institute of Management and Remuneration Economics (2001)

There is also evidence of a reversal of positive trends. The 1994 National Management Survey (Institute of Management, 1995) found a fall in the number of women managers from 10.2 per cent in 1993 to 9.8 per cent in 1994. A similar trend can be found in Scottish management figures; 35 per cent of managers and administrators were women in 1995 but by 1999 there were 32 per cent (Kay, 2000). The same trend can be found in the National Health Service where the proportion of women chief executives was 28 per cent in 1994 but 22.3 per cent in 1998. This happened in spite of the NHS being the first government department to join Opportunity 2000 (a business led campaign to increase the number of women at the top of organizations, launched in 1991) and the creation of a high profile NHS Women's Unit.

Just 9 per cent of ethnic minority females in the UK are to be found in the category 'professional, manager, employer, employees and managers – large establishments' compared to 11 per cent of white females (Davidson, 1997). Relative to white women, black and ethnic minority women continue to be under-represented in higher-grade employment (Bhavnani, 1994, 1996). Black women are less likely to become managers, but where they do, are more likely to be self-employed owner managers of very small units (Bruegal, 1994) or managers in the cash strapped public sector (Bhavnani and Coyle, 2000).

All the studies show a continuing problem for women who aspire to top management positions. Women are not seen to have the necessary characteristics for leadership in senior or middle management positions compared to men. Successful middle managers are perceived to possess those characteristics attitudes and temperament more commonly ascribed to men than to women (Schein, 1973; Harris, 2001). Schein's (1973) adage 'think manager, think male' appears to apply well in Britain. Not only are the characteristics held by a manager seen as similar to the conceptions of men, but also those who select managers are likely to see men as more plausible candidates for managerial jobs. The type of behaviour deemed appropriate coincides with images of masculinity and centres around rationality, measurement, objectivity, control and competitiveness (Pollitt, 1993; Kerfoot and Knights, 1996). Women are associated with 'feminine' characteristics such as caring, nurturing and sharing. Gender role stereotypes have a major impact not only on selection but also on promotion and evaluation of managerial performance (Vinkenburg et al., 2000). Women themselves may experience 'role conflict' in thinking of themselves as managers (Liff and Ward, 2001).

What other explanations are there as to why the proportion of women in top management has remained so small? Powell (2000) goes as far as to argue that women's presence at top levels of management violates the norm of male superiority. This is one explanation as to why women are likely to be sexually harassed; men are hostile to women who compete with them for jobs and can demonstrate that hostility in the form of sexual harassment (Wilson and Thompson, 2001). Women as a minority encounter difficulties in adjusting to and fitting into male managerial cultures (Kanter, 1977). They become 'tokens', their behaviour taken as an example of 'women's' behaviour and always in the spotlight. They face an unsupportive environment, the 'old boys' network, an unwillingness by those in power to confront and eliminate sexism and being assigned less influential projects (Nelson and Burke, 2000).

How do women in management perceive their situation? A survey by the Institute of Management (2001b) found that only around a third of the women managers who responded believed their organization discriminates against them in terms of pay policy while 47 per cent thought women suffer discrimination when their company makes decisions affecting their career progression. Twenty seven per cent pointed to family commitments as a career block. The old boy network was seen by over a third (35 per cent) as a major barrier. Similarly an Opportunity Now survey (2002) found that a third of their women respondents believed they were discriminated against at the point of promotion. The obstacles were greater for older women and those from ethnic minorities - 49 per cent of women from ethnic minorities cited direct discrimination. More than half the 1000 women surveyed think they have to put their career before family to win promotion in their organization. When the statistics show such inequity in numbers, one might expect to see far more women managers perceiving discrimination in their organizations.

In the face of stereotyping, how do women choose to lead? Where women managers are in a minority, working in male-dominated industries they tend to lead in a similar way to men (Gardiner and Tiggemann, 1999). In male-dominated industries women are prone to display a more stereotypically masculine style than males (Eagly and Johnson, 1990; Ferrario and Davidson, 1991). They probably do this to make themselves less visible or to lessen perceived differences and stereotyping by the men (Kanter, 1977). On the whole, it would seem that women managers see successful managers as masculine (Cames et al., 2001; Vinnicombe and Singh, 2002).

The research shows that managerial styles are not a fixed and unchanging function of an individual's sex. It may be that organizational traits, rather than personality traits, determine management style (Wajcman, 1998). It is interesting to note that Wahl (1998) studied a women dominated company and found that style depended on the functional position of the manager.

There is some suggestion from the research in Britain that women are rejecting the way in which managerial work is organized. Marshall (1995), in her study of women who left senior management jobs, found that these women no longer wanted to work in masculine work cultures. Liff and Ward (2001) in a study of a UK bank, found that management in general, and senior management in particular was a predominately male preserve where women represented only 2 per cent of senior managers and 10 per cent of middle managers. Only 5 per cent of applicants for a set of new, relatively senior posts were women. Liff and Ward discovered that women perceived senior managers in the bank as part super human workaholics, willing and able to accommodate enormous workloads and prepared to devote themselves entirely to the bank. In addition they viewed these senior managers as being able to impress the right people and be in the right place at the right time. The women believed that showing an interest in flexible working was risking being seen as a non-career person. Women who attempted to have a career were either seen as aberrant women (in the sense they put work before a family) or as having second class careers which advanced more slowly or disjointedly than men's. The situation could be described as 'think female manager, think childless superwoman' (Liff and Ward, 2001).

Formal provisions such as career breaks may not be taken up if women feel that it will be construed as evidence that they are not able to compete on the same terms as men (Liff and Ward, 2001) Many organizations have an ambivalence about employees family commitments. For example an Industrial Society report showed that while 55 per cent of managers said that enabling employees to balance home and work life was essential to ethical management, only 30 per cent said it was true in their organization (IRS, 1996). Balancing the demands of home and work is important for both men and women. However the total workload (including domestic as well as paid work) tends to be higher for women, and increases with the number of children in the family (Nelson and Burke, 2000).

While part time work is increasing, paradoxically excessively long working hours for managers have become the norm. This is due in part to work intensification and partly because long working hours have come to be an indicator of commitment (Corby, 1997). Work intensification has come about, in part, due to restructuring and downsizing (Simpson and Holley, 2001). Evidence of increasing managerial workloads is widespread. For example, an Institute of Management survey found that 84 per cent of managers claimed to regularly work in excess of their official working week and for 60 per cent this was always the case (Institute of Management, 1996). Half the respondents took work home and over 4 in 10 said they worked at weekends. A study by Wajcman (1996) of five large multinationals found that over 60 per cent of male and female managers worked on average 50 hours and 16 per cent of both men and women, more than 60 hours a week. Research has shown that a large and similar proportion of men and women would like to adjust the number of hours they work, mostly by working fewer hours in exchange for reduced earnings. Preferences for reduced hours are highest for men and women in the managerial and professional jobs (Fagan, 2001). Women and men who work long hours are least satisfied with the amount of time they have for family and leisure pursuits (Fagan, 1996). As a result of long working hours, men and women have to make a stark choice between work and families.

Delayering and restructuring can result in women managers being the losers. In depth case studies of three large organization who had experience restructuring found that unless it involved expansion of managerial positions, it is likely to disadvantage women managers as it leads to job losses where women are concentrated (Woodall et al., 1997).

Women entrepreneurs

Much has been made of the increasing number of women in self-employment but the statistics on which such claims are based present many problems (Allen, 1999). In Britain the Labour Force Survey and Inland Revenue adopt different criteria so regularly produce widely varying estimates of the numbers of self-employed and business owners. A survey in the EC found that the numbers of women who worked independently or ran their own business, or worked unsalaried in the partner's business was higher by some 10 million women than those recorded in official Eurostat figures (Allen, 1999). Notwithstanding the difficulties in interpreting the figures, the Labour Force Survey (1999) shows that women make up 25.9 per cent of the self-employed population in the UK. It is estimated that the number of women owned businesses in the UK is in the region of 952,750 (Carter and Anderson, 2001). These figures reveal the important contribution that women owned businesses make to the UK economy, but it is likely that this number under estimates the majority of women's entrepreneurial efforts which are dedicated to family businesses and masked by co-ownership. Overall, research findings suggest it is hard to ignore the linkages between women entrepreneurship and the family.

A number of researchers in the UK have suggested that women's entrepreneurship can be seen as a means of escaping the persistent inequalities and the occupational confines of the labour market (e.g. Marlow, 1997). However the literature suggests that women also face inequality in self-employment. For example, they have been found to be disadvantaged in their ability to raise start up finance (Carter and Cannon, 1992; Johnson and Storey, 1993; Carter and Rosa, 1998). Guarantees may be beyond the scope of most women's personal assets and credit track record. Finance for the ongoing business may be less available for female owned firms than it is for male enterprises and female entrepreneurs' relationships with bankers may suffer because of sexual stereotyping and discrimination. In comparison with men, women enter self-employment with fewer financial assets, less experience in management, with less network and family support. Furthermore a key issue is the extent to which the initial resource shortage affects long term business performance (Brush, 1997).

Researchers have asked if female entrepreneurs manage their firms in a qualitatively different way to men (Stanford et al., 1995). Buttner (2001) has reported that management styles of female entrepreneurs can be described as mutual empowering, collaborative, involving sharing of information, empathy and nurturing. Rosa et al.'s (1996) study looked specifically at the impact of gender on small business management. It found that women's businesses employed fewer core staff, were less likely to have grown substantially in employment (to more than 20 employees) after 12 months in business, had a lower sales turnover and were valued at a lower level than male owned businesses. Although these results appear to demonstrate gender differences in business performance, they should be treated with caution. Women have only recently emerged as an entrepreneurial group and their businesses are much younger and therefore less established.

Country legislation supporting women in the workforce

In Britain there are two major complementary pieces of legislation to deal with sex discrimination. These are the Equal Pay Act 1970 and the Sex Discrimination Act 1975. (Both laws have been amended - by the 1983 Equal Value Regulations, the Sex Discrimination Act, 1986 and Sex Discrimination (Gender reassignment) Regulations, 1999.) This domestic framework of legislation enacts various requirements in European law and continues to be profoundly influenced by rulings of the European Court of Justice.

The Equal Pay Act did not come into effect until 1975. It has had some, but limited effect. In 1971 women earned only 63 per cent of the average hourly earnings of full time male employees. By 1999, they earned 81 per cent (Sargent, 2001). The act asserts the principle that men and women should receive equal pay for equal work, including redundancy pay, pensions, severance pay, sick pay and paid leave. The legislation requires a comparator that can be 'like work', 'work rated as equivalent' and 'work of equal value'.

The Sex Discrimination Act covers discrimination on grounds of gender, marital status and gender reassignment. The provisions of the act apply to women, men and married persons. There are two main forms of discrimination recognized by the Act. Firstly direct discrimination where a person from one group is treated less favourably than those not in that group. This is the most blatant. An example would be where a woman is refused employment because she is a woman or on the grounds of pregnancy. The second is indirect discrimination where an apparently neutral employment practice has a disproportionately disadvantageous effect upon a particular group. There is indirect discrimination where an employer imposes a requirement or condition that applies equally to all, but can only be met by a considerably smaller proportion. For example age barriers in recruitment or requirements on length of service may indirectly discriminate against women who have taken time out of employment to bring up children.

There are exceptions to the Sex Discrimination Act, circumstances where it is lawful to discriminate with genuine occupational qualifications. This is where effective performance of a job requires a person of a particular sex or race. For example a certain physiology or authenticity may be needed in the case of models or actors. Privacy and decency may be preserved for women if a ladies health club restricts employment to female staff.

Positive discrimination is not permitted under British sex discrimination law but positive action is allowed. Under represented groups can be encouraged to apply for posts, and an organization can set targets for the number of women to be recruited. Family-friendly measures like career breaks, flexible working time and assistance with childcare help individuals carry the double load of paid work and domestic commitments. Access to single sex training can allow women to overcome earlier educational and training disadvantage and encourage them to move up a management hierarchy.

Initiatives supporting women in the workforce

A nation-wide voluntary business campaign, established in 1991, called Opportunity 2000, set key goals for tackling inequality through a broad based business driven policy approach. Senior managers are asked to drive change from the top, be seen as role models in leading equal opportunities, develop and address the issues as part of their business strategy. They are asked to make an investment, change behaviour, communicate and share ownership in developing new working methods to enhance business performance. Members of Opportunity 2000 (recently renamed Opportunity Now) are required annually to demonstrate how they have met their goals. Opportunity Now currently boasts a membership of over 350 organizations. Among Opportunity Now members, 28 per cent of managers are women.

A number of government initiatives have attempted to support the advancement of women. The government has given £44m to boost the number of childcare places offered by local councils (*The Guardian*, 15th October 1998). The continued existence of inequality has prompted the government to set up a Women's Unit 'to ensure that Government policies knit together properly to take account of the interests of women' (The Women's Unit, 1998).

Equal opportunities polices have been part of employment policy and business practice since the early 1980s. The majority of large UK organizations now have a formal equal opportunities policy (Liff and Cameron, 1997); recent evidence suggests that two thirds of workplaces have formal written equal opportunities policies (Culley et al., 1999). The public sector has been regarded as leading the way in the development of equal opportunities policy. Results in both the private and public sector have been very mixed. Research has found that line managers play an important role in either challenging or reproducing inequality (Kirton and Greene, 2000).

Individual companies too have introduced initiatives. Asda, the supermarket group has guaranteed that 10 per cent of its senior positions will be offered on a job share basis to encourage more women into store management (*The Guardian*, 1st October 1998). British Telecom and the Post Office have developed training to increase the numbers of women in senior positions (EOR 1996; 1999). Companies such as British Telecom, Anglia Television and Legal and General are encouraging women managers to go on executive development courses (The Guardian, 5th November 2001).

The future

The model of the successful manager is male and while these stereotypes remain, they succeed in perpetuating the dominant place for men in management. Management cultures are described as masculine, characterized by long work hours, lack of family friendly polices, bullying and harassment. While the traditional male career model of a full time career is the norm and some women and very few men step off the fast track to meet family responsibilities, women will continue to be at a competitive disadvantage. Organizational initiatives relating to family friendly policies should be directed at both men and women in organizations to facilitate a change but this change alone will not bring about equality for women in management in Britain.

References

Allen, S. (1999), Gender inequality and divisions of labour, in Beynon, H. and Glavanis, P. (eds), *Patterns of Social Inequality*, London: Longman.

Bhavnani, R. (1994), *Black women in the labour market: a research review*, Manchester: Equal Opportunities Commission.

Bhavnani, R. (1996), *Black and ethnic minority women in the labour market in London*, London: Fair Play.

Bhavnani, R. and Coyle, A. (2000), Black and ethnic minority women managers in the UK - continuity or change?, in Davidson, M.J. and Burke, R.J. (eds), *Women in Management: current research issues Volume II*, London: Sage.

Blackwell, L. (2001), Occupational Sex Segregation and Part time work in Modern Britain, *Gender, Work and Organization*, **8** (2), 146-161.

Bruegal, I. (1994), *Labour market prospects for women from ethnic minorities in Institute for Employment Research* (ed.), Warwick University: Labour Market Structures and

Prospects for Women, Institute for Employment Research/Equal Opportunities Commission.

Brush, C.G., 'A Resource Perspective on Women's Entrepreneurship: research relevance and recognition', Proceedings of the OECD Conference on Women Entrepreneurs in Small and Medium Enterprises: a major force in innovation and job creation, Paris, April 1997, 155-168.

Buttner, E.H. (2001), 'Examining female entrepreneurs' management style: an application of a relational frame', *Journal of Business Ethics*, February, 253-269.

Cames, I., Vinnicombe, S. and Singh, V. (2001), 'Profiles of 'successful managers' held by male and female banking managers across Europe', *Women in Management*, **16** (3), 108-117.

Carter, S. and Anderson, S. (2001), *On the Move: women and men business owners in the United Kingdom*, Washington DC: NFWBO and IBM.

Carter, S. and Cannon, T. (1992), *Women as Entrepreneurs*, London: Academic Press.

Carter, S. and Rosa, P. (1998), 'The financing of male and female owned businesses', *Entrepreneurship and Regional Development*, **10** (3), 225-241.

Corby, S. (1997), 'Equal Opportunities and Flexibilities in the United Kingdom's Public Services', *Review of Public Personnel Administration*, Summer, **17** (3), 57-68.

Culley, M., Woodland, S., O'Reilly, A. and Dix, G. (1999), *Britain at Work*, Routledge.

Davidson, M. (1997), *The Black and Ethnic Minority Women Manager: cracking the concrete ceiling*, London: Paul Chapman.

DFEE (2001), *Management Summary*, London: DFEE.

Eagly, A.H. and Johnson, B.T. (1990) 'Gender and leadership style: a meta-analysis', *Psychological Bulletin*, **80** (5), 389-407.

EOR (Equal Opportunities Review) (1996), 'Women in the Post Office', *Equal Opportunities Review*, **66**, March-April, 13-19.

EOR (Equal Opportunities Review) (1998), 'Women in the labour market', *Equal Opportunities Review*, **79**, May-June, 30-31.

EOR (Equal Opportunities Review) (1999), 'BT: championing women in a man's world', *Equal Opportunities Review*, **84**, March-April, 14-20.

Fagan, C. (1996), 'Gendered time schedules: paid work in Great Britain', *Social Politics: International Studies in Gender, State and Society*, **3** (1), 72-106.

Fagan, C. (2001), 'Time, Money and the Gender Order: Work orientations and working-time preferences in Britain', *Gender, Work and Organization*, **8** (3), 239-266.

Ferrario, M. and Davidson, M.J. (1991), 'Gender and management style: a comparative study', in Davidson, M.J. and Cooper, C.L. (eds), *Shattering the Glass Ceiling*, London: Paul Chapman.

Gallie, D., White, M., Cheng, Y. and Tomlinson, M. (1998), *Restructuring the Employment Relationship*, Oxford: Oxford University Press.

The Guardian (5 November 2001), 'None of their Business', Analysis by Nick Pandya.

Gardiner, M. and Tiggemann, M. (1999), 'Gender differences in leadership style, job stress and mental health in male and female dominated industries', *Journal of Occupational and Organizational Psychology*, **72** (3), 301-315.

Harris, H. (2001), 'Researching discrimination in selection for international management', *Women in Management Review*, **16** (3), 118-125.

HESA (Higher Education Statistical Agency) (2001), Students in Higher Education Institutions 199/2000, Cheltenham: HESA.

Institute of Management (1995), National Management Salary Survey, Institute of Management, Kingston Upon Thames.

Institute of Management (1996), Are managers under stress? A survey of management morale, IM: Corby.

Institute of Management (2001a), UK managers in tune with the spirit of the age, News release number 020 7497 0496, 21 June, IM: London.

Institute of Management (2001b), A Woman's Place? - a survey of female managers' changing professional and personal roles, IM: London.

Institute of Management and Remuneration Economics (2001), UK National Management Survey, Institute of Management: London.

IRS (1996), 'Hypocrisy rife in company ethics', *Employment Trends*, **619**, 2 November.

Johnson, S. and Storey, D. (1993), Male and female entrepreneurs and their businesses: a comparative study, in Allen, S. and Truman, C. (eds), *Women in Business: perspectives on women entrepreneurs*, London: Routledge, pp. 70-85.

Kanter, R.M. (1977), *Men, Women and the Corporation*, New York: Basic Books.

Kay, H. (2001), 'Women and Men in the Professions in Scotland', Scottish Executive, Central Research Unit (http://www.scotland.gov.uk/cru/kd01/red/men00.htm).

Kerfoot, D. and Knights, D. (1996), 'The best is yet to come: searching for embodiment in managerial work', in Collinson, D. and Hearn, J. (eds), *Men as Managers, Managers as Men: critical perspectives on Men, Masculinities and Management*, London: Sage, pp. 78-98.

Kirton, G. and Green, A.M. (2000), The Dynamics of Managing Diversity, Oxford: Butterworth-Heinemann.

La Valle, I., Finch, S., Nove, A. and Lewin, C. (2000), Parents' Demand for Childcare, DfEE Research Report RR 176, London: The Stationery Office.

Liff, S. and Cameron, I. (1997), 'Changing equality cultures to move beyond 'women's problems', *Gender Work and Organization*, **4** (1), 35-46.

Liff, S. and Ward. K. (2001), 'Distorted Views Through the Glass Ceiling: the construction of women's understandings of promotion and senior management positions', *Gender Work and Organization*, **8** (1), 19-36.

Marlow, S. (1997), 'Self-employed women - do they mean business?' *Entrepreneurship and Regional Development*, **9** (3), 199-210.

Marshall, J. (1995), *Women Managers Moving On: exploring career and life choices*, London: Routledge.

Millward, N. and Woodland, S. (1995), Gender segregation and male/female wage differences in Economics of Equal Opportunities, Humphries, J. and Rubery, J. (eds), Equal Opportunities Commission, Manchester.

Nelson, D.L. and Burke, R.J. (2000), 'Women, work stress and health', in Davidson M.J. and Burke R.J. (eds), *Women in Management: Current Research Issues Volume II*, London: Sage.

New Earnings Survey (2000), Tables A6.1 and A10.1 National Statistics Publication, Office for National Statistics.

(ONS) Office for National Statistics (2000), *Social Trends,* **30**, London: The Stationery Office.

Opportunity Now (2002), 'Sticky Floors and Cement Ceilings' - Report discussed in *Financial Times*, 5 March, Women held back by bullying, harassment and discrimination; and *Personnel Today*, 5 March, Putting family first holds back career women.

Pollitt, C. (1993), Managerialism and the Public Services: cuts or cultural change in the 1990s?, Oxford: Blackwell.

Powell, G.N. (2000), 'The Glass Ceiling: explaining the good and bad news', in Davidson, M.J. and Burke, R.J. (eds), *Women in Management: Current Research Issues Volume II*, London: Sage.

Rake, K. (ed.) (2000), *Women's incomes over the lifetime*, London: The Stationery Office.

Rosa, P., Carter, S. and Hamilton, D. (1996), 'Gender as a determinant of small business performance: insights from a British study', *Small Business Economics*, **8**, 463-478.

Rubery, J. and Fagan, C. (1994), 'Occupational segregation: Plus ca change...', in Lindley, R. (ed.), *Labour Market structures and Prospects for Women*, Institute for Employment Research, University of Warwick/Equal Opportunities.

Rutherford, S. (2001), 'Any Difference? An analysis of gender and divisional management styles in a large airline', *Gender, Work and Organization*, **8** (3), 326-345.

Sargent, M. (2001), *Employment Law*, Harlow, Essex: Pearson Education Ltd.

Schein, V. (1973), 'The relationship between sex role stereotypes and requisite management characteristics', *Journal of Applied Psychology*, **57** (2), 95-100.

Simpson, R. and Holley, D. (2001), 'Can restructuring fracture the glass ceiling? The case of women transport and logistics managers', *Women in Management Review*, **16** (4), 174-182.

Singh,V., Vinnicombe, S. and Johnson, P. (2001), 'Women Directors on Top UK Boards', *Corporate Governance: an international review,* **9**, forthcoming.

Stanford, J., Oates, B. and Flores, D. (1995), 'Women's leadership styles: a heuristic analysis', *Women in Management Review*, **10** (2), 9-16.

Vinkenburg, C.J., Jansen, P.G. and Koopman, P.L. (2000), 'Feminine leadership - a review of gender differences in managerial behaviour and effectiveness', in Davidson, M.J. and Burke, R.J. (eds), *Women in Management: Current Research Issues Volume II*, London: Sage.

Vinnicombe, S. and Singh, V. (2002), 'Sex role stereotyping and requisites of successful top managers', *Women in Management Review*, **17** (3/4), 120-130.

Wahl, A. (1998), 'Surplus femininity', paper presented at Gender Work and Organization Conference, Manchester, 9-10 January (cited in Rutherford, 2001).

Wajcman, J. (1996), 'Women and men managers: careers and equal opportunities', in Crompton, R., Gallie, D. and Purcell, K. (eds), *Changing forms of Employment*, London: Routledge, pp. 259-277.

Wajcman, J. (1998), *Managing Like a Man: women and men in corporate management*, Cambridge: Polity Press.

Wilson, F. and Thompson, P. (2001), 'Sexual harassment as an exercise of power', *Gender, Work and Organization*, **8** (1), 61-83.

Wilson, R. (1994), 'Sectoral and occupational change: prospects for women's employment', in Lindley, R. (ed.), *Labour Market structures and Prospects for Women*, Institute for Employment Research, University of Warwick/Equal Opportunities Commission, Manchester.

The Women's Unit (1998), *Delivering for Women: progress so far*, London: The Cabinet Office.

Woodall, J., Edwards, C. and Welchman, R. (1997), 'Organizational Restructuring and the Achievement of an Equal Opportunities Culture', *Gender, Work and Organization*, **4** (1), 2-12.

SECTION II
WOMEN IN MANAGEMENT –
EUROPEAN COUNTRIES

Chapter 8

Women in Management in Norway

Astrid M. Richardsen and Laura E. Mercer Traavik

Introduction

In March 2002 the Norwegian government passed legislation aimed at securing at least 40 per cent women on corporate boards of directors by the year 2005. In order to achieve this, the government introduced quotas in all public and public affairs enterprises within a year, whereas private sector companies were issued an ultimatum to achieve 40 per cent female representation by 2005, otherwise legislation will be introduced to enforce quotas.

The passing of the bill sparked a heated public debate in which a number of prominent business leaders, mostly men, spoke passionately against the use of quotas, whereas women were divided on the issue. Some women argued for recruitment based on competence and experience, and were concerned that selection by quota would create a perception that women were not as competent as men and could only secure a position by special treatment. Other women were in favour of some kind of incentives to reverse the current imbalance and give competent women the opportunity to sit on boards, and yet others emphasized the benefits of diversity.

The controversy over equality is not new in Norway, as several laws in favour of affirmative action in other areas of public affairs and business have previously set off passionate debates. What surprised a lot of people in the most recent argument was how traditional the rhetoric voiced by male business leaders still was, and the vehemence with which arguments against quotas were put forth. While obviously paying lip service to bringing in women on company boards, it became apparent that in reality the 'old boys network' is still going strong. Several business leaders publicly admitted that board membership is not just a matter of competence, but of friendship, confidence, diplomacy, compliance, team work, and purely subjective appraisals. The result has been a growing realization that despite a reputation as a progressive country in terms of gender equality, Norway has a long way to go compared to many other European countries, even countries that have been considered more traditional and conventional than Norway.

From the existing international literature on the topic of gender equality, it is clear that the glass ceiling, first described by Morrison, White and van Velsor (1992), exists not only in the US, but in many countries, including countries often associated with high equality, such as Norway. The literature also indicates that progress is slow (Davidson and Burke, 2000). The labour market statistics for Norway are similar to those in other countries, although many Norwegians are surprised that more progress has not been made with regards to women's advancement. One would hope that the focus on these issues will enhance awareness and demands for action, as we have witnessed in the current debates and controversies in Norway.

Norway has a population of 4.5 million people, and life expectancy for men is 76 years and for women 81 years. The average number of children per woman is approaching two, which is one of the highest rates in Europe, and 53 per cent of all children under five years old have either day-care, pre-school or kindergarten places. Single mothers are eligible for substantial government support until their child reaches 10 years of age and Norway has laws that ensure women's right to have an abortion on demand. Norwegian culture prioritizes family life and children, which is reflected in working hours and national holidays. The standard of living is one of the highest in the world, according to recent international reports, yet there continues to be substantial gender inequality. Norway is an excellent example of political initiatives and social welfare policies that promote equality, yet have failed to achieve the desired results.

This chapter will focus on gender equality in Norway and will use the latest labour market statistics available to report on labour force characteristics, women pursuing education, women in management, women entrepreneurs, country legislation and initiative to support the advancement of women. In the following sections we present the picture of Norwegian women, the advancements and the hurdles, and predictions and recommendations for future action and research.

Labour force characteristics

In the year 2000 women made up 46.6 per cent of the Norwegian workforce, while clear gender differences remained in the type and degree of participation in the labour market, as well as earning levels (Statistics Norway, 2001b).

Norway has the most gender segregated labour market within the OECD regions (Norwegian Gender Equity Council, 2001b). For example, women comprise a mere 8 per cent in the building and construction industry, yet make up 83 per cent in the health care and social services. Men continue to dominate fields such as engineering and women make up an overwhelming majority within primary and secondary education. The majority of Norwegian women work in the public sector, 66 per cent compared to 37 per cent in the private sector. The data reveal that within Norway occupational segregation between male and female jobs continues to be extremely pronounced. In Table 8.1 the percentage of women in the different industry sectors in the year 2000 is presented.

Table 8.1 Percentage of women in the industry sectors

Industry	Percentage of women
Health and social services	83
Teaching	65
Other social and personal services	56
Financial services and insurance	50
Retail, hotel and restaurant	49
Public administration and defence	43
Property management	39
Industry and mining	26
Agriculture, lumber and fishing	26
Oil and gas	21
Energy and water supply	20
Building and construction	8

Source: Statistics Norway, 2001b

As for participation in the labour market, between 1980 and 1998 the percentage ofr women in the workforce increased in all age groups. The latest statistics show that 87 per cent of men and 78 per cent of women are participating in the labour market (Vikan, 2001). Although women have increased their overall participation in the Norwegian labour market, the degree of their participation is different from men. 93 per cent of employed men compared to 60 per cent of employed women between the ages of 25 and 66 are working full time (Norwegian Gender Equity Council, 2001b). In fact, of all the OECD countries only the UK has a higher percentage of women working part time[1]. On average, women work 8 hours less per week in paid work compared to men. The number rather than the age of the children has the largest impact on whether women work full or part time: 57 per cent of women with several children work part time as compared to 43 per cent of women with only one child (Statistics Norway, 2001a). These statistics reveal that the Norwegian woman's participation in the labour market is strongly influenced by her family situation.

However, trends do indicate that the degree of participation among women is increasing. Since 1980 and right up until 1999 the number of men working part time has remained stable, whereas for women there has been a decrease from 52.5 per cent to 44.7 per cent in 1999 (Statistics Norway, 2001a). Over the last two decades participation of women with young children (under three years old) has increased by 20 per cent from 1980 to 1998. Women's participation in the labour market also increases as their children get older. Another positive trend is that differences between men and women in the number of hours worked are smaller among the younger and more educated members of the labour force. For men and women with college or university education there is only a 2 per cent difference in work activity, whereas a 20 per cent difference exists among those who only have junior high school education 1998 (Statistics Norway, 2001a).

Perhaps the most alarming labour force characteristics is the difference between men and women's earnings, which remains at the same level as 25 years ago. Women continue to earn only 65 per cent of what men do (Norwegian Gender Equity Council, 2001b). This gap is largely due to the difference in participation in the workforce, with three times as many women working part time. These differences are even more pronounced in the immigrant and first generation Norwegian groups (Statistics Norway, 2001a). In a recent United Nations report, Norway ranks seventh internationally in terms of income differences (Human Development Report, 2001).

The overall picture of the Norwegian labour market is that women are participating in increasing numbers yet they are not obtaining the same earning levels as men, nor entering into traditionally male dominated professions or jobs. Also, it appears that a woman's family situation greatly influences whether she participates in the labour market full time.

Women pursuing education

The labour market characteristics do not reflect the small revolution that Norwegian women have achieved in education. In the youngest age groups (25-29 years), 39 per cent of women have university or college level education compared to 30 per cent of men, and in 2000, 61 per cent of students registered for higher education were women (Norwegian Social Science Data Service, 2002). The increase has been dramatic, in 1980, 10 per cent of women had higher education compared to 14 per cent of men, whereas in 1998, 22 per cent of women and 23 per cent of men had higher education (Statistics Norway, 2001a). In addition, women are beginning to dominate the studies of law, medicine and the social sciences (Frønes and Brusdal, 2000).

Although women have made great progress in the numbers obtaining higher education, traditional gender differences still emerge in the choices of study. Technical studies continue to be dominated by men, whereas women make up the overwhelming majority in health and welfare studies. Of those who obtained an engineering degree in the years between 1997 and 1999, only 22 per cent were women (Norwegian Gender Equity Council, 2001b). Only 30 per cent of those who obtained the elite Norwegian business degree, civil economist, in the same years were women (Norwegian Gender Equity Council, 2001b). It should be noted that almost all top leaders in the Norwegian private sector have one of these two degrees (Kvålshaugen, 2001).

The proportion of women among academic and research staff continues to be low. In Norway post graduate education is often funded through scholarships. Women now account for 43 per cent of the recipients of this type of funding. Although more women are taking post graduate studies and qualifying for academic careers, currently only 12 per cent of professors and 27 per cent of associate professors in Norway are women (Norwegian Social Science Data Services, 2002).

The data show that while women are making great progress in many fields as well as in the sheer percentages actually obtaining higher education, there continues to be dramatic differences in choices of study, which reveals that women and men continue to choose gender-stereotyped fields.

Women in management

Statistics on women in management positions are usually reported separately for the public and private sectors. In terms of government, Norway is a country with one of the highest representations of women in national government (37 per cent in parliament); only Sweden has higher female representation (43 per cent) (Norwegian Gender Equity Council, 2001b). However, representation of women in parliament was reduced in the last election from 39 per cent. In terms of government ministries, the percentage of women cabinet ministers is now 42 per cent, and the percentage of women managers in the public sector increased from 26 per cent in 2000 to 29 per cent in 2001. The same gender segregation observed in the labour market can also be seen in the public sector. For example, Norway has never had a female minister of finance or foreign affairs, and the highest percentages of women managers are found in the areas of child and family services (51 per cent), health and welfare (51 per cent), and culture (42 per cent).

Since 1981 it has been established by law that all public governing boards, committees and councils should comprise at least 40 per cent of each sex. The percentage of women board and committee members in the public sector decreased from 42 per cent in 1999 to 41 per cent in 2000. In terms of the various ministries governing public affairs, the data indicate that about half of the ministries are not upholding the law. The lowest percentages of female representation occur in the departments of transport, defence, oil and energy, trade and foreign affairs; while the highest percentages are indicated in the departments of child and family services, education, regional development and culture.

In terms of the private sector, the percentage of women in management positions at all levels is 23 per cent, however, only 7 per cent of senior managers in private companies are women (Gender Equality Barometer, 2001). Of the people who indicate that they are the general manager of a company, 18 per cent are women. In companies with more than 250 employees, there are only 21 women managers compared to 467 men. These women senior managers earn approximately half the salary of their male colleagues (Statistics Norway, 2001b).

The percentage of women who hold a position as director of the board in any company is 11 per cent (Norwegian Gender Equity Council, 2001b). A recent report (Hoel, 2001) on 240 of the largest companies in Norway indicated that 26 per cent had no women in the management group or on the board of directors, 19 per cent had women only on the board and 22 per cent had women only in the management group. In terms of joint stock companies listed on the commodities exchange, only 6.4 per cent of board members are women, and only 3.6 per cent of the board members elected by shareholders are women. Companies within finance and publishing have the highest percentages of women on boards (19.3 per cent and 25.9 per cent respectively), and these industries also have the highest increase in women participation from 1999 to 2000. The Centre for Gender Equity has estimated that at the current rate of overall increase, it will take another 115 years before equality is reached on corporate boards, 62 years to achieve gender equity in senior management, and 39 years to achieve a balance in the number of men and women board of directors.

Small business in Norway, i.e., companies with less than 50 employees, represents 96 per cent of all firms, and employs 40 per cent of the private sector work force (Spilling, 1998). The Central Registry of Firms and Establishments indicates that not all registered companies provide data on leadership and gender. However, of the firms with records on the company manager and gender, general managers consist of 16 per cent women and 84 per cent men (Spilling and Berg, 2000).

The records for board chairmen in small businesses are also incomplete, but of those companies that that have records, the percentage of board chairmen is 10 per cent women and 90 per cent men. These figures compare well with data from a survey of approximately 1300 small and medium-sized businesses in Norway, which indicated that 15 per cent of the firms had women leaders (Spilling, 1997). In addition, the Central Registry data indicate that women tend to be managers for smaller companies than men. The companies led by women accounted for only 7 per cent of the total employment generated by the firms with registered managers, and accounted for only 5.3 per cent of the total turnover (Spilling and Berg, 2000).

The data also showed a gender-based segregation of labour that parallels general statistics from the labour market. Women have a significantly lower percentage of managers in manufacturing (6.4 per cent of women managers versus 12 per cent of male managers), construction (1.4 per cent of women managers versus 12.6 per cent of male managers), and financial and producer services (14.1 per cent of female managers versus 20.1 per cent of male managers); and have a significantly higher percentage of managers in retail trade, hotel and restaurants (52.4 per cent of female managers versus 37.5 per cent of male managers), and in public, social and private services (20.4 per cent of female managers versus 6.6 per cent of male managers). However, the relative distribution of male and female managers *within* each industry indicated that male managers are in majority in all of them, and so there is no industry which may be classified as 'typically female' in terms of management (Spilling and Berg, 2000).

Women entrepreneurs

The literature in the area of women in management indicate that the trend for women to start their own businesses is increasing world wide, and is quickly emerging as an area of growing research interest. However, research on women entrepreneurs in Norway is scarce and studies often have serious methodological limitations (Richardsen and Burke, 2000). In addition, it is almost impossible to accurately identify the exact number of women entrepreneurs and women-led firms (Holmquist, 1996; Brun, 1998; Spilling, 2001). Data sources concerning female entrepreneurs are few, because the Central Registry of Firms and Establishments has until recently not provided the gender of the business owner. In addition, while the variable in the population census called 'self-employed' will include a significant share of entrepreneurs, a number of self-employed individuals may have achieved that status by inheriting or taking over an existing business (Spilling and Berg, 2000). A number of entrepreneurs may also be formally employed by their own company, thus being recorded as an employee in the census. Nevertheless, the statistics on self-employed individuals will be reported here to provide information about women entrepreneurs.

Between 1980 and 1990 the number of self-employed women increased by 22 per cent, whereas there was a 10 per cent decrease in the number of self-employed men (Vangsnes, 1993). In 1990 women represented 24 per cent of the total number of self-employed, and an even higher per cent of self-employed over 35 years of age (Spilling, 1998). Between 1990 and 1996, the total number of self-employed people decreased, mostly among men (approximately 10 per cent), while there was a 6 per cent increase in self-employed women (Statistics Norway, 1997).

According to Statistics Norway's most recent labour market statistics (2001), the total number of people in Norway who are self-employed is 159,000, which constitutes 7 per cent of the total labour force. Of these, approximately 71 per cent (113,000) were men and 29 per cent (46,000) were women. In a study using the Norwegian VAT Register (Spilling, 2001), the data indicated that women make up 21 per cent of all new business registrations. The Central Registry of Firms and Establishments indicated that 18 per cent of all recorded managers were women, and in terms of registered sole proprietorships, data showed that 21 per cent of sole owners of companies are women. The majority of new registrations are organized as sole proprietorships, and among women entrepreneurs, over 70 per cent chose this type of ownership and only 26 per cent started limited companies (Spilling, 2001). Among men entrepreneurs, 54 per cent started sole proprietorships and 42 per cent started limited companies. Women also make up about 21 per cent in owner-managed firms.

There are still large differences between men and women in terms of the type of industry in which registrations are made (Spilling, 2001). While 54 per cent of male start-ups were in construction, primary industries and agriculture, producer services and transport, 64 per cent of female start-ups were in wholesale and retail trade, and community and social services. The majority of companies (88 per cent) started by women in Norway tend to be small with one or two employees, and they are in general smaller than those of men. Also, 50 per cent of companies led by men have more than 100 employees, while only 15 per cent of women-led firms employ that many. Survival rates of companies by gender indicate that companies registered to women have only marginally poorer survival rates between 1995 and 1999, as compared to companies registered by men.

In summary, data indicate that women's enterprises in Norway tend to be small with one or two employees, and tend to be concentrated in two commercial sectors, i.e., wholesale and retail trade, and community and social services. In addition, over 60 per cent of women leaders are concentrated in retail sales, child care centres and hairdressing and beauty care. As a rule, therefore, women-led enterprises are often operating in a local market economy and have only local competition. Women-led businesses are also more often sole proprietorships than businesses led by men, which more often tend to be limited companies.

Country legislation supporting women in the workforce

Norway prides itself on a strong social democratic tradition, which is based on the assumption that men and women should be treated equally and fairly. The Gender Equality Act was first passed in Norway in 1978 and put in practice in 1979 and has undergone many reformulations over the years (ODIN, 2002). This act provides the framework for ensuring that women have the same rights, obligations, and opportunities as men and vice versa. Norway has set up institutions to provide guidelines, such as the Gender Equality Ombudsman, however, there are few binding laws or mechanisms to ensure that these guidelines are followed.

In addition to the Gender Equality Act, there have been attempts to mainstream gender equality in all areas of public policy (Gender Equality Ombudsman, 1997). For example, Norway has one of the best parental leave legislation internationally. The parental leave period is 42 weeks with full pay and the opportunity to have unpaid leave for up to 3 years. There is a father quota where fathers are required to take 4 weeks of the total parental leave. Norway also has the Marketing Control Act which places responsibility on advertisers to ensure that their advertising is not discriminatory or derogatory of either sex. As well, women have control over their reproduction rights and the Abortion Act gives women the right for abortion on demand in the first 12 weeks of pregnancy.

The legislation that directly addresses gender equality and the peripheral but related legislation directed at giving women equal status and rights, have not been able to redress the imbalance between men and women in the workplace. Possible explanations for this situation are that the Gender Equality Act does not have the legal clout or ability to impose sanctions easily or in such a way to act as a powerful deterrent. Closely related to this point is the fact that the mechanisms for ensuring implementation of the act are largely based on voluntary cooperation and influence through information campaigns.

There are also examples of legislation that has had adverse effects on female advancement and equality. A few years back, the Christian Democratic government then in office, passed a bill to give families with children added financial support in order to give parents opportunities to spend more time at home with their children. Feminists have been opposed to the bill all along, claiming it would be a detriment to equality for women, and a recent report seems to support their claims (Statistics Norway, 2001b). As many as 8000 women have chosen to withdraw from employment since the reform was implemented, whereas the data show no change in men's employment. It is expected that the reduction in employment may reach as much as 18 per cent among mothers in the next few years. This will have adverse effects on the labour market, which will have problems filling vacancies in certain sectors and is a serious set-back for equality in the workplace. In sum, Norwegians in general have believed they were in the forefront of equality, yet the legislation has not brought about this result.

Initiatives supporting women in the workforce

To address the paucity of women on corporate boards, and in higher management, several initiatives have been implemented. However, individual private sector companies have started virtually no visible initiatives and instead the leaders for such actions are often the public sector or women themselves.

Financed by several different government departments and organizations, in 1999 a database was started called the Women's database (*Kvinnebasen*). The objective of the database is to provide information about women who have high competence in their respective fields and are interested in leadership and corporate board positions. The database is intended to be used by those organizations or individuals searching for highly qualified women, and currently 2700 women are registered from across the country. It is unclear what type of impact this database is having on the utilization of highly competent women in the private and public sector, however, it does provide valuable information for companies who want to increase the number of women in management and on corporate board positions. The database is linked to other databases in Norway, which helps to increase the dissemination of important information on highly qualified women.

Another initiative to assist the advancement of women in management was started in 1995 by the Confederation of Norwegian Business and Industry. They started a mentoring programme which aimed to promote women into leadership and corporate board positions. In 2000 the programme was outsourced to AFF, (a research and consulting firm) and is now run in cooperation with the confederation and a Norwegian government agency. At the end of the year 2000, 215 participants had completed the programme.

In order to counteract the 'old boys network' and its effects on important management decisions, a number of women in business have realized the need for women to create their own networks. New women's networks are growing fast[2], and many of these work actively to break the glass ceiling and help promote women in management. Women's networks have been established within politics, business, among students as well as in cultural areas, and they arrange a variety of activities, training and opportunities for sharing information. Examples are 'Women Show The Way', which arrange open conferences on selected topics; 'Women and Management', a network for women leaders in academia; 'Web Women', a network for women managers in marketing, media and communications; 'The Board Room', a network of women who have taken courses to gain board membership competence; and 'Association of International Professional and Business Women', a network for business women in Norway of international background. Common to all the fast growing networks is a belief that not much will change unless women themselves take action and build networks and contacts the way men do.

The future

Although Norway has enjoyed an excellent reputation for equality, the reputation hides the statistical truth that women still have a long journey towards equality in the workplace, especially in the private sector. Considering the most recent statistics, one has to conclude that despite a number of political initiatives and social welfare policies that promote equality, Norway has failed in the implementation of these policies and therefore not achieved the desired results. One has to question to what extent such initiatives and policies may have worked against progress by creating unwillingness from both men and women to uphold them. In the recent controversy over equality on corporate boards of directors, a majority of men expressed strong opposition to enforced recruitment practices as did a number of women. A number of women managers interviewed by the news media[3] nevertheless emphasized the need for incentives to reverse the current imbalance in management practices. Some of the interventions women would like to see are the following: Explicit action plans and interventions on the part of companies to promote women to senior management positions, long-term career planning for women to increase potential recruits to such positions, recruitment to management as well as senior positions based on real competence rather than acquaintance and personal chemistry, and organizational support in terms of practical assistance, such as cleaning help and day care centres, rather than traditional fringe benefits, such as company cars. In other words, women want companies to make commitments and implement changes in recruitment and advancement practices that will benefit women and actively promote diversity.

The Centre for Equality has also come up with several recommendations to increase the equality between men and women in Norway. Some of their suggestions are to remove the added financial support for parents staying at home with their children, and increase the percentage of parental leave that must be taken by the father. In addition, authorities must do more to encourage non-traditional choices in education, companies must produce concrete action plans for achieving equality, and there should be a statutory requirement of a statement on gender equality in annual reports.

The research in this area points to a number of obstacles to women's advancement to senior levels, and usually both chief executives and senior women agree on these factors (Morrison et al., 1992; Burke and McKean, 1995). The most common obstacles mentioned are lack of mentors, role models, visible jobs, and flexible work arrangements, and being excluded from so-called 'old boys' networks'. There has been relatively little research conducted in Norway concerning the barriers to women's equal participation in the labour market, but a few studies indicate that such barriers are related to career and job satisfaction, career advancement opportunities and health (Richardsen, Mikkelsen and Burke, 1997; Richardsen, Burke and Mikkelsen, 1999). Despite the increased knowledge of obstacles, the keys to success for women are largely unknown. Through interviews with successful women, some areas of importance are emerging, but the studies also suggest that there are individual differences among the women (White, 2000). It may be difficult to uncover universal key factors that will lead to equal status for women, because there are individual differences on many levels, e.g., background, work experience, values, and type of organizations. What may be more important is to expose the range of these individual differences, which women can use in their career planning. Some authors have argued that there is much more to be learned from studies of successful women than comparing women's career success with that of men (Morrison et al., 1992; White, 2000). Career development issues would be an important area of research in order to promote gender equality in Norway.

Through the growing international research findings on the issues of women in management, we understand more about organizational pressures and obstacles that maintain the glass ceiling effect in many professions and in many countries. Increasing knowledge of the effects of family-friendly organizational practices and values, ways to handle diversity, mentoring arrangements and visible job assignments will no doubt serve as guidelines also to Norwegian women on how to manage their careers in a corporate climate. However, there remains a need for empirical research that deal specifically with the challenges facing Norwegian women.

Notes

1 *Dagsavisen*, Dato, 2002.
2 *Aftenposten*, March 8, 2002.
3 *Aftenposten*, March 18, 2002.

References

Brun, C. (1998), 'Kjønn og entreprenørskap', in Spilling, O.R. (ed.), *Entreprenørskap på norsk*, Bergen: Fagbokforlaget.

Burke, R.J. and McKeen, C.A. (1995), 'Work experiences, career development, and career success of managerial and professional women', *Journal of Social Behavior and Personality*, **10**, 81-96.

Davidson, M.J. and Burke, R.J. (eds) (2000), *Women in Management: Current Research Issues, Volume II*, London: Sage Publications.

Frønes, I. and Brusdahl, R. (2000), *På sporet av den nye tid: Kulturelle varsler for en nær fremtid*, Bergen: Fagbokforlaget.

Gender Equality Ombudsman (1997), *Gender Equality by Law: The Norwegian mode*, Unpublished Official Pamphlet.

Hoel, M. (2001), *Kvinner i styrer og ledelse i norsk næringsli*, Oslo: Rådet for Ledelse Likestilling Mangfold, Report.

Holmquist, C. (1996), 'Women have always been entrepreneurs', in Nordic Council of Ministers, *Conference on women's enterprising*, TemaNord 1996:593.

Human Development Report (2001), *Making new technologies for human development*, United National Development Programmeme, http://www.undp.org/hdr2001

Kvålshaugen R. (2001), *The Antecedents of Management Competence: The Role of Educational Background and Type of Work Experience*, Unpublished doctoral dissertation, Sandvika, Norway: The Norwegian School of Management.

Morrison, A.M., White, R.P. and van Velsor, E. (1992), *Breaking the Glass Ceiling*, Reading, MA: Addison-Wesley.

Norwegian Gender Equity Council (2001a), *Minifacts on gender equality*, Summary of official statistics.

Norwegian Gender Equity Council (2001b), *The Gender Equality Barometer 2001*, Norwegian Gender Equity Council. Summary of official statistics.

Norwegian Social Science Data Service (2002), http://www.nsd.uib.no

ODIN (2002), *Norwegian Government electronic information service*, http://odin.dep.no.

Richardsen, A. and Burke, R.J. (2000), 'Women entrepreneurs and small business owners in Norway and Canada', in Davidson, M.J. and Burke, R.J. (eds), *Women in Management: Current Research IssuesVolume II*, London: Sage Publications.

Richardsen, A.M., Burke, R.J. and Mikkelsen, A. (1999), 'Job pressures, organizational support and health among Norwegian women managers', *International Journal of Stress Management*, **6**, 167-178.

Richardsen, A.M., Mikkelsen, A. and Burke, R.J. (1997), 'Work experiences and career and job satisfaction among professional and managerial women in Norway', *Scandinavian Journal of Management*, **13**, 209-218.

Spilling, O.R. (1997), *SMB 97 - fakta om små og mellomstore bedrifter i Norge*, Bergen: Fagbokforlaget.

Spilling, O.R. (1998), 'Kjønn og ledelse i SMB', in Spilling, O.R. (ed.), *SMB 98 – fakta om små og mellomstore bedrifter i Norge*, Bergen: Fagbokforlaget.

Spilling, O.R. (2001), 'Women entrepreneurship and management in Norway: A statistical overview', *Discussion Paper*, Norwegian School of Management BI.

Spilling, O.R. and Berg, N.G. (2000), 'Gender and small business management: The case of Norway in the 1990s', *International Small Business Journal*, **18**, 38-59.

Statistics Norway (1997), *Labour market statistics 1996*, Report on official statistics of Norway.

Statistics Norway (2001a), *Women and men in Norway 2000*, Report on official statistics of Norway.

Statistics Norway (2001b), *Labour market statistics 2000*, Report on official statistics of Norway.

Vangsnes, K. (1993), *Kvinner som selvstendig næringsdrivende 1980-1990*, Unpublished report, Norwegian Gender Equity Council.

Vikan, S.T. (2001), Likestilling i ujamnt tempo, *Samfunnsspeilet*, **4**.

White, B. (2000), 'Lessons from the careers of successful women', in Davidson, M.J. and Burke, R.J. (eds), *Women in Management: Current research issues, Volume II*, London: Sage Publications.

Chapter 9

Women in Management in Poland

Renata Siemieńska

Introduction

Women in Poland like elsewhere, are highly underrepresented in top positions in political and economic decision-making bodies. However, this chapter aims to demonstrate that some increases in the participation of women in these positions may be the result of a combination of different factors, including decreasing levels of discrimination. Nevertheless, in countries like Poland, undergoing a transformation of political and economic systems, we argue that the situation is less conducive to women entering the political and economic elites in substantial numbers. Furthermore, the presence of women in decision-making bodies is not directly correlated with the level of economic or social growth, nor with the development of democratic systems in individual countries (Norris and Inglehart, 2000). We propose that undoubtedly, cultural factors influence women's aspirations to becoming decision-makers and the level of support for women candidates in political parties, affect the electoral behaviour of both men and women.

Labour force characteristics

Changes in the Polish socio-economic and political system after World War II brought with them changes in the position of women in society and in perceptions of women's status and their aspirations. The centrally planned system created numerous opportunities for the manipulation of women as a new source of labour. Of every 100 married women, 13 worked in non-agricultural jobs in 1950, 42 in 1960, 68 in 1970, and about 74 in 1989. Following World War II, the authorities attempted to increase or decrease the number of women in paid employment in accordance with the country's economic growth rate. Childcare facilities (kindergartens, nurseries, and day care for older children) and paid maternity leave were either increased or limited by the state in various periods, depending on the economic goals adopted and available financial means. The manner in which women were mobilized through social, political, and economic pressure, together with overt propaganda emphasizing gender equality and difficult everyday conditions, created the double burden of family and paid employment which was especially hard for women. This duality consequently gave rise to the feeling of having 'too much equality'. Under the conditions of a newly created free-market economy after 1990, the number of kindergartens, day care centres etc. decreased.

It has been often stated (for instance, in the Annual Report of the European Commission 2000) that the high level of employment of women in countries that want to become members of the European Union is only an effect of a higher level of women's employment in the period preceding the transformation of the political and economic system. However, at the end of the 1990s, after the fall of the communist regime, the percentage of employed women in Poland kept systematically increasing. In 1990, women made up 46 per cent of the labour force, and in 1999, 48.2 per cent (Statistical Yearbook for the Republic of Poland, 2000). Drastic deterioration of the economic situation later caused a decrease in the employment rate, which amounted to 40.1 per cent for women and 53.5 per cent for men in the third quarter of year 2001. Therefore, as has been observed many times before, economic breakdown resulted in greater increases of unemployment among women than among men. During the third quarter of year 2001, the unemployment rate among women was equal to 19.7 per cent, and among men – 16.3 per cent (Monitoring of the Labor Market, 2001).

The proportions of individuals employed in the public and the private sectors are changing, with those employed in the private sector on the increase. In 1991, the private sector employed (including individual farms) 55.5 per cent of all employed, and the public sector – the remaining 45.5 per cent (Statistical Yearbook of the Central Office of Statistics 1993). In the year 2000, this has changed respectively to 73.3 per cent of all employees in the private sector and 26.3 per cent in the public sector. In the private sector, women made up 44.7 per cent of all employed, while in the public sector, 53.6 per cent. Polish women tend to prefer to work in the public sector because of relatively higher job security and, on average, lower number of work hours compared to conditions in the private sector.

Women constitute more than half of full and part-time employees (in main work place) in health and social work, education, public administration, defence, compulsory social security, financial intermediation, hotels and restaurants, trade and repair (Statistical Yearbook of the Republic of Poland 2001).

Salaries of employed women in Poland constitute about 80 per cent of those of men, and this disparity in pay between men and women was similar before the transformation of the political and economic system (see Table 9.1). The difference is especially visible among the most educated. Generally, one can conclude that despite women's higher levels of educational attainment over a long period, they are still underrepresented in top managerial positions in both the private and public sector.

Table 9.1 Full-time paid employees, average gross wages and salaries in selected highly skilled occupational groups in 1996 and 1999 (as part of total full-time employees)

Occupational groups:	Full-time paid employees in % in total in 1996*			Full-time paid employees in % in total in 1999**			Women's average gross wages and salaries as % of men's	
	Total	Men	Women	Total	Men	Women	1996	1999
Total	100.0	100.0	100.0	100.0	100.0	100.0	79.2	79.9
Legislators, senior officials and managers	5.1	5.7	4.6	4.8	5.6	3.8	75.4	74.1
Professionals	15.7	10.2	21.9	16.8	11.6	22.5	73.7	71.1
Physical, mathematical and engineering science professionals	2.2	3.1	1.3	2.5	3.5	1.3	74.1	76.9
Life science and health professionals	1.7	1.2	2.1	1.6	1.2	2.0	81.2	83.7
Teaching professionals	7.3	3.0	12.2	7.9	3.4	12.9	85.4	79.6

Source: *Statistical Yearbook 1997, GUS (p.155); **Statistical Yearbook 2001, GUS (p.167)

Women pursuing education

After Poland achieved independence in 1918, women gained the right to vote and pursue political and social equality with men. However, women represented 27.2 per cent of all students in 1928-1929, and 28.3 per cent in 1937-1938 (Small Statistical Yearbook, 1939). A particularly large proportion of women studied pharmacy and dentistry.

After World War II, the number of women being educated rapidly increased, which has been congruent with the ideology of the newly established communist system emphasizing equality as a way – among others – to enlarge a reserve labour force (Siemieńska, 1989). In the 1980s, the number of women exceeded the number of men enrolled in university-level studies. The further feminization of professions that were already female-dominated increased. Men had relatively less interest in university level studies and long-term studies because, contrary to the pre-war period, these forms of education did not guarantee well-paid jobs. Certain workers' professions or even setting up one's own small enterprise, opened up opportunities for earning larger incomes. For women who wanted to avoid vocational careers and were unwilling to perform 'dirty' and hard physical work, the white-collar work they could get with a secondary school or university-level education was attractive. Education has traditionally conferred high social status, even though in the post-war period it has not been associated with increased incomes (Slomczynski and Wesolowski, 1973). However, the economic crisis of the early 1980s came as a shock to Poland. The ability to earn a living became more pressing, and the social appeal that education had traditionally held, was eclipsed for some time (Jasinska and Siemieńska, 1983).

In some university institutions, until 1985 a quota was in effect relating to the number of women admitted in medicine and agriculture, regardless of their numbers among the candidates. In Poland, women account for a considerably large percentage of law students. However, among Poland's executive cadres, under the communist system (Siemieńska, 1983), graduates of schools of economics or technical universities or on the lower level of general and vocational secondary schools, dominated. Furthermore, the situation did not change much at the beginning of the 1990s (Siemieńska, 1994) (see Table 9.2).

Polish girls' selection of university subjects is still strongly dominated by traditional sex-role expectations (Bialecki, 1997). Parents still select technical education for males as the most preferable, with economics placed second. For females – economic professions and medicine are the most popular choices (Bialecki, 1997). However, interestingly, girls more often than boys, aspire to professional statuses higher than that of their parents.

Table 9.2 Women as a percentage of university students, by field of study, 1962-2000

	1962-63	1971-72	1985-86	1990-91	1996-97	1999-00
Total number of students in thousands	141,6	221,1	340,7	394,3	927,5	1431,9
% of women in total	38.3	47.5	50.9	51.4	56.6	56.9
Educ. profile (% of women in total):						
Engineering	14.2	25.2	19.8	17.4	20.6	20.9
Agriculture, forestry and fishery	31.3	42.8	45.2	43.9	55.1	56.4
Economic		63.6	56.6	55.1		
Law and administration	41.3	50.0	45.7	50.2		
Law					53.0	52.9
Commercial & business administration					60.1	62.6

Humanities	63.8	74.5	75.5	75.4	75.1	73.6
Math. Science	58.5	59.9	61.5	60.4		
Math. and computer science					51.3	40.5
Natural science					65.9	66.4
Medical science	59.6	65.8	62.3	63.8	64.8	69.9
Phys. education	--	37.5	35.8	37.3		
Fine and applied arts	45.2	46.9	51.3	50.8	60.5	62.3
Educ. Science and teacher training	--	70.4	--		83.9	78.2
Religion and theology				32.9	59.4	59.6
Social sciences					62.1	63.2
Architecture and town planning					49.4	53.5
Home economics					69.1	71.6
Transport and communication					7.2	10.9
Mass communication and document.					77.4	76.6
Services					64.3	68.3
Other					32.9	34.7
Specialities of higher vocation Schools					66.5	
Academies of the Ministry of National Defence						22.0
Academies of the Ministry of the Interior and Administration						6.4

Sources: For the years 1962-1986 Siemieńska, R. (1989) Poland, in Gail P. Kelly, International Handbook of Women's Education, New York-Westport, Connecticut-London, Greenwood Press, p.342; for the years 1990-1991 Small Statistical Yearbook 1991 (1991), Warsaw: Central Statistical Office, pp.132-133; for the years 1996-1997 Small Statistical Yearbook 1997 (1997) Warsaw, Central Statistical Office, p.192; for the year 1999-2000 Statistical Yearbook 2000 (2000), Warsaw: Central Statistical Office. pp.239-240

Women accounted for 35.5 per cent of doctoral students in 1970, 28.9 per cent in 1985 (Statistical Yearbook 1986), and 39.3 per cent in 1996/97 (Higher Schools in the School Year 1996/1997, 1997).

Creation of non-state university level schools after 1990 gave opportunities for cheaper education in smaller towns than was available in big city universities. Certainly, the path of higher education is one more often chosen by women than by men. In 1996 women constitute 54 per cent of students of evening studies and above 60 per cent of students of extramural and external studies (Higher Schools in the School Year 1996/1997, 1997: 2). In 1996/97 women constituted 66.7 per cent of the total number of university students. Moreover, 14.1 per cent of the total number of female graduates and 6.3 per cent of the total number of male graduates received their diplomas in non-state higher education institutions in 1996 (Higher Schools in the School Year 1996/97).

The number of women among students is still systematically increasing (in 1990, they made up 50.2 per cent of all students of private and public higher education institutions, and in 1999/2000 – 56.8 per cent) (Statistical Yearbook of the Republic of Poland, 2000). But at the same time, their percentage among students of non-state universities is decreasing (in 1999/2000 – 62.5 per cent) (Universities and their finances in 1999). The worsening financial situation in a large part of the Polish society, has the most negative effect on the education of women. Although their numbers are increasing, they are attaining the worse quality education, which will undoubtedly lead to decreases in opportunities for women in the labour market. In addition, this will exclude them from some types of careers, such as academia, where the potential staff are those who have the best academic background.

Women in management

Composition of the political, economic and cultural elite by gender

In 1989 the communist system collapsed in Poland. A question appeared at the time whether the changes in the system would be accompanied by an exchange of political and economic elite, or whether the old elite would be able to retain their influence in both or one of them. In various research projects concerning business elites in the nineties, from 130 to 700 people were recognized as members of the economic elite (Wnuk-Lipiński and Wasilewski, 1996; Drąg and Indraszkiewicz, 1994; Federowicz, 1998; Wasilewski, 1999). However, Jasiecki (2002) identified the strategic institutions in Poland constituting 800 of the largest production and trade companies, largest banks and insurance companies, and, within these, the major shareholders, presidents and members of boards of supervisors and managers, occupying the highest positions.

Observations made in Russia, Hungary and Poland in the early 1990s (Szelenyi, Treiman and Wnuk-Lipiñski, 1995; Wasilewski, 1992; Wasilewski and Wesolowski, 1992) have shown that in all of these countries, the political elite existed to a much greater extent than the economic elite, due to a gradual transformation of the socialist economy into one based on private ownership.

Research on the composition of the political, economic and cultural elite carried out in the early nineties in Poland on samples consisting of about 2000 individuals (including 1000 who were the members of the economic, political and cultural elite in 1993) showed that women constituted 12.1 per cent of the members of political elite (the members of parliaments and high officials on a central level). Moreover, among those holding high positions in administration, women constituted 21 per cent (Fodor, Jerzowa and Wnuk-Lipiński, 1995). In the cultural elite there were slightly less women by several per cent. The cultural elite included persons in the highest positions in the mass media, education, the largest publishing houses and the chair of creative associations, i.e. individuals holding strategic positions in the formal decision-making structure in the area of science and culture.

Furthermore, the percentage of women did not exceed 15 per cent in the new elite in privatized and private-owned enterprises. In state-owned enterprises it was 4 per cent, which corresponds to the percentage of women in state-owned firms in 1988, i.e. before the change of the system (Borocz and Rona-Tas, 1995).

The comparison of the number of men and women belonging to different socio-occupational groups reveals that the number of women who were top civil servants and managers increased between 1982 and 1999 from 0.3 per cent to 0.7 per cent. Moreover, among women a larger group of individuals is classified as non-technical intelligentsia (in 1999 – 4.6 per cent) than among men (3.3 per cent), while traditionally engineers were more widely represented among men (in 1999 – 4.2 per cent) than among women (0.5 per cent) (although the number of engineers has decreased for both men and women since 1982).

The Polish data from the late 1990s indicated that women made up about 30 per cent of all senior officials and managers (including women entrepreneurs and chief accounting officers) (Activity, 1999). Depending on the definition of business elites, the number of women included varied greatly. The more people included in the elite, the more women (relatively) were in the group. And so, for instance, in research conducted on the Polish business elite, including 588 people, women made up 10.9 per cent of all respondents (Wnuk-Lipiński and Wasilewski, 1996), while in the Polish business elite examined in 1998, which included 194 people (due to the application of a more restrictive criteria of defining elite), there were only 7.7 per cent of women (Wasilewski, 1999). Among managers working in banks, examined at the same time, there were many more women – 26 per cent of 130 respondents (Federowicz, 1998), similar to the regional business elite (21.2 per cent women among 716 people) (Drąg and Indraszkiewicz, 1993). The results of the research show that there were more women in the regional elite than in the national elite. Moreover, due to significant gender segmentation of the labour market, in some sectors, like banking, there were more women than in others. The analysis of the lists of 'the richest Poles', prepared annually by 'Wprost' weekly, gives similar results. Throughout the nineties, there were 3 to 7 women on the list, depending upon the year, and around 100 men (Jasiecki, 2002), which once again substantiates the fact that women very rarely become members of the elite.

Thus the change in the political and economic system, while creating good conditions for social mobility due to the restructuring of economy, also resulted in women not being too successful at entering the elites. Membership in the political and economic top management in the period preceding the beginning of the transformation was a very important advantage. Women were at that time, almost absent from higher positions in politics and economy (Siemieńska, 1990; 1991), so they could not have become beneficiaries of changes and new opportunities in the period of restructuring of the economy. These were open mostly to those who disposed of information and connections, who were part of the former nomenclature, and later also for members of the former opposition, who became part of the new establishment (Jasiecki, 2002).

Women in politics

Women's participation in politics in Poland, as in other the post-communist countries, is small. The number of women in the lower chamber of the parliament elected in the three elections 1991, 1993 and 1997 was respectively 9 per cent, 13 per cent and 13 per cent. Women constituted 8 per cent, 13 per cent and 12 per cent of members of the higher chamber. Formally speaking, the number of women has decreased compared to the communist period when it stood at over 20 per cent in 1985. At that time, they performed the role of 'tokens', persons present, but with much less influence than their representation in numbers might have suggested. Nor did they usually represent the overall interests of women. Moreover, under communist systems the parliament performed mainly decorative functions and was a 'rubber stamp' for the decisions made by the bodies of the communist parties.

In the 1990s, women deputies tended to have a higher level of education than their male counterparts. Women have more difficulty (compared to men), in getting themselves initially placed on a candidate list. The number of women elected for the first time in 1997 was lower (44.1 per cent) than men (52.4 per cent) (Siemieńska 1996; Wesołowski and Mielczarek, 1999).

After the last elections in 2001, the number of women in the lower chamber of parliament increased to 20 per cent and in the higher chamber to 23 per cent. Only two women were created members of the government after the last election: the Minister of Justice and the Minister of Education (Ministry of National Education and Sports).

Women in local self-governments

Women continue to be underrepresented on lower level local government authorities (Siemieńska, 1994a, 1996a, 1996b; Bartkowski, 1996; Jasińska-Kania, 1998; Wiatr, 1998; Siemieńska, 2000). During the nineties the number of women elected to local authorities grew slightly from 11 per cent in 1990 up to 13.2 per cent in 1994 (Elections to councils in districts – June 14, GUS 1994) and 15.7 per cent in 1998. In comparison in 1989, there were 22 per cent women in local councils. Consequently, the proportions by which the number of women decreased in the elective bodies at the beginning of the 1990s, are the same at both levels. As was the case of female parliamentarians, women elected to local councils in the

1990s were a little bit older and more educated than their male counterparts (Siemieńska, 2002).

Social structure and attitudes of men and women in the top management and political elites

Research conducted in 1996 by the author (as part of an international research project) on narrowly defined political and economic elites included 120 individuals (60 men and 60 women) and investigated their social structure and attitudes in detail (Vianello and Moore et al., 2000). The interviewed political elite consisted of members of the government, department directors, supreme court judges and persons managing the lower-level administrative units. A number were parliamentarians or persons functioning as leaders in parties. Members of the studied economic elite were presidents of large corporations, members of management boards of corporations, directors and vice-directors of company branches. Two individuals out of 60 attained the now-occupied positions before year 1990 (before the transformation) in the political elite, and in the case of the economic elite – it was 9 individuals out of 60 (including 4 men and 5 women). Half of the members of the analysed political elite had previously been members of one of the parties existing at the time (PZPR, SLD, PSL).

Although this was the period of transformation, when new people entered the elites and others moved from the political to the economic elite (some members of the former nomenclature), these individuals tended to have university education although sometimes they did not have prior similar job experiences. Also their parents, especially women's parents, were fairly well educated, with 48 per cent of fathers of members of the economic elite having had university education. Education of fathers of the political elite was slightly lower; 37 per cent had university education (including 30 per cent of fathers of men) and 43.3 per cent of fathers of women. There were greater differences between the two elites with regard to education of mothers. Mothers of members of the political elite less often had university education (15 per cent) than those of the members of the economic elite (43 per cent). In the political elite, more often mothers of women, and in the economic elite – mothers of men – had university education. In both elites about 70 per cent of people had spouses with university education or a Ph.D. Therefore, these results indicate that although the process of exchange in members of elites is taking place, they came mostly from social groups having a greater cultural capital (Bourdieu, 1984), strengthened by intergenerational transmission, thus differing greatly from the rest of the society.

This study also investigated whether gender made a difference in the attitudes of Polish top managers and politicians towards men and women's equality in public life. Table 9.3 clearly indicates that Polish women members of elites more often than men, perceived gender inequality in their work environment and, more generally, in society as a whole.

Table 9.3 Perception of gender inequality (in %)#

Men occupy top positions because:	Economic elite			Political elite		
	Total	Men	Women	Total	Men	Women
(1) women prefer men to occupy top positions*	53.3	46.7	60.0	35.0	30.0	40.0
(2) women lack specific training*	85.0	86.7	83.3	90.0	86.7	93.3
(3) women are isolated in a predominantly male environment	46.6	56.6	36.6	43.3	36.7	43.3
(4) women are prevented from reaching the top	31.6	43.4	20.0	35.0	23.3	40.0
(5) of how women are reared	46.6	40.0	43.3	48.3	60.0	36.7
(6) women lack informal contacts	25.0	20.0	30.0	28.3	16.7	40.0
(7) women are accepted in leadership positions in the field*	8.3	10.0	6.7	1.7	3.3	-
(8) men and women treated equally in my organization*	8.3	6.7	13.3	11.7	3.3	20.0
(9) women have to achieve more than men to receive recognition	31.6	23.3	40.0	51.6	26.7	76.7
(10) when jobs are scarce men should have more rights*	33.3	36.7	40.0	15.0	20.0	10.0
(11) the family suffers when women work full time*	50.0	36.6	63.3	51.6	43.3	60.0
(12) paid jobs are best for women's independence	76.7	66.6	86.7	85.0	86.7	83.3

Answers: 'strongly agree' and 'agree' or * 'strongly disagree' and 'disagree' depend on the question.

However, they perceived gender inequality less often than members of elites in countries of Western Europe or in the United States (Siemieńska, 2000a, 2000b). The roots of the perception are in the past. In post-communist countries there are particularly strong conservative attitudes towards inequality. Communist propaganda strongly emphasized the existence of equality between men and women in the labour market, women's opportunity to succeed at work and the absence of a conflict between household duties and professional life. Furthermore, people of the Catholic countries (in Poland about 90 per cent of inhabitants define themselves as Catholics) are more conservative in this respect (Inglehart, 1997). Nevertheless, it should be noted that attitudes toward women's presence in public life are changing among members of the elites as well as among members of the society generally (Siemieńska, 2000c).

Women entrepreneurs

The change of the political and economic system from one in which the public sector dominated under the communist system, to the situation where private sector employees constituted more than half of the labour force, contributed to the growth of entrepreneur business owners, especially among men (in 1982 2.4 per cent of men and 0.8 per cent of women; in 1999 8 per cent of men and 3.8 per cent of women (Domanski, 2000).

In the year 1990, women made up 44.9 per cent of employers and own-account workers, while in year 2000, slightly above 46.5 per cent (Statistical Yearbook, 2001). However, companies owned by women are usually much smaller (and often very small) or family businesses (Lisowska, 2000). Moreover, this category includes individuals persuaded by employers to take advantage of this form of employment in order to decrease their own costs of employment (social insurance in Poland increases the employment costs for the employer by more than 40 per cent).

Companies owned by women also tend to be concentrated in certain areas of economic activity. According to a study conducted in the late 1990s women owned mainly companies manufacturing food and wood products (37.5 per cent), textiles (35.3 per cent), and construction companies (12.9 per cent). Women did not own companies manufacturing machinery or chemical products (Gardawski, 2001).

Country legislation and initiatives supporting women in the workplace

The legal situation relating to men and women in the labour market as employees is more or less the same, with the exception of a retirement age (women retire at the age 60 years and men 65 years). Furthermore, both parents have similar rights regarding parental leave.

In relation to legislation aimed at equality of opportunity in the workplace, the Equality Act has been submitted to Parliament on several occasions during the last few years but has always been rejected in the early stages of debate. However, a new version of the Act is currently being discussed in the Senate (upper chamber of the Polish Parliament). The aims of the Act are to emphasize the principle of gender equality in public and private life which already exists in the Constitution and to introduce mechanisms for monitoring and implementing initiatives.

The most prominent initiatives supporting women in the workplace in Poland have been centred on Parliamentary initiatives. Here, women's increased presence was caused by a different set of different events and initiatives that occurred between the parliamentary elections in years 1997 and 2001:

- **The electoral law was changed.** In 2001, constituencies were larger and with a greater number of seats. Reduction in the number of constituencies was a result of their adaptation to the new administrative structure of the country. Thus, 'incidentally', this change resulted in an increase in the number of women listed as candidates: the more candidates there were per constituency, the greater were the chances for women to be listed as candidates (Siemieńska, 2000).
- **Attitudes towards women in politics changed.** In 2001, 60 per cent of women (compared with 50 per cent in 1997) and 40 per cent of men (compared with 28 per cent in 1997) do not agree with the opinion that 'men are better suited to politics that women' (Siemieńska, 2000; 2002).
- **The women's lobby became stronger.** This exerted more influence on political parties and on public opinion as a whole. Fifty organizations joined the Pre-Electoral Coalition of Women – an open agreement between women's organizations and groups, created a few months before the elections. The members emphasized the apolitical character of the coalition. The Pre-Electoral Coalition of Women (as well as other women's groups and feminist organizations), stood somewhere between the centre and the left wing, and were also supported by the Women's Parliamentary Group. Women-members of the Parliament organized an action entitled 'Women run, women vote' to convince the voters to vote for women. The participating women belonged to all parliamentary parties.
- **A gender quota was introduced by some political parties.** The coalition of SLD (postcommunist party)-UP, as well as UW (liberal-centre), accepted the rule that neither of the sexes should be represented by less than 30 per cent of all candidates, and lists presented for individual constituencies should be approved only when they comply with this condition. Moreover, even right wing parties such as the LPR were influenced by these changes.
- **The electoral preferences of the society changed.** In the 2001 Polish elections, the coalition SLD-UP obtained the highest number of votes (a shift from right to left) which was important from the point of view of women, since this coalition has, for a long time, been willing to take women into consideration in its political plans and reforms. As a result, the number of

women, listed as candidates was much greater than before. The number of elected women depended greatly upon the number of women, listed as candidates, their positions on the lists given them by party gatekeepers (positions 1-3 have been giving the higher chances to be elected), as well as the attitudes of the general population toward women's presence in politics in the different districts (see Table 9.4).

Table 9.4 Women among candidates and deputies to the Sejm (Lower Chamber of Parliament), 2001

Name of Party or Electoral Coalition	Candidates** Number of districts in which women were on the lists of candidates	% women in total number of candidates	% women on 1-3 positions on the lists of candidates	Elected*** Total	% total	Women	% women
Total		23.2		460		93	20.2
Democratic Left Alliance (SLD)*	41	36.3	18.7	200	43.6	50	25.0
Polish Peasant Party (PSL)	41	14.6	6.5	42	9.1	0	0.0
Labor Union (UP)*	41	36.3	18.7	16	3.4	5	31.3
Civic Platform (PO)	41	16.8	15.4	65	14.1	13	20.0
Self Defence of Polish Republic (SO)	39	20.3	13.0	53	11.5	9	17.0
Law and Justice (PiS)	40	17.9	12.2	44	9.6	6	13.6
League of Polish Families (LPR)	41	24.7	25	38	8.3	10	26.3
Social and Cultural Society of the German Minority in Silesia (MN)		16.7		2	0.4	–	–

*   SLD and UP (in bold) ran in an electoral coalition the Democratic Left Alliance.
**   Author's calculations. ***Source: www.ipu.org.
Orientation of the political parties: SLD and UP – left; PO – centre right; SO – populist; PiS LPR – right; PSL – peasant party.

In several regions, the percentage of women elected was higher than the percentage of women listed as candidates. In the regions with more votes for post-communist SLD, more women were elected. In the 1990s, there was a significant increase in the number of both women and men who voted for both women and men, as opposed to voting only for men. In 2001, 46 per cent of men in comparison with 31 per cent of women voted exclusively for men, but 39 per cent of men and 55 per cent of women voted for men and women (Siemieńska, 2000; 2002).

The future

After 1990, the proportion of individuals belonging to economic versus political elites began to change. Men and even more frequently women, come from socially advantaged groups culturally, often strengthened by intergenerational transmission. In this respect new elites differ greatly from the rest of the society. However, despite the large number of highly educated women, they are clearly underrepresented in political and economic elites. The experience over the past 10 years since the political and economic transformation started, has made many women (especially those active in politics), aware of the fact that their career opportunities are limited. Certainly, this recognition resulted in new initiatives and positive action, which led to increases in the number of women in parliament. However, the increase was not accompanied by a higher number of women in the government or regional authorities. In the case of the economic elite, there have been few attempts at building any support networks (other than ineffectual associations and clubs) to accelerate women's promotions in the economic elite.

We predict that the increase of men's and women's awareness of gender inequality in public life and attempts to introduce institutional mechanisms facilitating women's larger presence in elites and their genuine participation in the decision-making processes, will continue in the future. The process will be stimulated by internal changes in the country and also by the fact that Poland will become a member of the European Union where gender equality and the increase of women's presence in top political and economic management is considered an important part of common policy.

References

Annual Report of the European Commission 2000, Brussels.
Bartkowski, J. (1996), *Lokalne elity władzy w Polsce w latach 1966-1995* (Local Elite of Authorities in Poland 1966-1995), Warsaw: Interart.
Bialecki, I. (1997), 'Nierównosci w dostepie do ksztalcenia w Polsce powojennej' (Inequality in Access to Education in Postwar Poland), in R. Siemieńska (ed.), *Wokól problemów zawodowego równouprawnienia kobiet i mezczyzn* (About Problems of

Professional Equality of Women and Men), Warsaw: Foundation of Promotion of European Law - Scholar, 107-120.

Borocz, J. and Rona-Tas, A. (1995), 'Formowanie się nowej elity ekonomicznej' (Crystallisation of New Economic Elite), in I. Szelenyi, D. Treiman, E. Wnuk-Lipinski (eds), *Elity w Polsce, w Rosji i na Wegrzech. Wymiana czy reprodukcja?*, Warszawa: Instytut Nauk Politycznych Polskiej Akademii Nauk, 133-157.

Bourdieu, P. (1984), *Distinction: A Social Critique of the Judgment of Taste*, Cambridge, Massachusetts: Harvard University Press.

Central Statistical Office (1997), Education in the school year 1996-1997 (1997), Warsaw, Central Statistical Office, p.XXXVIII.

Central Statistical Office (1991), Education 1990-1991, Warsaw.

Domanski, H. (2000), *Hierarchie i bariery społeczne w latach dziewięcdziesiatych* (Hierarchies and Social Barriers in the Nineties), Warsaw: Instytut Spraw Publicznych.

Drąg, Z. and Indraszkiewicz, J. (1994), *Regionalna elita władzy w Polsce* (Regional Governing Elite in Poland), Warsaw: Friedrich Ebert Foundation.

Federowicz, M. (1998), *Kariery bankowców w Polsce* (Careers of bankers in Poland), Warsaw: Instytut Spraw Publicznych.

Fodor, E., Jerzowa, N. and Wnuk-Lipiński, E. (1995), 'Nowe elity kulturalne i polityczne' (New Cultural and Political Elites), in Szelenyi, I., Treiman, D. and Wnuk-Lipiński, E. (eds), *Elity w Polsce, w Rosji i na Węgrzech. Wymiana czy reprodukcja?* (Elites in Poland, Russia and Hungary. Exchange or Reproduction?) Warsaw: Institute of Political Studies - Polish Academy of Science, pp. 159-186.

Gardawski, J. (2001), *Powracajaca klasa. Sektor prywatny w III Rzeczypospolitej* (Social Class Coming Back. Private Sector in the III Polish Republic), Warszawa: Wyd. IFiS PAN.

Inglehart, R. (1997), *Modernization and Postmodernization, Cultural, Economic and Political Change in 43 Societies*, Princeton: Princeton University Press.

Jacquette, J.S. (ed.) (1991), *The Women's Movement in Latin America*, Boulder-San Francisco-Oxford: Westview Press.

Jasiecki, K. (2002), *Elita biznesu w Polsce* (Business Elite in Poland), Warsaw: IFiS PAN.

Jasinska, A. and Siemieńska, R. (1983), The Socialist Personality: A Case Study of Poland, *International Journal of Sociology*, **13**, 1-84.

Jasinska-Kania, A. (1998), 'Kim są przedstawiciele lokalnych elit władzy?' (Who are the representatives of local authorities?), in Wiatr, J. (ed.), *Wladza lokalna w warunkach demokracji* (Local Authorities in Conditions of Democracy), Warsaw: Institute of Sociology, University of Warsaw; Scholar, 35-45.

Lovenduski, J. and Norris, P. (eds) (1993), *Gender and Party Politics*, London: Sage.

Maly Rocznik Statystyczny 1939 (Small Statistical Yearbook, 1939), Warsaw: GUS.

Monitoring Rynku Pracy 21.11.2001 (Monitoring of Labour Market), Warsaw: GUS.

Norris, P. and Inglehart, R. (2000), 'The Developmental Theory of the Gender Gap: Women's and Men's Voting Behavior in Global Perspective', *International Political Science Review* **21** (4), 441-463.

Rocznik Statystyczny 1993 (Statistical Yearbook 1993), Warsaw: GUS.

Rocznik Statystyczny 1997 (Statistical Yearbook 1997), Warsaw: GUS.

Rocznik Statystyczny Rzeczypospolitej Polskiej 2000 (Statistical Yearbook of the Polish Republic 2000), Warsaw: GUS.

Rocznik Statystyczny 2001 (Statistical Yearbook 2001), Warsaw: GUS.

Siemieńska, R. (1983), 'Local Party Leaders in Poland', *International Political Science Review*, 4 (1).

Siemieńska, R. (1989), 'Poland', in Kelly, G.P. (ed.), *International Handbook of Women's Education*, New York, London: Greenwood Press, pp. 323-347.

Siemieńska, R. (1994a), 'Women Managers in Poland: In Transition from Communism to Democracy', in Nancy J. Adler and Dafna N. Izraeli (eds), *Competitive Frontiers, Women Managers in A Global Economy*, Cambridge-Oxford: Blackwell, pp. 243-262.

Siemieńska, R. (1994b), 'Women in the Period of Systemic Changes in Poland', *Journal of Women's History*, 5 (3), 70-90.

Siemieńska, R. (1996a), 'Women's Political Participation in Central and Eastern Europe: A Cross-Cultural Perspective', in Wejnert, B., Spencer, M. and Drakulic, S. (eds), *Women in Post-Communism*, Greenwich, London: JAI Press.Inc., pp. 63-92.

Siemieńska, R. (1996b), *Kobiety: nowe wyzwania. Starcie przeszłości z teraźniejszością* (Women: New Challenges. A Clash of the Past and the Present), Warsaw: Institute of Sociology, University of Warsaw.

Siemieńska, R. (1999), Elites and Women in Democratising Post-Communist Societies, *International Review of Sociology*, 9 (2), 197-219.

Siemieńska, R. (2000a), *Nie mogą, nie chcą czy nie potrafią? O postawach i uczestnictwie politycznym kobiet w Polsce* (They Can't, They Won't or are They Incapable? About Attitudes and Women's Political Participation in Poland), Warsaw: ISS UW and F. Ebert Foundation, UNESCO Chair 'Women, Society and Development' UW. Wyd. Naukowe 'Scholar'.

Siemieńska, R. (2000b), 'Elites' Value Orientations', in M. Vianello and G. Moore (eds), *Gendering Elites. Economic and Political Leadership in 27 Industrialised Societies*, New York-London: Macmillan Press, pp. 247-267.

Siemieńska, R. (2000c), 'Factors shaping conceptions of women's and men's roles in Poland', in M.E. Domsch and D.H. Ladwig (eds), *Reconciliation of Family and Work in Eastern European Countries*, Frankfurt am Main-Berlin-New York: Peter Lang, pp. 117-136.

Slomczynski, K.M. and Wesolowski, W. (eds) (1973), *Struktura i ruchliwosc spoleczna* (Social Structure and Mobility), Warsaw: Ossolineum.

Szelenyi, I., Treiman, D. and Wnuk-Lipiński, E. (eds) (1995), *Elity w Polsce, w Rosji i na Węgrzech. Wymiana czy reprodukcja?*, (Elites in Poland, Russia and Hungary. Exchange or Reproduction?), Warsaw: Institute of Political Studies, Polish Academy of Science.

Universities and their Finances in 1999, Warsaw: GUS.

Vianello, M. and Moore, G. (eds) (2000), *Gendering Elites. Economic and Political Leadership in 27 Industrialised Societies*, New York-London: Macmillan Press.

Vianello, M., Siemieńska, R. et al. (1990), *Gender Inequality. A Comparative Study of Discrimination and Participation*, London-Newbury Park-New Delhi: Sage.

Wasilewski, J. (1992), 'Dilemmas and Controversies Concerning Leadership Recruitment in Eastern Europe', in Lewis, P. (ed.), *Democracy and Civil Society in Eastern Europe*.

Wasilewski, J., (1999), 'Socjologiczny portret polskiej elity potrasformacyjnej' (Sociological Portrait of the Polish Postransformation Elite), in Wasilewski, J. *Elita polityczna 1998* (Political Elite 1998), Warsaw: ISP PAN.

Wasilewski, J. and Wesolowski, W. (eds) (1992), *Poczatki parlamentarnej elity: Poslowie kontraktowego Sejmu* (The Beginning of Parliamentary Elite: Deputies of the Contract Parliament), Warsaw: IFiS.

Wesołowski, W. and Mielczarek, P. (1999), 'Zmienność i stabilizacja warstwy politycznej: cztery Sejmy okresu transformacji' (Change and Stabilization of Political Strata: Four Sejms of Time of Transformation), *Studia Socjologiczne*, **3**, 37-82.

Wnuk-Lipiński, E. and Wasilewski, J. (1996), 'Formowanie się elity w Polsce' (Formation of Elite in Poland), in Wnuk-Lipiński, E. (ed.), *Demokratyczna rekonstrukcja. Z socjologii radykalnej zmiany społecznej* (Sociology of Radical Social Change), Warsaw: PWN.

Chapter 10

Women in Management in Russia

Andrew Gale and Larissa Polnareva

Introduction

The aim of this chapter is to describe current labour force characteristics in Russia and their determinants including professional workers and unemployment. Also, the structure and trends in women's employment are discussed, with reference to the significance of education and training, childcare and changes in the Russian legislative environment. The chapter introduces the importance of women's associations and their developing role in Russian society. The emergence of Russian women entrepreneurs and business leaders is addressed and government initiatives are assessed.

Between 1917 and1990 Russia was one of the largest republics in the former USSR. During this period a specific stereotype of women in paid work was formulated and characterized by the following main features. Firstly, from amongst the overall number of known workers in Russia in 1988, 51 per cent were women. As a comparison, the figure for the UK was 42 per cent, USA 44 per cent, France 39 per cent, and for neighbouring Finland 48 per cent. Secondly, there was free secondary and tertiary education for all women, leading to a higher number of educated women specialists in comparison to men by the end of the Soviet period. Another interesting point to note is that in contrast to the majority of western countries, certain occupations were traditionally male dominated in Russia. For example, by the end of the 1980s the percentage of accountants who were female was 89 per cent. In addition, Russian women constituted 87 per cent of economists, 67 per cent of doctors and 58 per cent of engineers (Iljin, 1997).

Arguably, professions in which there were high proportions of women were low status. It could be inferred that teachers and librarians are low status in Russia as women represent 70 per cent and 91 per cent respectively. Those employed in these professions lost out in their ability to gain top jobs in the communist party and state bodies. The top jobs were taken by men, from heavy industry and the army.

The female professional role stereotypes can be traced back to the end of the USSR in the 1980s. It is explained in relation to a number of controversial government policies connected with the regulation of 'gender problems' (Iljin, 1997; UNICEF, 1999; United Nations, 2000).

Although under the law women were considered to have equal rights, in reality this was never realized and was due to the closely guarded patriarchal culture of society. In traditional patriarchal societies the woman plays the role of keeping the home fires burning. 'Domestic' rather than 'economic affairs' are considered by society and the government as a woman's priority.

In spite of the fact that women surpassed men in education and achieved better results in their different fields and professions (UNICEF, 1999; United Nations, 2000), employers representing state companies and organizations were not very interested in investing in the professional development of women. The limited opportunities afforded women to improve their qualifications led to women being unable to develop their careers. According to statistical data, men received better salaries, had more power and prestige, as well as having better prospects for career development (Iljin, 1997; UNICEF, 1999).

In spite of the declaration of social equality in all national sectors, the state monopolized economic system was built on the separation of leading and secondary branches of the economy. The gender selection of professional personnel approved by the state for the group of leading branches began at the stage of entrance into higher education. Higher education prepared 'specialists' for those branches of the economy where the large majority were men. Specialists are highly qualified experts in their field, equivalent, for example, to corporate members of chartered professions in the UK.

Rising women's unemployment was associated in the past with the economic crisis and latterly due to perestroika in the economy. Peristroika means in Russian: 'rebuilding' and was the name given to the last Soviet Five-Year Plan. In the period of 1990-1995 alone, those working in Russia decreased by 10.9 per cent. The reduction in the number of working men and women did not occur proportionally. The employment of men decreased by 1.6 per cent and of women by 19.4 per cent. Also, Russia has a developing dual-sector labour market.

Taking into account the situation for women in Russia mentioned above, it is not surprising that during the Soviet period, women in leadership positions were not the norm. The authors of this chapter were directly involved in needs analysis, design and delivery of continuing professional development programmes for middle and senior managers in the construction sector in Russia pre and post 1992. Out of all the managers trained (over 200) there were no senior women managers and only two or three junior middle managers. Arguably the construction sector in Russia has a very masculine culture (Gale and Holden, 1995).

In 1989 in Russia, only 6.5 per cent of women were in leadership positions, one of the highest figures among the Soviet republics (5.6 per cent on average). It should be remembered that the word 'leadership' included the personnel of the state or communist party organizations with a wide sphere of power and authority, as well as directors of those industrial and non-industrial organizations with the more 'female' professions. It is clear that only a small percentage of women occupied high-level positions during the pre-perestroika period in Russia. The role played by women in the leadership of the USSR up until the beginning of the 1990s was nominal.

Labour force characteristics

The beginning of the 1990s was known as the start of the political and economical reforms in Russia, which led to a socio-economic system other than socialism. Following the 'Russian reforms' a number of changes can be observed in relation to proportions of women in the workforce, professional segregation and income, unemployment, the labour market sector and the work orientation of women.

A change in the percentage of economically active women

During the years of reform, the general involvement of women in the economy dropped. In 1992, up until the moment of the fall of the USSR and the formation of the new Russia, women represented 48.6 per cent of all those employed. In 1995, the figure dropped to 46.9 per cent. This process affected, in a significant way, young women (under 30 years old) with pre school age children.

The continuous reduction in the percentage of employed women was noticed throughout the 1990s amounting within the decade to more than 19 per cent. However, a significant reduction of women in employment occurred before 1995, after which the situation stabilized. This tendency of a drop in women's employment in Russia at the beginning of reform was due to some logical factors. Firstly, removal of 'forced labour' in production and the acquisition of the right to freely choose whether or not to be employed, facilitated a free exit of part of the labour force from being employed. Secondly, the increase in the pressure on the labour market and growth in unemployment led to an unavoidable exit of those weaker groups who had lower competitive strength in the labour market. Today, the level of women employed significantly lags behind the level of men employed (55.9 per cent against 69.4 per cent respectively) (Baskakova, 1998; Mezentsev, 1998).

Professional segregation and income

The decrease in the activity of women in the economy was followed by an intensive redistribution of Russian women workers across sectors of the economy. During this, researchers noted the close ties between the rate of increase in income in sectors and the displacement of women workers from those sectors. In particular, the number of women working in the so-called 'female' professions such as retailing, catering, banking and insurance dropped by 15-17 per cent. And, at the same time, in these sectors in the middle of the 1990s, a faster growth rate in wages was noticed.

This process can be easily illustrated in the example of banking where in 1990-1995 the number of working women dropped from 90 per cent to 77 per cent, when at the same time there was a rise in wages (for example, in 1993 the average monthly wage in banking was 2.5 times higher than the average in all sectors of the domestic economy). The outcome was an influx of a significant number of men into banking activities and a correspondingly significant drop in the number of women (Chetvernina and Dunaeva, 2000).

In the overall drop in the number of working women for 1992-1998, the highest cutbacks were seen in the higher paid jobs, in such sectors as communications (from 71 per cent to 60 per cent) finance (from 86 per cent to 71 per cent), and regulatory bodies (from 68 per cent to 48 per cent). In the traditional lower paying sectors, working women either decreased insignificantly (agriculture, culture and public health), or somewhat increased (education). In 1998, 60.2 per cent of women (1.6 times more than men) were working in sectors with income below the average in Russia as a whole (Chetvernina and Dunaeva, 2000).

Table 10.1 shows the trend in the changing number of women employed in some sectors of the Russian economy and changes in the level of income in those sectors between 1992 and 1998.

Table 10.1 Percentages of women in sectors of economy and average monthly income

Year	Number of women by sector (%)				Correlation between average monthly income in sectors to the average in Russia (%)			
	1992	1994	1996	1998	1992	1994	1996	1998
Industry	45	43	41	38	118	104	110	115
Agriculture	36	35	34	32	66	50	48	45
Construction	25	25	24	24	134	129	122	127
Transport	26	26	26	26	146	150	144	144
Communication	71	69	62	60	91	123	130	140
Retailing	73	65	62	62	81	79	77	82
Services	48	44	46	46	82	96	106	105
Public Health	83	82	82	81	66	76	77	69
Education	79	81	82	80	61	69	70	63
Art and Culture	70	68	69	68	52	65	62	62
Science	53	52	51	50	64	78	83	99
Finance and insurance	86	75	74	71	204	208	193	199

Source: Goskomstat, 1999

The question of wage discrimination for women is more difficult. Some researchers (e.g. Goskomstat, 1999) consider that women in Russia receive on average almost 50 per cent less than men, although in the 1980s this index was 68-70 per cent.

Goskomstat (1999) published evidence showing women in Russia, as a whole, received 65 per cent income compared with men. However, official statistics consider only the so-called average monthly wages and do not consider supplementary income such as bonuses and subsidies that were often used by Russian companies as incentive payments.

This is interesting when one considers the findings obtained by a group of researchers (Chetvernina and Dunaeva, 2000). As a result of conducting a survey in 1999, results showed that a large majority of men and women *believe* that they receive as much as the opposite sex occupying the same position. Only 14.3 per cent of men indicated that they had higher salaries than women, and almost as many women (14.7 per cent) stated that their salaries were lower compared to men in the same positions. Such agreement may indicate the starting of a process of the equalization of wage levels for men and women, for equal work as part of a rational economic order. Therefore, one could conclude that perceptions about gender and pay equality in Russia may be in sharp contrast to the reality of the situation.

Unemployment

In Russia in recent years, a considerable drop in female employment has occurred. In the Russian Regions at the end of the 1980s about 92 per cent of women of working age were employed. By the end of 1996, according to Goskomstat (2001), this had dropped to 75.7 per cent.

This change was associated in the past with economic crisis. Perestroika has also lead to unemployment of women too. Between 1990 and 1995 employment in Russia decreased by 10.9 per cent (employment of men decreased by 1.6 per cent and women by 19.4 per cent).

The fact that unemployment mainly affected women was obvious from the moment unemployment was officially recognized in Russia; in July 1991. Information from the State Unemployment Agency shows that the number of women among registered unemployed is significantly higher than the number of men. In 1993 it was 72 per cent, gradually decreasing to 67 per cent in 1994, and to 64 per cent in 1998. Although, until now, the number of unemployed women has tended to decrease, the employment structure itself continues to have some negative features, such as (Anon, 2000a; Chetvernina and Dunaeva, 2000):

- An increase in the average duration of unemployment amongst women: 9.1 months in 1999 compared with 8.5 months for men.
- The decrease in the number of women, from the number unemployed for long periods, who found a job within the period of registering their unemployment.

- A lowering in the probability of finding work amongst long term unemployed women. In 1993 the number of long term unemployed women who found work was 63 per cent and decreased to 55 per cent by the year 2000.

The formation of a dual-sector model of the labour market

The situation presently in Russia, is that there is a gradually developing dual-sector labour market. In the primary sector, jobs are characterized by relatively high salaries, stable work, good working conditions and career opportunities. Conversely, in the secondary sector – the opposite is the case, and jobs are characterized by low salaries, the absence of stable work and poor career development prospects and bad working conditions.

In the modern Russian economy, the primary sector corresponds to non-state or privately owned organizations, whereas the secondary sector gradually moves in the direction of state companies characterized by often withholdings wages (employees being paid frequently up to six months in arrears) and a high level of latent unemployed (Baskakova, 1998; Mezentsev, 1998; Anon, 2000a; Chetvernina and Dunaeva, 2000).

In this bifurcation of the labour market, it is possible to observe the tendency for an increase in the proportion of women in the secondary sector. The bifurcation process can be observed in such sectors as public health, jurisprudence and insurance having a traditionally high proportion of women. In recent years organizations presenting services at higher market rates and offering a high level of wages against the background of a general decline in the level of wages, are actively developing. Most of the workers moving into the primary sector of the economy are men.

Work orientation of women

The structure of female employment in modern Russia is influenced not only by material circumstances presented in the generalized way above, but on subjective factors of choice. Most women have a high commitment to stability and avoid risk when choosing employment. In practice, this work orientation means choosing to work in the state (or secondary) sector of the economy (68 per cent women) (Mezentsev, 1998).

Women pursuing education

As was mentioned before, during the Soviet period, women had sufficient opportunity to obtain an education. According to a census of the population in 1989, 46 per cent of working women had secondary and higher education, while in the same period the figure for men was 34.2 per cent (Varfalvi, 1999).

Women maintained their interest and determination to obtain vocational training, even after the economic reforms began in 1992. In 1997, the State Statistics Committee (Goskomstat, 2000) published figures, which confirmed that 60 per cent of employed women specialists had secondary and tertiary education compared with men at 46 per cent. In Russia the term 'specialist' is used to denote a person with professional training in a specific field such as medicine or a branch of engineering. This trend has been constant up until today. For example, in 2000, according to Goskomstat (2000), 55 per cent of all students amongst state specialist academies and higher education institutions were women. In this way, one may confirm that in the USSR and subsequently in the new Russia, women's access to education was a reality, at least in principle. In spite of this, the problems connected with education were not solved completely. In particular two can be highlighted:

- a surplus of labour; and
- imbalance in the educational system.

The first problem – surplus of labour – is connected with the peculiarities of Soviet economics (still not completely eradicated during the period of reform) where the rate of training specialists was ahead of the rate of the technical development in manufacturing. As a result, the number of graduates outnumbered the number of job vacancies on the labour market. This was why a good deal of qualified specialists were forced to find work in fields other than in their own specialist fields, or take on job positions where they were over qualified. Although during the Soviet period statistics on unemployment (as a result of a labour) were not gathered, it is known that women formed a higher proportion of unemployed than men. The after-effects of such a surplus are felt even now. For example, in 2000 in the Nizhny Novgorod region (one of the most developed in Russia) among those registered unemployed with a tertiary education, 46 per cent were women and 35 per cent men. Although women comprised 70 per cent of the total unemployed, they could lay claim to no more than 33 per cent of the job vacancies, with low pay and low prestige (Varfalvi, 1999).

The second problem – imbalance in the educational system – mostly concerned tertiary education. Since the direction for education and specialization in universities was regulated not by market demand but by the state, the system was slow to react to the changes in requirements for specialists in various branches of the economy. As a result, higher education institutions continued to produce a labour force for those branches of the economy that could not take them in, and were late in setting new curricula for branches of the economy that were in desperate need of qualified specialists.

The situation was well illustrated in the 1990s when western business people arrived in Russia and were amazed at the number of engineers (in particular women engineers). In reality the 'supernormal' development of the engineering profession in Soviet Russia was an outcome of government policy in the sphere of tertiary education, as the result of which a polytechnic institute was opened in every regional centre. In the beginning, this was due to the forced industrialization of the economy in the 1920s to 1930s, and then later, in the 1950s to 1960s, with the development in the Urals and Siberia (Varfalvi, 1999).

The system of tertiary education in Russia kept the same characteristics even after the beginning of economic reforms – right up until the 1990s. Only in the second half of the nineties, when the new market reform mechanisms regulating the qualifications of the labour force were put into practice, was a change in the balance of educational system noticed mostly through a lessening of women interested in the engineering professions. In 2000, information on gender distribution in education was published by Goskomstat (2000) (see Table 10.2). In recent years, a drop in the number of women choosing engineering as a profession (under 30 per cent) as well as an increase in the number of women choosing careers in economics and management (71 per cent) is noticeable.

Table 10.2 The gender distribution amongst students of state tertiary education institutions according to groups of fields of specialty, beginning academic year 1999/2000

Specialty	Gender distribution (%)	
	Women	Men
Education	82	18
Art and culture	73	27
Technology of food processing	72	28
Economics and management	81	29
Public health	69	31
Human and social sciences	67	33
Natural sciences	66	34
Ecology and conservation	64	36
Services	41	59
Geology and geotechnology	40	60
Construction and architecture	36	64
Metallurgy	35	65
Computer science and computerization	27	73
Mechanical engineering and metal works	25	75
Electronic engineering, radio engineering and communications	22	78
Power engineering	19	81
Aerospace and missile industry	18	82
Technology of production machinery	15	85

Source: Goskomstat, 2000

Women in management

When considering the representation of Russian women in the sphere of management, it is necessary to address a number of issues. Firstly, during the existence of the USSR, the meaning of the word 'management' was understood in a different social context than it is today. The words 'management' and 'manager' were understood as a higher category of party and state service that was included in a special social class, a so-called party-administration 'nomenclature'. The first person in a group of people administering any area of the economy – from big factories to small day nurseries – had to go through a procedure of confirmation by the corresponding party and state system, i.e. have a 'permit' to one of the levels of nomenclature (Ajrapetova, 2000).

The nomenclature administration of the economy was the foundation for the totalitarian government that controlled not so much the economic productivity, but the political loyalty of its administrators. The nomenclature, administration and other supporting institutions of Soviet society, were basically oriented towards men. According to statistic directories, by the end of the 1980s, no more than 7-8 per cent of women having higher education occupied leading positions in companies. The same index for men was 2.5 times higher (Cirikova, 1998).

In the reform period at the beginning of the 1990s the Russian economy went through a phase of 'privatization': as a result a significant proportion of enterprises moved from the state into private ownership. Correspondingly, part of the administration which earlier belonged to the Soviet nomenclature moved to the private sector where they acquired new attributes of modern management in comparison with the former methods of administration. In this process of transformation of nomenclature into managers, women showed a distinct conservatism, and according to figures, by the end of 1993 (when the main privatization had already been completed) 37 per cent of women managers stayed working in state enterprises as compared to 21 per cent of men. In 1993 the State and private sectors, the main contingent of female managers was distributed according to the more traditional 'female' professions, amongst which retailing led (48 per cent of all women managers), then social services (21.1 per cent), and catering (16 per cent) (Babaeva, 1996).

As it was before the economic reform, women were represented mostly amongst the junior and middle echelons of management. At top management level, representation of women drops sharply. For example, according to figures in 1996, amongst the top leaders in companies, women in industry constituted 11 per cent, in agriculture 8 per cent, and in construction 1 per cent. The overall percentage of women in top management in companies covering all branches of industry in the Russian economy in 1996 was 5.6 per cent (Babaeva, 1996). According to Goskomstat (2000) 32 per cent of managers in Russia were employed in management positions but according to the Trade Unions, only around 7 per cent were in top management positions.

It is difficult to say what trends are emerging in Russian society today from the point of view of women's role in the management of the economy. Above all, the absence of a systematic sociological and statistical data on this subject, does not allow a confident prediction. In domestic sociology the female manager has not yet become the centre of much attention, which indirectly is an expression of general weakness of feminism in modern Russia.

Nevertheless, even on the basis of the fragments of facts gained recently by researchers studying the problem from different angles, the following suppositions can be made:

- In the near future, a significant influx of women graduating with higher education in management (a relatively new subject for Russian universities) onto the labour market is expected. Official statistics have recorded women exceeding 70 per cent of students studying in this field (see Table 10.2). Although the figures are a combination of management and economics, it can be suppose that soon companies seeking graduates in management will have to become gender inclusive.
- Certain sectors are emerging where women are represented in top management positions. Here undoubtedly the financial spheres are the leaders and a survey of 62 of the largest banks in Russia revealed that the chairpersons of 11 banks were women (17.7 per cent). A survey in 1996 found that three women worked in government in the following top positions: First Vice President of the Central Bank of Russia, Vice Minister of Finance and Vice Minister of Defence (dealing with the army budget) (Babaeva, 1996).
- Today the old Soviet principle of the nominal presence of women in economic leadership has virtually been eliminated. Women are not nominated to management positions on the basis of political decisions anymore, they achieve those positions through competing against men. In the long term, this should radically affect the Russian mentality, which still preserves a patriarchal attitude and paternalism towards women with professional business careers (Babaeva, 1996).

As an example of the change taking place, the publication of a list of the business elite of Russia in 2000 indicates 11 out of 130 posts were occupied by women. The absolute value of this result may be conservative (8.5 per cent). However, the women have a presence among successful top managers in the national economy and this may speak of the opening of new career opportunities for women (Chirikova, 1998).

Women entrepreneurs

The changes, which took place in the years of reform in Russia, influenced the ratio of the number of employed in state and non-state sectors. Within the period

1992-1996 alone, employment in the private sector rose from 18 per cent to 38.2 per cent. In the private sector 25 per cent of those employed were entrepreneurs or self-employed.

The rise in the number of women entrepreneurs was noticeable already in 1990-1991, the last years of the existence of the USSR when on the eve of the break up of the Soviet Union, there was an attempt to overcome state totalitarianism by creating a plural economy. The main proportion of women working in business were spokespersons of engineer-technical professions, coming from scientific-research institutes, technical laboratories, and design-construction agencies. Their chosen sphere of work more often than not had nothing in common with the profession for which they trained in higher education. According to Babaeva (1996), the most common businesses developed by women were found in sectors such as:

- consulting services
- training
- magazines and publishing
- agriculture
- small-scale production
- small-scale commerce.

When examining the higher echelons of the old soviet nomenclature there were few women, and they did not stay with the management of large enterprises. The most valuable assets of state property did not fall into the hands of women during the period of privatization. The bulk of women entrepreneurs concentrated on small and medium sized enterprises (Babaeva, 1996).

According to the figures given by Goskomstat in 1994; among joint owners of closed corporations (at that time more than 900,000 of this type of company were registered in the country) 39 per cent were women and among members of production and agricultural cooperatives 23 per cent, were women. The percentage of women working as employers was between 17-19 per cent, as farmers about 20 per cent and the self-employed, more than 33 per cent (Goskomstat, 1994). According to Goskomstat (2000) in one year only (1997) the percentage of women employers increased from 21 per cent to 30 per cent and by the end of 1999 was 31 per cent (see Table 10.3).

Table 10.3 Percentage of women and men classified as employers, 1997

Classification of entrepreneurs	Grouping according to sex (%)	
	Women	Men
Employers	31	69
Member of production cooperatives	35	65
Self-employed	42	58
Mean of all entrepreneurs	36	64

Source: Goskomstat, 2000

In the last few years the development of a wider diversity of women entrepreneurs in Russia has been noted. One survey of 200 companies found that about 25 per cent belonged to women or women had co-ownership (Babaeva, 1996).

What was considered as a business typically dominated by men is now becoming shared with women, who as a rule, occupy the second position of vice-president or chief administrator. The same survey, mentioned above, revealed that out of one hundred corporations engaging in industrial production, 18 per cent had women on their board of directors (Babaeva, 1996).

Country legislation supporting women in the workforce

In Soviet Russia legislation regulating gender addressed chiefly the question of women in professional careers. Laws which could have supported working women in the social sphere and in family relations significantly lagged behind. This type of policy started in the communist regime immediately after the revolution in 1917 and continued right up until the 1970s.

At the beginning of the 1970s women formed a higher proportion of the labour force in the USSR than any other country in the world. However, to achieve this position a high price was paid: a significant decrease in the birth rate. Foreseeing the future severe demographic crisis, the state in a relatively short period (International Labour Organization, 2001) approved a package of socially oriented legal measures amongst which the most substantive were:

- Giving women, with children up to the age of eight years of age, the right to undergo retraining and refresher courses whilst maintaining their present job position and average monthly salary for the period of training (1979).
- The introduction of part-paid leave (maternity leave) whilst caring for a child until the age of one year (1981).
- Giving women, with two or more children up to the age of 12, an extra three days paid leave and two weeks unpaid leave per annum (1981).

- A provision issued by the state committee for labour on the adoption of a flexi-time work schedule for women with children (1984).
- The introduction of part-paid leave to care for children up to ages of one and a half years of age and unpaid leave until a child is three years old (1989).

In the area of labour legislation Russian legal specialists distinguish between three groups of effective enactments: international legislative documents, ratified firstly by the USSR and then by Russia as a legal successor of the USSR constitute the first group. Primarily, this is the Conventions of the International Labour Organization (Baskakova, 1998):

- *ILO Convention No. 45 (1935)* 'The use of women in underground work in mines of any kind'
- *ILO Convention No. 100 (1951)* 'The equal pay of men and women for equal work'
- *ILO Convention No. 103 (1952)* 'The protection of motherhood'
- *ILO Convention No. 111 (1958)* 'Discrimination in the work place'
- *ILO Convention No. 122 (1964)* 'Work policies'
- *ILO Convention No. 156 (1981)* 'Equal treatment and equal opportunities for working men and women: working with family responsibilities'.

In the second group are the legislative acts formulated in accordance with international legislative documents. This large group represents, as a whole, the results of incorporating international regulations into Russian national law. Its characteristics were that in the Russian labour law international regulations as a rule are interpreted broadly, giving more benefits to women than was actually meant by international documents.

The third group represents the legislative acts regulating the work of women and does not have a parallel in international documents. As lawyers have commented, introducing the laws, of this group as a whole, into Russia is a channel for international legislative processes, reflecting in particular, the formulation of ILO documents:

> Every member of the ILO can in consulting with representative entrepreneurial and labour organizations determine that.....specific events directed at satisfying special needs of people who because of sex, age...family circumstances...are usually recognized as in need of special protection or help, will not be considered as discrimination (*ILO Convention No. 111 (1958)* 'Discrimination in the work place').

Examples of such acts can be considered, in particular, as law on 'State guarantees and compensations for persons working and living in the extreme north and other areas equated with it' (1993) or 'The provision of working and rest time for sailors on ships' (1996) etc.

Although in general Russian legislation on gender is sufficiently up to date and progressive, and in the state constitution, as in family and labour codes, the guarantee of gender equality in labour, society, politics, and the cultural spheres, as well as in education and professional training is secured. Nevertheless, the application of these laws in practice is not trouble-free.

As noted by lawyers, there are two major problems. Firstly, Russian law does not clearly define the procedure for the effective defence of women against discrimination. Because of the absence of a state mechanism for court defence, legal process in Russia is not yet oriented to addressing different types of sexual discrimination occurring in the work place (Kravchuk and Lukashevsky, 2000).

Secondly, a consequence of the first problem, is that in Russia there are no judges specialized in dealing with social and labour rights (cases on pension, employment, social benefits, etc.). Taking into account the generally overloaded courts the situation does not help women to use the rights provided by recent legislation (Kravchuk and Lukashevsky, 2000).

Initiatives to support women in the workforce

The two main categories of initiatives directed at the support and development of professional opportunities for women are initiatives arising from State bodies and initiatives arising in society.

State initiatives

From the point of view of women participating in management and entrepreneurial activity, among state initiatives the most interesting are the following: *National Action Plan* to improve the position of women and increase their role in society approved by the state in 1996 and *A Conception of Legal Development for the Provision of Equal Rights and Equal Opportunities for Men and Women* approved by the Russian lower parliament in 1997.

Both documents are interesting. In particular, it is of interest to analyse the premise where the present situation after reform of the laws affecting gender in Russia. In the *National Action Plan*, among measures taken by the state directed at the development of the social status of women, the following initiatives were planned:

- Inspection of the conformity the Russian Federation Law to labour code to ensure that the industrial relations system in Russia should provide for the training and retraining (CDP) of women 'returners' after maternity leave.
- A legislative proposal on a supplement to the Federal programme on support for small businesses in the Russian Federation. This would support women entrepreneurs, as well as family businesses.

- The organization of a series of training seminars entitled: *Starting your own business* on the development of entrepreneurial activities based on family members having a share in the business.
- The recruitment of women diplomats to work in Russian Consulates and Embassies overseas, in permanent representatives of the Russian Federation in the United Nations and other international organizations.
- Interdepartmental comprehensive programme of social support for students. In particular women students and students' families.

The *Conception of legal development...* highlights the future direction of legislation on gender policy. It suggests that the priority when planning the passing of the new legislation or changing it in parliament should include:

- The right to equal participation of men and women in making decisions at all levels of legislative, executive and juridical authorities and in local government bodies.
- The improvement of electoral legislation towards creating the conditions for involving more women in actualizing the right of choice.
- The improvement of legislation on state and municipal services with a view to the formalization of gender equality in according with international standards.
- The right to education and professional courses.
- The right to conduct entrepreneurial activities.

Both initiatives (the 'National Action Plan' and 'A Conception of Legal Development for the Provision of Equal Rights and Equal Opportunities for Men and Women') are not completed or effective yet. The State programme was considered for the period up to 2000, but as all the decisions can not be achieved without the provision funding, the 1998 financial and economic crisis put this and other social programmes back by years.

Nevertheless, it should be acknowledged that in Russia, in the medium term, state initiatives should have an effect on sex equality, extending from the Federal to regional and local levels.

Women's associations and clubs

As with many Russian social institutions, women's movements have not as yet gained a clear institutional form. In Russia there is still no strong political party that would include gender equality as a priority in its programme. Women's social movements do not have centralized management and today present a patchy picture of uncoordinated initiatives. However, in comparison to the past; 'nominal' women in pre-reform Russia, contemporary women's initiatives can be considered as a big step forward (Mashkova and Loginova, 2000; Solonicheva, 2000).

Although, regular statistical data on women's organizations are neither systematically nor routinely gathered, publications dedicated to the activities of women's associations and clubs indicate that they exist in every large regional centre – independent of the level of economic development. Amongst organizations representing business women, a certain competition is noticed, especially in the capital; Moscow, and in the second largest city, St. Petersburg. These organizations, as a rule, strive to develop in two directions: cooperation with international women's associations, and opening branches in the regions.

For example, the association 'Women and business in Russia' was founded in 1991 in St. Petersburg and entered the World Association of Women Entrepreneurs (FCEM) in 1995 and then opened its branches in Moscow and three other Russian cities. In a similar way, the association 'Club of Business and Professional Women, BPW' founded in 1993 in St. Petersburg is developing and in 1997 opened a club in Moscow and its mission today is 'the establishment of contacts between European BPW and Russian clubs, as well as assistance in the organization of new clubs'.

Similar approaches are being made by other women's organizations. For example, the 'Club of Business Women' (GEN-club) operating since 1989 under the auspices of the 'Economic News' in Moscow and the 'All-Russian Society, 'Business Women of Russia'. This last one, judging by its form of legal registration and method of forming regional branches, probably plans to get involved in politics and take part in elections, as is another movement with a similar name, 'Women of Russia' which was successful in the all-Russian elections of 1993.

The main emphasis of activities of business women's associations are: legal consultations, creating conditions for useful contacts, dialogue with state and local bodies and conducting cultural and educational events. Based on published information (Mashkova and Loginova, 2000; Solonecheva, 2000; Artamanov, 2000; Anon, 2000b) about projects which different women organizations were involved in during 2000, their interest in various questions concerning gender relations is shared in the following way:

- Legal gender issues – 48 per cent of all projects.
- Economic problems – 16 per cent of all projects.
- Cultural events – 21 per cent of all projects.
- Educational training programmes – 15 per cent of all projects.

The future

Reviewing general world trends it could be expected that similar ones would evolve in Russia (Babaeva, 1996; Russian Federation Government 1996a and b; KARAT Coalition, 1999). However, keeping in mind the position in which Russia finds itself today, economically and politically, the following picture is suggested for the next 5-10 years.

Firstly, there may be a greater number of women than men with management qualifications in the labour market, and because of the potential surplus of highly qualified managers, women may turn more often to starting up their own businesses. The women with experience of practical entrepreneurship will take charge of business women's associations. Furthermore, we believe the number of these associations could be expected to reduced, through merger and competition, and their activities will be focused on issues pertinent to the moment.

Secondly, it is unlikely in the near future that a strong women's political party will emerge, but women's associations may increasingly support political parties that have the strongest social programmes. On a final optimistic note, undoubtedly wider discussions of gender issues in Russian society are likely to develop which may influence changes to the traditional patriarchal attitude towards women's professional development in Russia.

References

Anon (2000a), 'Problems of gender policy on the labour market', *Conference in St. Petersburg*, International Labour Organization, Russian Office.

Anon (2000b),'Resolution of the Forum', Press release of the International Forum of CIS Assembly women, Saratov, September, 14-15.

Ajrapetova, N. (2000), 'Will women come to the big politics?' Independent Newspaper (Nezavisimaya Gazeta), 25 October.

Artamonov, V.S. (2000), 'Case Study on gender problems of employment of the graduates of higher education in the Murmansk Region', Conference in St. Petersburg, International Labour Organization, Russian Office.

Babaeva, L.V. (1996), 'Women in Russia in the conditions of a social turn', in *Collection of Scientific Reports*, Russian Scientific Foundation, No. 34.

Baskakova, M.E. (1998), 'Equal opportunities and gender stereotypes on labour market', *Project: Gender Expert*, Moscow Centre for Gender Studies, Moscow.

Chetvernina, T. and Dunaeva, N. (2000), 'Women in the Russian transitional economy', Report, *Conference in St. Petersburg*, International Labour Organization, Russian Office.

Chirikova, A. (1998), *A woman in charge of a firm*, Moscow.

Gale, A.W. and Holden, N.J. (1995), 'Russian Construction Project Management in Transition: Issues and Arguments for Radical Change' in *Proceedings of the Internet Symposium, St Petersburg*, Russia, 14-16 September, pp. 89-93.

Goskomstat: Sate Statistical Committee (1994), *Men and Women of Russia in 1994*.

Goskomstat: Sate Statistical Committee (1999), *Men and Women of Russia in 1999*.

Goskomstat: Sate Statistical Committee (2000), *Men and Women of Russia in 2000*.

Goskomstat: Sate Statistical Committee (2001), *Men and Women of Russia in 2001*.

Iljin,V. (1997), *State and social stratification of the Soviet and Post-Soviet societies (1917-1996)*, Moscow.

International Labour Organization (2001), *Labour Law Reform in Russia, 9th Issue*, Russian Office, Moscow.

KARAT Coalition (1999), 'National mechanism to improve the status of women in the Central European and Eastern European countries', Report, *The UN Commission on the Status of Women*, 43rd session, New York, March 3.

Kravchuk, N.V., Lukashevsky, S.M. (2000), 'Human rights in the regions of the Russian Federation', Report on observance of the women's rights in Russia, The Moscow Human Rights Conference.

Mashkova, E. and Loginova, E. (2000), 'Analysis of gender stereotypes on the Russian television', Sociological Studies, N11, Moscow.

Mezentsev, E. (1998), Women in the area of employment and on labour market, Moscow Centre for Gender Studies, Moscow.

Russian Federation Government (1996a), 'Order N 6', Concept of improvement of the status of women in the Russian Federation, January 8, Moscow.

Russian Federation Government (1996b), 'Order N 1023', National programme to improve the status of women and to enhance their role in society in the Russian Federation, August 29, Moscow.

Solonicheva, V.Y. (2000), 'Gender aspects of the regional labour market and realisation of the active policy of women employment promotion (the Nyzhny Novgorod Region)', Case Study, Conference in St. Petersburg, International Labour Organization, Russian Office.

UNICEF (1999), 'Regional Monitoring Report' (MONEE), UNICEF Research Centre, Innocenti, Italy.

United Nations (2000), 'Four International Conferences on the Status of Women Central and Eastern European countries between 1975-1995', Article, 23rd Special Session of the UN General Assembly, June 5-6.

Varfalvi, L.V. (1999), Gender studies and their integration into the higher education, Khabarovsk State Academy of Economics and Law, Khabovsk.

Vovchenko, O.M. (2000), 'Gender equality as a social philosophical problem', Moscow.

SECTION III
WOMEN IN MANAGEMENT –
NORTH AND CENTRAL AMERICA

Chapter 11

Women in Management in Canada

Ronald J. Burke and Rekha Karambayya

Introduction

This chapter provides a profile of the changing status of women in management in Canada. The evidence suggests that women have achieved huge gains along a number of dimensions in the past two decades. Women now make up 46.2 per cent of all the job holders in Canada (*Globe and Mail*, 2002). Women have not been as hard hit as men by job losses during a period of downsizing and restructuring, in part because they are underrepresented in the sectors that were hit hardest during economic downturns. In addition, women have reaped benefits from job gains following those years of downsizing. Between 1996 and 2001 the Canadian economy created 1.6 million new jobs of which 52.7 per cent went to women. Women now hold 49.6 per cent of the professional jobs in Canada, up from 38.3 per cent in 1987. Although still far from parity, women now hold 20.5 per cent of the jobs in the science and engineering fields. However, women experienced a marginal decrease in the percentage of managerial jobs from 36.9 per cent in 1996 to 34.8 per cent in 2001 (*Globe and Mail*, 2002).

Despite the encouraging picture reflected in the above numbers, women are not yet facing a level playing field. A look beyond the numbers suggests that women still face a number of difficult hurdles that significantly hinder their advancement into the highest ranks of organizations. Those hurdles include exclusion from informal organizational and professional networks, high visibility as a result of token status at senior levels, lack of sponsorship and support, and even gender discrimination. Outside the workplace women still have to contend with the limitations imposed by traditional gender roles, the challenges of 'second shift' work, and the absence of viable role models.

In this chapter we begin with a discussion of the representation of women in the labour force, in educational institutions and in managerial ranks. We outline government legislation and organizational initiatives designed to support women in the workplace, and comment on their success. We conclude with some of the challenges and hurdles that remain, and make recommendations regarding future directions for research and practice in this area.

Labour force characteristics

Between 1976 and 1999, the total number of employed women increased 83.6 per cent from 3,630,700 to 6,665,300, while the total number of employed men only increased 28.0 per cent. The percentage of women employed also increased 12.6 per cent, from 42.0 per cent to 54.6 per cent, while the percentage of men employed decreased 5.9 per cent from 72.7 per cent. All this has led to a greater gender balance in the total number of employed persons. Whereas in 1976, 37.1 per cent of those employed were women, this increased to 45.9 per cent by 1999. The labour force participation rate for women ranged between 78.2 per cent for women aged 25-54 to 39.4 per cent for those between the ages of 55 and 64. During the same period the unemployment rates for men and women were comparable at around 7.5 per cent (Statistics Canada, 2000).

In 1999 women were employed more in service industries (86.4 per cent) than in goods-producing ones (13.5 per cent), and have shifted slightly (+2.0 per cent) towards the former since 1987. Men have also favoured service industries (63.3 per cent) over goods-producing ones (36.7 per cent), but they have done so less than women. These trends may reflect economic trends and employment opportunities rather than a preference for a particular sector (Statistics Canada, 2000).

Between 1987 and 1999, the percentage of women employed in 'business and finance' occupations increased from 1.9 per cent to 3.1 per cent and surpassed men (2.1 per cent to 2.7 per cent). As a result, women have come to represent 49.4 per cent of those employed in business and finance occupations, up from 44.6 per cent in 1994 and 40.7 per cent in 1987.

Since 1987, the percentage of employed women in 'senior' management positions has remained stable at 0.4 per cent, while the percentage of men employed as senior managers has decreased from 1.6 per cent to 0.9 per cent. With regard to employment in 'other' management positions, the percentage of women has increased from 5.8 per cent to 6.9 per cent, while the percentage of men has increased from 10.0 per cent to 10.6 per cent. The percentage of 'senior' managers who are female has increased from 16.9 per cent to 26.8 per cent, and the percentage of 'other' managers who are female has increased from 30.6 per cent to 35.7 per cent with corresponding decreases in the percentage of men at both levels (Statistics Canada, 2000).

Between 1976 and 1999, the total number of women employed part-time increased 116.7 per cent from 862,200 to 1,868,300. The percentage of women employed part-time also increased 4.3 per cent from 23.7 per cent to 28.0 per cent. While the percentage of men employed part-time has always been lower, it almost doubled over this time, increasing 4.4 per cent from 5.9 per cent to 10.3 per cent. The gender split in the total number of part-time employees has remained virtually unchanged, changing marginally from 70.2 per cent female in 1976 to 69.7 per cent in 1999 (Statistics Canada, 2000).

The reasons for part-time employment for women have changed over the past 25 years, some quite significantly. For example, 'illness and disability', 'personal and family responsibilities', and 'going to school' as reasons for part-time work increased marginally. The reason 'only being able to find part-time work', however, changed more significantly, increasing from 10 per cent to 24 per cent. The reason 'not wanting to work full-time' also changed and decreased substantially from 39 per cent to 27 per cent (Statistics Canada, 1997).

Between 1970 and 2000, the average annual employment income across all occupations increased from $3,199 to $30,130 for women, and from $6,574 to $37,556 for men. Whereas in 1970, women's income was 49 per cent of men's, it increased to 80 per cent by 2000.

Between 1970 and 1990, the average employment income for occupations in public-sector management increased from $4,638 to $31,716 for women, increasing from 43 per cent of men's income to 73 per cent. During the same time the average employment income in private-sector management increased from $7,179 to $28,054 for women, going from 39 per cent of men's income to 58 per cent by 1990. Average income for 'management occupations' was $38,136 for women and $57,796 for men, with women's income at 66 per cent of men's (Statistics Canada, 1997).

Women pursuing education

Women have continued to account for large numbers of university students. In 1996 56 per cent of university students were female, representing a 15 per cent increase from 24 years earlier when 41 per cent of university students were female. In 1972-73 there were 105,100 women enrolled in university. By 1981-82 that number had grown to 169,400, and by 1998-99 it was at 468,881. While full-time university enrolment of men in universities fell 3.3 per cent between 1994 and 1999, full-time university enrolment of women grew 4.5 per cent during the same period (Statistics Canada, 2001). In 1998-99 there were 319,475 and 149,406 women enrolled in full-time and part-time university programmes respectively, compared with 260,901 and 96,579 men.

The remarkable pace of women enrolling in business studies has narrowed the gender gap in business studies almost completely. According to the latest figures, (1996), 51 per cent of business students were male and 49 per cent were female. This represents an incredible 37 per cent shift from 24 years earlier when only 13 per cent of business students were female. Over this period as well, the number of women enrolled in business studies increased 46,225 or 1046 per cent whereas the number of men only increased 21,549 or 70 per cent. Finally, between 1972 and 1996 the proportion of female students enrolled in business studies (*vis-à-vis* all other disciplines) increased from 1/25 to 1/7, whereas the proportion of male students only increased from 1/7 to 1/6.

In 1996, there were more women than men at the undergraduate and master's levels across all disciplines, and at the undergraduate level in business studies. Men still dominated women, however, at the doctoral level across all disciplines, and at the master's and doctoral levels in business studies. This represents an incredible shift from 24 years earlier when there were more men than women at each level, across all disciplines and in business studies.

While the numbers of women in professional programmes such as law and medicine has risen gradually over the past two decades to about the same level as men in those programmes, the percentage of women in MBA programmes appears to be stalled at about 30 per cent on average. A study conducted by Catalyst suggests that a key barrier to women's enrolment on MBA programmes is the absence of role models (Catalyst, 2000). Another barrier may be the admission requirement recently introduced by some programmes that applicants have several years of relevant work experience. Women with management experience may be unable or unwilling to take two years out of their personal and professional lives to pursue an MBA.

Women in management

Catalyst (1999), a New York City based research and advocacy group on women in management, undertook a census of women who hold corporate officer positions in the 560 leading Canadian corporations. They found that women represented twelve per cent of corporate officers in Canada as of March 31, 1999. Almost half (44 per cent) of these companies had no women officers; one quarter (28 per cent) had one woman officer; and one quarter (28 per cent) had multiple woman officers. Women held only 3.4 per cent of the 'clout' titles such as Chair, CEO, Vice Chair, President, COO, SEVP and EVP.

Interestingly, Canadian companies having multiple women on their boards of directors also had multiple women officers. Similarly, companies with no women directors were more likely to have no women officers. In addition, companies with multiple women officers were more likely to have multiple women in line positions.

Women's representation as corporate officers was highest in financial institutions (18 per cent), biotechnology and pharmaceuticals (17 per cent), life insurance (17 per cent), gas, electrical utilities and pipelines (16 per cent) and multi-media (16 per cent). Women corporate officers had the lowest representation in engineering (5 per cent), mining, metals and minerals (5 per cent), steel production (5 per cent) and construction (6 per cent).

Women on Boards of Directors

In 1998, Catalyst undertook the most comprehensive study of women on boards of directors of Canadian companies. A total of 560 organizations were studied; companies on the *Financial Post* 500, the top 20 financial institutions, the top 20 life insurance companies and the top 20 crown corporations (Catalyst, 1999a).

Of the 560 top Canadian companies, less than half (41.7 per cent) had women board members. Of these, 17 per cent had more than one woman on their board. Only 36 per cent of the FP500 companies had any women directors, 87 per cent of the other 60 companies did. Only 11 per cent of the FP500 had more than one woman director compared to 62 per cent of the other 60 companies.

Women held 7.5 per cent of board seats in Canada, including 6.2 per cent of the FP500 board seats and 14 per cent of seats on the other 60 companies. Larger companies, based on revenue, had more women on their boards and often more than a single woman director. Publicly-owned companies were almost twice as likely to have at least one woman on their boards, as were privately-owned companies (44 per cent vs. 24 per cent, respectively).

Women and men directors had some similarities. Both typically came from the corporate sector (63 per cent of women and 66 per cent of men). Both typically held one board seat (87 per cent women and 85 per cent of men). Women fared best in financial institutions, life insurance, broadcasting and cable, information technology, utilities and pipelines, engineering, pharmaceuticals and publishing and printing, all with more than 10 per cent female representation. In Crown corporations, covering a variety of industries owned by government, women represented 21 per cent of all directors. Women fared less well in chemicals and fertilizers, oil and gas field services, import/export, high tech manufacturing, and construction with less than 3 per cent board representation.

Brown and Brown (1998) examined board practices in Canada over a 25 year period. Although their methodology and source of data was not provided, they stated that over 70 per cent of boards include at least one woman, but women only occupy 10 per cent of all directors positions.

Women's career experiences

Catalyst (1997) undertook a study of successful managerial and professional women (N=417) and the views of CEOs (N=159) supplemented by phone interviews with 17 senior women and 14 CEOs. Most women were between 40-44 years of age (30 per cent), married (76 per cent), had children (65 per cent), had university education (87 per cent), earned between $100,000-200,000 (54 per cent), worked in service producing organization (51 per cent), with revenues between $200 million to $1B (25 per cent). CEOs were typically between 50-54 years of age (31 per cent), married (94 per cent), worked in goods-producing organizations (50 per cent) with revenues between $200M to $1B (38 per cent).

This Catalyst study was the first systematic look at the question of why so few women are at the top of Canadian organizations. While both senior women and CEOs believed women were making progress, senior women held less positive viewpoints. CEOs saw lack of time in the pipeline and lack of significant general management or line experiences as more significant barriers than senior women did. Senior women saw male stereotyping and preconceptions of women's roles and abilities, and exclusion from informal networks of communication as more significant barriers compared to CEOs. More senior women than CEOs also believed that family responsibilities had a negative impact on women's careers.

Nevertheless, senior women and CEOs agreed on the strategies needed by organizations to support women's advancement. The top three were: identifying and developing high-potential women; providing women with high visibility assignments or clients; and cross-functional or developmental job rotation. Over half the senior women indicated the importance of career development strategies such as mentoring, women's networks, identification of high-potential women, in-house leadership training, high visibility assignments and succession planning. Over a third endorsed strategies to promote work-family balance. The gap in perceptions between senior women and CEOs needs addressing. Women see the problem as an unsupportive work environment; CEOs see the problem as deficiencies in women's experiences and time in the pipeline.

Orser (2000) reported the results of a study of women in management with data from 393 senior women, 130 HR professionals and 107 CEOs. These data were supplemented with telephone interviews with 40 women executives, 26 HR professionals and 28 CEOs having high proportion of women on their senior management team. Using four items, Orser created a gender diversity progress scale. CEOs rated their organizations more favourably on that scale than did women executives. Public sector organizations were seen by both CEOs and senior women as making more progress. Senior women reported significantly more attitudinal barriers than did CEOs. This lack of awareness of barriers by CEOs needs to be addressed if continued progress in advancing women is to be made.

The most critical factor senior women identified in supporting women's advancement was the CEOs commitment to women's advancement. This included: making explicit statements about the need for women's advancement, recognizing gender differences in contribution and management style, basing promotions on merit, taking part in initiatives designed to help women and not accepting excuses for a lack of women at all organizational levels. Work life balance also emerged as a priority for women executives.

Women entrepreneurs

In 2000, 832,000 or 35 per cent of self-employed persons in Canada were women. While historically, there have always been more self-employed men, over the past 25 years, the number of self-employed women has increased at faster rate than men (172 per cent versus 78 per cent), and the percentage of self-employed persons who are women has increased (+9 per cent) whereas it has decreased for men. Working for oneself is still nowhere near as popular as working for others for women (12 per cent versus 88 per cent) or for men (19 per cent versus 81 per cent).

The dominant type of self-employment for women continues to be unincorporated business without paid help (61 per cent). Unpaid work in family business, which was the second most dominant type of self-employment for women in 1976 (34 per cent), dropped almost entirely by 2000 (–30 per cent), and now more closely resembles the percentage for men (2 per cent). In its stead, unincorporated business with paid help increased (+2 per cent), as did incorporated business with and without paid help (+9 per cent and +6 per cent).

Self-employed women have continued to shift out of the goods-producing sector (14 per cent) and into the services-producing one (86 per cent). While the same is true for men, the percentage of men in the goods-producing sector is higher (35 per cent) than the percentage for women entrepreneurs. The top industry sectors for self-employed women are health care and social assistance (16 per cent), other services (15 per cent), trade (14 per cent), and professional, scientific and technical services (12 per cent). In contrast to women, the dominant areas of self-employment for men are construction 16 per cent, professional, scientific, and technical services 14 per cent, trade 13 per cent, and other services 7 per cent. The collection/breakdown of data on sectors and areas of self-employment was only started in 1987 however.

The three biggest increases for self-employed women over the past 13 years have been in the areas of professional, scientific and technical services (+7 per cent), management of companies and administrative and other support services (+5 per cent), and finance, insurance, real estate, and leasing (+2 per cent). The same is true for men although the increases are not as significant as for women (+6 per cent, +3 per cent, and +1 per cent).

Country legislation supporting women in the workforce

Broadly speaking, Canadian legislation to support women in the workplace is enshrined at the constitutional, federal, provincial, and international levels. Federal employment and labour laws, which cover less than 10 per cent of the Canadian workforce, include the Canada Labour Code (1965) and the Canadian Human Rights Act (1977). Provincial laws, which cover the majority of the Canadian workforce, include employment standards legislation, labour relations legislation, health and safety legislation, workers' compensation, and human rights legislation. Canada has also been signatory on three pieces of international legislation. These are the Equal Remuneration Convention in 1972, the International Covenant On Economic, Social, & Cultural Rights in 1976, and the Convention On The Elimination Of All Forms Of Discrimination Against Women in 1981.

Given the large domain/scope of legislation supporting women in the workplace, this section will focus on four major areas of legislation: employment equity, pay equity, sexual harassment, and maternity leave.

In 1983, the federal government announced the establishment of a Royal Commission on Equality in Employment chaired by Judge Rosalie Silberman-Abella, whose mandate it was to 'explore the most efficient, effective, and equitable means of promoting equality in employment for four groups: women, Native peoples, disabled persons, and visible minorities'. Judge Silberman-

Abella's recommendations led the enactment of the first Employment Equity Act in 1986.

The Act applied to federally regulated private employers with 100 employees or more, representing about 620,000 employees and about 410 employers. In the same year the Federal Contractors Program For Employment Equity was enacted to apply to employers with 100 employees or more, contracting on grants valued at $200,000 or more with the federal government. At present, this Act applies to about 1.1 million employees and about 845 employers.

In 1991, the Act was reviewed and several shortcomings were identified in a report entitled A Matter of Fairness. In order to correct these shortcomings, the Act was amended in 1995 to include the two key changes. First, coverage was extended to federal public service employers, representing about 150,000 employees in about 66 departments. Second, employers were made responsible for proactively administering their own employment equity programmes. Enforcement of compliance through audits was made the responsibility of the Canadian Human Rights Commission. Specifically, employers would now be required to follow a twelve-step program which included conducting a workforce survey, undertaking a workforce analysis, conducting a review of its human resources policies and practices, preparing an employment equity plan, and reporting annually to the government.

Between 1987 and 1998, the representation of women in workplaces covered by the Act has increased from 40.9 per cent in 1987 to 44.3 per cent in 1998. In 1998, women accounted for 41.4 per cent of all hirings in the workforce under the Act and won 55.0 per cent of all promotions.

At the federal level, pay equity finds its source in both domestic and international human rights law. Section 11 of the 1977 Canadian Human Rights Act states 'It is a discriminatory practice for an employer to establish or maintain differences in wages between male and female employees employed in the same establishment who are performing work of equal value'. In 1970, the Female Employees' Equal Pay Act was incorporated into the Canada Labour Code, and in 1986, the Canadian Human Rights Commission issued the Equal Wage Guidelines to assist employers with the interpretation and administration of Section 11.

Pay equity legislation in Canada is complaint based. Since 1977, the Canadian Human Rights Commission has dealt with slightly more than 400 pay equity complaints. Of these, a majority were dismissed, while others were resolved through negotiated settlements totalling some $8 million and covering approximately 1500 employees. The complaint brought against the federal Treasury Board by the Public Service Alliance of Canada was the largest pay equity settlement in Canadian history. When the case was finally resolved in 1999, the government agreed to pay some $3.5 billion in back wages and interest to some 200,000 current and former public service employees.

In 1983, the Canadian Human Rights Act was amended to prohibit sexual harassment in the workplace, as stated under section 14. In 1985, the Canada

Labour Code was amended to include division XV.1 on sexual harassment. Section 247.1 defines sexual harassment as:

> ...any conduct, comment, gesture or contact of a sexual nature that is likely to cause offence or humiliation to any employee that might, on reasonable grounds, be perceived by that employee as placing a condition of a sexual nature on employment or on any opportunity for training or promotion.

Section 247.2 entitles every employee 'to employment free of sexual harassment'. Sections 247.3 and 247.4 hold employers responsible for being proactive in preventing sexual harassment in the workplace; and for creating workplace policy concerning sexual harassment.

Legislation providing for maternity leave and benefits in Canada dates as far back as 1921 when the province of British Columbia enacted the country's first maternity leave legislation. In 1971, the federal government amended the Canada Labour Code to establish a seventeen-week maternity leave. In 1993 the Canada Labour Code enacted an additional 37 weeks of 'parental' (formerly 'paternal') leave.

The legislation stipulates that pregnant or nursing women who are able to work are entitled to job modification with no alteration in wages and benefits where their current job functions put them or their foetus at health risk. Where this is not possible, or when pregnant or nursing women are unable to work, they are entitled to a leave of absence.

Legislation enacted into the Canada Labour Code in 1978 forbids employers from dismissing, suspending, laying off, demoting, or disciplining an employee because she is pregnant or has applied for a leave of absence. While on a leave of absence, employees are entitled to notification of all employment, training, and promotion opportunities, and are also entitled to continued coverage and accumulation of pension, health, and disability benefits, as well as seniority. Under the Employment Insurance Act, employees are entitled to 55 per cent of their weekly insurable earnings, with a cap at a weekly net of $413. Upon return from a leave of absence, employees are entitled to reinstatement in their original position, and where not possible, in a similar position, without loss of wages or benefits. Maternity and parental leave apply to adopted children as well.

Initiatives supporting women in the workforce

Several Canadian organizations have undertaken initiatives to support women's career advancement during the past 10 years. Three of these efforts, described in more detail in the published literature, will be profiled here.

Christie (1997) describes the integrated approach taken by Deloitte & Touche, beginning with the development of a strategic plan for the 1990s. The firm clearly recognized that their human resources were their main competitive advantage, and since 50 per cent of recruits were women, issues of retention and development loomed large. A firm-wide culture survey suggested that the best way to promote gender equality was to develop systems that created a fairer and more supportive environment for everyone.

An advisory group on the Retention and Advancement of Women was created in January 1994, chaired by the firm's Managing Partner. The three biggest concerns facing women were balancing multiple commitments, the work environment and career advancement. The Advisory Group published a report titled 'A Partnership for Change' in 1995, proposing several major initiatives including communication, changing the firm's culture, alternate work arrangements and the coaching and mentoring of top talent.

The Royal Bank Financial Group has been particularly active in addressing the work/family interface (Tombari and Spinks, 2001; Spinks and Tombari, 1999). RBFG has 55,000 employees with women constituting 75 per cent of the total workforce. RBFG's work family initiatives evolved through three stages: strategy design and development, strategic implementation, and continuous improvement, communication and evaluation. Key initiatives undertaken included dependent care programmes, flexible work arrangements and training and support. At any period of time, 35-50 per cent of their employees use a component of the work-family life initiatives.

Two impact assessments (1994 and 1997) showed overwhelmingly positive responses. Data were collected from users, their immediate managers and non-user co-workers. Eighty-one per cent of users said that flexible work arrangements (FWAs) made them more effective in managing work/family responsibilities. Employee health and well-being were also influenced by FWAs; 70 per cent reported less stress, 65 per cent reported having more energy. FWAs also emerged as an important retention tool; 36 per cent would leave if these options were not available. Users of FWAs did not believe their use would limit advancement (users, 78 per cent, non-users, 84 per cent; managers, 90 per cent).

The Bank of Montreal has been actively putting policies and programmes in place in support of workplace quality for over a decade (Jafri and Isbister, 2001; Kinsley, 1993; Totta and Burke, 1995). In 1991, the President created an employee task force for the advancement of women in the bank. By the end of the year, the task force issued a *Report to Employees* identifying the main barriers to the advancement of women and recommending 26 action plans to remove them.

Five elements contributed to the success of the task force and its impact:

- *Executive sponsorship* – a senior executive led the task force which went a long way in generating interest.
- *Getting the facts out* – the task force examined the myths underlying many of the barriers to the advancement of women, and got this information out to all employees.

- *Inclusive approach* – while focussing on barriers faced by women, the task force had as its goal the removal of barriers and the creation of opportunities for *all* employees.
- *Accountability and integration* – Action plans ensured both managerial accountability and an integrated approach to implementation.

Of the 26 action plans, only three were aimed solely at women: a gender awareness workshop, and two action plans mandating a 50 per cent participation rate for women in two training programmes that are feeder routes to senior positions. Both women and men expressed a need to take charge of their own career development, as well as a desire for support in balancing commitment to work, family, community and education. The former were addressed by the creation of an online career information network listing all new job openings and an executive advisor programme that matches people seeking career guidance with more senior people; the latter by employee-initiated FWAs.

A position of VP for Workplace Equality was created to function as the catalyst for the implementation and integration of all the bank's workplace equality initiatives. BMO was also active in dealing with potential and actual backlash to their equality efforts by continuing to communicate with knowledge and facts through intensive and targeted educational training programmes. The evidence (Jafri and Isbister, 2001) shows a dramatic increase in the numbers of women at all levels of management within the bank.

The future

The patterns in the data presented here suggest dramatic changes for women in the workplace in Canada in the past two decades. There has been a significant increase in the numbers of women entering the workforce, so that in 1999 women represented 45.9 per cent of employees. It is clear that the numbers of women in business and management has also steadily increased. However, the data clearly indicate that as we move up to senior levels in organizations the representation of women tends to fall dramatically. Women represent only 26.8 per cent of senior managers and only 6.4 per cent of corporate officers. The situation appears as bleak if not more so on boards of directors. There are very few corporate boards with more than one female director, and still large numbers with none at all. So while women seem to be getting in to organizations in large numbers, they do not seem to be making it to the top ranks of these organizations.

Two competing arguments have been provided to explain this pattern: that women 'do not have (or want) what it takes' to make it to senior organizational positions, or that they are not allowed access to those positions because of subtle barriers in the workplace. The first explanation suggests that women either do not have the right sorts of skills and experience, or do not want to pay the personal price demanded by senior corporate jobs. The second explanation points out that women often lack the connections, mentors and access to training and 'feeder routes' that these positions require.

Perhaps one of the biggest hurdles women will face in the workplace is the fact that there are huge differences in the perceptions regarding which of these two explanations rings true (Ragins, Townsend and Mattis, 1998). Senior managers seem to believe that women do not want to make it to the top, while women feel that they are denied access to the top. What little data there is on the subject appears suggest that women are often denied opportunities in the workplace because stereotypical assumptions are often made about their career commitment and ambition. The data collected by the Bank of Montreal (Totta and Burke, 1995) suggests that most executives based their explanations for why women were not getting ahead on stereotypical 'myths' that were easily debunked. Perhaps more organizations should begin the process of uncovering and addressing these misconceptions.

While there is little Canadian data on this, it may also be true that women pay an enormous personal price for career success. Hewlett (2002) in a study of successful career women in the U.S., points out that 42 per cent of high earning career women in corporate America between the ages of 40 and 55 are childless, compared to 25 per cent of men in similar jobs. These women often lamented the lack of balance in their lives, and reflected on their choices and options with some regret.

Another indicator of women's career success is income. Here the pattern is a familiar one, suggesting that while women have achieved huge gains in the last twenty years, they have not achieved parity with men. Despite pay equity legislation and the women's movement, women still make on average 80 cents on the dollar earned by men. Even after taking into account a large number of personal and work-related differences (such as gender differences in education, work experience, full-time/part-time status, occupation, marital and family status) about half of the gender gap in wages remains unaccounted for (Drolet, 2000).

One explanation for the income differential is that despite their skills and experience there are systemic patterns in the labour market that disadvantage women. Another explanation is that there are 'shadow negotiations' around work and compensation that women do not pay adequate attention to (Kolb and Williams, 2000). In order to achieve equal footing with men women may need to become aware of the subtle interpersonal dynamics, and hidden agendas that determine 'worth' in the workplace.

Evidence shows that women are over-represented in universities relative to their numbers in the population at large. However their numbers in some programmes, such as the MBA, have plateaued for reasons that are not obvious. Since these programmes tend to be important feeder routes to the top levels of organizations, it may be important to explore reasons for these trends.

Seventy per cent of all part-time workers are female. Part-time work is often more unpredictable, less well compensated, and often not career oriented compared to full-time employment. While popular opinion suggests that women engage in part-time work because they are not career committed, or because they have family commitments, the data here suggests that a significant proportion of the women working part-time have not been able to find full-time work.

Meanwhile, women tend to cluster and prosper in some sectors of the economy such as the services sector, financial institutions, information technology, and the public sector. These may be relatively new sectors in which women may not experience old patterns of discrimination and exclusion. Clearly we need more data on why these patterns exist and what they might predict for the future.

The evidence presented here suggests that women now have unprecedented access to work and organizations, and even to management. That access unfortunately does not extend to the most senior levels of corporations. Perhaps it is time to shift the focus from broad-based affirmative action and employment equity programmes to explore and address the more subtle pressures keeping women out of the executive suites and boardrooms of corporate Canada. In order to do that we need a broader, more integrative, focus on a combination of career and life issues faced by women, and a recognition of the range of career and life choices they entail, as well as the gender stereotypical attitudes (which are often unfounded) still held by the senior male executive gatekeepers.

Acknowledgements

Preparation of this chapter was supported in part by the School of Business, York University. We acknowledge the assistance of Joe Krasman in collecting information for this project. Louise Coutu prepared the manuscript.

References

Brown, D.A.H. and Brown, D.L. (1998), *Success in the boardroom: 25 years of Canadian directorship practices: 1973-1998*, Ottawa: Conference Board of Canada.
Catalyst (1997), *Closing the gap: Women's advancement in corporate and professional Canada*, New York: Catalyst.
Catalyst (1999a), *Women board directors of Canada*, New York: Catalyst.
Catalyst (1999b), *Catalyst census of women corporate officers in Canada*, New York: Catalyst.
Catalyst (2000), *Women and the MBA: Gateway to opportunity*, New York: Catalyst.
Christie, K. (1997), 'Deloitte & Touche takes an integrated approach to the advancement of women', *Equal Opportunities International*, **16**, 14-22.
Drolet, M. (2000), *The persistent gap: New evidence on the Canadian gender wage gap*, Ottawa: Statistics Canada, Business and Labour Market Division.
Globe and Mail (2002), *It's True: Women are gaining ground in every job category*, Bruce Little, March 4, 2002.

Hewlett, S.A. (2002), *Creating a life: Professional women and the quest for children*, New York: Miramar Books.

Jafri, N. and Isbister, K. (2001), 'A decade of diversity', in Burke, R.J. and Nelson, D.L. (eds), *Advancing women's careers: Research and practice*, London: Blackwell Publishers, pp. 37-89.

Kinsley, M.J. (1993), 'A pragmatic approach to workplace equality', *Business and the Contemporary World*, **5**, 171-184.

Kolb, D.M. and Williams, J. (2000), *The shadow negotiation: How women can master the hidden agendas that determine bargaining success*, New York: Simon and Shuster.

Orser, B. (2000), *Creating high performance organizations: Leveraging women's leadership*, Ottawa: Conference Board of Canada.

Ragins, B.R., Townsend, B. and Mattis, M. (1998), 'Gender gap in the executive suite: CEOs and female executives report on breaking the glass ceiling', *Academy of Management Executive*, **12** (1), 28-42.

Spinks, N.L. and Tombari, N. (2001), 'Flexible work arrangements: A successful strategy for the advancement of women at the Royal Bank Financial Group', in Burke, R.J. and Nelson, D.L. (eds), *Advancing women's careers: Research and practice*, London: Blackwell Publishers, pp. 220-242.

Statistics Canada (2000), *Women in Canada 2000: A gender-based statistical report*, Ottawa: Statistics Canada.

Statistics Canada (1997), *Labour Force Historical Review*, Ottawa: Statistics Canada.

Tombari, N. and Spinks, N. (1999), 'The work/family interface at Royal Bank Financial Group: Successful solutions – a retrospective look at lessons learned', *Women in Management Review*, **14**, 186-193.

Totta, J. and Burke, R.J. (1995), 'Integrating diversity and equality into the fabric of the organization', *Women in Management Review*, **10**, 46-53.

Chapter 12

Women in Management in Mexico

Gina Zabludovsky

Introduction

As in other parts of the world, women in Mexico and the rest of Latin America have made impressive gains in both education and employment since 1970. In line with international trends, the rates for females in the work force have increased, as has the ratio of women to men in the economically active population.

Women's efforts to bring about change did not occur in a vacuum. As a result of the revolutionary changes the world has undergone, such as the globalization of markets for both capital and labour, technological and scientific development, better and faster communications, the second half of the twentieth century witnessed drastic shifts in the gender division of labour throughout the region. There have been changes in family composition and dynamics and an increased participation of women in the labour market of Latin America as a whole, resulting in the situation where one in five families is now headed by a woman (Brasileiro and Judd, 1996).

The growing insertion of women is reflected in every area of the economy, notably in education, which has begun to have a bearing in leadership positions worldwide. The following chapter is an analysis of women's participation in the Mexican labour force, the growing numbers of women pursuing education and the share women hold of leadership positions in the private and public sectors, as managers, officials, members of boards of directors and entrepreneurs. Finally, we will analyse some of the initiatives to support the advancement of women coming from the government and public sectors and from women's associations.

Labour force characteristics

The rise in women's participation in the Mexican labour force has been one of the fastest growing in Latin America, increasing from 20.6 per cent in 1970 to 35.2 per cent in 2000 in an economically active population of 39,633,842 in the latter year, comprised of 26,073,520 men and 12,560,000 women.

The aforementioned percentage is even higher in the urban areas of the country where women comprise 37.2 per cent of the total economically active population of 17,757,743. However, as shown in Table 12.1, over the last decade, this percentage has been steadily increasing.

Table 12.1   Male and female labour force (urban areas) in 1991, 1995, 1997 and 2000

	1991	1995	1997	2000
Men	65.5	64.0	63.0	62.8
Women	34.5	35.9	36.9	37.2
TOTAL	100.0	100.0	100.0	100.0

Source: Developed by Gina Zabludovsky, data from INEGI Encuesta Nacional de Empleo (National Employment Survey, urban areas) 1991, 1995, 1997 and 2000

Women have an especially important presence in such lines of business as restaurants and hotels (48.9 per cent), other services (49.5 per cent) and commerce and trade (42.9 per cent). In contrast, females have an extremely low participation in traditionally masculine sectors, such as construction (5.1 per cent), mining (5.9 per cent), transportation and related services (8.2 per cent) and agriculture and livestock (12.6 per cent) (see Table 12.2).

Table 12.2 Male and female labour force by industry categories

Industry categories	Men	Women
Agricultural and animal	87.6	12.5
Mining and quarry	94.1	5.9
Oil production & refining	75.9	24.1
Manufacturing	67.1	32.9
Electric power	82.1	17.9
Construction	94.9	5.1
Commerce	57.1	42.9
Hotels, restaurants	50.4	49.6
Transportation and services	91.9	8.12
Communications	69.8	30.2
Financial and business services	62.0	38.0
Other services	50.5	49.5
Public management	64.2	35.9
Non specified	74.0	26.0
TOTAL	62.8	37.2

Source: Developed by Gina Zabludovsky, data from INEGI Encuesta Nacional de Empleo (National Employment Survey, urban areas) 2000

Despite women's growing participation in the labour force, it is interesting to note that disparities still exist between the earnings of women and men. Table 12.3 shows that the percentage of women earning less than the minimum wage reaches 13.6 per cent, while the percentage of men at this income level is only 5.5 per cent. Among women earning the equivalent of one minimum wage up to twice this amount, the percentage is 32.4 per cent, while for men it is 26.8 per cent. In contrast, although 6.2 per cent of men earn the equivalent of 10 times the minimum wage, the number of women in this group is barely 2.5 per cent.

Table 12.3 Male and female labour force in relation to the minimum wage

Salary	Men	%	Women	%
Less than 1	656,980	5.5	971,246	13.6
1 to 2	3,232,492	26.8	2,314,086	32.4
More 2 to 3	2,946,070	24.4	1,399,653	19.6
More 3 to 5	2,420,422	20.1	1,043,905	14.6
More 5 to 10	1,398,985	11.6	584,995	8.2
More than 10	764,134	6.2	177,829	2.5
Without ingress	234,983	1.9	456,333	6.4
Non - specified	429,330	3.4	186,494	2.6
Total	12,065,396	100	7,134,541	100

Source: Developed by Gina Zabludovsky, data from INEGI Encuesta Nacional de Empleo (National Employment Survey, urban areas) 2000

Women pursuing education

On an international level, in the 1990s the percentage of women enrolled in higher education has exceeded that of men in many countries. In the last two decades, the numbers of women in university degree programmes have also risen in traditional male domains, such as science and technology (Avelar and Zabludovsky, 1996).

In Mexico, however, despite the significantly greater numbers of females now enrolled in higher education, the percentage of women still falls short of that of men. According to national statistics, the proportions of males and females among college graduates in the major cities are 54.6 per cent men and 45.4 per cent women (INEGI 2000-1). Nevertheless, it is also worthwhile to note that trends in higher education have changed significantly. If one examines 'freshers' and the returning classes of college students in the year 2000, we find that the index of difference between men and women has decreased, since 51.3 per cent of this population is male, while 48.72 per cent is female, a minimal 3 point difference (see Figure 12.1).

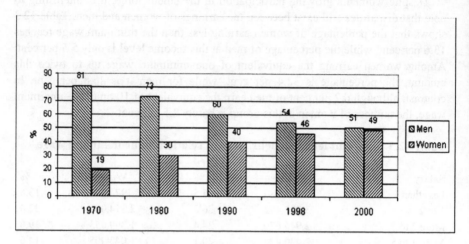

Figure 12.1   Men and women enrolled in higher education, 1970-2000

Source: Developed by Gina Zabludovsky, data from Anuarios Estadísticos de la ANUIES

These data indicate that the gap between the number of men and women in higher education is closing. Thus, for example, if we view the percentage distribution in higher education by sex starting as of 1970, significant changes can be observed, since the student population in that year was 19 per cent female, rising to 30 per cent in 1980, 40 per cent in 1990, 46 per cent in 1998 and 49 per cent in 2000.

The degree programme with the highest female population is Accounting (18.3 per cent of the total women university graduates for that year and 14.3 per cent of the total men); followed in second place by Business Administration (13.5 per cent of the women and 10.3 per cent of the men) and in third place by Law[1] (11.4 per cent of the women and 12.9 per cent of the men). Thus, it is interesting to note that the most important areas of study for women are those related to business administration.

Apart from the above-mentioned degree programmes, each of the others account for less than 5 per cent of the female student body. The fourth ranked degree programme for women is Psychology (4.8 per cent of the female population), closely followed by the MD programme (comprising 4.64 per cent of the total female population and 1.13 per cent of the total male). The fourth most popular degree programme for men is Industrial Engineering (5.3 per cent of the total male population vs. 2 per cent of the female population), a figure of some importance since very few women presently take a degree in this area. Therefore, despite the fact that women have entered the various fields of engineering, these areas do not yet constitute the most often selected degree programmes for females, so that neither industrial engineering, civil engineering nor mechanical engineering ranks in the list of the most popular degree programmes.

Women in management

As previously mentioned, the female component of the economically active population in the urban areas of Mexico is estimated at 37.2 per cent however, women only represent 24.6 per cent of the employment category considered by the Census Bureau which is stated to be officers and directors in the public and private sectors. Nevertheless, these data should not be taken at face value, since these echelons are comprised of pay levels which do not generally rank among the salaries paid to executives. If we include only those officers paid over ten times the minimum salary (the others could hardly be considered officers with any decision-making responsibility), the inequity becomes even more acute, since women comprise only 17.3 per cent of this group.

Although this percentage remains low, if we compare it to that of the economically active population, the data indicate that, as in the rest of the world, women account for a growing share of the positions of leadership, both in institutions and society at large. As Brasilerio and Judd (1996, p.3) indicated: 'An examination of the experience of women's leadership at all levels sheds light on the creation and functioning of new spaces for women's participation, in both private and public institutions'. In Mexico, a significant advance is evident in the presence of women holding officer positions over the last decade (in the private and public sectors), rising from 14.8 per cent in 1991, to 19.6 per cent in 1995 and to 24.6 per cent in 2000. This increase is also notable in the ranks of executives earning over ten times the minimum salary, in which women officers increased by 10 percentage points, from 7.1 per cent in 1991 to 17.3 per cent in 2000. This rise is especially relevant if we compare it to the general economically active population over the last 9 years, where the increased presence of women was much lower (around 2.7 per cent).

Another important point to consider is that the presence of women in officer and director positions varies with respect to different fields of activity. Thus, we note that of the total population of women holding officer and director positions, 46.9 per cent of them were in services (in contrast to 33.1 per cent of the men) and 20.4 per cent in commerce. In relation to the total amount of officers, the highest percentage of women officers (31.6 per cent) was in the services industry, while the lowest percentage of women officers (only 14.3 per cent) is in construction.

With respect to women's participation in national government and elected offices, information from 1999-2000 shows that in the public sector, women held 27 per cent of middle management positions. However, the number of women in directive positions decreases significantly, so that by the year 2000 women only held 14.3 per cent of the government minister and similar positions (INEGI, 2000-2). In relation to elected offices, based on data showing the composition of legislatures for the 2000-2003 period, women comprise 16 per cent of the seats in the chambers of representatives of the nation's federal and state governments. In the federal judicial branch women account for 36.1 per cent of a total of 4,790 middle and top management positions, while in the Supreme Court, women comprise 51.4 per cent of the 2,073 administrative officers. Nevertheless, there is only one woman among the eleven judges sitting on the Supreme Court (CONMUJER, 2000; INEGI, 2000-2).

The number of women in top management positions in private enterprise is even lower than in the government and in elected offices of the legislative branch. Recent data support previous research findings that women are more likely to hold directive level positions in the government and public sector, than in the private sector. The authors own analysis, based on the directories of the 500 largest companies in Mexico (Expansión, 2001), showed that in 2001, only four general directors (CDOs) were women (the equivalent of only 1 per cent of this echelon). If we consider the next 12 highest positions ranking below general directors (the directors of administration, merchandising, purchasing, distribution, finance, business, logistics, manufacturing, marketing, operations, human resources, information systems and traffic), we see that women represented 8.9 per cent of management positions in Mexico in 2001 (see Table 12.4).

Table 12.4 Top management positions (500 largest companies)

General Direction	% Men	% Women
CDO	99	1
Administration	94	6
Merchandising	93	7
Purchasing	85	15
Finance	92	8
Logistics	93	7
Manufacturing	98	2
Marketing	79	21
Operations	95	5
Human Resources	85	15
Information systems	95	5
Traffic	83	17
Sales	94	6
TOTAL	91	9

Source: Developed by Gina Zabludovsky, data from Expansión

If we compare these data with previous studies (Zabludovsky, 2001), we find that compared to 1994 (when women represented 5.9 per cent of directive positions), there has been a 3.1 per cent increase in women's participation at director level positions. However, the preceding should not be interpreted as comprising a trend towards an increasing number of women holding these positions, since data from 1997-1998 show that the percentage of women had already reached 10 per cent, so that in fact there has been a small decrease since then. The area where a growth trend does seem to exist is in the number of companies that have at least one women at the highest director positions, so that while in 1994 these companies comprised 24.2 per cent of the total companies among the top 500, the figure shot up to 40.6 per cent in 1998 and 52 per cent in 2001. Based on the preceding data it can be stated that, despite the fact that the percentage of women holding director positions has not grown significantly, a growing number of companies do have women in these top management echelons.

The 'vertical segregation' which we have been able to detect so far (meaning the presence of women in hierarchically lower level jobs) is tied to 'horizontal segregation' (women concentrated in certain fields and occupations). Thus, the data show that the highest presence of women as General Directors is in Marketing (21 per cent), Traffic (17 per cent), Human Resources (15 per cent) and Purchasing (15 per cent). The levels immediately below these, where women hold director positions, show a sharp drop, with an 8 per cent presence in Finance, 7 per cent in Merchandising and Logistics and only 1 per cent in Manufacturing.

Research also illustrated that there is an inverse correlation between the size of a company and the probability that executives in the upper management echelons will be women. Thus of the 63 per cent of the companies with women in top management positions none are included among the 250 largest companies in the nation (rather they place among those ranking from 251 to 500). In this regard, female executives' status in Mexico is similar to that of their counterparts in other countries. Some studies conducted in places a diverse as the United States, Argentina and Japan (e.g. Gallos, 1989; Heller, 1994; Steinfoff and Tanaka, 1995) have shown that women prefer to work for small organizations where there is less occupational segregation and where structures are less hierarchical and bureaucratic. In addition to the factors of the size of the company and the type of management job, the presence of women depends on the company's organizational structure. There is a greater chance that female executives will be found in companies having a less pyramidal and decentralized management model, one that provides opportunities for independence and flexibility.

As far as women on 'corporate boards are concerned', a review of the boards of directors of companies listed on the Mexican Stock Exchange (Bolsa Mexicana de Valores, 2000) showed that females have a significantly lower presence there than in other environments, since women represent only 3.1 per cent of total positions on the Boards of Directors. Moreover, no woman held the position of Chairman of the Board (in companies where they own stock) and only one woman was Vice President and one a Treasurer. The company accounting for the largest number of women (1 is the owner and 5 are alternate members of the board) was engaged in radio broadcasting and (as could be observed by the fact that several members of the board shared the same last name), this operation was a family-owned company. All of the other companies where several women sat on the Board of Directors also proved to be family companies. Nevertheless, the author has indicated in previous articles, the importance of women in family business in Mexico is not limited to major companies quoted on the stock exchange but also includes all sizes of women-owned business (Zabludovsky, 1998).

Women entrepreneurs

In addition to their participation in the work force as salaried employees, women in Mexico are also entering the ranks of remunerated work as independent owners of small businesses in Mexico. Women of all ages and economic levels are running their companies alone or with their husbands or other relatives (Grabinsky, 1996; Grabinsky and Zabludovsky, 2001).

With regard to entrepreneurship, women represent 31 per cent of the business owners of the country (including own-account workers and employers) (INEGI 2000-1). This figure has increased in recent years, so that while in 1991, the percentage of women was 25.3 per cent with respect to the total number of entrepreneurs, in 1995; it reached 28.4 per cent, increasing to 30.3 per cent in 2000.

However, due to the great differences between employers and own-account workers, for purposes of the different surveys that we have conducted in the country, we have considered women entrepreneurs to be comprised solely of those women business owners who are employers, meaning that they hire at least one employee apart from themselves. This definition coincides with that adopted in Mexico's statistical instruments and allows us to make adequate comparisons. Under this definition, women comprise 17 per cent of the total number of business owners. The percentage of women employers has also shown a gradual increase in recent years, rising from 13.6 per cent in 1991, to 15 per cent in 1997, to 17 per cent in 2000 as illustrated in Figure 12.2.

Women entrepreneurs in Mexico are particularly important as the owners and directors of micro businesses, which is the size that accounts for the largest number of businesses in Mexico. According to national statistics, 80 per cent of entrepreneurs (men and women) employ up to 5 persons. However, this figure is higher among women than among men. Based on data from 2000, whereas 75 per cent of men employers hire up to 5 persons, among women the percentage increases to 83 per cent. As the number of employees increases in a company, the probability of finding women employers decreases. In firms employing 16 or more workers the presence of women entrepreneurs drops to 1.5 per cent. This situation was also confirmed by other kinds of studies we have conducted in various years (Zabludovsky, 1994; Zabludovsky in collaboration with NFWBO, 1998). Thus we can conclude that, as has occurred in other countries women-owned firms in Mexico are predominantly micro businesses. However it is also true that, in line with world trends, women entrepreneurs in Mexico have also grown in employment terms in recent years, with a larger presence in small and medium-sized businesses (Carter in collaboration with NFWBO, 2001; Zabludovsky 2002).

In relation to the different sectors of activity, the percentage of women entrepreneurs shows sharp variations in relation to different types of business. In 2000, the highest rate of women entrepreneurs compared to men was found in hotels, restaurants and similar areas (where they comprise 42 per cent), followed by commerce (24 per cent) and other services (19 per cent). In contrast, there were very few women entrepreneurs in such areas as mining and construction[2]. These data confirm previous studies where similar trends were detected (see for example the study of women business owners in the United Kingdom by Carter and Anderson (2001)).

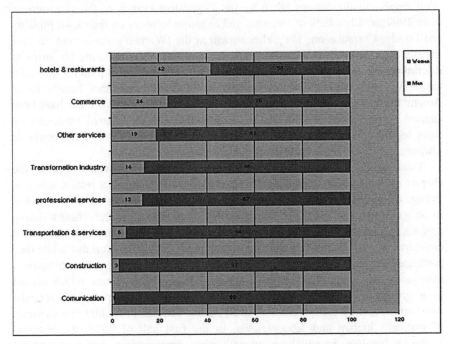

Figure 12.2   Male and female employers by industry categories

Source: Developed by Gina Zabludovsky, data from Encuesta Nacional de Empleo (National Employment Survey, urban areas) 2000

However, recent data also show that women-owned businesses are becoming increasingly diversified. The presence of women is no longer restricted to traditional sectors. There are many activities in which the percentage of women approaches 17 per cent, which is their representation in the total number of businesses in the metropolitan areas (Zabludovsky, 2002). Currently, more women are involved in a wider variety of sectors, including such industrial activities as durable manufacturing, a field where very few women were active up to just a few years ago. Our previous studies show that there is an increasing participation of women in manufacturing. In the transformation industry the presence of women grew from 8 per cent in 1997 to 14 per cent in 2000. Another fact of importance is that as of March 2002, the National Chamber of the Transformation Industry was headed by a women, which was an unprecedented event in the country, since every chamber and business organization had been presided over by men.

Country legislation supporting women in the workforce

With respect to the actions taken by the Legislative branch of the government, since 1997 the Chambers of Deputies and Senators have set up their own Equality and Gender Commission. They also organized the 'Women's Parliament' to give impetus to a national legislative agenda to contribute to eliminating all forms of discrimination against the female sex and promote government policies that fully ensure women's rights and the application of programmes that benefit them. Among the legislative results of these actions, various laws and decrees have been enacted corresponding to the Beijing Action Plan and are centred especially on ways to prevent and prosecute acts of violence against women (Parlamento de Mujeres, 1998; PRONAM, 2000).

There have been no changes to the Federal Labour Law with respect to the chapter on women for several decades and the law now in effect relates solely to matters of pregnancy, maternity and breast-feeding. These laws forbid companies to oblige women to carry out activities that could endanger their health during pregnancy and grant a six-week leave prior to and another six-week leave after childbirth, as well as two extraordinary rest periods during the workday while they are breast feeding. In practice, to avoid granting these benefits, some companies have resorted to pregnancy tests as a requirement for hiring women, which has led to a growing number of protests and campaigns in the press by feminist associations and by the government itself stating that this procedure is a violation of women's human and labour rights. In the first half of 2002, the National Women's Institute, in collaboration with other organizations, has proposed the drafting of bills to amend the Labour Law and allow, among others, the incorporation of measures against sexual harassment and job discrimination. These proposals, however, are still at the drawing board stage (Ley Federal del Trabajo, 1996; INMUJER, 2000-2).

Initiatives supporting women in the workforce

On a government level, the awareness of the importance of promoting the advancement of women is largely the result of the agenda and effects of the world conferences on women, since in 1975 Mexico was the host country of the World Conference of the International Women's Year. Five years later (1980), the first government programme specifically oriented to integrating women into development was implemented and subsequently (1985) a commission was created to coordinate the activities organized in Mexico in relation to the country's participation in the Second World Conference on Women held in Nairobi. However, these programmes established extremely limited objectives and scopes of operation, since the commission was placed under the National Population Council (of the Programa Nacional de la Mujer). For the Fourth Women's Conference in Beijing in 1995, a National Coordinating Committee was created to present Mexico's platform, the organization of which would lead to the establishment and implementation of the National Women's Programme, PRONAM, and the National Women's Commission (set up as a decentralized administrative agency within the Secretary of the Interior). The purpose of this committee was to coordinate initiatives oriented to the advancement of women and the elimination of obstacles to their participation in every area and level of the social order. However, from the standpoint of the administrative organization of the federal government, this programme was clearly much more advanced than the earlier ones. It continued to operate within the Secretary of the Interior but was not assigned a significant budget until 2001, when the National Institute of Women was created as an autonomous decentralized government agency, with its own legal status and funding (PRONAM, 1999; Senado de la República, 2000; INMUJER, 2002-2).

With respect to the government budget allocated to gender affairs, very little has been achieved outside health issues, although some programmes for education and the alleviation of poverty have been set up, such as PROGRESA, which contributes to reversing the trend of girls' higher rate of school drop-out of school than boys' by granting females slightly larger scholarships than males. Others areas of the government have recently started up actions to consolidate and extend the scope of technical and financial aid to develop technological and managerial skills in micro, small and medium-sized businesses, where, as we have seen, women have a very significant presence (Senado de la República, 2000). In 1998 a programme was implemented, in coordination with the *International Labor Organization*, entitled 'More and Better Jobs for Women', the objectives of which were to promote micro businesses and establish an inter government ministry organization to achieve common goals. It should also be noted that some of the programmes started up by the development banking institution, NAFINSA, provided credit opportunities, business development courses and other types of support aimed specifically at micro, small and medium-sized business, including a trust and a credit union to support some groups of women micro entrepreneurs. Other international organizations, such as the Women's Bank, have also established programmes in Mexico. Nevertheless, despite the fact that these measures are commendable, they have had an extremely limited scope and the population that benefited from them has been minimal.

In relation to the measures implemented by the private sector for business leadership positions, in general terms, the companies operating in Mexico have not taken any specific steps to incorporate and advance the careers of women in management positions and consider that they have no responsibilities in this area. In a previous study, the author found that in 1999 only two important companies (Motorola and IBM) had implemented diversity programmes to prompt the hiring of women and promoting them to higher positions, through programmes to balance family and work responsibilities and different mentorship and leadership development programmes (Zabludovsky, 2001).

In view of the very small number of initiatives implemented by government agencies and private corporations, one of the most significant changes in recent years has been the growing importance of women's organizations and particularly the fact that women business owners and executives are striving to establish support networks and enhance the level of education and relationship networks among their members. Thus, the Association of Women Executives was founded in 2000, with the backing of Motorola, to carry out various projects. The aim of the association is to promote the professional development of women executives and facilitate their entry into top managerial positions. The members meet at least once a month to discuss various topics.

Female business owners have several worldwide women's organizations, that are represented in Mexico. One is the Association of Women Company Heads (AMMJE, an affiliate of Femmes Chefs D'Entreprises). Some of the association's objectives are: to promote the exchange of information, experience and knowledge; contribute to the development of professional skills through conferences, seminars and workshops; extend the communications and support networks; offer assessment in the legal, trade and promotional areas and create financial instruments such as the Credit Union and foster the development of its women business owner members. Although the organization's membership remains small, AMMJE has grown significantly in recent years, from eight city chapters in 1998 to twenty-two at present, while the membership base of 400 in 1998 has increased to 1,500 in 2002. One of the AMMJE's activities is the holding of national and international congresses. The latest world congress held by the Femme Chefs D'Entreprises took place in Mexico City in January 2002, attended by the President of Mexico and other important figures.

Women's participation in business was evident in other international events. In March 1999, the FIDE Congress (International Federation of Hispanic Women Entrepreneurs or Federación Internacional de Mujeres Empresarias Hispánicas) was held in Mexico for the first time, in the port city of Acapulco. Federal and state governments and private organizations provided support in organizing this congress, particularly the Association of Women Entrepreneurs of Guerrero, an independent organization, as well as representatives of Nacional Financiera, the development banking institution. FIDE held its following congress in the city of Mérida, Yucatán.

Another international association active in Mexico is the National Federation of Women's Professional and Business Clubs, some of the objectives of which are to promote the interests of its members and coordinate the activities of the member organizations. Women also belong to specific business owner organizations, such as the Mexico City Chamber of Commerce and the National Chamber of the Manufacturing Industry (CANACINTRA).

Also, since 1997, women's associations have been founded within important business chambers. One is the membership of women from the State of Mexico in the Employers Confederation of Chambers of the Mexican Republic (COPARMEX) and the Women Industrialists of the CANACINTRA that held a national meeting in the first half of 1998. Since then, several national congresses have been held in different Mexican cities, directed by various associations.

Although it is difficult to evaluate and foresee what the future holds for these organizations, it is clear that the steps already taken point to the possible consolidation of forces among women's organizations, in order to achieve an ever growing presence, not only in the economy but also in the arena of social and political participation. With respect to training programmes specifically directed towards women in decision-making positions, as of the second half of the 1990s, various associations have begun to implement courses in this area, such as the Diploma Course for Women's Leadership that has been taught since 1998 in the 'Instituto Tecnológico Autónomo de México' and in the 'Centro de Liderazgo de la Mujer' (Women's Leadership Center or CELIM). The objectives of this programme are to 'develop leadership, strategic and management skills in women' which comprises part of CELIM's activities and objectives, an organization founded and supported by the directors and members of the Mexican Association of Women Entrepreneurs (AMMJE). As of 1998, another leadership training programme for women got underway at the Universidad del Valle de México. This project was developed by the women business owners of COPARMEX.

Other training programmes have also been developed recently in civil associations acting independently from government programmes and women's entrepreneurs organizations, such as the Simone de Beauvoir Institute for Women's Leadership, created as a civil association for the purpose of providing women with the 'theoretical-conceptual tools that allow them to review and restate traditional leadership models on different bases and contribute to generating social leadership permeated with gender viewpoints' in public and private environments. To meet these objectives, the institute has four axes: 'information and knowledge', 'subjectivity', 'image' and 'advocacy' (Simone de Beauvoir Publicity Bulletin).

The initiatives carried out by these latter associations are most interesting and will play an important role in the future, however at present, since they have just recently been founded, it is still difficult to evaluate their impact.

The future

As this chapter shows, Mexican women are playing a larger role in the economy outside the home, as well as in the educational sphere. Increasing numbers of women are enrolled in the professional schools of universities and significantly more women have come to hold officer positions in companies over the last decade (a 10 per cent growth). The data indicate that the future outlook for females is more promising, not solely due to their increased participation in top management positions, but also as a result of the founding and consolidation of government organizations and associations for women. These organizations seek to promote and achieve a more visible role for them in decision-making areas, provide the training and skills required for the development of women in leadership positions and generate awareness of the importance of furthering the well-being of women and eliminating the various types of discrimination.

However, despite the advances attained, much still remains to be done in the achievement of gender equality. We have noted significant disparities in Mexico with respect to the earning power of men and women and, at the decision-making levels, women clearly account for only a small percentage of this echelon: from 14 per cent to 18 per cent of top management positions, depending on the areas involved; 14.3 per cent of government ministers and similar positions; 16 per cent of the seats in chambers of representatives; 17 per cent of public and private officers (at the earnings level equivalent to 10 times the minimum salary); 18 per cent of women entrepreneurs-employers. When considering women's participation in top positions of major corporations, the percentage of females is even lower, only 9 per cent and the respective figure drops even more drastically in relation to their numbers on the boards of directors of companies listed on the stock exchange, a scant 3.5 per cent, a figure comparable to the number of women mayors, in the political arena.

Therefore, it is imperative to establish links between the developing women's associations, government representatives, the academic world, labour unions, employers' organizations (governmental, private, academic, representatives from the media and the community) to build awareness of the topic, bring down the remaining barriers and promote the role of women in positions of leadership.

Many actions could be implemented to achieve these ends. Among others, there are the following: perfect the database on women in economic decision-making; build public awareness of individual organizational and institutional behaviour which hinder women's advancement to decision-making positions in government; promote the entry of women into non-traditional careers; create enforcement mechanisms as a means of eliminating barriers to women's advancement to decision-making positions and advocate the position that value diversity in leadership ranks as a strategy for sustainable growth and as a benefit for organizational performance.

It would also be important to be in a position to monitor policies and practices to fill vacancies at decision-making levels; to strengthen leadership training institutes for women in business and government as well as the Equity and Gender units now existing in the Chamber of Deputies and the Labour Ministry; and women's presence in employers' associations.

The preceding proposals comprise just a few examples of the array of actions that must be implemented to achieve the advancement of women in directive positions. However, the success of these actions, in the end, depends on ensuring that governments, as well as corporations and society at large, become conscious of the fact that the full utilization of the talent pool represented by women is a prerequisite for organizations in their endeavours to maintain sustained, human-centred development and achieve a competitive edge in local and global marketplaces.

References

Avelar, S. and Zabludovsky, G. (1996), 'Women's Leadership and Glass Ceiling Barriers in Brazil and Mexico' in *Women's Leadership in a Changing World,* New York: UNIFEM, pp. 31-41.

ANUIES (2000), *Anuario Estadìstico*, México, D. F.

Brasileiro, A.M. and Judd, K. (1996), Introduction, *Women's Leadership in a Changing World*, New York: UNIFEM.

Bolsa Mexicana de Valores (2000), *Annual, Financial Facts and Figures*, México. D.F.

Carter, S. and Anderson, S. (2001), in collaboration with NFWBO, *Women and Men Business Owners in the United Kingdom,* Underwritten by IBM, NFWBO, Washington, D.C.

CONMUJER (2000), *Plataforma de Acción* , Pekìn+5, México, D.F.

EXPANSION (2001), *Las 500 Empresas más importantes de México*, México, D.F.

Fielden, S., Davidson M.J., Gale, A. and Davey, C.L. 'Women , equality and construction' in *The Journal of Management Development, Developing Women in Managers*, Burke, R. and Nelson, D. (eds), Emerald Library, Cambridge, Mass.

Gallos (1989), *Exploring Women's Development: Implications for Career Theory, Practice and Research*, Cambridge University Press, UK.

Grabinsky, S. (1996), 'Crisis in Mexico: its effects in family owned business', *Journal of Entrepreneurship Culture* **4** (3).

Grabinsky, S. and Zabludovsky, G. (2001), *Mujeres, Empresas y Familias,* Del Verbo Emprender, México, D.F.

Heller, L. (1994), *Relaciones asiméricas entre hombres y mujers en las organizaciones*, Buenos Aires, Argentina, 1994, mimeo.

INEGI (1991), *Encuesta Nacional de Empleo*, México, D.F.

INEGI (1995), *Encuesta Nacional de Empleo,* México, D.F.

INEGI (1997), *Encuesta Nacional de Empleo*, México, D.F.

INEGI (2000-1), *Encuesta Nacional de Empleo*, México, D.F.

INEGI (2000-2), *Hombres y Mujeres en México*, México, D.F.

INMUJER (2002-1), *Propuestas del Instituto Nacional de las Mujeres para incorporar la Perspectiva de Género en la Modernización de la Ley Laboral*, México, D.F.

INMUJER (2002-2), *Proequidad*, México, D.F.

Ley Federal del Trabajo Actualizada (1996), McGraw-Hill, México, D.F.

Parlamento de Mujeres (1998), *Parlamento de Mujeres de México*, México, 2000.

PRONAM (1999), *Alianza para la Igualdad, Informe de Avances de Ejecución*, México, D.F.

Senado de la República (2000), *Agenda de Género de la Legislación Federal 1995-2000*, México, D.F.

Steinfoff, P. and Tanaka, K. (1994), 'Women Managers in Japan', in *Competitive Frontiers, Women Managers in a Global Economy*, Adler, L.N. and Izraeli, D., Cambridge, Mass: Blackwell Publishers.

UNIFEM-CONMUJER (1999), *El enfoque de género en la produccion de Estadísticas Educativas en México*, Serie Estadísticas de Género, México, D.F.

Zabludovsky, G. (1994), *Presencia de la mujer empresaria en México*, Documento de Trabajo, CIDE, México.

Zabludovsky, G. in collaboration with NFWBO (1998), *Women Business Owners in Mexico, an Emerging Economic Force*, UNAM-IBM, México, D.F.

Zabludovsky, G. (2001), 'Women managers and diversity programs in Mexico', *The Journal of Management Development, Developing Women in Management*, R. J. Burke and D. L. Nelson (eds), **20** (4), UK: MBC University Press.

Zabludovsky, G. (2001-2), 'Ejecutivas en México' en Zabludovsky y Avelar, *Empresarias y Ejecutivas en México y Brasil*, UNAM México, D.F.

Zabludovksy, G. (2002), 'Trends in women's participation in Mexican Business', *Journal of Entrepreneurship and Innovation*, UK.

Notes

1 The areas graduating the largest number of students are Accounting, Law and Business Administration. These three areas alone comprise 40.44 per cent of the entire student body (for both men and women).
2 Studies in other countries have also found that the construction industry is the most male-dominated of all industries (see Fielden, Davidson, Gale and Davey, 2001).

Chapter 13

Women in Management in the USA

Debra L. Nelson and Susan Michie

Introduction

Our aim in this chapter is to present a portrait of women managers in the United States. There is considerable diversity within the group, and the picture we present shows both encouraging progress and formidable challenges. We begin by profiling the U.S. workforce and showing trends in education. We then turn to two groups of particular interest, women managers and women entrepreneurs, to examine the progress that has been made. Next, we describe the legislation and initiatives that target women managers. We conclude with a look at women's entry into non-traditional careers as a focus of future attention.

Labour force characteristics

The proportion of women in the U.S. labour force climbed steadily throughout the 20th century, but seems to have levelled off between 1990 and 2000 (see Figure 13.1). Women's share of the labour force reached 46 per cent in 1994 and has remained close to this level (Women's Bureau, 2000a). In contrast, the rates for men have steadily declined except at the older ages. Older men are almost twice as likely as older women to be in the civilian labour force. Among those individuals age 65 and over, the ratio of men working in executive, administrative and managerial occupations is 50 per cent higher than the ratio of women in similar positions (U.S. Census Bureau, 2000). Working women in the 65 and over age group tend to hold administrative support jobs, and they have a higher poverty rate than older men (11.8 per cent versus 6.9 per cent). This situation serves as a stark reminder of the past under-representation of women in management, and emphasizes the importance of the gains they have made in recent decades.

Men's labour force participation by age appears as an inverted 'bowl', rising through the prime working years of 25-44 and then slowly declining. Historically, women's labour force participation by age was represented by an 'M' curve. Women would enter the labour force, leave to care for their families, and then return to work later in life. By the early 1980s, the 'M' curve for women had virtually disappeared, and women's labour force participation by age became an inverted 'bowl' similar to that of their male counterparts (Women's Bureau, 2000a).

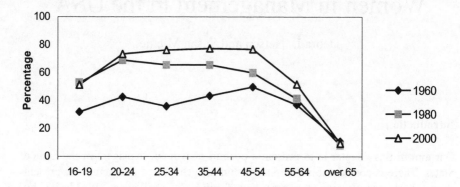

Figure 13.1 Labour force percentage participation rates for women, 1960-2000

Source: U.S. Dept. of Labor, Monthly Labor Review, *Labor Force Participation*, December 1999, and *Labor Force Projections to 2010*, November 2001

Several factors contributed to reshaping labour force participation for women over the past two decades. Family make-up has changed significantly in the U.S. in recent years. An increasing number of women are choosing not to have children. The proportion of women 40-44 years of age without children steadily increased during the 1980s and 1990s and now stands at almost 20 per cent. In addition, the per centage of married couple families is decreasing, while households headed by single women are on the rise. In fact, as illustrated in Table 13.1, working mothers accounted for much of the increase in women's overall labour force rates in recent years, and the older the children, the more likely women will participate.

Table 13.1 Labour force percentage participation rates of mothers by children's age group

Age of children	Mother's participation rate
14 – 17	78.9
6 – 13	78.3
Under age 6	64.4
Under age 3	60.7

Source: U.S. Dept. of Labor, Bureau of Labor Statistics, *Facts on working women*, March 2000

Although labour force participation for all female minority groups has increased substantially since 1980, participation rates for Black women surpassed all others during the 1990s. Higher education levels and the upsurge of new businesses owned by Black women account for some of the rate increase. Welfare reform in the mid 1990s and lower labour force attachment for young black males may also have contributed to the rise of black women in the labour force (Murray, 1999). In 1998, single black women maintained 47 per cent of black families (Women's Bureau, 2000b) (see Table 13.2).

Table 13.2 Labour force percentage participation rates for women and men by race, 1988-2000

	Women					Men				
Year	Total	Black	White	Asian & Other	Hispanic	Total	Black	White	Asian & Other	Hispanic
1980	51.5	53.2	51.2	55.4	47.4	77.4	70.6	78.2	74.5	81.4
1990	57.5	58.3	57.4	57.4	53.1	76.4	71.1	77.1	74.9	81.4
2000	60.2	63.2	59.8	58.9	56.9	74.7	69.0	75.4	74.9	80.6

Source: U.S. Dept. of Labor, Monthly Labor Review, *Labor force projections to 2010*, November 2001

One in five Americans has a disability, and more than half of them are women. During the 1980s, the proportion of women with work disabilities in the U.S. labour force rose from 23.5 per cent in 1981 to 27.5 per cent in 1988 (Women's Bureau, 1992), but seems to have levelled off in the 1990s, with 28.5 per cent of disabled women working or looking for work in 1998. In comparison to men, more women with disabilities are employed in service, managerial, or professional occupations (Jans and Stoddard, 1999).

Employment in the public sector has declined for both women and men since 1980. The declines were especially pronounced for Black and Hispanic workers. Still, in 1998 almost one in five of all women, and 22 per cent of Black women held a public job (Bernhardt, Dresser and Hill, 2000). Though many believe the public sector provides better access to professional and managerial occupations for women, Bernhardt et al. (2000) found that if teachers are separated from other professional and managerial occupations, the public sector does not appear to provide greater opportunity for women.

Though women's participation in the work force has increased substantially in recent years, the occupations women hold, and the areas of work they manage, have remained fairly constant. More women are employed as teachers (excluding post secondary), secretaries, cashiers, and managers over female employees than in any other areas of work (Women's Bureau, 2000b).

Women pursuing education

Educational attainment is a strong and reliable predictor of labour force participation. Generally, the higher the level of education, the more likely a women will be in the labour force. Women have made considerable progress in attaining post secondary degrees. In each year since the early 1980s, women earned more than half of all bachelor's degrees, and by the 1999-2000 academic year, they were attaining a record 57 per cent (NCES, 2001). However, women still earn considerably less than half of bachelor's degrees in technology-related fields where job demand is the highest, such as, physical sciences (40 per cent), computer and information sciences (28 per cent), and engineering (20 per cent).

Women have made progress at the graduate level as well. In 1999-2000 women were awarded 58 per cent of master's degrees, but the most substantial gains for women in education are at the doctoral level. Women earned 44 per cent of all degrees in 1999-2000, compared to 14 per cent in the early 1970s. The type of doctoral degrees earned by women ranged from 15 per cent in engineering to 67 per cent in psychology. Since 1980, women have obtained an increasing per centage of many professional degrees, for example, law (46 per cent), medicine (43 per cent), pharmacology (66 per cent), veterinary medicine (69 per cent) and optometry (53 per cent). Over 50 per cent of all professionals are women, but the largest occupational group of women remains the 4.4 million teachers who make up nearly 40 per cent of all women with professional degrees (Women's Bureau, 2000a).

Women in management

The advancement of women in management in the U.S. has, in some respects, been encouraging. In 1900, only 4.4 per cent of managers were women. By 1999, 45 per cent of the 19.6 million managers in the U.S. were women, a ten-fold increase. As with women professionals, women managers tend to gravitate towards certain specialties. These include medicine and health care, human resources, education, and management-related occupations, such as underwriters and accountants. In 1999, 32.3 per cent of all employed women were managers or professionals, compared to 28.6 per cent of employed men (Women's Bureau, 2000a).

While the overall number of women managers is on the rise, the progress of women managers into top-level positions has been quite slow. Among the Fortune 500 companies, only 12.5 per cent of the corporate officers are women. Of these top-level women executives, very few occupy the positions of chief executive officer, president, chief operating officer, or executive vice-president (Catalyst, 2000a). While 83 companies had women corporate officers who were top earners, overall women represented only 4.1 per cent of all top earners in 2000. Among top-level managers, line corporate officers with profit-and-loss or direct client responsibility hold the most decision-making power. Managers in staff positions provide support to the line operations, and hence are less influential. Men hold 92.7 per cent of all line officer jobs (Catalyst, 2000a), while the majority of female corporate officers are in staff roles, such as human resources and public relations. Because these jobs do not make or break the bottom line, they rarely, if ever, lead to the top CEO position. Among the Fortune 1500, 95 to 97 per cent of jobs that are vice-president level and above are held by men.

Women's representation on corporate boards of directors is slowly increasing. In 2001, 87 per cent of the Fortune 500 companies had at least one woman director. The per centage of board seats held by women in the Fortune 500 is 12.4, a slight increase (from 11.2 per cent) over 1999. Among the Fortune 1000 companies, women hold 10.9 per cent of all board seats, and 74 per cent of these companies have at least one woman director. Women of colour hold only 2 per cent of board seats (Catalyst, 2001a).

Women are also making strides in elected offices in U.S. government. In 2001, women held 73 of the 535 seats in the 107th U.S. Congress – 13, or 13.0 per cent of the 100 seats in the Senate, and 60, or 13.8 per cent of the 435 seats in the House of Representatives. In addition, two women serve as Delegates to the House from the Virgin Islands and Washington, DC. In 1981, women held only 4 per cent of seats in the U.S. Congress, and only 6 per cent in 1991 (CAWP, 2001). Adler (1999) noted that while corporate and political leadership are not the same, both types of leadership involve well-defined, elite role-based positions that affect societies' well-being and success.

This data represents progress for women in management, albeit slow. Societal forces played a clear role in women's advancement over the past two decades (Burke and Nelson, 2002). By steadily increasing their education levels, women became more attractive candidates for managerial jobs. Lower birth rates led to fewer candidates for all jobs (Powell, 1999). Changes in gender role expectations made it more acceptable for women to work, and to develop long-term career commitment. The presence of more women in managerial jobs provided mentors and role models to encourage women at lower levels of the organization. In addition, equal opportunity and affirmative action legislation led to organizational initiatives aimed at advancing women in management.

The data also reveals that formidable barriers to women's advancement remain. The glass ceiling, an invisible barrier that prevents women from rising into top-level management in organizations, remains intact with only a few women able to shatter the barrier (Nelson and Burke, 2000). Glass walls still isolate women in staff/support roles, and inhibit their movement into more powerful line management positions. These barriers persist for several reasons. Chief among them are structural discrimination in organizations that allows individual discrimination by the majority toward the minority. 'Good managers' are associated with male or masculine characteristics (especially by men). Women managers are often deemed as less competent, active, emotionally stable, independent, and rational than male managers (Heilman, et al., 1995). Because women live and work in a society that is patriarchal in nature, sex stereotyping often prevails in managerial jobs. Common organizational practices that perpetuate discrimination include lack of developmental opportunities for women, appraisal and compensation systems that favour men, and the failure to hold managers responsible for advancing women (Nelson and Burke, 2000). Companies have focused on moving women into management, but not on grooming them to become leaders (Conlin and Zellner, 1999).

Many advantages can be gleaned when women take on leadership roles in the U.S. Women lead in ways that are relational, inclusive, and transformational. Rosener (1990) examined the leadership styles of women in medium-sized, non-traditional organizations. Her interview data revealed that women and men describe their leadership styles and influence tactics very differently. Women's styles evolve naturally from feminine characteristics, and are centred on four themes: consensus building/power sharing, win-win solutions in conflict management, building a supportive climate, and promoting diversity. Rosener also noted that women are more likely than men to make subordinates feel important, included and energized. Hampden-Turner (1994) argued that American women's value systems are more in synch with other cultures, internationally, than are the values of American men. Therefore, advancing women in U.S. organizations should serve the country well in international business.

Women entrepreneurs

One of the notable trends among women in management in the U.S. is their increased participation in entrepreneurial ventures. Between 1992 and 1997, the number of majority-held (51 per cent), women-owned businesses increased by 16 per cent compared to 6 per cent for all U.S. firms, and women-owned companies totalled approximately 5 million in 1997 constituting 25 per cent of entrepreneurs (U.S. Census Bureau, 2001) (see Figure 13.2).

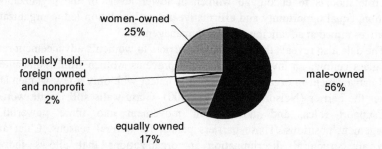

Figure 13.2 Percentage distribution of all U.S. firms by gender of ownership, 1997

Source: U.S. Census Board (2001), Census Brief: Survey of Women-Owned Business Enterprises, Washington DC: CENBR/01-6

This trend is expected to continue. Between 1997 and 2002, women-owned businesses are projected to grow 14 per cent compared to 7 per cent nationwide, and sales revenues will increase by 40 per cent. By 2002, 6.2 million women-owned businesses in the U.S. will employ more than 9.2 million people (up 30 per cent from 1997), and generate more that $1.15 trillion in sales (Center for WBR, 2001c). This growth points to the substantial economic impact of women-owned businesses. While almost half of these women-owned firms are located in major metropolitan areas, women entrepreneurs are represented in all 50 states, with the fastest growth rates occurring in smaller states without a major metropolitan centre.

Women-owned firms in the U.S. are heavily concentrated within the service sector. This sector encompasses not only business and engineering services, but also professions such as accounting, medicine, and law. There are also indications that women entrepreneurs are moving into non-traditional industries, such as construction, agricultural services, transportation, and communication, among others (Center for WBR, 2001b). Since 1992, sales for women-owned businesses in agricultural services and construction have increased by close to 100 per cent.

One question of interest is whether today's women entrepreneurs are similar to, or different from their predecessors. Labelled as 'traditionals', early women entrepreneurs identified with traditional female roles and work values. Their enterprises were small sole proprietorships with slow growth. The second generation of women entrepreneurs or 'moderns' emerged in the 1980s, and displayed values more similar to male entrepreneurs. They headed corporations rather than sole proprietorships, and were more growth-oriented (Moore, 1999). Studies indicate that the 'new generation' of female business owners (those who started their companies within the past decade) are focusing on growth and expansion, and are achieving success faster than their female predecessors. In this respect, women entrepreneurs are growing more similar to their male counterparts, and they are narrowing the revenue gap (Center for WBR, 2001b). Among businesses started within the past decade, research indicates no gender gap in firms with $500,000 or more in revenues.

'New generation' women entrepreneurs are more educated, and have more previous management experience, than the women who started their businesses 20 or more years ago. They are also more likely to start a venture that is related to their previous career, which increases the probability of success for the new business.

Businesses owned by women of colour are growing in number at rates exceeding all women-owned firms and the national average (Center for WBR, 2001a). Approximately one in every five woman-owned firms is headed by a minority. Afro-American women are the fastest growing minority segment, but Hispanic women represent the largest group by heading over 470,000 firms. By 2002, 1.2 million businesses will be owned by women of colour, with 822,000 employees and over $100 billion in sales. Greater participation in entrepreneurship by women from a wide variety of backgrounds is increasing diversity among women business owners.

Beginning in the late 1980s, a growing number of women left organizational jobs to become entrepreneurs. Many factors may have contributed to these departures. Glass ceilings, glass walls, and outright discrimination make entrepreneurship an attractive alternative to corporate life for some women. Desire for autonomy, flexibility, independence, and increased income are cited by both women and men as reasons for starting their own businesses (Moore, 2002). Interestingly, money is not the most important driving force for entrepreneurs of either gender. For women, a primary motive for starting a business is to 'do the work they wanted to do' (Srinivasan et al., 1994).

'Corporate climbers' are one group of women who leave corporate America to become entrepreneurs (Moore and Buttner, 1997). These women had aspirations to become top-level managers in large organizations, but became disillusioned with corporate life and the barriers to women's progress. Among women business owners, corporate climbers are a smaller group in comparison to 'intentional entrepreneurs' who join corporations for different reasons. Intentional entrepreneurs have lifelong ambitions of owning their businesses, and take corporate jobs to gain experience that will later help them to become successful business owners. Whether they are labelled as corporate climbers or intentional entrepreneurs, similar experiences caused these women to leave their organizations. Restructuring, reorganization, and other organizational barriers, such as inhospitable corporate cultures, left many women with few opportunities for advancement.

Much of the research on men and women entrepreneurs has emphasized their similarities. One gender difference among entrepreneurs concerns the career paths they follow to business ownership. Among fast-growing firms, men owners are more likely to have executive-level experience, while women owners are more likely to come from a profession (Center for WBR, 2001b). More men than women have owned another business prior to their fast-growth firm. Women owners are less likely than men to have a mentor, but more likely to seek counsel from outside sources on business issues. Typically, the outside source is an accountant, family member, or other entrepreneur.

Another important difference between men and women entrepreneurs has emerged from research concerning work and family issues. Women, more so than men, elect to become entrepreneurs in order to balance work and family life (Cheskin, 2000). Independence and flexibility may allow entrepreneurial women to better meet family demands, despite the stressors they face in the struggle for business success, such as demanding work schedules, and the financial and personal risks inherent in business ownership. Given the challenging economic conditions for families in the U.S., and the continuing barriers to women's advancement, entrepreneurial life will remain a viable option for women in management.

Country legislation supporting women in the work orce

The passage of the 19th amendment to the Constitution of the United States in 1920 granted women the right to vote. This single act of legislation provided the precedent for other laws aimed at improving the conditions of women, but substantial changes for working women did not occur until the 1960s.

Equal Pay Act of 1963

In 1960 women in the U.S. earned approximately 60 cents for every dollar earned by men. The Equal Pay Act of 1963 required that men and women be paid equal wages for equal work. However, the law applied only to situations where women and men were employed in the same, or very similar jobs. It did nothing to remedy the low pay of women in 'female occupations' that rarely employ men. The law also did not apply to situations where male and female jobs were essentially different, but required similar levels of skill, effort, and responsibility. Though the gender pay gap has been narrowing slowly since 1973, today women still earn only 77 cents for every dollar earned by men in the U.S. (Women's Bureau 2000b).

Title VII of the Civil Rights Act of 1964

This act included a chapter subdivision called Title VII that prohibited employment discrimination on account of race, creed, national origin, or sex, and provided women with a powerful tool for challenging employment inequalities. Some of the earliest casualties under Title VII were state laws created to 'protect' working women (Cushman, 2001). Various laws banned night work for women, limited the number of hours they could work, or the amount of weight they could lift on the job. Women's groups initially supported many of these laws, but others saw them as barriers rather than protections, especially poor women working out of dire necessity, and women of colour who faced economic barriers due to both race and sex. Title VII provided several forms of judicial relief, including hiring, reinstatement, and back pay with interest. In 1991, an amendment to Title VII added compensatory and punitive damages as well.

Following the passage of the Civil Rights Act, the proportion of women working in many non-traditional (male dominated) occupations steadily increased. Women in skilled professions such as medicine and law accounted for most of the gain, while blue-collar jobs involving manual labour continued to be segregated by sex. Beginning in the late 1960s, affirmative action programmes were designed to advance women and minorities in many jobs from which they had long been excluded. For example, Executive Order 11375 banned sex discrimination, and required affirmative action by federal contractors and subcontractors in 1967. Whether or not affirmative action programmes had a positive impact on the advancement of women in the U.S. workforce is still a very controversial topic.

Title IX of the Education Amendments of 1972

The passage of this act prohibited sex discrimination in the public education system. As a result, women gained the opportunity to educate themselves for a number of occupations and professions from which they had previously been barred.

Family and Medical Leave Act (FMLA) of 1993

This act guaranteed *both* male and female employees up to twelve weeks of unpaid job-protected family or medical leave per year. The law applies to companies with more than fifty workers, and requires continuation of group health benefits during the unpaid leave. By recognizing the family care obligations of both mothers and fathers, this act implied that employers should not see child or elder care as solely a woman's responsibility (Cushman, 2001).

Initiatives supporting women in the workforce

Legal actions against sex discrimination and shortages in the labour force during the 1990s prompted many companies to develop initiatives for recruiting, retaining and advancing women in management. Important areas of focus include women's leadership development, women of colour, work/life balance, globalization, and women on boards.

In 1999, Merrill Lynch settled a massive sex-discrimination class action suit involving 900 female employees. As a result, the company started a high-profile campaign to make internal advancement of women a top priority across its entire global operation. Companies that avoid litigation often use accountability mechanisms to ensure that managers and staff meet equal opportunity objectives for promoting women within their organizations. At Charles Schwab hiring, retention, turnover, time in grade, and participation rates in training programmes are all tracked by race and gender. Women comprise 36 per cent of corporate officers and two of the company's five vice-chairpersons. IBM launched an international initiative that specifically targets women and minorities for leadership development. Since 1995, women's representation at executive levels in IBM has increased from 1 per cent to 8 per cent in the Asia-Pacific region; from zero to 5 per cent in Latin America; and from 2 per cent to 8 per cent in Europe, the Middle East, and Africa (Catalyst, 2000b).

At the time of its merger with J.P. Morgan in 2000, 22 per cent of Chase Manhattan's senior level management and 19 per cent of its corporate officers were women. Every J.P. Morgan Chase & Co. business unit creates a formal diversity plan that includes mentoring, networking, work/life programmes and career development. Each unit is evaluated according to the plan, and results are tied to the managers' bonuses (Catalyst, 2001b). Other firms where managerial and executive bonuses and/or salaries are linked to women's advancement include Gannet, Knight Ridder, Northern Trust and Prudential. At Advantica, 25 per cent of senior-manager pay is tied to hitting goals for advancing women. Since 1994, after the company paid over $54 million in a discrimination lawsuit brought by its customers, the proportion of women officers has increased from 7 per cent to 27 per cent (Cleaver, 2000).

Catalyst, a well known and respected non-profit organization working to advance women in management, recommends that companies use the following initiatives to maximize the potential of their female workforce:

- Measure women's advancement
- Move women into line positions
- Find mentors for women
- Create women's networks
- Make culture change happen
- Promote women
- Get women into non-traditional work
- Promote women in professional firms
- Support customized career planning
- Make flexibility work.

Balancing work and family life continues to be a growing challenge for women as they move up in the ranks of management. Work-family programmes are a long-standing fixture in corporate America, and the most popular ones for women, include flextime, telecommuting, job sharing, compressed work weeks, and child/eldercare resources and referral (Martinez, 1998). The best companies know that child care benefits and flexible work arrangements are not an end in themselves, but a means to help women advance in the organization. Work-family programmes fall short, if women are induced to work longer hours, but they still get passed over for promotion (Cleaver, 2000).

Catalyst maintains a web site with links to over 35 professional non-profit and for profit organizations. These groups provide resources and information concerning career development, business ownership, job search, and workplace issues for women. The largest organization for women professionals and business owners in the U.S. is the National Association for Female Executives (NAFE). For the past 30 years, NAFE has benchmarked the success of women in the workplace. Their publications profile successful women as business role models, and provide annual lists of top companies for female executives and working mothers. To make the grade, companies must show that their initiatives, culture, and most of all, results blend to create a supportive environment for achievement-oriented women.

The future

Among women in management in the U.S., there is reason for optimism. Progress has been slow, but steady. One avenue that could be targeted for improvement is the lack of women in 'non-traditional' career fields such as information technology. Initiatives that encourage women to enter non-traditional industries seem to be lacking in many respects. For example, during the 1990s, information technology (IT) had the fastest employment growth of all industries, and IT is predicted to create almost 2 million more jobs by 2008. Despite this incredible upsurge, women represent only 15 per cent of computer engineers and 28 per cent of computer scientists. Thus, women are underrepresented in the occupations most likely to lead to top-level management in IT. As one CEO in the industry so bluntly stated, 'a "women's view" [as a board member] on how to run our semiconductor company does not help us, unless that woman has an advanced technical degree and experience as a CEO' (Dalton and Daily, 1998). This statement epitomizes the career barriers women managers face in many non-traditional industries. First, women tend to choose academic career paths that do not lead to executive positions. Second, they often face a catch-22 standard that does not apply to men (i.e. women executives must have CEO experience to serve on the board, and they need board experience to become CEOs). Third, in many corporate cultures, women executives are plainly not welcome.

Our portrait of women managers in the U.S. reminds us that the journey, for most women, continues. Although more women are working, and more women are earning college degrees, they remain clustered in certain industries and occupations, often in support positions. Although there are more women managers, they have not attained the top-level, line responsibility positions that lead to CEO jobs. Women's participation on corporate boards, an important source of organizational influence, has been increasing at a snail's pace. Surveying this challenge, Bella Abzug remarked 'The test for whether or not you can hold a job should not be the arrangement of your chromosomes' (Turkington, 2000, p.198).

References

Adler, N.J. (1999), 'Global leaders: women of influence', in Powell, G.N. (ed.), *Handbook of Gender and Work*, Thousand Oaks, CA: Sage, pp. 239-261.

Bernhardt, A., Dresser, L. and Hill, D. (2000), *Why Privatizing Government Services Would Hurt Women Workers*, Institute for Women's Policy Research, Washington DC: IWPR #B234.

Burke, R.J. and Nelson, D.L. (2002), 'Advancing women in management: Progress and prospects', in Burke, R.J. and Nelson, D.L. (eds), *Advancing Women's Careers*, Oxford, UK: Blackwell, pp. 3-14.

Catalyst (2000a), *2000 Catalyst Census of Women Corporate Officers and Top Earners*, New York, http://www.catalystwomen.org/research/censuses.htm.

Catalyst (2000b), *2000 Catalyst Award Winners Focus on Corporate Culture Changes*, New York, http://www.catalystwomen.org/Press_Room.htm.

Catalyst (2001a), *2001 Catalyst Census of Women Board Directors of the Fortune 1000*, New York, http://www.catalystwomen.org/research/censuses.htm.

Catalyst (2001b), *2001 Catalyst Award Winners Focus on Corporate Culture Changes*, New York, http://www.catalystwomen.org/Press_Room.htm.

CAWP (2001), Center for American Women and Politics, Eagleton Institute of Politics, Rutgers University, http://www.cawp.rutgers.edu.

Center for Women's Business Research (2001a), *Minority Women-Owned Businesses in the United States, 2002*, Washington DC, http://www.nfwbo.org/Research.

Center for Women's Business Research (2001b), *New Generation of Women Business Owners*, Washington DC, http://www.nfwbo.org/Research.

Center for Women's Business Research (2001c), *Women-Owned Businesses in 2002: Trends in the U.S States*, Washington DC, http://www.nfwbo.org/Research.

Cheskin Research (2000), *Women entrepreneurs study*, Santa Clara University Center for Innovation and Entrepreneurship and Center for New Futures, http://www.cheskin.com.

Cleaver, J. (2000), 'Top 25 companies for executive women', *Working Woman*, **25**, 48-60.

Conlin, M. and Zellner, W. (1999), 'The CEO still wears wingtips', *Business Week*, New York (November 22), 82-90.

Cushman, C. (2001), *Supreme Court Decisions and Women's Rights*, Congressional Quarterly Press, Washington DC.

Dalton D.R. and Daily, C.M. (1998), 'Not there yet', *Across the Board*, **35**, 16-20.

Hampden-Turner, C. (1994), 'The structure of entrapment: Dilemmas standing in the way of women managers and strategies to resolve these', *The Deeper News: Global Business Network Publication*, **5**, 3-42.

Heilman, M.E., Block, C.J. and Martell, R.F. (1995), 'Sex stereotypes: Do they influence perceptions of managers?' *Journal of Social Behavior and Personality*, **10**, 237-252.

Jans, L. and Stoddard, S. (1999), 'Chartbook on Women and Disability in the United States. An Info Use Report', Washington, DC: U.S. National Institute on Disability and Rehabilitation Research.

Moore, D.P. (1999), 'Women entrepreneurs approaching a new millennium', in Powell, G.N. (ed), *Handbook of Gender in Organizations*, Thousand Oaks, CA: Sage, pp. 371-389.

Moore, D.P. (2002), 'Boundaryless transitions: Global entrepreneurial women challenge career concepts', in Burke, R.J. and Nelson, D.L. (eds), *Advancing Women's Careers*, Oxford, UK: Blackwell Publishers, pp. 245-261.

Moore, D.P. and Buttner, E.H. (1997), *Women entrepreneurs: Moving beyond the glass ceiling*, Thousand Oaks, CA: Sage.

Martinez, M.N. (1998), 'An inside look at making the grade', *HR Magazine* (March): 61-65.

Murray, C. (1999), 'And Now for the Bad News', *Wall Street Journal*, New York (2 February), p. A22.

NCES (2001), National Center for Education Statistics, U.S. Department of Education, *Postsecondary Institutions in the United States: Fall 2000 and Degrees and Other*

Awards Conferred: 1999 – 2000, Washington DC: NCES 2002 – 156, by L.G. Knapp, et al.

Nelson, D.L. and Burke, R.J. (2000), 'Women executives: Health, stress and success', *Academy of Management Executive*, **14**, 107-121.

Powell, G.N. (1999), 'Reflections on the glass ceiling: Recent trends and future prospects', in Powell, G.N. (ed.), *Handbook of Gender and Work*, Thousand Oaks, CA: Sage, pp. 325-345.

Rosener, J.B. (1990), 'Ways women lead', *Harvard Business Review*, **68**, 119-125.

Srinivasan, R., Woo, C. and Cooper, A.C. (1994), 'Performance determinants for male and female entrepreneurs', in Bygrave, W.D., Birley, S., Churchill, N.C., Gatewood, E., Hoy, F., Keeley, R. and Wetzel, W.E. Jr. (eds), *Frontiers of entrepreneurship research*, Babson Park, MA: Center for Entrepreneurial Studies, pp. 43-56.

Turkington, C. (2000), *The Quotable Woman*, New York: McGraw-Hill.

U.S. Census Bureau (2000), *The Older Population in the United States: March 2000*, Washington DC: PPL-147.

U.S. Census Bureau (2001), *Census Brief: Survey of Women-Owned Business Enterprises*, Washington DC: CENBR/01-6.

Women's Bureau (1992), *Facts on Working Women: Women with Work Disabilities,* (March) Washington DC: U.S. DOL/92-2.

Women's Bureau (2000a), *Women at the Millennium, Accomplishments and Challenges Ahead*, Washington DC: U.S.DOL/00-02.

Women's Bureau (2000b), *20 Facts on Women Workers: March 2000*, Washington DC: U.S. DOL/00-02.

SECTION IV
WOMEN IN MANAGEMENT –
AUSTRALASIA

Chapter 14

Women in Management in New Zealand

Judy McGregor

Introduction

Women's power in New Zealand currently achieves high visibility and is part of the swirl of popular commentary. This is because New Zealand has its first elected female Prime Minister Helen Clark, (who followed the first female Prime Minister Jenny Shipley), a female Attorney General Margaret Wilson, a female Chief Justice Sian Elias and a female Governor General Dame Silvia Cartwright. While the feminization of the country's top constitutional positions points to women's progress in status and influence, it disguises a more fragile reality. That is the slow progress of women at the top in the private business sector both at management and governance levels, as opposed to the public realm which pays greater attention to equal opportunities.

Paradoxically, the media attention focussing on 'women on top' in New Zealand as an 'extraordinary phenomenon' (Stirling, 2000) has stimulated a male backlash, a Save the Males campaign. Former Member of Parliament turned newspaper columnist, Michael Laws, writes that women in New Zealand have 'gone and stuffed everything that ever made us a Kiwi'. Lamenting that the feminization had meant that the nation's iconic rugby team the All Blacks had 'lost their mongrel' Laws asked sardonically, 'Isn't it time that males were given our own indigenous space where we can be our natural, inarticulate, unfeeling and expressionless selves'(Laws cited in Stirling, 2000). More significantly, though, it can be argued that the media attention has indirectly served to reduce public interest in, and policy attention to, the continuing inequality of the sexes below the top rungs. Women's progress and the structural barriers they face need to clamber back on the political agenda.

Labour force characteristics

Given the visibility of women in public office, and perceived backlash, is the labour market awash with women? No. At the last census the labour force participation rate for women was 57.9 per cent, while the rate for men was 73.5 per cent (Statistics New Zealand, 1998). While the gender gap for participation is narrowing, women's work in New Zealand is punctuated by career interruption and characterized by pay differentials between men and women, occupational segregation and by unpaid work. To take the difference in career trajectories first. Men's experience of the labour force is characterized by stability with participation reaching 90 per cent by age 25 years and staying there until age 55 years. By contrast, women's participation suggests much interruption with participation peaking around age 25 years at 70 per cent, falling, then peaking again around age 45 years at a high of 80 per cent (Statistics New Zealand, 2001).

While women's overall participation has increased dramatically in the past 40 years, the rise hides the fact that business views the age band of 25 to 45 years as prime employing ages (Wallace, 2001). This is precisely the age band that women have children and interrupt their careers, which impacts on a lack of progression into senior management (Lawrence, 1996).

There are, too, structural pay differentials between sexes. Pay differences between men and women are also at their greatest for this 'prime age-group' of 25 to 45 years. For example, Statistics New Zealand (1999) shows that for the 40 to 49 age band, the average male income is approximately NZ$40,000 compared to NZ$24,000 for women.[1] Only in the 15-19, and the over 70 year age groups, does women's income ever come close to matching men's income. Overall, women's income is 64 per cent of men's pay.

Looking at the salaries of graduates by gender at the end of 2001, males in commerce/business earned on average NZ$52,279 and females earned NZ$41,271. Even in areas dominated by women such as health and social/behavioural sciences, men out-earn women at NZ$61,305 to NZ$44,396 and NZ$42,154 to NZ$38,545 respectively (University Graduate Destinations, 2001).

There is nothing unique about the occupational segregation of women at work in New Zealand. Just under half of all employed women work in two occupations: clerks (24.5 per cent) and service and sales workers (20.8 per cent) according to census statistics. The top ten occupations by gender are uncannily similar to those of other developed countries as illustrated in Table 14.1.

Table 14.1 Top ten occupations of women and men

Women	Men
Salespersons and demonstrators	Corporate managers or managing director
Office clerks	Livestock producers
Secretaries	Salespersons and demonstrators
Waiters and bartenders	Labourers
Nursing and midwifery professionals	Supply and distribution managers
Supply and distribution managers	Carpenters and joiners
Personal care workers	Machinery mechanics and fitters
Caretakers and cleaners	Heavy truck drivers
Receptionists and information clerks	Technical and commercial sales representatives
Primary teaching professionals	Crop and livestock producers

Women work in a narrower range of occupations than men, are more likely to work part time, are more likely than men to be multiple job-holders and have a higher unemployment rate (8.3 per cent compared to 7.2 per cent), (Statistics New Zealand, 1998).

Women pursuing education

New Zealand was the first country to award a woman a Bachelor of Arts degree in the British Empire in 1877 (Stirling, 2000), a source of as much feminist pride as the country's distinction as the first nation state to grant women the vote. Women's educational status has improved dramatically in the years since the Second World War. For example, there is roughly equal gender distribution of females across all types of primary and secondary schooling (Status of Women in New Zealand, 1998). However, more females than males are participating in both full- and part-time tertiary study (21.7 per cent women, 19.4 per cent men full-time of the 18-24 age group; 6.8 per cent women, 6.6 per cent men part-time). Females outnumber males graduating with Bachelors and Bachelors with Honours degrees with a total of 9686 women compared to 6998 males in 2000 (University Graduate Destinations, 2001). The dominant ethnic group of the graduates is European/Pakeha at around 70 per cent, with Asian at 15 per cent and New Zealand Māori (indigenous people) at five per cent.

At postgraduate level females outnumber males as masterate graduates, but slightly less than half the doctorate graduates are women. Female graduates are equally represented by gender in commerce/business, over-represented in health, humanities, social and behavioural sciences and visual and performing arts. They are under-represented in mathematics and information sciences, the physical sciences, and technology and engineering (see Table 14.2).

Table 14.2   Field of tertiary study by gender of graduates in 2000

	Male	Female
Architecture/Building/Planning/Surveying	82	65
Biological Sciences	265	407
Commerce/Business	994	1124
Health	221	677
Humanities	248	627
Mathematics and Information Sciences	287	159
Physical Sciences	125	85
Social and Behavioural Sciences	639	2024
Technology and Engineering	260	142
Visuals and Performing Arts	62	116
TOTALS	3183	5426

Source: University Graduate Destinations, 2001

Māori women do not fare as well as their European/Pakeha counterparts although gains are being made at the tertiary level. Overall the disparities between Māori and non-Māori are greater than the disparities between Māori women/girls and Māori men/boys. An enduring pattern throughout compulsory education in terms of participation, achievement and progress is that non-Māori girls tend to do best, followed by non-Māori boys, Māori girls and Māori boys in that order (Ministry of Women's Affairs, 2001).

In the 1990s, however, Māori women made the greatest gains in tertiary enrolments proportionate to the population. As a proportion of all those aged 15 years and over, Māori women were more likely than any other group to be enrolled in a tertiary education institution in 1999 (ibid).

Because successive New Zealand Governments have adopted 'user pays' policies in relation to tertiary study, considerable gender inequity attaches to women's increased educational status. This is likely to have serious future consequences for women's progress in public and private spheres. For example, undisputed figures produced by the New Zealand University Students' Association show the average women graduate would take 28 years to pay off her student loan while the average male graduate would take 14 years, with the women paying $NZ12,481 interest compared with the male $NZ7924. This reflects women's decreased earning power and women's interrupted career paths for family reasons. The 'user pays' regime seems disproportionately harsh for women even though they may be more debt averse and not take out so much of a loan during study. There is also some suggestion that female students disproportionately work in menial jobs in the hospitality, call centre or cleaning sectors, at the expense of achieving better grades, to help pay for tertiary studies. 'User pays' tertiary study may also influence women to select cheaper university courses in 'softer' disciplines, which perpetuates a cycle of women's under-representation in science and technology.

Women in management

The promotion of a younger woman, Theresa Gattung, to the top of one of the world's top 500 companies, the telecommunications giant Telecom, has significantly raised the profile of women in management in New Zealand (McGregor, 2000a). Her elevation at age 37 years made her the only female chief executive of a listed New Zealand company which had revenue of NZ$3.4 billion at the time she was appointed. Her promotion prompted unprecedented media interest and Ms Gattung was forced to defend both her youth, 'I'm not too young for the job' (Love,1999) and her career-first aspirations. She was asked by male reporters if she was planning a family (Bedford,1999) which drew the following response from the female editor of the country's leading information technology weekly:

Some of the questions at the press conference announcing Ms Gattung's appointment were utterly astonishing. She was asked if she intended to have babies. Would this question ever be asked of a man taking on a top corporate job?... these questions needless to add, came from males only, who seemed gobsmacked by her appointment (Perry, 1999).

Ms Gattung's appointment prompted prediction by expert commentators of a 'dramatic acceleration in girl power' (McClinchy,1999) in the nation's boardrooms in the next ten years. More recently, another woman, Rosemary Howard joins Theresa Gattung at the top of the telco tree in New Zealand as CEO of the newly merged TelstraClear, with approximately 1500 staff.

But outside of the nation's large telecommunications industry, what is the status of women in management in New Zealand? This chapter reports on new findings from a study undertaken in 2000, which replicated a 1993 benchmark Women in Management survey (McGregor, Thomson and Dewe, 1994). The top 500 companies by numbers of employees were surveyed by mail questionnaire and the nationwide survey covered all industries, approximately a third of respondent organizations were in the public sector, and it achieved a response rate of 139 companies, 27.8 per cent, similar to the previous response rate of 28.5 per cent.

Benchmark Women in Management Study (2000)

The findings reported in this section are previously unpublished and compare the new survey results with previously reported figures to provide a picture of progress over time. Respondent organizations employed a total of 82,074 employees with 43,427 (52.9 per cent) males and 38,647 (47.1 per cent) females, a higher female participation rate than the previous study but 42 per cent of the women worked part time compared with only 20 per cent of men. Of the 43,427 men employed, 15 per cent held management positions and represented 72.8 per cent of the total management structure of respondent organizations. Of the 38,647 women employed, a total of 6.5 per cent held management positions representing 27.1 per cent of the total management of organizations that participated in the study. The good news is that this shows a rise in both the actual numbers of women in management and in the percentage of females in the total management structures, over the 1993 study (see Table 14.3).

Table 14.3 Comparison of women and men in management, 1993-2000

	1993 Male	2000 Male	1993 Female	2000 Female
Number of managers	6637 (14.3 per cent)	6774 (15 per cent)	1236 (5.2 per cent)	2520 (6.5 per cent)
Proportion of management group	84.3 per cent	72.8 per cent	15.7 per cent	27.1 per cent

However, while these figures reveal improved participation for both women and men, the bad news is the stagnant position of females in management hierarchies. In seven years, as shown in Table 14.4, there has been little improvement. Women remain over-represented in junior management and are fairly static at senior management levels.

Table 14.4 Management composition of participating organizations - position of men and women employed at each management level

	1993 Male	2000 Male	1993 Female	2000 Female
Junior management	32.5	42.0	53.6	57.0
Middle management	47.5	36.0	38.6	34.0
Senior management	20.0	22.0	7.8	9.0
	100.0	100.0	100.0	100.0

A comparison of median remuneration packages of men and women managers again reveals similar structural inequities now to those that existed in the early 1990s (see Table 14.5).

Table 14.5 Median remuneration packages of men and women managers (in 000s)

	1993 Male	2000 Male	1993 Female	2000 Female
Junior management	$40,000	$57,000	$36,000	$ 52,500
Middle management	$51,000	$ 7,000	$46,500	$ 66,000
Senior management	$80,000	$122,000	$68,000	$107,000

Women at every level of management are still substantially underpaid despite New Zealand passing equal pay legislation in the early 1970s and progress toward equal opportunities initiatives in the public sector. Depressingly, the differential at middle and senior management has, in fact, increased. Even at the top of our biggest company the pay differential applied. When Theresa Gattung was appointed to Telecom she was reputed to have secured a million dollar salary. This prompted a letter writer to Wellington's morning newspaper, *The Dominion*, to suggest it was ironic that Ms Gattung, replacing a male CEO, was considered to be worth only half his salary. This was 'strange in a country that has been touting pay equity for as long as I can remember, if not actually practising it' (*The Dominion*, 5 October, 1999).

The age distribution of management personnel in the latest study shows that women managers are younger, 78 per cent in the 45 years and under category, compared with 66 per cent of men, reinforcing women's likely concentration in junior management. Global structural shifts have impacted on New Zealand's labour market like other Western developed societies, resulting in the rise of knowledge work and service industries at the expense of traditional manufacturing and agricultural production. Redundancy, restructuring, early exit, and retirement policies have accompanied the changing nature of work (Drucker, 2001). The latest study confirms earlier research (McGregor et al., 1994) that women have not necessarily been disproportionately disadvantaged by recent employment structural change. About a third of the respondent organizations indicated that they had reduced their workforce in the previous 12 months (1999). There was a net loss of 907 male managers reported (−62 in 1993) and a loss of 13 female managers (+243 in 1993). The figures reflect that downsizing and restructuring impacts most heavily on middle to senior managers, where women are under-represented, as company and organizational structures flatten out. Men are disadvantaged most by redundancy and retrenchment in management, partly because there are more of them at middle and higher levels (Schulz, 2001).

The findings of the latest study reveal a picture of progress for women in management in terms of participation, an ominous *status quo* against enthusiastic predictions that 'it was only a matter of time' in terms of status and money, and indications of regression in terms of philosophical commitment towards women's advancement. This is graphically illustrated by the findings from questions asking companies and organizations whether they had a policy of identifying female employees who had management potential. While 28 per cent indicated in the affirmative in 1993, the proportion had slumped to 18 per cent in 2000, a worrying sign that many companies and organizations either believe the gender battle has been won or they believe that affirmative action is passé. Slight reassurance is gained from the findings that 98 per cent of respondents said they adopted the same promotion criteria for men and women, similar to the results of the 1993 benchmark Women in Management study.

Women in Governance

The first female head of state in New Zealand, Prime Minister Jenny Shipley, promised to improve the proportion of females on statutory boards to 50 per cent by 2000. Shipley, now no longer Prime Minister or National Party leader, made the promise as part of the Government's follow-up to the Beijing Women's Conference in 1995. It is no comfort to have predicted (McGregor, 2000b) that Shipley's radical experiment with the nation's boardrooms would fall well short of the 50 per cent mark by the turn of the century.

New Zealand has two sorts of statutory boards. The first type imitates the private sector and operates akin to a private company ruled by the Companies Act, 1993. There are currently about 60 Crown companies that have converted to the corporate model with compelling legislation that prioritizes profitability over social responsibility. Currently there are 205 directors positions on Crown Company boards and at the end of February 2002, 67 (33 per cent) were female and 138 (67 per cent) were men, according to figures provided by the Crown Company Monitoring and Advisory Unit (CCMAU) (personal correspondence).

The second type of statutory boards include community, public service agencies that are less corporate and include more 'social responsibility' in their objectives, usually funded directly by public monies with devolved budgets, and therefore less like private companies in character. According to the draft report to the United Nations on the Status of Women in New Zealand (2001), a total of 37 per cent of appointments or reappointments were women in 2000.

Taken together the proportion of women appointed to statutory boards in New Zealand in 2002 is 35 per cent, a steady climb from 31 per cent in 1996 and 25 per cent in 1993. CCMAU state the Government has expressed its desire and commitment for board representation to reflect the make-up and diversity of New Zealand society.

So why hasn't Jenny Shipley's brave target of equity in the boardroom been achieved? First, the pattern of homosocial reproduction, the selection of new directors on the basis of social similarity, so prevalent in the private sector, is equally alive and well in the public sector. Second, the extent of political bias in crown company appointments warrants further analysis. Names of suitable candidates are forwarded to share-holding ministers for consideration and they then have to meet with Caucus approval. Under New Zealand's newer proportional representation system, the Labour Coalition Government needs to win the backing of the parties and factions that comprise the coalition, about appointments. While there is no empirical evidence on these invisible political processes, it is intuitively reasonable to suggest that coalition trade-offs and deals influence who is appointed and reappointed and who is not considered for a further term because they were appointed under the previous National Government.

Third, there are some women who after training to be directors adopt a risk-averse attitude towards appointment. This is because crown company directors are required to meet the same obligations as directors of private sector companies, in addition to any obligations contained in legislation specific to the company in question. In New Zealand the liabilities of directors have been hardened up by changes to the Companies Act, 1993, following public and parliamentary concern about the role and performance of directors in company collapses. After attending director's training myself I reported on the observations of other potential female directors (McGregor, 2000). One wrote, 'I had been provided with enough information to create considerable doubt in my mind as to the personal value versus input and risk in relation to directorships in New Zealand. I have in the past considered it a natural professional, progression but am now somewhat sceptical of the role'.

In the private sector women are making even slower progress. While the business case argument (Bilimoria, 2000) is generally accepted as a valid rationale for the value of women in corporate governance, the resilience of male boardroom cultures cannot be under-estimated. Reliable data on gender in governance in the private sector is notoriously hard to gather in New Zealand because crown companies are included in most studies and therefore inflate percentages. With this caveat in mind, figures provided by the Institute of Directors show that 17 per cent of its membership in 2002 were women up from 15 per cent in 2000 and 10 per cent in 1997 (personal correspondence). A survey conducted for the IOD shows that the percentage of non-executive directors across all types of companies (Crown, listed etc) shows 9 per cent of women in 1997, 11.7 per cent in 2000 and 12.4 per cent in 2001. While the IOD has three women on its 7-person council, it remains conservative about diversity in the boardroom. Discussing the idea that the legal framework for Crown companies could be altered to allow for non-commercial merit criteria, the Institute strongly opposed the idea and said that the government should not move away from merit criteria for crown board selection. The performance of these commercial organizations was vital for the country's economic wellbeing and 'there is no evidence to suggest that their performance is affected by a lack of diversity, real or perceived, on their boards' (Institute of Directors, 2002, p. 1). Equally, of course, there is no evidence that performance is improved by sameness and lack of diversity, either.

Women entrepreneurs

While definitions of entrepreneurship are contested, in New Zealand the concept is uniquely identified with self-employment and micro-business. The smallness of the country, at 3.79 million total population, means almost everyone employs themselves or each other. Approximately 85 per cent of the 355,000 businesses employ five or less people. An island nation which is geographically distant from most other global markets, New Zealand cultivates business self-reliance. The indigenous metaphor (itself gendered) for entrepreneurial activity is No 8 Wire, a particular strand of farming fencing wire, that apocryphal New Zealanders are expected to carry around in their back pockets and to use ingeniously and imaginatively to make new products and fix problems.

Given that New Zealanders believe they are entrepreneurial, what is the status of women? The number of women who are self employed has risen dramatically. Those who are self-employed without employees increased 24.3 per cent to 70,000 between 1995 and 2001, compared to a 21.1 per cent rise in their male counterparts (to 155,200) (Status of Women in New Zealand, 2001, draft). Those with staff, though, fell by 3.0 per cent to 37,700 over the same time period, although less than the 4.5 per cent fall in male employers.

A number of factors influence the rise in female self-employment. A greater number of younger women are starting their own business, 19.6 per cent under 34 years of age compared with 10.7 per cent of men (McGregor and Tweed, in press). Most women business owners are concentrated in one of the fastest growing sectors, the service sector, and some of the growth has come from managerial ranks. When mid-career women cannot meet their need for challenge, flexibility, career advancement and a compatible organizational culture, many opt for self-employment. Significantly, too, self employment offers women autonomy in terms of their family-work life patterns so they are not at the mercy of corporate expectations of straight-trajectory career paths.

A large recent study of small business in New Zealand identified a quite distinct profile of a new generation of female small business owners who are networked through WISE (Women into Self-Employment Network). They are younger, identify self-confidence as an inhibitor to business start-up, and are more likely both to have, and to want, mentorship. These networked women also have greater expansionist intentions than other women in small business (McGregor and Tweed, in press).

Country legislation supporting women in the workforce

What compels countries to advance women's progress at work? Female political champions can be instrumental and so, too, can a general moral commitment to equity founded on New Zealand's social welfare traditions. But as New Zealand moved more quickly to labour market deregulation through the 1980s and 1990s than most other developed countries, progress for women at work was jeopardized by the dismantling of collective bargaining in favour of individualized contracts. Only now, with the rolling back of de-regulation by the Labour Coalition Government, has the Employment Contracts Act been replaced by the Employment Relations Act 2000. The new labour law is predicted to be more likely to act in favour of women's pay and conditions in the formal labour market and redress the inequality of bargaining power.

Another determinative factor in New Zealand improving its statutory framework is its international obligation to periodically report to the United Nations Committee on the Elimination of all Forms of Discrimination Against Women (CEDAW) against audited outcomes. For example CEDAW criticized New Zealand for its absence of paid maternity leave and the status of women in armed combat. In its upcoming report the New Zealand Government will report that paid parental leave will be introduced in 2002. Eligible women will be entitled to 12 weeks' paid parental leave, funded by the Government, which they can transfer to their partners (including same sex partners) (Status of Women 2001, draft report). It will also report that the Chief of Defence Force lifted all restrictions on women in combat roles in 2000 and women are currently serving in East Timor.

Initiatives supporting women in the workforce

Formal and informal measures are supporting the advancement of women. The informal initiative of New Zealand's biggest company, Telecom, reveals the power of mentorship for women in senior management. Senior men have for years advanced male protégés both in terms of succession planning and as a consequence of homosocial reproduction. As more women attain CEO status are we likely to see similar 'girl's clubs', but will this process be more influential in improving the numbers and status of women at the top of corporate companies? Theresa Gattung has appointed three women to the companies more senior line leadership positions: Australian head, head of esolutions and head of corporate communications, and in doing so has broken the mould of senior women in support roles only. Gattung collects and refers to a clipping file of articles about women she admires, mostly women who have advanced equality. She states 'I'm keenly aware that I've got where I am through the efforts of people who have been before me' (Stride and Mandow, 2000, p. 41). The appointment of senior women provided other women with role models and demonstrated female capability.

Government initiatives are generally aimed at disadvantaged women in the labour market rather than high flyers. For example a women's strategy has been developed by the Community Employment Group of the Department of Labour and it focuses on addressing barriers for particular women such as Māori, Pacific peoples, rural and urban women. Its features include:

- updating women's skills
- reaching out to women isolated by location or at home with children
- assisting women to re-enter the workforce
- building on cottage industries
- developing enterprises using arts and culture
- increasing women's skills and familiarity with new technologies
- providing role models and mentoring support
- using family and support networks for Māori and Pacific peoples women to build on existing initiatives and build new ones
- assisting women with strategic planning for new ventures.

Another formal initiative, the Equal Employment Opportunities Trust, which aims to influence employers' behaviour for the better about diversity issues in general, has been perhaps the most influential lobby in New Zealand for women at work in the past decade. It uses Government funding to work on specific projects such as EEO workshops for small businesses and valuing working parents and effective retention strategies, runs an effective outreach programme of publicity and promotion, and guides and leads a range of government policy related to diversity. Largely because of its employer membership and its successful operational marriage of pragmatism and idealism in its training and education work, the trust has a high profile and effective track record. The EEO Trust identifies future socio-economic issues and demographic trends that will impact on diversity. For example, it is currently working with university research partners on equity issues involving older workers, including mature female job-seekers, in anticipation of the 'grey wave workforce'.

The future

In New Zealand the rhetoric about women's power is upbeat. Familiar 'power' females adorn not just women's magazines but the covers of financial magazines and the lead stories in business pages. The reality, though, is much more complex than this rhetoric suggests. While New Zealand women celebrate the success of other females, the challenge is to acknowledge the deep structural barriers that still exist and devise appropriate frameworks for action.

The enduring chestnut in terms of women's status, particularly women in management, remains pay equity. For women at the top, at the bottom and in the middle of corporate and private sector ladders the gender pay gap is a visible expression of value and worth. Even before female graduates begin work they can anticipate earning less on the basis of gender only. While the Ministry of Women's Affairs is currently undertaking a pay equity programme this will again identify and evaluate possible policy options – a well trodden path in New Zealand that does not suggest a proactive Government approach. This is despite recent research proving that indirect discrimination in the operation of pay systems is widespread and that the value of women's contributions are not properly estimated. Pressure from the women's lobby will be required to ensure pay equity becomes a political issue not just a women's issue.

More research is needed, too, on women's progress in the less visible sector in New Zealand, the private sector. For example, quantifying the numbers of women on private sector boards excluding Crown companies is urgently needed to compare data from the 1990s when there were optimistic predictions of women storming the male bastilles. Only by systematic measuring can the emotional hype that attaches to the female front-runners be matched by a more sober and objective reality check on women's progress at work. New Zealand women should be flattered by their high profile which marks a new maturity in media interest, particularly when journalists move beyond youth and babies. But they should not be seduced by headlines into believing the battle for equality is won.

References

Bedford, D. (1999), 'Simply the best – and right under their noses', *Evening Post*, 13 August, p. 11.

Bilimoria, D. (2000), 'Building the business case for women corporate directors', in Burke, R.J. and Mattis, M.C. (eds), *Women on Corporate Boards of Directors*, The Netherlands: Kluwer Academic Publishers, pp. 25-40.

Drucker, P.F. (2001, 3-9 November), 'The next society', *The Economist*, **361**, pp. 3-20.

Institute of Directors (2002), 'Report to CCMAU on Diversity on crown boards, panels and councils by Dr. Brent Wheeler'
http://www.iod.org.nz/opinion/mediareleases/WheelerReport.html accessed 16 May, 2002.

Lawrence, B.S. (1996), 'Organizational age norms: Why is it so hard to see one?', *The Gerontologist*, **36** (2), pp. 209-220.

Love, P. (1999), 'I'm not too young for the job-Gattung', *Evening Post*, 13 August, p. 1.

McClinchy, A. (1999), 'Women to take lead', *National Business Review*, 24 September, p. 5.

McGregor, J. (2000a), 'Stereotypes and symbolic annihilation: press constructions of women at the top', *Women in Management Review*, **15** (5/6), pp. 290-295.

McGregor, J. (2000b), 'The New Zealand Experiment – Training to be On Board As A Director', in Burke, R.J. and Mattis, M.C. (eds), *Women on Corporate Boards of Directors*, The Netherlands: Kluwer Academic Publishers.

McGregor, J., Thomson, M. and Dewe, P. (1994), *Women and Management in New Zealand: A Benchmark Survey*, Women in Management Series, working paper 19, University of Western Sydney.

McGregor, J. and Tweed, D., 'Profiling a new generation of female entrepreneurs in New Zealand: networking, mentoring and growth', accepted for forthcoming publication in *Gender, Work, and Organization*.

Ministry of Women's Affairs (2001, September), Māori *women: mapping inequalities and pointing ways forward*, Wellington, New Zealand.

New Zealand Vice-Chancellors' Committee (2001), *University Graduate Destinations 2001*, Report No. 5 (Second Series).

Perry, A. (1999), 'Gattung looked a shoo-in to get top Telecom job', *NZ Infotech Weekly*, 16 August, p. 33.

Schulz, J.H. (2001), *The economics of aging* (7th edn) Westport, Conn: Auburn House.

Statistics New Zealand (1998), *New Zealand Now-Women (1998 Edition)*, Wellington: Statistics New Zealand.

Statistics New Zealand (1999), *Labour Market Statistics – 1999*, Wellington: Statistics New Zealand.

Statistics New Zealand (2001), *Labour Market Statistics – 2000*, Wellington: Statistics New Zealand.

Status of Women in New Zealand, 1998, Ministry of Women's Affairs
http://mwa.govt.nz/women/status/cedaw010.html

Status of Women in New Zealand, 2001, Draft Report to the United Nations Committee on the Discrimination of all Forms of Discrimination Against Women, Ministry of Women's Affairs.

Stirling, P. (2000, 9-15 September), 'Women on top', *New Zealand Listener*, pp. 18-22.

Stride, N. and Mandow, N. (June, 2000), 'Look who's running the show now', *Unlimited*, pp. 41-44.

Wallace, P. (2001), *Agequake: Riding the demographic rollercoaster shaking business, finance and our world*, Naperville, Il: Nicholas Brealey Publishing.

Note

1   The NZ$ equalled .3079pound sterling at the time of writing.

Chapter 15

Women in Management in Australia

Leonie V. Still

Introduction

Australia ranked in the top ten on a number of indices purporting to measure gender equity in the International Labour Organization Report, 'Breaking through the Glass Ceiling: Women in Management' (Wirth, 2001). For a small developed country, this was a reasonable achievement. However, drawbacks exist in using such indices to establish local performance relative to global benchmarks because some countries have fundamental flaws in collection procedures and the time periods are not always comparable.

Similar comparison problems on equity performance also exist internally in Australia. There is no doubt that women have made significant inroads into management. Women comprised 23 per cent of managers and administrators in 2000, with 10 per cent being generalist managers, 25.5 per cent specialist managers, and 27 per cent farm managers (Australian Bureau of Statistics [ABS], 2000a). However, it is difficult to know whether these figures represent a substantial improvement on the past as the method of collecting government statistics has altered twice since 1986. Most commentators acknowledge that the employment status of women has improved substantially in the public services, both at State and Commonwealth level, and those private sector companies covered by The Equal Opportunity for Women in the Workplace Act (1999) that replaced the former Affirmative Action Act (1986). However, in companies not covered by the Act, the Equal Opportunity for Women in the Workplace Agency (EOWA) considers that change has generally stood still and could have actually regressed (EOWA, 2000a).

The Public Services in Australia are generally viewed as the exemplar organizations in the pursuit of gender equity. Awareness of women's less than equal employment status and representation first occurred with the Royal Commission into Commonwealth Public Sector Administration in 1975 and has been on the agenda ever since. Chief Executive Officers of Government agencies, as part of their performance reviews, are now charged with ensuring that their Departments or agencies achieve certain equity objectives. A climate of action imperatives pervade the services and women are now making sure and steady progress in the Senior Executive Services, with some attaining Departmental Head level.

However, a similar climate for gender equity does not exist in the private sector. While a number of major Australian companies have made considerable advances in progressing women into senior management, the lack of an effective general data base and consistent reporting on progress makes it difficult for any true assessment to be made of the private sector. The Equal Opportunity for Women in the Workplace Agency (EOWA) receives annual reports from private sector organizations, group training schemes, unions, community organizations, non-government schools and higher education institutions with 100 or more employees (EOWA, 2001a). Those organizations with less than 100 employees are not covered by the Act. Hence, while EOWA can keep track of some 2600 organizations there is no overall coverage of the private sector.[1] The result is that the Australian Bureau of Statistics is the only consistent source of statistics on women managers, and even here the method of reporting has changed twice since 1986.

Given the above context, what is the situation for women in management in Australia? The following review, which uses the year 2000 as the main benchmark, summarizes progress across a number of areas, while also pointing out other areas that still need attention.

Labour force characteristics

According to the Australian Bureau of Statistics (ABS, 2000a) nine million Australians were currently employed in November 2000, with the female labour force participation rate being 55.4 per cent compared to 72.4 per cent for men. This is a considerable improvement on 1970 when 40 per cent of women were in the labour force compared with 83.4 per cent of men.

As is well known, female labour force participation rates vary by age, partly reflecting periods of life when women take on caring responsibilities. In November 2000, the female labour force participation rate was highest (at 77.6 per cent) for women aged 20-24 years, lower (69.2 per cent) amongst those aged 25-34 years before rising to 71.4 per cent for those aged 35-44 years. Despite this traditional M-shaped curve, women comprised approximately 42.7 per cent of all people employed, in contrast to 1964 when they comprised only 28 per cent of employed persons.

In 2000 women made up 34 per cent of the full-time labour force and 72 per cent of the part-time labour force (ABS, 2000a). Over the past decade there has been a big shift from full-time to part-time employment in Australia. The number of persons employed part-time increased by over half (51 per cent) in the 10 years since October 1991, standing at 2.6 million in October 2001 (ABS, 2001). Women have borne the brunt of this employment change, which has been brought about by the impact of globalization, labour market reform, the relative growth in service industries and the introduction of new technologies.

The Australian labour market is one of the most highly segregated of the OECD countries, both vertically (in terms of hierarchical levels) and horizontally (occupations). There has been little change in this situation for the past 40 years, with women's employment predominating in three main occupational areas: services, sales and retail. In fact, 56 per cent of all employed women are concentrated in two occupations – clerks and sales, and personal service workers (EOWA Equity Statistics, 2001b).

Despite various enquiries over the years there is still a significant earnings gap between men and women. The biennial Employee Earnings and Hours survey is considered to provide the most reliable and comprehensive source of data on the level of, and movements in, relative earnings for males and females. In December 2000, the ratio of female to male average weekly ordinary time earnings for full-time adult managerial employees was 75.1 per cent, and the ratio for adult non-managerial employees was 89.7 per cent (EOWA, 2000b). Other surveys of managerial women have found them to receive, in some cases, two-thirds the pay rate of men for the same job (Hall, 2000; Still, Bellman and Kok, 2001). Overall, women, whether managerial or non-managerial, have less access than men to overtime, over-award payments, allowances, bonuses and other employment benefits despite enterprise bargaining, workplace agreements and individual contracts – all part of recent labour market reform.

Thus while women's workforce participation has increased considerably over the years, they are still segregated into a small number of occupations and industries and receive less than equitable remuneration. For such a developed country, then, women still have a long way to go to achieve gender equity in terms of employment, status and reward.

Women pursuing education

The acquisition of, and exposure to, education is viewed by many as a prerequisite for improving women's employment status.

According to the Commonwealth Office of the Status of Women (OSW, 2000), more girls than boys are finishing high school and going on to university. In 1999 there was a 78.5 per cent retention rate for girls completing education to Year 12 level (University matriculation level) compared with 66.4 per cent for boys.

Women make up 58 per cent of students commencing a Bachelor degree at university compared to 52 per cent in 1998. The proportion of women in post-graduate studies increased from 43.5 per cent to 52.7 per cent between 1996 and 1999 (OSW, 2000).

However, just like the workforce, women continue to concentrate in disciplines such as education (76 per cent of enrolments), health (74 per cent) and arts and humanities (69 per cent), and less in engineering (15 per cent of enrolments) or architecture (38 per cent) (EOWA, 2001b). In 1998, 83 per cent of women's enrolments were concentrated in Arts/Humanities, Business/Economics, Education and Health degrees (OSW, 1999a).

Currently, employed women are more likely to have qualifications at the basic vocational, undergraduate diploma, and postgraduate diploma levels. Employed men are more likely to have qualifications at the skills, vocational and higher degree levels. However, this is changing as the pipeline effect of women's increasing educational participation begins to bear fruit. Some recent surveys have shown women managers to hold more tertiary qualifications i.e. multiple degrees, than their male counterparts, if not necessarily at the same level e.g. post-graduate diplomas versus master's degrees (Still, 2001a).

Women in management

As indicated earlier, it is difficult to obtain a trend-line on the progress of women in management in Australia because official government statistics were altered in 1986 and again in 1996. Comparisons between pre-1986, 1987 to 1996, and post-1996 are therefore difficult to make.

According to EOWA (2001b), men outnumbered women in managerial and administrative jobs by more than three to one in December 2000. Of the 633,400 managers and administrators on Australia's payroll in 2000, 77 per cent were male and 23 per cent were female. Women still do not make up a quarter of the managerial category. Of the generalist managers, 90 per cent were men and 10 per cent women. Approximately 74.5 per cent of specialist managers were men and 25.5 per cent women, while for farm managers 73 per cent were men and 27 per cent were women (EOWA, 2001b).

A more detailed analysis of the situation for women in management in Australia is gained by a consideration of the private versus the public sectors.

Private sector

EOWA, through its annual reporting mechanism of 2600 organizations with over 100 employees, compiled some figures on women's representation between 1995 and 1998. Tier 1 managers are those typically at the most senior level in an organization. Tier 2 managers represent those immediately below the top level, while Tier 3 managers are defined as being directly responsible for the work of operating employees, but are more senior than supervisors (see Table 15.1).

Table 15.1 Women's percentage representation in management by management tier, 1994-1998 (private companies)

Year	Tier 1	Tier 2	Tier 3
1994	8.0	15.0	24.0
1995	10.0	14.0	26.0
1996	10.0	16.0	27.0
1997	11.0	18.0	28.0
1998	12.0	19.0	31.0

Source: Adapted from EOWA (2000a), *Women in Management*

While these figures seem promising they hide a number of defining characteristics of women in management in Australia. For example, women have reached middle management, but are not yet in senior and executive management in any great numbers. The ILO (2000 Executive Summary), summarizing Wirth's (2001) report, found that Australia had the lowest number of female managers of all industrialized countries, with just 1.3 per cent of senior executive positions held by women. Similarly to their female counterparts in the general workforce, women managers are segregated into particular occupations, professions and management support roles rather than mainstream areas which lead to decision-making and power. While some women have broken through these constraints, the majority of women managers, by and large, are still located in peripheral management support areas.

Although women now represent 23 per cent of the total managerial workforce, their representation is also uneven across various industries, with some industries such as cultural and recreational services showing considerable gains, others slightly declining (retailing), and other remaining much the same (EOWA, 1999). In those industries not covered by The Equal Opportunity for Women in the Workplace Act [1999], EOWA believes that little progress has been made in advancing women in management (EOWA, 2000a).

Public sector

As mentioned earlier the public services in Australia, both at Commonwealth and State level, are considered to be the exemplar organizations in advancing women in management. As illustrated in Table 15.2, in June 2000 25.3 per cent of permanent on-going employees in the Senior Executive Service (SES) of the Australian Public Service (APS) were women. This represents a significant improvement over 18.3 per cent in 1995 and about 9 per cent in 1988. Various initiatives have been introduced to encourage women into senior positions in the APS. The numbers are also expected to increase as the 'pipeline effect' of greater women's representation in non-SES positions flows through the system.

**Table 15.2 Percentage of women in the senior executive service, 1992-2000
(Australian Public Service; relates to ongoing staff)**

Year	Band 1*	Band 2*	Band 3*	Total SES
1992	16.0	8.0	5.0	13.8
1993	17.4	11.4	5.0	15.5
1994	19.1	13.2	6.0	17.1
1995	20.8	12.8	4.0	18.3
1996	22.1	13.4	7.0	19.5
1997	22.5	13.6	8.0	20.0
1998	24.6	17.3	9.0	22.2
1999	27.0	18.7	9.0	24.6
2000	28.1	19.8	13.0	25.3

Source: Adapted from Public Service & Merit Protection Commission: State of the Service:
Australian Public Service Statistical Bulletin, 2000-01, Table 5 Ongoing Staff:
Classification by Gender, 30 June 1992 to 30 June 2001
Note: The Bands relate to SES levels. Band 1 is the entry level; Band 3 is the highest level

Board representation

The main source of information for women's representation on private sector
boards is the annual Korn/Ferry International Survey of Boards of Directors. In
1993 fewer than 20 per cent of the 200 largest Australian companies had at least
one woman on their boards. This proportion rose to 24 per cent in 1994, 26 per
cent in 1995 and 28 per cent in 1996 (Burton, 1997), while more recent figures
reveal a continuing upward trend to 42 per cent. The 2000 Korn/Ferry Report states
that over 40 per cent of government enterprises in Australia have female non-
executive directors on their boards, with government services, financial services
and the insurance industry contributing 47 per cent of all non-executive positions
held by women. In addition companies with an annual turnover of over $1 billion
have the highest number of women on the board, followed by companies with $501
million to $1 billion turnover (Korn/Ferry International, 2000). Table 15.3 below
details the percentages of women, where available.

Table 15.3 Percentage of women on private sector boards, 1994-2000

Year	Top 200 Companies - At least one woman on their board	Women Non-Executive Directors on Australian Boards	Women Executive Directors on Australian Boards	Total Women Board Members
1994	24.0	N/A	N/A	4.0
1995	26.0	N/A	N/A	4.0
1996	28.0	4.0	1.0	4.0
1997	28.0	7.3	1.0	6.0
1998	34.0	9.7	1.3	7.6
1999	42.0	10.3	1.3	8.3
2000		13.7	2.9	10.0

Source: Table compiled from information drawn from Korn/Ferry International Annual Reports
Reprinted with permission of Korn/Ferry International

The improved trends can be attributed to a heightened awareness of the issue and a determined action by Commonwealth and State women's offices to make the appointment of women to boards a priority issue. Nevertheless, the figures (particularly those relating to executive directors) also indicate that increasing the representation of women in management or on boards in the private sector does not appear to be a high priority for the majority of leading companies

Women entrepreneurs

In Australia the word 'entrepreneur' is often another euphuism for the term 'small business operator'. Such applies in the case of self-employed women. There is no collection of statistics concerning women entrepreneurs. Instead, self-employed women are included in official Government statistics as small business operators.

The Australian Bureau of Statistics (2000b) defines a 'business operator' as a proprietor of a sole proprietorship, partners in a partnership, or the working director(s) of an incorporated company. According to the Bureau there is no standard definition of a 'small business operator', but it acknowledges that the expression is one that is often used in research and policy debate and is generally taken to include the above group of people. The Bureau's ancillary 1999 review of the way businesses should be defined by size recommended three particular categories for the small business sector: non-employing businesses – sole proprietorships and partnerships without employees; businesses employing between 1-4 people (Micro-businesses); and businesses employing between 5-19 people (ABS, 1999). This change is also in line with research in Australia and has been used since November 1999 in the Bureau's Characteristics of Small Business Survey.

Of the 1.4 million small business operators in Australia as at November 1999, 67 per cent were male and 33 per cent were female. Between February 1997 and November 1999, the number of male small business operators increased at an average 2.8 per cent per annum, while the number of female operators declined slightly (down a little less than 1 per cent per annum). This represented a reversal of the trend established over the previous two years where the number of women small business operators was increasing at 2.6 per cent per annum compared to 1.5 per cent for males (ABS, 2000d). The new trend for women was a surprise, as previously it had been assumed that, if women continued to enter self-employment at their previous rate, they would soon account for 50 per cent of small business operators.

Given the above scenario, what are the characteristics of women small business operators in 2000? As at November 1999 32 per cent were aged under 30; 34 per cent were aged between 30 and 50 years; and 30 per cent were more than 50 years of age. Women thus tended to be fairly evenly distributed across the full age range (ABS, 2000c).

Approximately half the women had completed secondary school but did not have a degree, diploma or vocational qualification. Twenty per cent had a basic or skilled vocational qualification, while another 26 per cent held a degree or diploma. Some 44 per cent of women small business operators worked full time, the majority working between 35 to 50 hours a week. Women accounted for 65 per cent of all part-time operators.

Self-employed women tend to be either a sole trader or the operator of a micro-business (up to 4 employees). Consequently, the majority of women operators are involved in just one business. However, 7 per cent of women were involved in two or more businesses as at November 1999.

Seventeen per cent of small businesses in Australia in November 1999 were operated predominantly by women compared to 53 per cent by males. When the number of businesses operated by both a male and a female are considered, women have an influence in approximately 47 per cent of businesses. The non-employing business group was the most common business size for both predominantly female operated businesses (66 per cent) and predominantly male operated businesses (52 per cent). Businesses operated by equal numbers of male and female operators were spread fairly evenly over the three categories of business size (ABS, 2000c).

In November 1999, 43 per cent of home-based businesses were operated predominantly by women, with a further 26 per cent being operated by equal numbers of males and females. Female home-based business operators were more likely to work part time in their business with 60 per cent working less than 35 hours (ABS, 2000c).

Despite efforts by the Commonwealth Government and others to encourage women to 'grow their businesses', most still prefer to be either a sole trader or a micro-business operator. Two significant reasons for this are lifestyle (combining work and family) (Still and Soutar, 2001) and 'wanting to make a difference' such as providing quality products or services, being part of the community, looking after clients and other more socially-oriented objectives as opposed to the male-preferred pure economic objectives of growth and wealth creation (Still and Timms, 2000a; Still and Soutar, 2001). The growth cycle of a woman's business is also affected by other cycles in her life – for instance, family, education and care of the elderly (Still and Timms, 2000b). Women's businesses are not homogeneous enterprises; neither are women small business operators a homogenous group (Still and Timms, 2000b). This diversity means that women do not necessarily follow the same growth trajectories as men in business because of some of these attributes and conditions.

However, there are signs that younger women entering the field, the 'second generation entrepreneurs', are more inclined to be growth oriented in their businesses, are less risk averse than their older counterparts, and are even seeking venture capital and business 'angels' (Walker, 2000). Changes to the current profiles of women small business operators and their businesses are thus expected in the future.

Country legislation supporting women in the workforce

Between 1983 and the present Australia passed an extensive list of legislation to promote equal opportunity for women and to eliminate discrimination.

Australia ratified the United Nations Convention on the Elimination of All Forms of Discrimination Against Women (CEDAW) in 1983. This was followed by the passing of the Sex Discrimination Act 1984 (preceded by the Sex Discrimination Act, 1975 in South Australia) which prohibited discrimination in employment on the basis of sex, marital status or pregnancy; the Affirmative Action (Equal Employment Opportunity for Women) Act 1986; and the Commonwealth Human Rights and Equal Opportunity Commission Act 1986.

In 1990 the Commonwealth Government ratified International Labour Organization Convention 156 on Workers with Family Responsibilities (ILO 156). Two years later the provisions of the Sex Discrimination Act 1984 relating to sexual harassment were strengthened and the Act was extended to industrial awards.

A number of other protective Acts quickly followed. For instance, in 1992 the Disability Discrimination Act (HREOC) was passed, followed by the Industrial Relations Reform Act 1993. This act prevented discrimination on a wide range of grounds and required the Industrial Relations Commission to take into account ILO 156 (workers with family responsibilities), among others. Similarly in 1993 the Commonwealth Sex Discrimination Act 1984 was strengthened by the following amendments: dismissal on the grounds of family responsibilities became a ground for complaint under the Act; the Act was extended to cover Commonwealth industrial awards and workplace agreements; and amendments were made to the definition of sexual harassment so that complainants no longer needed to show that they suffered a disadvantage or detriment.

In 1996 the Federal Workplace Relations Act 1996 was passed, which retained equal remuneration and parental leave provisions, and prohibited discrimination on a number of grounds including sex, marital status, family responsibilities and pregnancy. Finally, The Equal Opportunity for Women in the Workplace Act 1999 replaced the Affirmative Action Act 1986 to dispel the notion of quotas (affirmative action was often mistaken for the US style system of quotas).

With this impressive array of legislation it could be assumed that women would now be treated fairly in the workplace and have their potential recognized. However, the workplace has become much more dynamic since these changes were first introduced with the result that much of the legislation is not producing the desired result although certain improvements can be documented. The current dynamism, it is felt, has three impacts on women in management.

First, recent research reveals that the systemic discrimination inherent in most organizational cultures is still one of the biggest hurdles for career-oriented women (Still, 1997; Meyerson and Fletcher, 2000; Rutherford, 2001). Although procedural change has impacted overt discrimination in recruitment and selection procedures, it is ineffective against the various cultural nuances and informal systems that operate in most organizations. Women are still considered to be 'outsiders' especially at executive management level. It is almost impossible to legislate against systemic discrimination as this varies from organization to organization, job to job, and occupational level to occupational level. The implementation of procedures to provide guidelines for action is also an impossibility. The best solution appears to lie in education and an understanding of how organizational culture can impact the careers and lives of employees.

Secondly, the Australian workplace has changed since the early 1980s due to globalization, technological advances, 'downsizing', labour market reform, and other such changes. A bi-polar effect is currently operating in the workplace. Many employees are now concerned about job security (Forster and Still, 2002), while organizations, in a quest for 'generational change' in management, are concerned about the lack of commitment exhibited by younger workers, the so-called 'Generation X', while at the same time engaging in a 'war for talent'. The employment situation is extremely fluid and most employees are fearful of the impact of continual change.

Third, careers themselves are also altering (Still, 2001b) bringing with them new benchmarks and parameters. Vertical careers are being replaced by horizontal or lateral careers, while full-time employment is being superseded by part-time work, casual jobs, short-term contracts, volunteerism, and combinations of these alternatives. Measures of 'success' are also altering. Where once it was assumed that most ambitious employees would follow traditional 'upward mobile' career paths to achieve power, prestige, reward and recognition, modern-day concepts of 'success' now also embrace work and family balance and self-actualization (Still, 2001b). These last two concepts, by their very nature, often conflict with the traditional view of success. The result is that many young employees no longer follow traditional career paths; nor are they prepared to be as committed to the organization as their predecessors.

Legislation can only lay down certain principles and compliance standards. If change is relatively slow, legislation will be seen as progressive. If change is relatively fast, then legislation becomes outdated much sooner and needs constant review. Australia appears to be approaching this latter position. In one sense, everything is in place to ensure that women will attain equal opportunity in management in the future. In another sense, the dynamics of the situation are such that they demand a review, a radical rethinking of the situation and some new strategies to ensure that women in management do not begin to regress.

For women in management, then, radical change, or even a reasonable rate of incremental change, is thus not an outcome of the legislation to date.

Initiatives supporting women in the workforce

The position of women in leadership and decision making in the public sector is a relatively recent priority area for the Commonwealth Government's Office of the Status of Women. In 1995 the Federal Cabinet endorsed a strategy to reach a target of 50 per cent representation of women on Commonwealth Boards, Councils and Authorities by the year 2000. However, it was not until 1998 that the Government assumed total discretion over the appointment and selection process and was able to exert more influence on the situation. Previously it had a shared discretion with various producer bodies and other constituent groups.

With the resolution of the discretion issue, the Office of Status of Women introduced a range of initiatives to improve the representation of women. The percentage of women on Commonwealth Boards, Councils and Authorities increased from 28.3 per cent in 1995 to 32.2 per cent in 2000. However, the Government still has some way to go before the target of 50 per cent representation of women in reached.

Politics

Australia was the first country in the world to give women both the right to vote and the right to stand for Parliament when the Commonwealth Parliament passed the Commonwealth Franchise Act in 1902. However, it took forty-one years before women were elected to the Commonwealth Parliament, creating the longest time lag in the western world between women's right to stand and their achievement of parliamentary representation (Parliament of Australia, 1999).

Some idea of women's progress in being elected to the Commonwealth Parliament is given in Table 15.4.

Table 15.4 Women in the Parliament of Australia, 1987-2001

Year (Election dates)	House of Representatives (Lower House)		Senate (Upper House)		Total	% of Total Seats
	No.	%	No.	%		
1987	9	6.1	17	22.4	26	11.6
1990	10	6.8	18	23.7	28	12.5
1993	13	8.8	17	22.4	30	13.5
1996	23	15.5	23	30.3	46	20.5
1998	33	22.3	22	28.9	55	24.5
2001	38	25.3	23	30.2	61	27.2

Source: Women in Parliament, Statistics on House of Representatives and the Senate, Parliamentary Library, Parliament of Australia, 2001. www.aph.gov.au/library/

Following the 1993 election a concerted effort was made by women of all political persuasions to improve women's opportunities of being elected to Parliament.

For instance, in 1994 the Australian Labour Party adopted a motion to guarantee women a 35 per cent share of winnable State and Federal seats by the year 2002, and established Emily's List in 1996 as a fundraising and support organization for Labour women candidates and MPs. The Party's target is for women to make up 50 per cent of Labour candidates and eventually 50 per cent of Labour parliamentarians (Gilchrist, 2001). Similarly, Australia's conservative party, the Liberal Party, established a Woman's Candidates Forum to attract female candidates for Parliament, with strategies focusing on the provision of training, support and community education to encourage women candidates and potential candidates. After the 1998 election the Coalition Government had four women ministers, five women Parliamentary Secretaries in the Ministry, and a woman Senator was President of the Senate. However, the Australian Democrats, the main minor party, are the only political party in Australia to have had a woman leader. Of the seven leaders between 1978 and 2000, five have been women.

Despite these improvements, Australian women have a long way to go before they have 50 per cent representation in the country's parliaments, either Commonwealth or State. However, more women are now prepared to put themselves forward as candidates, and to go through gruelling pre-selection procedures, while others are receiving various forms of political education through election to local government office, serving on the executive of political parties, and other similar activities.

The future

A number of challenges remain regarding the future progress of women in management in Australia.

First, full acknowledgement of both the slow rate of change and a lack of impetus for change needs to be made by both the public and private sectors. Since the election of the Federal Coalition Government in 1995 women have become 'mainstreamed', rather than treated as a special category requiring attention, in official government policy. As a result women's issues now have a low profile, and women's policy offices deal more with domestic violence and sexual abuse programmes than employment equity.

Secondly, while pay equity is a perennial issue the impetus for improvement is virtually non-existent. Despite the New South Wales Pay Equity inquiry (1998) and the Equal Remuneration and Other Conditions of Employment Test Case (2000), there is essentially no national impetus for improvement. The labour market reforms of the latter part of the 1990s appear to have deflected this with their emphasis on individual contracts and trade-off agreements of already established working conditions for wage increases.

Thirdly, the current emphasis on appointing women to boards suggests that women's general representation in management has been solved. However, women's board representation is not a panacea either, as only a few women will be appointed to this level and many of those will hold multiple appointments like their male counterparts, a trend already occurring (Macken, 2001).

Fourth, women's attitudes themselves are changing partly as a result of new generations entering the workforce. While mature women still see the need for reform, and are aware of possible erosions of hard-earned gains, many young Generation X women in their 20s and early 30s believe that gender equity exists in the workplace and that feminism and activism are relics of a past era. They are not sensitive to gender issues or wish to be involved in drives for improvement.

Finally, there are few issues that currently galvanize women in management. Twenty years ago the issues were quite clear. Nowadays, the more obvious have been either remedied or diminished, while the remainder have either merged or become blurred with the pace of external change. Women are building their careers and striving to achieve their goals. While some are aware of the problems in some organizational cultures, most are still isolated from this issue. Pay equity and child-care are perennial issues, and some small incremental changes occasionally take place. However, the situation for women in management in Australia appears to have plateaued for the time being and little dramatic change can be expected in either numbers or opportunities in the immediate future under present circumstances unless new issues or new leaders emerge.

References

Australian Bureau of Statistics (1999), 'Labour: Special Article: Concordance between First and Second Editions of the Standard Classification of Occupations', January, (www.abs.gov.au).

Australian Bureau of Statistics (2000a), *Labour Force*, Cat. No. 6203.0.

Australian Bureau of Statistics (2000b), *Small Business in Australia 1999*, Cat. No. 1321.0.

Australian Bureau of Statistics (2000c), *Characteristics of Small Business*, 8127.0, (www.abs.gov.au/aussstats).

Australian Bureau of Statistics (2000d), *Women Turn Away From Small Busines*, 8127.0, (www.abs.gov.au/ausstats).

Australian Bureau of Statistics (2001), *Labour Force, Australia*. Cat. No. 6203.0, October.

Burton, C. (1997), *Women's Representation on Commonwealth and Private Sector Boards*, research paper for the Office of the Status of Women, Department of the Prime Minister and Cabinet, August (www.dpmc.gov.au/osw/).

Equal Opportunity for Women in the Workplace Agency (1999), *Action News*, Issue 40, December (www.eeo.gov.au).

Equal Opportunity for Women in the Workplace Agency (2000a), *Women in Management* (www.eeo.gov.au).

Equal Opportunity for Women in the Workplace Agency (2000b), *Equity Statistics* (www.eeo.gov.au).

Equal Opportunity for Women in the Workplace Agency (2001a), *Building Successful Partnerships, Annual Report 2000/2001*, Canberra: Commonwealth of Australia (www.eeo.gov.au).

Equal Opportunity for Women in the Workplace Agency (2001b), *Equity Statistics* (www.eeo.gov.au).

Forster, N. and Still, L.V. (2002), *All Work and No Play? The Effects of Occupational Stress on Managers and Professionals in Western Australia*. Research Monograph No. 1, Centre for Women and Business, Graduate School of Management, The University of Western Australia.

Gilchrist, M. (2001), 'More Women MPs but still short of 50pc quota', *The Australian*, December 19, p.6.

Hall, P. (2000), 'Work and Family Issues: Trends and Projections', Paper delivered at *Catalyst for Change Programme*, Equal Opportunity for Women in the Workplace Agency, March.

International Labour Organization (2000), *Breaking Through the Glass Ceiling: Women in Management*, Executive Summary, Geneva, ILO.

Korn/Ferry International (2000), *Annual Board of Directors Study in Australian and New Zealand*, Korn/Ferry Australasia.

Macken, J. (2001), 'Missing in Action', *The Australian Financial Review Magazine*, October, 49-54.

Meyerson, D.E. and Fletcher, J.K. (2000), 'A modest manifesto for shattering the glass ceiling', *Harvard Business Review*, **78**, 127-136.

Office of the Status of Women (1999), *Facts About Women*, March 1999 (www.dpmc.gov.au/osw).

Office of the Status of Women (2000), *Women 2000*, Commonwealth of Australia.

Parliament of Australia: Senate (1999), *Women in the Senate*, Senate Brief No. 3, September (www.aph.gov.au/senate).

Parliament of Australia, Parliamentary Library (2001), *Women in Parliament: Statistics on House of Representatives and The Senate* (www.aph.gov.au/library).

Public Service & Merit Protection Commission (2001a), *State of the Service, Australian Public Service Statistical Bulletin, 2000-01*, Commonwealth of Australia, October.

Rutherford, S. (2001), 'Organizational Cultures, Women Managers and Exclusion', *Women in Management Review*, **16**, 371-382.

Still, L.V. (1997), *Glass Ceilings and Sticky Floors: Barriers to the Careers of Women in the Australian Finance Industry*, Sydney: Human Rights and Equal Opportunity Commission.

Still, L.V. (2001a), *Generational Change Amongst Women Managers Aged 30 to 59*, Unpublished paper, Centre for Women and Business, Graduate School of Management, The University of Western Australia.

Still, L.V. (2001b), *Recasting Careers for Managerial and Professional Women: The New Scenarios*, Paper No. 7, Centre for Women and Business, Graduate School of Management, The University of Western Australia.

Still, L.V. and Timms, W. (2000a), 'I Want to Make a Difference - Women Small Business Owners: Their Businesses, Dreams, Lifestyles and Measures of Success', *Proceedings of 44th International Council of Small Business World Conference* [CD-ROM, ISSN 0646-49636-6].

Still, L.V. and Timms, W. (2000b), 'Women's Business: The Flexible Alternative Workstyle for Women', *Women in Management Review*, **15**, 272-282.

Still, L.V. and Soutar, G.N. (2001), 'Generational and Gender Differences in the Start-Up Goals and Later Satisfaction of Small Business Proprietors', *Proceedings of Australian and New Zealand Academy of Management Conference*, Auckland, New Zealand, December.

Still, L.V., Bellman, S. and Kok, J. (2001), *How Do You Fare? Career Outcomes of MBA Graduates 1977-2001* [Executive Summary], University of Western Australia: Graduate School of Management.

Walker, E. (2000), *The Changing Profile of Women Starting Small Businesses*, Paper No. 6, Centre for Women and Business, Graduate School of Management, The University of Western Australia.

Wirth, L. (2001), *Breaking Through the Glass Ceiling: Women in Management*, Geneva: International Labour Office.

Note

1   EOWA (2002) is currently engaged in conducting the *Australian Women in Leadership Census*, which it is hoped will clarify both the status of women on boards in Auatralia's top 200 organizations as well as women corporate officers and top earners in Australia.

SECTION V
WOMEN IN MANAGEMENT – ASIA

Chapter 16

Women in Management in China

Fang Lee Cooke

Introduction

China is a large country with more than half a billion women, over 50 per cent of whom are in full-time employment. The female workforce as a whole contributed to 38 per cent of the country's GDP (8940 billion yuan) in the year 2000 (Liu, 2001). However, knowledge about these Chinese women in general and women's management careers in specific, remains very limited. The aim of this chapter is to review the positive role of the state in promoting women's education and employment since the founding of Communist China in 1949. It identifies patterns of gender inequality which exist throughout the process of employment such as recruitment, promotion and retirement in China. It explores the political, social and economic factors which influence women's upward career mobility. The intention is to identify barriers to women's career progression. Some of these barriers may be unique to organizations in China and so will require special attention if they are to be eradicated, whereas others may be more generic, transcending differences of occupational sector or society.

Labour force characteristics

In China, women's participation in employment on a large scale is a phenomenon which emerged following the establishment of socialist power in 1949. Today, sharing employment, income and housework has become a widely accepted way of life for many urban husbands and wives, albeit in part because of the low wage system in China which makes it necessary for a dual wage to support a family. As Stockman observed, 'crude measures of gender inequality in urban China reveal no greater inequality than in industrial capitalist societies, in fact possibly greater equality, and a marked reduction in inequality over the period of the building of the communist regime, up to the mid 1980s' (Stockman, 1994, p.771).

For many years, China has had a far higher women's employment rate than the world average (see Table 16.1). In 1997, for example, China had a female workforce of 0.33 billion, representing 47 per cent of its total workforce, which was 11 per cent higher than the world average (*China Statistics Year Book*, 1998).

According to official statistics, around 7 million new workers have been employed each year in the past few years, about 40 per cent of whom are women (Guo, 2000). The scope of industries in which women find employment is expanding into new sectors such as computing, communication, environmental protection, engineering design, estate property, finance and insurance, legal institutions, etc. The number of women employed in these sectors has grown by five to ten times of that before 1980 (Guo, 2000). Moreover, this is closely related to the rising education level of women.

Table 16.1 Labour participation rate (estimate value) of China and other countries in 1995

Country	15-64 years old		10-19 years old	
	Male	Female	Male	Female
	%	%	%	%
China	96	80	45	43
Hong Kong	86	50	31	36
South Korea	76	41	14	16
India	90	31	30	16
Japan	84	53	10	10
North Korea	75	65	21	21
United States	86	60	24	20
Germany	87	57	27	24

Source: *1995 World Bank Report: workers in the globalised world*, China Financial and Economic Publishing House, 1995: 144-147

Meanwhile, unlike their counterparts in the Western economy who are likely to drop out of the labour market during their childbearing and childrearing years, women of childrearing age in China have the highest participation rate in employment (see Table 16.2). Career breaks for women to have children appear to be the exception rather than the norm, although some may argue that this is not necessarily positive, as it increases the social and family pressure on women when they are in their childcaring period. In addition, most working women are full-time workers because there are no established arrangements for part-time work in China to accommodate working mothers. The consequence of these two facts is the complete contrast between the pattern of economic activity of Chinese women and that typically found in the capitalist industrial societies (Stockman et al., 1995). The one-child per-married couple policy implemented in the early 1980s in China, also serves to reduce the childcare burden of working women.

Table 16.2 Women's participation rate in employment at different ages

Age	15-19	20-24	25-29	30-34	35-39	40-44	45-49	50-54	55-59	60-64
Participation rate in 1990*	70.50	91.22	91.38	91.21	91.20	88.28	81.10	61.80	44.94	27.21

Sources: *The Fourth Census of China*, 1990; * Participation rate figures in percentage
Note: The finding of The Fifth Census of China (2000) was still not available yet by the time this chapter was submitted.

All these employment records show that women have increasingly played an indispensable part in modern China's economy. However, the half a century's state intervention in women's employment has largely focused on protecting women's labour rights and increasing their share in employment quantitatively, whereas little provision exists which aims to ensure and improve the quality of women's employment prospects. Statistics on occupational segregation show that a lower proportion of women are professionals or managers, and that a higher proportion are in clerical and lower-level manual work (see Table 16.3). This is despite the finding that China has 'the least occupational gender segregation' in Stockman et al.'s (1995, p.73) comparative study of China, Japan, the UK and the USA. Men make up the majority of employees in most of the occupations and in state-owned sectors where average earnings are highest. For example, in 1997, 65.3 per cent of males worked in the formal sectors of the economy whilst only 34.7 per cent of females worked in them (*China Statistics Year Book*, 1998). Amongst the 60 million workers who worked in non-formal, private and individual businesses, over 50 per cent were females (Jiang, 2000). Working for the non-formal sectors is often associated with lower wages and pensions, less job security, lower employment welfare, reduced training opportunity and even fewer promotion opportunities.

Table 16.3   Proportion (%) of female employees by ownership and sector (end of 1995, 1999)

Item	Total		State ownership		Collective ownership		Other ownership	
	1995	1999	1995	1999	1995	1999	1995	1999
National Total	38.6	38.0	36.1	36.5	44.6	41.1	48.3	42.4
Farming, Forestry, Animal Husbandry, Fishery	37.6	37.6	37.8	37.9	31.9	25.9	37.2	34.1
Mining & Quarrying	25.9	26.5	24.4	26.4	42.1	37.4	22.8	21.6
Manufacturing	45.2	43.4	40.9	39.5	53.1	49.3	49.7	45.6
Electricity, Gas & Water Production & Supply	31.4	32.1	31.5	32.3	32.1	32.4	28.8	31.1
Construction	19.4	18.5	20.7	20.1	17.8	17.4	14.2	15.0
Geological Prospecting & Water Conservancy	25.0	26.4	25.0	26.3	26.5	30.1	38.3	22.2
Transport, Storage, Post & Telecom	26.5	28.0	25.9	27.4	29.4	30.4	24.2	31.7
Wholesale & Retail, Trade & Catering	46.3	46.3	44.9	44.6	47.5	46.1	56.4	52.9
Banking & Insurance	40.0	42.7	39.3	41.9	41.9	42.0	46.0	50.9
Real Estate Trade	33.7	33.8	34.1	34.6	33.2	33.9	31.9	31.6
Social Services	46.7	44.4	45.8	44.4	49.4	47.2	46.8	42.1
Health Care, Sports & Social Welfare	55.6	56.9	56.6	57.7	49.5	51.4	55.9	49.1
Education, Culture & Arts, Radio, Film & TV	40.4	43.4	40.4	43.4	42.7	43.8	45.1	39.9
Scientific Research & Polytechnic Services	33.9	32.9	34.1	33.7	31.5	25.8	30.9	25.7
Governmental & Party Agencies, Social Organizations	22.6	24.1	22.5	24.1	35.0	40.7	30.0	n/p
Others								36.8
	37.2	36.3	32.3	34.6	45.9	42.7	42.8	

Source: *China Statistics Year Book*, 1996 and 2000

Women pursuing education

To some degree, the disproportional presence of women in the less advantaged sectors may be explained by their marginally lower levels of education compared to those of men in general. This is particularly true in rural areas and contributes to the much lower proportion of women in management than men and of their municipal female counterparts (see next section for further discussion). But women's education levels have been rising at a faster rate than, and approaching those of, men (see Table 16.4). A random sample survey carried out by the Ministry of Statistics in 1996 shows that the average education received by workers was 7.6 years, in which the male average was 8.1 years while the female average was 7.0, 1.1 years lower than that of men. However, compared with the figures of 1990, the average years of education of the working population has risen by 0.5 years, in which the female average has risen by 0.5 years while the male average has only risen by 0.4 years (Yuao and Chen, 1997).

Table 16.4 Women's educational levels in China*

Item	1980	1985	1990	1995	2000	2001
Female students to total students (%)	43.0	43.4	44.9	46.5	47.1	47.1
Higher educational institutions	23.4	30.0	33.7	35.4	41.0	42.0
Specialized/technical secondary schools	31.5	38.6	45.4	50.3	56.6	57.4
Regular secondary schools	39.6	40.2	41.9	44.8	46.2	46.5
Vocational secondary schools	32.6	41.6	45.3	48.7	47.2	47.5
Primary schools	44.6	44.8	46.2	47.3	47.6	47.3

* Figures refer to percentage of female students to total students in education in given year.
Source: The Ministry of Statistics of China, 2002, *China Statistics Yearbook*, China Statistics Press

Similarly, the participation of women in higher education has been increasing at a faster rate than that of men (see Table 16.4). For example, in 1980, only 23.4 per cent of university graduates were women. This figure had risen to 33.7 per cent by 1995 and 42.0 per cent by 2001 (The Ministry of Statistics of China, 2002). Thirty-seven point seven per cent of scientists were women. As younger generations of women are becoming increasingly well-educated and well-qualified, (inferior) education levels may not be a convincing reason to justify the lack of women on the management ladder, at least for organizations where university qualifications have been the requirement for job entry.

However, discrimination against women starts in the recruitment selection to higher education institutions, which will have a cumulative effect on their subsequent career advancement. For women to enter the same courses as men in the same universities, they may have to demonstrate better performance records. For example, science, engineering and medical courses are traditionally considered to be subjects for men, dominated by male students. Fewer women apply for those subjects and if they do, they need higher scores than men because it is believed that women's 'abstract thinking ability' will slow down once they are in their late teens.

This form of discrimination against women continues when female graduates seek employment (Cooke, 2001). In the 1980s and early 1990s when the allocation of graduates was carried out by the state, the unwillingness of employers (many of them state-owned enterprises) to accept women graduates was already becoming apparent. Some state-owned companies even refused to accept women university graduates assigned to them by the state simply because they were women. This problem became much more widespread in the mid-1990s when the state withdrew its role in graduate allocation. Generally speaking, female university graduates and post-graduates now face more difficulties obtaining employment than their male counterparts. No legal mechanism is available for female graduates who suffer discrimination to seek justice.

Women in management

To a large extent, the long-term state intervention in gender equality in China has been 'positive action' based upon the recognition of gender differences, with measures devised to address the disadvantages that women experience as a result of those differences (Rees, 2000). So far, this has been the predominant conceptual framework underpinning the making of equal opportunity regulations and policies. The extensive provision of equal opportunity legislation and the high female employment rate mask a very central problem in women's employment - barriers to career progression. Although women already make up 47 per cent of the labour force in China, few play a part in management, even when defining management in the broadest possible way. Governmental organizations are no exception, where the state is the employer and has a direct responsibility to demonstrate its commitment to gender equality in employment as part of a wider effort towards gender equality in society. Due to the limited data available, we have not been able to obtain meaningful statistics on the private sector in China to enable us to compare practices between the state-owned sector and those of the private sector. The rest of this section will focus on governmental organizations.

Exploring women's participation in the administration of government and political affairs both in quantitative and qualitative terms is a useful way to measure gender equality in career development in China. Perhaps not surprisingly, few women work as senior or middle ranking state cadres in governmental organizations. The distribution of women managers in the management hierarchy takes the shape of a pyramid, with the majority of them occupying only low level positions within the organizations. The statistics in Table 16.5 show that only a small proportion of women are in managerial positions in governmental organizations of all levels. The higher proportion of women in central governmental organizations than those in the lower levels of governmental organizations is necessarily a result of the direct state intervention to promote (token) women in order to be seen championing the gender equality policy. The reality is that very few women (less then 10 per cent) are in ministerial or higher positions. The proportions of women in the lowest levels (township and community) of governmental organizations are even lower where state influence is weak.

Table 16.5   Percentage of women managers in governmental organizations, 1990

Level	Total (person)	Men	Women	Percentage of women
Central	17,546	14,261	3,285	18.7
Provincial	66,795	59,837	6,958	10.4
Municipal	324,197	287,741	36,456	11.2
Township	624,068	582,386	41,682	6.7
Community	324,783	306,052	18,731	5.8
Total	1,357,389	1,250,277	107,112	7.9

Source: *The Fourth Census of China, 1990*, China Statistics Publishing, 1993

China's state-owned enterprises and public sector organizations typically operate in an internal labour market system in which jobs are rarely advertised and promotion decisions are made internally, if not confidentially, by superiors. Criteria for promotion are seldom laid down or adhered to. In the last fifteen years, increasing emphasis has been placed on the (higher) education qualifications of the candidates. In fact, university graduates are recruited each year into governmental organizations where they start from the bottom rank as a cadre and make their way up gradually. By 1999, 84.9 per cent of the female cadres in governmental organizations had at least one advanced diploma or university degree qualifications, more than double that of 1990 (Liu, 2001).

Although a relatively large proportion (about 40 per cent) of women graduates are recruited into governmental organizations annually, women in these organizations, as well as in other types of organizations, progress more slowly than men from the same entry point. Women graduates often have lower status jobs, more limited promotion prospects and earn significantly less than men. Statistics show that women fall behind men in their careers quite early – certainly far too early to put the blame on having children. Even when women find the right track to a management career, they still fail to be promoted as quickly or as frequently as men.

Men in China also experience greater upward mobility when they change jobs (Bian, 1994). A survey conducted by the Women's Research Institute of the All-China Women's Federation shows that 'women's mobility in their life-long career tends to be horizontal while men's mobility is upward' (Zheng et al., 1995, p.73). So far, the majority of women in political careers end up in their positions by coincidence or by default (of being a woman). Over 60 per cent of the women in managerial positions in governmental organizations were appointed by the higher level of authorities and only about 4 per cent of them won their position through leadership campaigns or recruitment assessment (Yang, 1999).

Women entrepreneurs

It is difficult to capture the total number of women entrepreneurs in China, given the current radical restructuring of ownership and the fast development of the private and self-employed economy (see Table 16.6). An added problem is that national statistics often fail to detail gender differences, especially in the employment related data, making gender statistics study extremely difficult (Zheng, 2001). Nevertheless, we can make reasonable assumption that the number of women entrepreneurs is growing, albeit not at the same rate as the growth of employment in the non-state sectors. According to the Second National Sample Survey (taken on 1st December 2000) of Women's Social Position in China (2001), 6.1 per cent of women, compared with 8 per cent of men, in urban employment were in managerial positions. This was an increase of 3.2 per cent from that of 1990. Among the women entrepreneurs surveyed who were in the senior managerial positions in enterprises, 95 per cent of them were promoted to the managerial positions since the 1980s. In addition, 57 per cent of them were promoted to their senior managerial position in the 1990s, a figure close to that of men. Among the women entrepreneurs surveyed, 58 per cent of them made investment and established their businesses successfully since the 1990s. This indicates that more and more women are becoming entrepreneurs in the non-state sectors at an increasing speed.

Table 16.6 Employment growth in the private sector and other forms of ownership between 1990-1999

Year	National growth*	State-owned growth (%)	Collective-owned growth (%)	Foreign-owned growth (%)	Self-employed growth (%)	Private-owned*	Private-owned growth (%)
1990	155.1	2.35	1.34	40.43	8.45	1700	3.66
1991	13.9	3.07	2.23	150.00	9.64	1840	8.24
1992	11.7	2.11	-0.19	33.94	6.93	2320	26.09
1993	12.5	0.28	-6.30	30.32	19.12	3730	60.78
1994	12.4	2.69	-3.18	40.97	28.44	6480	73.73
1995	11.1	0.42	-4.20	26.35	22.19	9560	47.53
1996	13.3	-0.15	-4.16	5.26	8.73	11710	22.49
1997	10.9	-1.78	-4.41	7.59	8.45	13500	15.29
1998	5.1	-17.98	-31.91	1.03	12.37	17100	26.67
1999	9.0	-5.37	-12.79	4.26	2.08	20220	18.25
Average growth	11.1	-2.06	-7.78	28.07	12.84		31.67

*figures in thousand
Sources: China Statistics Year Book, 2000; *Forty Years of China Industry and Commerce Administration Management*, 2000, China Statistics Publishing House

The All-China Women's Federation conducted a postal questionnaire survey at the end of 1999 targeting 1,750 women entrepreneurs in non-public sectors in the whole country (with 1,124 returned valid questionnaires, 61 per cent of them from large and medium-sized cities). The survey found that the majority of the entrepreneurs were younger women (90.3 per cent below 50 years of age and 49.3 per cent between 36-45) and had higher educational levels than the national average for women. The vast majority worked in private-owned enterprises (74.4 per cent), whereas others worked in share-ownership companies including joint ventures (18 per cent) or were self-employed (5 per cent). The majority of the companies they worked in employed 11-50 employees, while less than a quarter of the companies had fewer than 10 employees. Over 30 per cent of these companies were in commercial businesses, 16.4 per cent in catering and entertaining, 14.6 per cent in clothe manufacturing, 11.7 per cent in social services, and 11.5 per cent in other light industries. Over 89 per cent of the respondents were married (82.9 per cent were in their first marriage), 84.4 per cent of them felt that their husbands were a great source of support in their career and 52.7 per cent of them operated the business together. These respondents felt that they were inferior to men in their physical strength (60.3 per cent), readiness to challenge (28.8 per cent), determination (36.9 per cent), strategic decision-making (27.4 per cent), analytical ability (20 per cent) and innovativeness (18.9 per cent). They also believed that quality deficiency of women themselves and social bias were the major causes for lack of women entrepreneurs in China (All-China Women's Federation, 2000).

Country legislation supporting women in the workforce

Since the founding of socialist China in 1949, Chinese governments have gradually established a legal system which aims to protect the rights and interests of female employees. This legal system consists of a series of legal and administrative regulations based on the Constitution of the People's Republic of China. Major pieces of legislation include:

- Labour Insurance Regulations of the People's Republic of China (1953).
- Announcement on Female Workers' Production Leave by the State Council (1955).
- Female Employees Labour Protection Regulations (1988).
- Regulations of Prohibited Types of Occupational Posts for Female Employees (1990).
- The PRC Law on Protecting Women's Rights and Interests (1992); and
- The Labour Law of China (1994).

In addition, China has agreed and signed up to a number of International Labour Conventions related to the protection of women and equal opportunities in employment, for example the UN Convention on the Elimination of All Forms Discrimination Against Women; ILO Convention No. 45 concerning the Employment of Women on Underground Work in Mines of All Kinds (1935); and ILO Convention (1951) No. 100 concerning equal pay for men and women workers of equal value.

This framework of legislation is supported by a number of official policies for increasing the participation of women in employment. In drawing up the legislation and official policies, special attention was paid to protecting women both in finance and in working arrangements during pregnancy, maternity or while breast-feeding. In 1995, the State Council issued 'An Outline of Chinese Women's Development 1995-2000' (*Xinhua yuebao*, 1995) which stipulates: '(China should) more or less realize social security for female workers' childbearing costs in urban areas (in that period)'.

Despite decades of equal opportunities legislation and administrative policies, women have not made significant inroads in management careers and remain concentrated in lower level jobs in all sectors. There are two reasons for which the impact of employment legislation on women's career advancement has been limited.

Firstly, the legal and constitutional recognition of gender equality was not followed by public campaigns for the furtherance of that equality in practice, especially in terms of career opportunities. In spite of the fact that recent laws (e.g.

The Labour Law) clearly state that women should have equal employment rights and benefits with men in terms of pay and conditions, promotion opportunities, pay rises, and housing, it rarely happens in practice. This is largely due to the lack of a legal monitoring mechanism to ensure the implementation of the relevant legislation, and in part due to the way jobs are gendered, often to the disadvantage of women (Cooke, 2001).

Secondly, there is a strong element of gender bias in certain aspects of the employment legislation itself, particularly its promotion, selection and retirement policies which close off women's access to the top management ladder. Since the 1990s, the state employer has implemented an age-related policy for management training and development with the aim of injecting new blood to its vast management team. Young talent of below thirty-five years old are selected for management training for the succession plan. Any potential candidates above the age of thirty-five will not be considered for their first promotion. This means that women in their thirties who are ready for career progression when their child-rearing responsibility has eased off, may not have the chance to progress as they have passed their 'sell-by date'. For those who are in the junior rank of management, once they are above the age of forty for women and forty-five for men, they will not be nominated for further promotions. This 'anti-ageing' policy of promotion to keep the management force young results in the decrease of proportion of women managers over 45 years old. For example, over 82.6 per cent of the female cadres in governmental organizations in 1999 were below 45 years of age (Liu, 2001), compared with that of about 60 per cent in 1990.

In addition, since 1951 China has followed a retirement policy in which female workers in general retire five years earlier than their male colleagues in the same occupations (at the age of fifty for blue-collar female workers and fifty-five for white collar). This legislative discrimination against women exists not only at the mass level, but also at the elite level where there is obvious incentive for the state to amend the regulations. In order to retain and utilize expertise more effectively, the Ministry of Personnel has, in the last two decades, issued a number of documents (e.g. Document 153/1983; Document 141/1983; Document 5/1990) which stipulate that professorial experts can carry on working till the age of sixty if they wish and their health permits. These documents also stipulate that a minority of female experts can carry on working after they are sixty if they are needed by their organization (Luo, 2000). Although these documents have provided legitimacy for intellectual and professional women to extend their working life, the opportunity to do so is largely controlled by their employing organizations.

The situation is worse for female managers and cadres in governmental organizations who have to step down at the age of fifty (fifty-five for men), whether they like it or not and irrespective of their rank. Those who are below a certain rank have to retire at fifty-five (sixty for men) while those who are above a certain senior rank can stay until they are sixty. This means that few female managers and cadres can make it to the top level and if they do, they are not likely to stay there for long.

Initiatives supporting women in the workforce

Initiatives to support career progression of women in China have been limited to a number of state-sponsored high profile public campaigns from time to time. Back in the 1950s and 1960s, Mao's motto 'women can hold up half the sky' was widely promoted, albeit based on the misconception of equal opportunities. Women were encouraged to perform strenuous tasks which were conventionally carried out by men, such as working in mines, under cold water, etc. Elite teams of women workers were formed and their achievements were broadcast in order to set examples for the nation. This practice was stopped after the Cultural Revolution.

Another initiative includes the annual road show of 'female model workers' on the 8th March (Women's Day in China) when hard working women role models are selected for the celebration ceremony. Less politically oriented initiatives have been that of 'model husband' and 'model family' which are essentially light-hearted social events aimed to encourage husbands to give more support to their working wives (often career women) by sharing (more) housework.

More practical initiatives to support working women come from company policies on childcare arrangements. Many state-owned organizations in both public services and enterprises have long adopted a state-initiated policy in arranging their shift system to accommodate the childcare responsibility for couples with young children. For example, if one of the spouses has to work a night shift, then the other one will not be scheduled to work at night. Efforts have been made by the state to relieve the burden of housework for female workers through the provision of childcare facilities at very low cost, often sponsored by and located in the organizations for which the parents worked. These company policies, however, have largely not been adopted in the private sector. Nor have the private companies promoted, according to public knowledge, gender equality initiatives to remove barriers to women's career progression. Current high unemployment rates and the relatively low level of human resource management knowledge (a new field to Chinese management which is gradually gaining attention in China) may be largely accountable for the situation. In addition, women have not been able to form a pressure group to exert influence in the private sector and indeed at the national level to advance their case of gender equality in career progression.

The future

Five decades of state intervention in equal opportunities in China has had a positive effect on increasing the employment rate of women. However, the hiring pattern reflects the global tradition of female predominance in the lower levels of work with few promotion opportunities. To the disappointment of many, equality remained an elusive ideal in China and women still face considerable challenges in climbing up the managerial ladder. Some of these challenges are historically embedded whilst others are emerging as (temporary) outcomes in a period of radical social, economic and institutional changes, a period which also brings new opportunities to women.

Firstly, there remains a lack of social expectation and, to a certain extent, tolerance that women should be a boss supervising men, or a wife should be more advanced than a husband in her career. Chinese couples often decide that the man's career takes precedence (Korabik, 1994). This may act as a disincentive for women to seek career advancement. Those who break away from the deeply ingrained normative foundation for gender segregation and subordination may have to pay a price. 'China's growing ranks of career women are facing increasing difficulties in attracting the country's eligible men, whose idea of the perfect wife is a homemaker, not a breadwinner' (*Sunday Telegraph*, 24 April 2001).

Secondly, compared with those of Japan, the UK and the USA, Chinese institutions are, to the greatest extent, structured around gender sameness, with a norm of permanent full-time work for all adults irrespective of sex, and a high degree of egalitarianism in family roles (Stockman et al., 1995). Chinese women tend to work through their life as men do and tend not to see their marriage as an obstruction to their working life, especially for younger women who are affected by the one-child policy and where childcare facilities are highly accessible. This provides a context within which women in China with young children may not find themselves confronted with the dual burden of employment and family life to the same extent as women in other countries. It has been argued that, for historical reasons, management jobs in the West have been specifically designed for married men who were able to cope with the long hours and dedication that management careers demand because they had the support of their full-time home-making wives. If long hours, continuous employment, significant geographical mobility and a series of highly challenging jobs are the price that women in the Western countries have to pay for their management positions, then the Chinese women candidates for managerial jobs, at least in the public sector organizations, are handicapped by the more ideological and organizational factors.

Thirdly, the rapid expansion of private companies and the growth of self-employed businesses have brought new opportunities for women to develop their entrepreneurship and managerial careers. China's entry to WTO will undoubtedly bring new product markets to the economy and therefore new employment opportunities for women. It is predicted that the service sector will be a new focus in China's economic development for which women may be in an advantageous position. However, new skills will be needed if women are to benefit from these new career opportunities.

Compared with their counterparts in governmental organizations, women in these sectors may find that managerial competency, rather than the quality of 'network' relationship, is the key factor in their career progression. Like many third world societies, informal social relationships, or *Guanxi* as it is called in Chinese, provides the lubricant for the Chinese to get through life. This presents particular difficulties for women in China, especially in the public sector where social morality and loyalty to the Communist Party play as much of a role in the promotion criteria as technical competency. Since there are few women in senior management to act as role models or mentors, a female managerial candidate in the public sector may have to look for a man to be her mentor and to establish her network relationship in a network dominated by men. Given the level of intimacy that the relationship naturally engenders (Vinnicombe and Colwill, 1995), women may find themselves embraced by rumours which can be highly damaging to their career because of the relatively low tolerance of the Chinese society of close relationships between men and women outside marriage. However, there is a compelling need for further research on the career prospects for women in the private sector in order to compare and contrast their situations with that in the state sector.

Finally, the gaps in gender inequality at different stages of employment are widening as a result of the weakening power of state administrative intervention, the development of the market economy, the looseness of the legislation and the discriminatory nature of some of the regulations themselves. In some ways, the new and/or recurring discrimination against women workers represents a setback to what was achieved under the planned economy of the socialist China in its early years of development. Without a strong political will to enforce the constitutional and legal rights of women, and without an independent legal procedure through which women can challenge the employment policies of managements, it will be difficult to achieve real gender equality (Stockman, 1994). The Chinese government thus faces tough tasks ahead in establishing and carrying out the state's legal responsibility to combat rising gender inequalities in employment accompanying economic reform.

Acknowledgements

Parts of this chapter come from the author's two journal articles: Cooke, F.L. (2001), 'Equal opportunities? The role of legislation and public policies in women's employment in China', *Journal of Women in Management Review*, 16:7, pp. 334-348, and Cooke, F.L. (forthcoming, 2003), 'Equal opportunity? Women's managerial careers in governmental organisations in China', *International Journal of Human Resource Management*.

References

All-China Women's Federation (2000), 'The Situation of Women Entrepreneurs in Non public Sectors', *Research in Women*, 2, 34-39.

Bian, Y. (1994), *Work and Inequality in Urban China*, State University of New York Press, Albany, New York.

China Statistics Year Book (1996), The Ministry of Statistics of China.

China Statistics Year Book (1998), The Ministry of Statistics of China.

China Statistics Year Book (2000), The Ministry of Statistics of China.

China Statistics Year Book (2002), The Ministry of Statistics of China.

Cooke, F.L. (2001), 'Equal opportunities? The Role of Legislation and Public Policies in Women's Employment in China', *Journal of Women in Management Review*, 16 (7), 334-348.

Forty Years of China Industry and Commerce Administration Management (2000), China Statistics Publishing House.

The Fourth Census of China (1990), The Ministry of Statistics of China.

Guo, H.M. (2000), 'Gender Discrimination in Women's Employment and the Completion of Relevant Laws and Regulations', Paper presented at the *International Seminar on the Legal Protection of Women's Employment Rights*, April, Shanghai, China.

Jiang, Y.P. (2000), 'State Intervention in the Employment of Urban Women', Paper presented at the *International Seminar on the Legal Protection of Women's Employment Rights*, April, Shanghai, China.

Korabik, K. (1994), 'Managerial Women in the People's Republic of China: The Long March Continues', in Adler, N. and Izraeli, D. (eds), *Competitive Frontiers: Women in a Global Economy*, Oxford: Blackwell, pp. 114-126.

Liu, Y. (2001), 'Chinese Women in Politics in the New Century', *China National Conditions and Strength*, 107 (11-12), 28-29.

Luo, P. (2000), 'Retirement Age and Protection of Women's Employment Rights', Paper presented at the *International Seminar on the Legal Protection of Women's Employment Rights*, April, Shanghai, China.

The Ministry of Statistics (1996), *Gender Statistics in China, 1990-1995*, China Statistical Publishing House.

Rees, T. (2000), 'Models of Equal Opportunities: Tinkering, Tailoring, Transforming', Paper presented at the *International Seminar on the Legal Protection of Women's Employment Rights*, April, Shanghai, China.

'The Second National Sample Survey of Women's Social Position in China: Project Report' (2001), *Collection of Women's Studies*, 42 (5), 4-12.

Stockman, N. (1994), 'Gender Inequality and Social Structure in Urban China', *Sociology*, 28 (3), 759-777.

The Sunday Telegraph, 24 April 2001.

Vinnicombe, S. and Colwill, N. (1995), *The Essence of Women in Management*, London: Prentice Hall.

The World Bank Report 1995: Workers in the Globalised World (1995), China Financial and Economic Publishing House.

Xinhua Y. (1995), 'An Outline of Chinese Women's Development 1995-2000', 10, 48-55.

Yang, F. (1999), 'Increasing five types of awareness for women in politics', Human Resource Development, 2, 36-37.

Yuao, X.G. and Chen, L. (1997), 'On the Management of Labour Market Demand and Supply', Management World, Beijing, China, June, 174-182.

Zheng, X.Y. (2001), 'Census and Gender Statistics', Collection of Women's Studies, 40 (3), 11-15.

Zheng, X.Y., Jiang, L.W. and Zheng, Z.Z. (1995), Women Population Issues and Development in China, Beijing University, Beijing.

Chapter 17

Women in Management in Malaysia

Azura Omar and Marilyn J. Davidson

Introduction

The plural society of Malaysia provides an interesting backdrop to investigate the experiences of women in organizations and in management. Malaysia - often referred to as an 'Asian microcosm' (Gomes, 1998) – has three main ethnic communities - Malays, Chinese and Indians. Ethnic differences between the three communities are deep, as reflected in the language they use, the code of dress and behavioural norms and patterns (Gomes, 1998). Besides this, ethnicity is critical, as it is used as the basis to define the country's economic development policies. The country's economic growth is achieved through policies with strong social restructuring underpinnings. In recent years, Malaysia's economic prosperity has created more employment opportunities for all Malaysians including women, especially in the urban economic arena.

Despite these advances, investigations about women managers in Malaysia are still in its infancy. Research on Malaysian women has grown moderately since the 1970s and thus far, much of the work is scattered in various fields such as Sociology and Anthropology, Education, Extension Education and Community Development, Rural Development, Law and Politics (Maimunah, 2001). In the field of economics however, there are few systematic investigations and large scale studies about Malaysian working women. Most research on women's role in Malaysia's expanding economy has so far, tended to focus on the study of the socio-economic status of women as factory workers in the labour intensive industries (see Ariffin, 1982; Khoo and Pirie, 1984; Lee and Sivananthiran, 1992) and on the changing roles of women in rural economic activities (see Ng, 1999; Maimunah, 2001). Drawing from these few economic sources and one on-going research study being carried out by the authors on women in management, this chapter looks at the broad picture on women in management in Malaysia.

Labour force characteristics

The Malaysian government, in both the Seventh Malaysia Plan (1996-2000) and theEighth Malaysia Plan (2001-2006) identified women as an important resource that can be 'mobilized to achieve national development agenda' (Malaysia, 2001). Women account for 48.9 per cent of Malaysia's 23.3 million population and they form a substantial force in the economy since Independence in 1957. Between 1975 and 1990 for example, female labour force participation rates averaged at 45 per cent (Muzambar, 1994). Between 1995 and 1997, the rates registered at 43.5 per cent and 45.8 per cent respectively, but declined in 1998 to about 44 per cent due to economic recession (Malaysia, 2001). In 2000, with economic recovery, this rate increased to about 44.5 per cent.

Despite these encouraging trends, working women accounted for only a third of Malaysia's 5.5 million women in the working age population of 15-64 years. According to the Seventh Malaysia Plan (1996-2000), these low rates prevailed, despite the fact that women were receiving better education and the labour market was buoyant. The government claimed two factors contributed to the under-utilization of women in the economy: (1) inadequate affordable child care facilities and (2) inflexible working patterns.

The literature on Malaysian working women showed that prior to industrialization, women's work was largely confined to rural economic activities. Malaysia's industrialization altered women's structural employment, with substantial shifts away from agricultural sectors towards urban industries and the service sectors (Ariffinet al., 1996). The export-oriented strategy adopted in the 1970s in particular, triggered the most significant changes for women, creating many labour intensive industries such as in textiles and electronics. These industries favoured women, as they were the cheapest and the most flexible labour forces in the market (Ariffin, 1992; Bernasek and Gallaway, 1997). It was estimated that women's employment in these industries increased by 200 per cent in the late 1980s (Brokefieldet al., 1994). Official statistics (see Table 17.1) indeed confirmed that women are assuming greater roles in urban industries. In 1980, 40.1 per cent of the total women labour force was in manufacturing, 29.3 per cent in wholesale, retail trade, hotels and restaurant, 29.5 per cent in finance-related services and 29.4 per cent in other services. By 2000, the proportion of women's labour force in these sectors increased to 41.1 per cent in manufacturing, 39.3 per cent in wholesale, retail trade, hotels and restaurant, 39.9 per cent in finance-related services and 45.3 per cent in other services.

Table 17.1   Percentage of employment distribution of Malaysian women within key economic sectors, 1980-2000

Sectors	1980	1985	1990	1995	2000
Agriculture, Forestry, Livestock & Fishing	39.0	38.4	34.4	28.6	26.8
Mining & Quarrying	10.3	10.5	12.6	17.9	13.0
Manufacturing	40.1	43.1	46.4	42.8	41.1
Construction	7.5	3.4	6.9	6.5	6.0
Electricity, Gas & Water	7.1	5.6	4.3	9.6	9.5
Transport, Storage & Communications	6.3	0.4	11.1	12.1	13.1
Wholesale, Retail Trade, Hotel & Restaurant	29.3	37.7	38.6	38.7	39.3
Finance, Insurance, Real Estate & Business Services	29.5	35.1	34.2	39.9	39.9
Other Services	29.4	36.8	37.9	40.0	45.3
Total	32.7	34.6	35.0	33.9	34.5

Source: Sixth Malaysia Plan (1991-1995), Seventh Malaysia Plan (1996-2000) and Eighth Malaysia Plan (2001-2006)

On aggregate, Malaysian women's labour participation rates are similar to those in the Philippines, Indonesia, Korea and Thailand (Horton, 1996). More careful desegregation of the statistics, however, revealed clear differences by race, age and marital status. In 1971, for example, unmarried women tended to be more economically active than married women and most of the working married women had better educational and socio-economic background (Muzambar, 1981). Employment of Malay women were lower than for Chinese women, reflecting perhaps the stricter code of conduct for Malays as Muslims and this trend has changed very little over the years, as indicated in research by Ariffin et al. (1996). The age-participation profile of Malay women between 1975 and 1987 was flatter than that of Indian and Chinese women. Differences were also recorded at some of the age categories. For example, in the age group of 17 to 23, participation level of Malay women was 14 per cent point lower than that of Chinese women (Ariffin, 1992). In a more recent study, Bernasek and Gallaway (1997) found evidence supporting the above findings. Their analysis of the Second Malaysian Family Survey (SMFS) data revealed that Malay women were less likely to hold paid employment than were Chinese and Indian women. The ethnic composition of paid employees sampled in SMFS differed from that of the Malaysian population, whereby the Malay women made up only about 40 per cent of the sample (vs. 58 per cent of the Malaysian population).

Women pursuing education

An important factor that contributed towards the economic and hence social development of Malaysian women was the huge investment in educational facilities accompanied by the provision for equal access to educational opportunities. The Eighth Malaysia plan (2001-2006) reported that female primary and secondary enrolment in government-sponsored educational institutions reflected the gender ratio of the population. At primary and secondary levels, female students accounted for almost half of the total enrolment in 2000, while at upper secondary level, female students accounted for about 66 per cent of total enrolment in 2000.

Not surprisingly, there have also been significant increases in the number of females entering public universities in recent years. In 1970, for example, female students accounted for only 29.1 per cent of the student population at public universities but in 2000, the percentage increased to about 55 per cent (Malaysia, 2001). Additionally, female enrolments in courses such as medicine, law, economics, business and management have increased in recent years. In 1998, female students constituted 54 per cent and 64 per cent of the total university intake in law and business-related courses respectively. However, despite these encouraging trends, female students are only making small progress into engineering and technology based courses but continue to dominate in arts and humanities. In 1998, 68 per cent of the total enrolments in arts and humanities studies were female, while it was only 29 per cent in technology and engineering courses (Department of Statistics, 2000).

Women entrepreneurs

In recent years, entrepreneurship has become one of the fastest growing sectors of employment for Malaysians. The economic slowdown, coupled with high levels of unemployment and better educational attainment, made self-employment (hence entrepreneurship) a major option for unemployed graduates (Maimunah, 2001) in mid-1980s. More significantly, these circumstances paved the way for Malaysian women to be entrepreneurs. In 1996, 400,000 Malaysian women entrepreneurs (including sole proprietors and business partners) accounted for almost 25 per cent of the total self-employed population in Malaysia (Department of Statistics, 1996).

Research on Malaysian women entrepreneurs first emerged in the 1970s. One of the earliest studies on women entrepreneurs by Daud (1975) provided a profile of Malay women entrepreneurs in Kuala Lumpur. She reported that most of the women entrepreneurs were in the 34-44 age group, were married, came form large families and were likely to be first-born. Moreover, the majority of these women were housewives before they started their businesses and they were motivated by the prospects of better income. These women were either in hawking (i.e.

peddling), retailing or wholesaling, as these businesses were less risky and required little capital and skilled manpower.

In a recent study of 33 women entrepreneurs, Maimunah (2001) found that the women entrepreneurs had a mean age of 39.6 years and were likely to be married with less than three children. About half of the respondents had tertiary education and came from families with business backgrounds. Interestingly, this study also identified economic reasons as being the prime motivator for women to be entrepreneurs. A total of 66.7 per cent of the respondents claimed that they had ventured into businesses because it was an opportunity to increase income. Moreover, 42.4 per cent of the women said that they liked the freedom of having control over their working lives and almost one-third of the respondents believed that owning a business was the best option for any woman who wanted to have both a career and a family. In terms of their entrepreneurial needs, the women indicated that they required better access to entrepreneurial business skills. In order for their businesses to improve, the women claimed that they needed skills training in planning, financial and business management, and some form of mentoring system which would get them in contact with successful entrepreneurs. The women in the study believed that having role models were important for inspiration and in helping them build up their self confidence.

Women in management

Ascertaining the progress of women in management in Malaysia is difficult given, the non-existence of longitudinal data on women as managers. Even the labour statistics on Malaysian women managers must be used with caution, as it defined administrative workers as managers, thus giving the impression that more women are in management positions than is actually the case. Nevertheless, the occupational structure statistics of Malaysian women showed that women are making slow headway into managerial jobs. Compared with many other women globally, however, the proportion of women in management and administrative jobs is still extremely low and has only increased from 0.6 per cent 1990 to 2.2 per cent in 2000 (Malaysia, 2001), as shown in Table 17.2.

Table 17.2 Percentage of occupational structure of Malaysian women, 1990-2000

Occupational Categories	1990	1995	2000
Professional & Technical	9.4	12.7	13.5
Administrative and Managerial	0.6	1.8	2.2
Clerical & Related Workers	14.1	17.5	15.5
Sales & Related Workers	11.4	11.6	12.1
Service Workers	14.1	14.4	17.4
Agriculture	28.1	16.6	14.8
Production & Related Workers	22.3	25.4	22.6

Source: Seventh Malaysia Plan (1996-2000) and Eighth Malaysia Plan (2001-2006)

Apart from these labour statistics, very little is known about Malaysian women who are managers as there are few systematic and empirical investigations on how well these women are doing at work and in management. To date, there is only one detailed study on the specific obstacles that women managers face. In a comprehensive review of women managers in the Administrative and Diplomatic Division of the Malaysian Civil Service, Syed Ahmad (1997) found that women were not getting enough opportunities despite the dramatic improvements in educational attainment and an increase in the number of women applicants. Undoubtedly, this study is significant as it is the first of its kind. However, it was restricted to public sector employment where women were granted longer maternity leave and were not subjected to wage discrimination (Ariffin et al., 1991). Generalizing what was found in her study to the bigger Malaysian picture is dangerous because the labour market is heavily segmented by ethnicity (Ariffin et al., 1996; Ng, 1999). Positive discrimination policies imposed by the government ensured that Malays dominate the public sector, while the Chinese and Indians were more likely to be in the private sector (Sendut, Madsen, and Thong, 1989; Sieh, Phang, Lang and Mansor, 1991; Ariffin, 1992). Ng and Yong (1999) estimated that in a typical government agency, some 78 per cent of all employees were Malays, 9 per cent Chinese and 11 per cent Indian.

More recently, Ng and Yong (1999) carried out a case study research project on a privatized government telecommunication agency and disclosed that while more women were in executive positions, men held all top decision making posts. Women in the agency needed an average of 9.7 years of experience to be promoted but men required only 4 years. Compared to the previous research on women in the Malaysian Civil Service, this study indicated that women were no better off even in private sector employment.

A new study

Recently, the authors have commenced a two-staged, detailed study of Malaysian women managers, covering aspects ranging from their socio-economic background to an analysis of how their work and personal lives differ from that of men in similar job positions. This study is an important step forward for research in Malaysia as it addresses the knowledge gap about Malaysian managers in general and women managers specifically. Moreover, this study is critical, as it is also designed to probe into the impact of ethnicity on the experiences of Malaysian women managers and to determine how comparable the experiences of Malaysian women managers are compared to those of the Western women managers.

Method In the first stage of the study, a total of 58 managers – 38 females and 20 males – were interviewed. The managers interviewed represented a cross-section of industries such as banking, health care, engineering, and education. Although this stage was successfully completed, it must be noted that securing participants for the study was difficult because there are no working database about Malaysian women and men managers. The participants of the interviews were contacted through a network of personal contacts and referrals.

The interviews took the form of a semi-structured format to ensure that all participants were asked the same of questions in the same manner. The questions were guided by the literature and were organized into a number of sections which included (1) personal demographic data, (2) childhood and family background, (3) educational background, (4) career history, (5) present job, (6) motivation, (7) managerial skills and work relationships and (8) work and family responsibilities. The semi-structured format of the interviews was critical, as it allowed the researchers to gain deeper understanding about the experiences and perceptions of the interviewees on women as managers.

With the sample size of only 58 managers, it is not possible to make generalization about women managers in Malaysia. Nevertheless, analysis of the interviews did reveal some interesting facts about the Malaysian women and men managers, as discussed below. Content analysis of these interviews, in conjunction with the review of the literature, was used to design a quantitative instrument that will be administered to a wider sample of Malaysian managers in the second stage of this ongoing study.

Career plans and goals The analysis of the interviews revealed that while almost all the men had some form of career plans, only five out of the thirty eight women actually planned their careers. The majority of the women suggested that they had free flowing careers with minimum planning and said that while they did accept promotions, they did not actively pursue them. A few of the women even suggested that their career choices were unintentional and that their subject choices at universities were based on what they excelled in, as indicated in the following comments:

It was not my plan to have a career in this industry. It was very much the case of me doing a chemistry course because I knew that I could do well. It was an elimination process. The same thing happened when I had to find a job. It was more like finding out where the vacancies are and then see if I like it (Female Senior Technical Manager, Chemical Company).

I joined this company because it was the first company to offer me a full-time and permanent job. I applied for 6 jobs and attended 5 interviews! Beggars can't be choosers! The important thing was to find a job – any job – and do it. Then I just stayed here and had a career (Female Audit Manager, Research and Development Company).

In terms of career goals, the majority of the women said that their goals were to do well and to achieve personal satisfaction on having done a good job. Only three women manager set their sights on the highest managerial positions and believed that they would one day get to that level. Thirty three women on the other hand said that it was very unlikely for women in their organizations to make it to top in their lifetime. These women however, did dream of holding high senior managerial jobs but maintained that they were unlikely to get these jobs. The typical comments included:

I don't think I can go any further.

Yes, I would like the opportunity to try. But having said that, I don't think I will get it. I am not unhappy about that. I have done my best.

Work relationships   All but one of the women interviewed, pointed out that they preferred to work with men rather than with women. The one manager that had no such preference, said that she had no choice but to work with women as there were only women in her organization. More significantly however, is the fact that both the women and men expressed views that were similar – they suggested that women are their own worst enemy:

When you put a man and a woman together, the job gets done. When you put a man and a man together, you get the job done. But with a woman and a woman together, it is difficult. They will either gossip or fight! (Male CEO, Manufacturing).

Women executives are very competitive. It is not easy for us to get promotions and we watch each other like a hawk. Some ladies go as far as sabotaging other ladies. Once, I had a 'friend' who turned against me. She wrote a poison pen letter about me and circulated it to everybody (Female Audit Manager, Research and Development Company).

Women need to learn to work together. That is important. I think we are prone to jealousy and that does not help (Female CEO, Architectural Firm).

Despite the stated preferences to work with men, a number of the women managers admitted that they initially found it difficult to build positive working relationship with men, as shown by these comments:

I did get picked on because I am a lady. At the beginning it was quite bad. There were eight men and one woman – me – at senior level and they tried to find fault in everything I do. But gradually, as I showed that I could do what I had to do, things got better (Female Human Resource Director, Petrol Chemical Company).

Being a woman is tough. Some senior managers – the men of course – tend to look at you. They don't say anything but you can see it in their body language, in the way they say things. They wonder if I can do this job. They monitor my work closely (Female Regional Research and Development Manager, Chemical Company).

In our company, when you get promoted to senior level, they will always have a function in your honour. When I got my promotion, we had the function but two senior managers refused to attend because they did not like the idea of having a woman in senior management (Female Regional Managing Director, Chemical Company).

Work vs. family responsibilities   Within Asian societies, marital expectation presents a great challenge for working women. Marriages and motherhood are social imperatives (Bank and Vinnicombe, 1995; Kausar, 1995; Omar and Davidson, 2001) and women do not have real choices between being married, having families and pursuing careers. Davidson (1997) in her study on black and ethnic minority women managers in the UK found evidence to support this thesis. She noted that women of Asian origin faced intense pressure to marry in their late twenties. Not surprisingly, the interview findings also supported this – Malaysian women, especially the Malays, reported that they too faced intense pressure to marry and have children:

I got married at 34 – rather late. I guess in our society, women are expected to be married and then have children. In my time, it was 24. When my younger sister got married, people in my village asked me "When are you getting married?" Of course they had to ask in such a rude manner! (Female Regional Manager, Transport Company).

I got married 2 years ago at 26. Everybody was so worried when I did not marry at 24 like my sister. Now, their favourite question is when I am going to have a baby? (Female Investment Manager, Venture Capitalist).

The importance of being married for Malay women is further demonstrated by the divorced women managers. Two of the eight divorced women managers revealed that no one in their organizations knew they were divorced. The women asserted that their work life would be even tougher if people knew they were divorced, as they would then be classified as 'dangerous' women. Indeed, a number of the married female Malay managers supported this viewpoint and one married female manager even suggested that 'it is better to be in a bad marriage than to be divorced'. Interestingly, none of the nineteen married Malay managers could identify the disadvantages of being married. Typical answers to the questions 'What are the disadvantages of being married?' were:

> There is no disadvantage. Being married and having a family is useful. I can mix with anybody – man and woman – because I am married. If I am single, I cannot do that because people will look at me differently.

> I can't say there is any. I think life is better for me since I got married.

Women as managers   One of the biggest problems faced by the women interviewed was the perception of others that women were not suited to be managers. A number of the men interviewed asserted that women lacked the qualities needed to be good managers. In fact, two Malay men in senior management argued that Malay women should not be top managers, because it is against Islamic teachings. Interestingly, a Malay woman in middle management shared this viewpoint, claiming that a woman cannot head an organization because a woman is not allowed to lead men in prayers.

Eleven of the twenty men managers interviewed suggested that Malay women were too conservative to be effective managers. These men also stressed that Malay women were on the losing side because Islamic regulations prevent women from 'entertaining' clients. Without the ability to entertain, the men said that Malay women could not be effective as managers. In contrast to what was said by the men, ten of the nineteen Malay women interviewed, believed that having Islamic regulations helped them to be 'professionals' in their managerial jobs. These women maintained that there is nothing wrong with 'entertaining' clients because it usually took the form of business lunches and dinners. Additionally, the women asserted that they were treated with greater respect by their bosses and clients when they defined their working boundaries based on Islamic regulations (i.e. prayer breaks, restricted mixing between males and females, wearing Islamic hijab clothing, etc.).

Country legislation supporting women in the workforce

Since Independence in 1957, the legal position, status and rights of women in Malaysia is largely determined by the Federal Constitution. According to Article

8(1) of the Constitution, 'All persons are equal before the law and entitled to the equal protection of the law'. The Constitution also recognized and safeguarded Malaysian women's right to participate in the political and administrative aspects of the country.

The Employment Act of 1955 (Revised 1981) regulates the conditions of work for all employees. The Act specifically defines 'employee' to include women and has provisions that apply exclusively to women – Part VIII (Employment of Women) and Part IX (Maternity Protection) – under the guise of 'protecting' women workers.

Part VII (Employment of Women)   Section 34(1) prohibits night work for women in the industrial or agricultural sector between the hours of ten o'clock in the evening and five o'clock in the morning. The Section also stipulates that a female employee is not allowed to commence work without having had a period of 11 consecutive hours free from work. However, a provision to the Section empowers the Minister of Human Resources to exempt in writing any female employees from these restrictions.

Part IX (Maternity Protection)   According to Section 37(1), a female employee is entitled to a minimum of 60 consecutive days of maternity leave. Maternity allowance for this eligible period is given to women with fewer then five surviving children. In recent years, the government has made an important step to extend the 60 days' paid maternity to women in government services and in statutory bodies. Under the previous law, government servants were at a disadvantage as they were entitled to 42 days' maternity leave.

In addition to these provisions in the Employment Act, Malaysian working women enjoy the same benefits as their male counterparts under the 1951 Employees' Provident Fund Ordinance, The Pensions Act and the 1952 Workmen's Compensation Act. However, it is pertinent to note that the law does not prohibit employers to pay women employees less than their male counterparts for doing the same amount of work. Additionally, there is no minimum wage legislation, which places women at a disadvantage since women are the preferred workers in the labour-intensive and low-wage industries (Ariffin, 1992; Bernasek and Gallaway, 1997).

Initiatives supporting women in the workforce

Recognizing the economic and managerial potentials of women, the government has taken numerous measures to improve female participation in the labour market. For the first time in a Malaysia Plan, a National Policy on Women in Development was specified in the Seventh Malaysia Plan (1996-2000). This policy, among others, outlined the agenda for meaningful participation of women in the workplace, in order to develop the country so that it could achieve the status of an industrialized nation within the next two decades (Malaysia, 1996). To encourage greater female participation, especially housewives, the Employment Act 1955 was amended in 1998 to include clauses on flexible working hours and part-time working. The government also outlined provisions for tax deductions to employers for the establishment of child-care centres near or at the workplace. In the year 2000, the government made the significant move of upgrading the Secretariat for Women's Affairs in the Prime Minister's Department (HAWA) into a full ministry with a Cabinet Minister. This move was regarded by many as appropriate as HAWA has been in existence since 1991 but remained a mere appendix in the Prime Minister's Department.

The future

While the measures taken by the government to increase female participation in the economy are indeed important, more needs to be done if Malaysia is serious about utilizing women's economic potential. To begin with, the government must ensure that 'Equal Pay for Equal Work' applies to all sectors. 'Equal Pay for Equal work' is not a law but the government has adhered to the policy for almost 40 years (Ariffin et al., 1996). In the private sector however, it has long been hypothesized that women are subjected to wage discrimination as there is no legal recourse, although to date, due to lack of research and monitoring, there exist no empirical evidence to support this claim.

Beyond the legal and legislative undertakings, Malaysians are faced with an even greater challenge of altering societal attitudes about working women. Initial finding from the authors' interviews of 58 Malaysian managers suggests, that while women were readily accepted in the workplace, they experienced prejudice once they climb the managerial hierarchy. According to one senior female manager:

> I think it is okay if we just simply work. Men can accept us. But once we move up, the men, and some women for that matter, take a different attitude. I think men are threatened by us. They do not like receiving instructions from a woman.

On the same issue, a Malay female manager commented:

> It is not easy for ladies to be successful at work. Our culture is shy of success. When a Malay lady gets to the top, she will be shot down definitely, simply because it does not fit in with our culture. I have a friend in this situation and things are really tough for her.

It should be noted that these findings about the experiences of Malaysian women in management are not conclusive. At this stage, it is not possible to put forward recommendations for strategies to help Malaysian women managers, as so much more needs to be known about these women's experiences. The key for moving forward at this point of time, is to fill the knowledge gap about working Malaysian women in general and women managers specifically. More research is needed. Future research in these areas must attempt to obtain bigger sample sizes, as well as take account of the influences of ethnicity, culture and gender differences – comparing work experiences of Malaysian women and men. The authors are the process of redressing some of these issues and are currently carrying a comparative large scale quantitative survey of female and male Malaysian managers. Hopefully, this will act as an impetus for numerous subsequent research studies to follow.

References

Ariffin, J. (1982), 'Industrialization, female labour migration and the changing pattern of Malay women's labour force participation', *Journal of South East Asian Studies*, **19**, 412 –25.

Ariffin, J. (1992), *Women and Development in Malaysia*, Kuala Lumpur: Pelanduk Publications.

Ariffin, J., Horton, S. and Sedlacek, G. (1996), 'Women in the labour market in Malaysia', in Horton, S. (ed.) *Women and Industrialization in Asia*, London/New York: Routledge.

Bank, J. and Vinnicombe, S. (1995), 'Strategies for change: Women in Management in the United Arab Emirates', in Vinnicombe, S. and Colwill, N.L. (eds) *The Essence of Women in Management*, London: Prentice Hall.

Bernasek, A. and Gallaway, J.H. (1997), 'Who gets maternity leave? The case of Malaysia', *Contemporary Economic Policy*, **15**, April, 94-104.

Brookfield, H., Double, L. and Banks, B. (eds) (1994), *Transformation with Industrialisation in Peninsular Malaysia*, Kuala Lumpur/Singapore: Oxford University Press.

Daud, F. (1975), *Penyertaan Wanita Bumiputra dalam Bidang Perniagaan and Perusahaan di Kuala Lumpur* (The Participation of Malay Women in Business and Industry in Kuala Lumpur), Master's Dissertation, Kuala Lumpur: University Malaya.

Davidson, M.J. (1997), *The Black and Ethnic Minority Women Manager: Cracking the Concrete Ceiling*, London: Paul Chapman.

Department of Statistics (1996), *Statistical Handbook of Malaysia 1996*, Kuala Lumpur: Department of Statistics.

Department of Statistics (2000), *Labour Force Survey Report*, Kuala Lumpur: Department of Statistics.

Gomes, A. (1998), 'People and Cultures', in Kaur, A. and Metcalfe, I. (eds), *The Shaping of Malaysia*, London: MacMillan Press Ltd., New York: St. Martin's Press Inc.

Horton, S. (ed.) (1996), *Women and Industrialisation in Asia*, London/New York: Routledge.

Kausar, Z. (1995), *Women in Feminism and Politics: New Directions Towards Islamization*, Selangor: Women's Affairs Secretariat, International Islamic University Malaysia.

Khoo, S.E. and Price, P. (1984), 'Female rural to urban migration in Peninsular Malaysia', in Fawcett, J.T. (ed.), *Women in Cities of Asia: Migration and Urban Adaptation*, Boulder, CO: Westview Press.

Lee, A.C. and Sivananthiran, A. (1992), *Report on employment, occupational mobility and earnings in the Kuala Lumpur labour market with special reference to women in the manufacturing sector*, Kuala Lumpur: Faculty of Economics and Administration, University Malaya.

Maimunah, I. (2001), *Malaysian Women in Rural Development and Entrepreneurship: From Rural Producers to Urban Entrepreneurs*, London: Asean Academic Press.

Malaysia (1991), *Sixth Malaysia Plan 1991-1995*, Kuala Lumpur: Government of Malaysia Printing Press.

Malaysia (1996), *Seventh Malaysia Plan 1991-1995*, Kuala Lumpur: Government of Malaysia Printing Press.

Malaysia (2001), *Eighth Malaysia Plan 2001-2006*, Kuala Lumpur: Government of Malaysia Printing Press.

Mazumbar, D. (1981), *The Urban Labor Market and Income Distribution: A Study of Malaysia*, New York: Oxford University Press.

Mazumbar, D. (1994), 'Labour markets in structural adjustment in Malaysia' in Horton, S., Kanbur, R. and Mazumbar, D. (eds), *Labour Markets in an Era of Adjustment*, Washington, DC: World Bank EDI.

Ng, C. (1999), *Positioning Women in Malaysia: Class and Gender in an Industrializing State*, London: MacMillan Press Ltd., New York, St. Martin's Press Ltd.

Ng, C. and Yong, C. (1999), 'Information technology, gender and employment: a case study of the telecommunication industry in Malaysia', in Ng, C. (ed.), *Positioning Women in Malaysia: Class and Gender in an Industrializing State*, London: MacMillan Press Ltd., New York: St. Martin's Press Ltd.

Omar, A. and Davidson, M.J. (2001), 'Women in Management: A Comparative Cross-Cultural Overview', *Cross Cultural Management: An International Journal, Women in Management: Cross Cultural Research*, **8** (3/4), 35-67.

Sendut, H., Madsen, J. and Thong, G.S. (1989), *Managing in a Plural Society*, Singapore: Longman.

Sieh, L.M.l., Phang, S.N., Lang, C.Y. and Mansor, N. (1991), *Women Managers of Malaysia*, Kuala Lumpur: Faculty of Economics and Administration, University Malaya.

Syed Ahmad, S.Z. (1997), *Women Managers in the Malaysian Civil Service, with Special Reference to the Administrative and Diplomatic Service*, Unpublished Ph.D. Thesis, Leeds: University of Leeds.

Chapter 18

Women in Management in Turkey

Hayat Kabasakal, Zeynep Aycan and Fahri Karakaş

Introduction

The Republic of Turkey has 68 million inhabitants, and covers an area of 297,000 square miles. It is situated at the middle eastern part of the world, located mainly in Anatolia (west Asia) and partly in the Balkans (southeast Europe). The country has been a convenient bridge between east and west for all periods of history. The analysis of women in society and in management positions conveys the simultaneous influence of eastern and western cultures on the Turkish context.

Turks migrated to Anatolia in 10th century from central Asia and had frequent contact with Muslims, which facilitated their conversion to the Muslim faith. They established the Ottoman Empire in the 13th century, conquering and expanding into north Africa, east and central Europe and the Middle East. After the defeat of the Ottoman Empire in the World War I, under the leadership of Mustafa Kemal Atatürk, Turks won the War of Independence and established the Republic of Turkey in 1923. The new republic achieved a series of social, political, linguistic, and economic reforms that were led by Atatürk. These reforms had serious implications for the modernization and emancipation of Turkish women.

The series of reforms and Kemalist principles that were established by Atatürk, carried values of secularism, nationalism, and modernism and tried to incorporate westernization into society. Women were assigned an important part in this modernization project and their progress was interpreted as a significant measure of success in attaining modernity (Arat, 1999). Based on the new state ideology, the emancipation of women from their inferior role during the Ottoman Empire would go hand in hand with the development of the nation and westernization. On the other hand, the duality between secularism and religiousness and the patriarchial middle eastern values still exists in contemporary Turkish society.

The cornerstones of the emancipation of women in the Turkish Republic were widely distributed education, legislative and administrative reforms, political rights, public visibility, and professionalism. The impact of the reforms has been significant among middle- and upper-class families, while their influence has been only partial among lower socioeconomic groups and in rural areas.

Despite the significant attempts at the modernization of women, some conflicting and traditional roles are simultaneously present in Turkish society, even among middle and upper classes as part of middle eastern culture. These traditional roles promote segregation of gender roles, the role of women as mothers and wives and traits that are considered to be feminine.

Labour force characteristics

In order to understand women's labour in the Turkish context, it is necessary to categorize labour force as market vs. non-market labour (Özbay, 1994). In Turkey, women's participation in agriculture as unpaid family labour is officially considered to be market labour. On the other hand, there is a large informal sector in Turkey and a sizable number of women are working in the informal sector that is not reflected as women's market labour.

Census data, in Table 18.1, shows that in 1955, 83.7 per cent of the population over 12 years of age was economically active, while this ratio dropped to 60.7 per cent in 1990. The drop in the economically active population over the years can be explained by massive migration to urban areas where there are not enough job opportunities as paid workers. The economically active population rates for women were 72 per cent in 1955 and 42.8 per cent in 1990, and for men these rates were 95.3 per cent in 1955 and 78.3 per cent in 1990 (SIS, 1994). While census data after 1990 is missing, Household Labour Force Survey Results, which is a nationwide study conducted by the State Institute of Statistics, portray more recent findings regarding labour force participation based on gender for the post 1990 period (SIS, Household Labour Force Survey Results, 1989-1999). Table 18.2 reflects these more recent statistics, where women's participation in labour force was 30.3 per cent in 1995 and 29.7 per cent in 1999, and these ratios were 70.2 per cent in 1995 and 68.3 per cent in 1999 for men. In 1995, 14.9 per cent of adult women in urban areas were economically active and this ratio increased slowly to 15.8 per cent in 1999. In rural areas, 48.4 per cent of women were economically active in 1995 and this ratio dropped to 47.6 per cent in 1999.

Table 18.1   Economically active population rate, 1955 and 1990

	Population over 12 years of age (%)		
	Total	Female	Male
1955	83.7	72.0	95.3
1990	60.7	42.8	78.3

Source: SIS, *Center for Population*, 1994

Table 18.2   Participation in labour force (1995 and 1999)

Years	Turkey		Urban		Rural	
	Women	**Men**	**Women**	**Men**	**Women**	**Men**
1995	30.3	70.2	14.9	66.6	48.4	75.9
1999	29.7	68.3	15.8	64.3	47.6	73.7

Source: SIS, *Household Labour Force Survey Results*, 1989-1999 April

The labour market in Turkey experienced two major changes after 1955 (Özar, 1994). First, as a consequence of massive mechanization in agriculture, there has been significant migration from rural to urban areas, leading to an increase in the urban labour force. Second, industrial and services sectors grew at high rates after the 1960s. As a result of these two trends, the agricultural labour force dropped significantly and the non-agricultural labour force portrayed an upward trend. Parallel with the fall in the agricultural labour force, the women's percentage in the total labour force dropped from 43.1 per cent in 1955 to 35.0 per cent in 1990 (SIS, Center for Population, 1995 and 1990). Furthermore, the Household Labour Force Survey results revealed a declining trend in women's participation in the labour force from 34.0 per cent in 1990 to 27.4 per cent in 1999.

Women's share in the agricultural labour force was 53.3 per cent in 1955 and 55.0 per cent in 1990 and their share in non-agricultural labour force was 8.3 per cent in 1955 and moved up to 14.4 per cent in 1990. Moreover, women constituted 12.3 per cent and 13.8 per cent of industrial workers in 1955 and 1990, respectively, while these figures were 6 per cent and 14 per cent in the services sector for the two respective periods. Household Labour Force Survey results show that 56.8 per cent of economically active women were employed in the agricultural sector, 28.8 per cent were employed in the services sector, and 14.4 per cent were employed in the industry in the year 2000.

The above statistics show that the agricultural sector continues to be the main source of employment for Turkish women. The growth in the non-agricultural sectors was not able to absorb women who migrated to urban areas in a way to change the labour composition. In general, it can be concluded that a majority of women who are considered to be economically active, work as unpaid family workers in agriculture. In 1990 the SIS Population Census statistics showed that 74.8 per cent of economically active women work as unpaid family workers, while only 17.3 per cent of men work unpaid in the family.

Participation of both men and women in the labour force is high in rural areas. The majority of rural women work in agriculture and the number of women in agricultural workforce is higher than men. Participation of rural women in non-agricultural activities is limited. The most frequent non-agricultural participation takes place in weaving, while they earn very little in exchange for very hard work (Berik, 1987). It is also possible to see women engage in economic activities like cotton production, tea and hazel nut production (Özbay, 1982). Women usually engage in these productions in their homes and do not generally demand higher wages as they combine several house duties with economic activities.

Urban women engage in various economic activities that are not reflected in formal market statistics, and there are few studies that investigate urban women's participation in these informal sectors. These studies show that waged domestic labour is very common among urban women from lower socio-economic groups (Zeytinoğluet al., 1997; Kalaycıoglu and Rittersberger, 1998). These women are typically first or second-generation migrants, have little or no education, and work without social security or legal protection. Although they contribute, on average, 42 per cent of the total family income, they regard their self-contributions as only minor. Kalaycıoğlu and Rittersberger (1998) point to the commonality of this perception regarding female earnings in Turkey. Given the fact that women's earnings are mainly used for daily needs rather than investments and purchase of durable goods, they are perceived as unimportant and minor.

Another pilot study in a lower income rural area of Istanbul points to a high percentage of migrant women working in the informal sector (Ilkkaracan, 1998). In this study, 530 women were interviewed and it was found that 22.6 per cent were economically active while 69.2 per cent of the men in their families were working. Of those economically active women, 57.8 per cent were blue-collar workers in the textile and ready-made garments sectors. Moreover, 62 per cent of the working women were wage earners in a formal private company, while 27 per cent were working either at their home or at somebody else's home. Only one-third of these women were covered by the social security system and the rest were not registered as labourers. In addition, those women who were working at home were receiving very low wages (İlkkaracan, 1998). Another study (Eyüboğlu et al., 1998) that included 5,646 women living in four major Turkish metropolises showed that 54 per cent of women who had work experience were employed without social security and only 6 per cent were union members.

Women who are from lower socio-economic groups and who have little or no education, usually work in adverse conditions. A study conducted in the ready-made garments sector showed that very few women have any social security, work under undesirable environmental conditions and have little work satisfaction (Eraydın, 1998). These conditions probably contributed towards the negative attitudes these women had towards work, as most women surveyed indicated that they preferred not to work (Eyüboğlu, Özar, and Tanrıöver, 1998). Furthermore, the majority of Turkish women prefer to stop working after they get married or give birth. In Ilkkaracan's (1998) study, 'family-related' reasons were cited most frequently as a reason for leaving work. These studies are in parallel with role perceptions and expectation regarding women's role in family and society as wives, mothers, and home care-takers. Society as well as women themselves, perceive women's main role as restricted to inside the house rather than participating in economic activities.

Parallel with the state ideology that promotes women's progress as part of the modernization project, the public sector employs significant numbers of women. In the years 2000 and 2001, women constitute 33.1 per cent of labour employed in the public sector (KSSGM, 'Women in Turkey', 2001). Moreover, this relatively high percentage of women in this sector is significant, since they are covered by the social security system and have relatively more favourable working conditions, compared to those working in the public sector.

Wage differences based on gender

A nationwide study conducted in 1987 points to a large wage gap between men and women, where women receive as little as 60 per cent of men's wages (Tan, Ecevit, and Üşür, 2000). Part of the reason for differences in the incomes of paid workers could derive from their concentration in different sectors (Tekeli ,1982). Turkish women are mainly concentrated in labour-intensive and low paying jobs, like textile and ready-made garments industries. In addition, the wage gap is likely to be a manifestation of the glass ceiling phenomenon, where women are concentrated at lower hierarchical levels in organizations.

It is interesting to note that the wage gap decreases as education level of employees increases. When wages of men and women with an elementary school diploma are compared, it is seen that women receive only 41.8 per cent of men's wages (Tan, Ecevit, and Üşür, 2000). Among university graduates, women's wages increase to 59.1 per cent of men's wages. Therefore, while education helps in improving female wage, there is still a big gap based on gender.

A comparison of the wage gap between men and women in different sectors shows interesting findings regarding the prevalence of discrimination in different types of sectors and organizations. As seen in Table 18.3, women directors, entrepreneurs and managers earn nearly as much (95.6 per cent) as their male colleagues in the public sector. Although comparably lower, women managers' wages are 84 per cent of men managers in the private sector. The wage gap increases among groups with lower education and in lower status jobs. The gap is biggest in the agricultural sector, where women receive 23 per cent and 40 per cent of men's wages in the public and private sectors, respectively.

Other than in the agricultural sector, the wage gap between men and women increases in the private sector, particularly at large organizations with more than 20 employees. These statistics are striking in the sense that private sector organizations, which have more discretion regarding the levels of wages, discriminate significantly more against women in terms of their earnings.

Table 18.3   Women's wages as percentage of men's wages

	Public Sector	Private Sector
Entrepreneurs/directors/upper level managers	95.6	84.0
Workers in agricultural sector	23.0	40.0
Scientific/technical/professional workers	85.6	66.0
Organizations having 10-19 employees	76.5	64.0
Organizations having more than 20 employees	80.0	47.0

Source: State Planning Organization, 2000

Women pursuing education

Kemalist principles and state ideology that aims to improve women's position in society has achieved some success in providing widespread education for Turkish women. Primary education is compulsory for both girls and boys; parents who do not send their children to school are liable to imprisonment. Primary education has been increased from 5 years to 8 years in 1997 and it is expected that the years of formal education received will increase for both girls and boys in the coming years.

In the early years of the republic, the rate of literacy was very low among women and throughout the years there has been a significant increase in the rate of literate women. In 1935, only 9.8 per cent of women and 29.4 per cent of men were literate, while in 1955 the literacy rate increased to 25.6 per cent for women and to 55.9 per cent for men and in 1990, 72.0 per cent of women and 88.8 per cent of men were literate (SIS, Population Census, 1935-1990). Furthermore, in 1999, combined primary, secondary and tertiary gross enrolment ratios were 55 per cent for women and 68 per cent for men (Human Development Report, 2001). In the same year, enrolment to universities was 3.7 per cent for women and 6.2 per cent for men (SIS, 1999) and women constituted 40.6 per cent of all students studying at Turkish universities (Gürüz, 2001).

Despite the improvements in women's education, there are a few points that need to be addressed. Although primary education is compulsory for both girls and boys, the discrepancy in the literacy and primary enrolment ratios of girls and boys show that laws are not always applied and more boys are sent to school. This is related to the dominant patriarchal values in society, which perceive women's role as restricted to duties and roles at home rather than achievement in the public arena. When a family's income is restricted, the scarce resource that is to be spent on sending children to school is likely to be allocated to boys rather than girls.

The influence of patriarchal values is observed in other aspects of education, such as the textbooks, curriculum, vocational schools, and area of subject choice at universities. There are studies that show that textbooks assigned at primary and secondary education are gender biased and portray women in the role of mothers and housewives and that a genderized curriculum was used in applied courses where boys spent more time on creative subjects such as handcrafts and calligraphy and girls spent more time for sewing and home economics (Tan, 1979; Gök, 1990; Arat, 1994; Gümüşoğlu, 1998). Gender roles are particularly distinct at vocational schools, where girls are placed in schools that can be considered to be consistent with the traditional female role, such as home economics, child rearing and sewing, and boys are placed in schools that provide skills with a higher market value, such as electricians and carpenters.

Gender roles are apparent in university education as well, as there are distinct differences between the concentration areas of female and male students, where the ratio of female students in engineering is significantly lower compared to social sciences (Tan, 1979). In the 1999/2000 academic year, women constituted 57.8 per cent of university students in language and 55.2 per cent in arts, while their representation fell to 23 per cent in technical sciences (ÖSYM, Higher Education Statistics, 2000). These figures show that women students are concentrated in non-technical occupations. When more specific statistics regarding education in the management departments are considered, women made-up 35 per cent of all students in this area in 2000/2001 (ÖSYM, Higher Education Statistics, 2001).

Women in management

As part of the modernization project of the republic, professionalization of women was of significant importance. Beginning with the early years of the republic, middle- and upper-class families placed a high importance on the education of their daughters in highly prestigious professions. The percentage of women in high status professions can be considered to be a high ratio even in comparison to industrialized western societies. Considering some of the prestigious professions, 60 per cent of pharmacists, 19 per cent of physicians, 30 per cent of dentists, 34 per cent of lawyers, and 23 per cent of professors are women in Turkey (Koray, 1991; Gürüz, 2001). In general, there are 46 women per 100 men in scientific, technical and professional workers (SIS, 1990). Table 18.4 shows the percentage of women in professions.

Table 18.4   Percentage of employed population by occupation, 1990

Population over 12 years of age

	Scientific, technical, professional workers	Admin., managerial workers	Clerical and related workers	Commercial and sales workers	Service Workers	Agricult., forestry, fishermen, hunters	Non-agricultural production & related, transport equipment
Male	5.9	1.5	4.2	8.1	8.7	37.6	34.0
Female	4.8	0.2	3.9	1.1	1.6	82.1	6.4
Women per 100 men	46	8	51	8	10	123	11

Source: SIS, *Population Census*, 1990

The success of women in prestigious occupations is not reflected in the same proportions when decision-making positions are taken into account, with only 8 women per 100 men in administrative and managerial positions (SIS, 1990). While women are accepted into high skill and technical professions, when it comes to decision making for others, their representation drops sharply (Kabasakal, 1998; 1999). For example, Koray (1991) compared the rate of women in professions with their representation at the chamber boards of the professions and found that the rate of women at chamber boards fell to 20 per cent in pharmacy, 6 per cent in medicine, 9 per cent in dentistry, and 7 per cent in law. A similar trend is perceived in the education sector where women have high representation rates. Although women made up 44 per cent of the teachers employed by the Ministry of Education, only 7 per cent of school principles were women (Kadınlar, 1990).

Women managers in the public sector

In the Turkish bureaucracy and public sector, women bureaucrats constituted 27.5 per cent of all supervisors, middle and upper level managers in 1996. As portrayed in Table 18.5, the representation of women at managerial ranks decreases sharply as one goes up the hierarchy from supervisory level to middle and upper levels. While women's representation at supervisory levels was 37.1 per cent, it fell to 13 per cent for department heads, 7.6 per cent for general managers, and 2.1 per cent for general secretary of ministries.

Table 18.5 Women managers in the public sector

Positions	%
General Secretary of Ministries	2.1
Ass. General Secretary of Ministries	4.8
General Managers	7.6
Department Heads	13.0
Supervisory Levels	37.1
Total	27.5

Source: Directorate of State Personnel, *Public Personnel Survey Results*, 1996

Table 18.6 Women in managerial positions in some occupations in the public sector

	Women	Men	Women %
Chief Ambassador	8	179	4.3
Ambassador	8	30	21.1
Governor and Assistant Governor	0	573	0.0
District Manager	7	714	1.0
Rector	3	76	3.8
Dean	49	451	9.8

Source: KSSGM, *Women in Turkey*, 2001

An analysis of the key managerial positions in the public sector reveals that women's representation in the higher levels of the public career ladder is rather low. Table 18.6 illustrates the percentage and number of women holding some managerial positions in the foreign affairs, public administration, and education sectors. At the level of ambassadors, there are 8 women out of 38 (21 per cent), while the ratio of women chief ambassadors decreases to 4.3 per cent. Women's representation in public administration is almost non-existent. There are no women assigned to the position of governors and assistant governors, whereas the percentage of women district managers is only 1 per cent. In the 79 public universities in Turkey, 9.8 per cent of all the deans are women while only 3.8 per cent of rectors are women.

Women managers in the private sector

Although there is no census data that portrays the percentage of Turkish women managers in the private sector, there are several small-scale studies, which shed light on the women managers' status in this sector. All of these studies point to the sharp decline in women's representation as one goes up the managerial hierarchy. A survey of manufacturing firms in the 1970s in a highly concentrated industrial area showed that women constituted 25 per cent of all employees in these firms, while their ratio decreased to 14 per cent in middle management and to 4 per cent in top management positions (Özbaşar and Aksan, 1976). Later in the 1980s, Tabak's (1989) study of the 500 largest manufacturing companies in Turkey showed that in the firms that employed more than 100 people, women made-up 17 per cent of all employees and 15 per cent of managers, whereas the ratio dropped to 3 per cent among top managers.

Women's labour distribution shows that following the agricultural sector, the second highest concentration of women is in the services sector. Thus, one would expect that there would be a higher representation of women in upper levels of the hierarchy in the services sector compared to the industrial sector. However, this hypothesis was not supported by a study conducted in the banking and insurance sectors (Kabasakal, Boyacıgiller, and Erden, 1994). This investigation included more than half of the banks and insurance companies operating in Turkey and showed that women constituted 43 per cent of all employees in these firms, yet their representation in middle management was 26 per cent, and in top management fell to 4 per cent.

Glass ceiling phenomenon

National and pilot studies show that women's representation in managerial positions is low in respect of their numbers as employees. There is a sharp decline in women's percentages as one goes up the managerial hierarchy in both public and private sectors. The number of women in senior executive positions is particularly low, pointing to the existence of the glass-ceiling phenomenon. In the public sector, only 7.6 per cent of general managers and 2.1 per cent of general secretaries of ministries are women. Several studies conducted in the 1970s, 1980s, and 1990s point to the fact that the percentage of women senior executives does not surpass 4 per cent in the private sector. Although not comparable, these statistics imply that there has been no increase in the percentage of senior management positions filled by women during these three decades.

When one analyses the representation of women managers at general assemblies of prominent chambers, it is seen that women constitute 8 per cent of the members in the Istanbul Chamber of Commerce and 0.6 per cent in TUSIAD (Turkish Industrialists and Businessmen's Association). There are no women represented on the boards of directors of these two institutions. Considering the fact that these associations have influential power over the government for shaping economic policies and sectoral strategies, it is significant that firms appoint their male managers as their representatives in these strategically important organizations.

Based on a comparison of women's representation at senior management positions as opposed to other prestigious professions, it is seen that women's high numbers in professional occupations significantly diminishes at key managerial positions. The more strategic the position becomes, the lower the representation of women, such as in key political positions, senior administrative positions in public offices, boards of chambers, and senior executive positions in profit-oriented private organizations.

Women in politics

Turkey was the first Islamic country to grant women the right to vote and to be voted. Women were given political rights in the 1930s – the right to vote and to run in municipal elections in 1930, and in national elections in 1934. Turkish women were granted these rights much earlier than their counterparts in many western countries. On the other hand, parallel with the above argument that women are uncommon in positions that are related to making macro decisions, the proportion of women elected to the Turkish parliament in 1999 was only 4 per cent ('Women in Statistics', 1927-1992, SIS). When the history of parliament is considered, the highest number of women was reached in the first parliament (4.6 per cent) but was as low as 0.6 per cent in 1950. In politics women have mainly been of symbolic importance and only in periods when the emphasis on modernization and westernization was stronger, women's representation in politics increased (although not in a way that would threaten male dominance) (Güneş-Ayata, 1994).

Women parliamentarians in Turkey carry mainly an 'elite' background (Tekeli, 1982; Arat, 1984, 1989). Probably because of their elite status, rather than promoting women's rights, they were involved in non-female areas such as modernity, nationalism, and westernization (Güneş-Ayata, 1994). The elite background is also common amongst women ministers who took posts in cabinets. The first women minister was assigned in 1971 and until 1999, a total of 20 women ministers assumed a post in Turkish cabinets. There are no women presidents in the history of the republic yet, whereas there is only one prime-minister, T. Çiller, who served in this post in the mid 1990s.

The representation of women in local politics follows a parallel picture to national politics. Only a symbolic number of elected posts in local elections were granted to women. In 1999, only 5.5 per cent of mayors and 1.6 per cent of municipality commission members were women (Higher Election Committee, 1999).

The socio-cultural context: gender roles

Turkish society is simultaneously characterized by traditionalism versus modernity, religiousness versus secularism, and eastern versus western values. These dynamics create role conflicts and identity crisis on the part of professional women. Professional women face the issue of satisfying the sex-role stereotypes that are prevalent in society and the role of a professional woman.

Based on GLOBE data, including 61 countries, Kabasakal and Bodur (2002) compared the cultural practices and norms that are prevalent in the Turkish-Arabic cluster with other nine clusters in the world. The cluster including Turkey, Egypt,

Morocco, Qatar, and Kuwait is found to be significantly higher in gender inequality and is characterized by highly masculine practices and norms compared to other country clusters in the world. The dominant masculine practices in these Islamic middle eastern societies may partly be explained by verses of the Koran. It can also be argued that the masculine middle eastern cultures promote a more masculine emergence and interpretation of the Islam religion (Kabasakal and Dastmalchian, 2001; Kabasakal and Bodur, 2002). Thus, Turkish women professionals are operating in a highly masculine society that shares masculine practices and values, yet at the same time the dominant Kemalist ideology of the Turkish state is promoting a more western and modern status for women in society. As a result of the westernization and modernization project of the state, there are relatively high percentages of women in highly prestigious professions, like medicine, law, pharmaceuticals, or academics. On the other hand, it is not possible to see a high percentage of women at executive and decision-making positions, including senior managerial positions, as members of parliament, or as entrepreneurs. It is most likely that the sharp differences in gender roles and dominant sex role stereotypes in society, serve as barriers for women to assume roles that require use of power and influence on others.

Gürbüz (1988) analysed the pervasive sex-role stereotypes and social desirability of these traits in Turkish society. She found that six socially desirable characteristics – ambitious, analytical, enterprising, forceful, insisting on one's rights, and risk taker – and three socially undesirable characteristics – dominant, jealous, and autonomous – were identified as masculine. Four socially desirable characteristics – loves children, dependent, elegant, and thrifty, – and five socially undesirable characteristics – submissive, cowardly, weak, insecure, and naïve – were identified as feminine characteristics. This study indicates that femininity in Turkish society is associated more with negative attributes and with passivity. Thus, the concept of a relatively negative and passive femininity is likely to be incompatible with managerial roles.

A study conducted among business administration senior students at a prominent Turkish university, highlights the perceived incompatibility between the traits associated with femininity and management (Türk-Smith, 1991). In this study, students were provided with a sex-role inventory and were asked to evaluate the characteristics of an ideal manager, an ideal female, an ideal male, an ideal female manager, and an ideal male manager based on this inventory. Findings show that characteristics of a manager were perceived to be compatible with characteristics of an ideal male and an ideal male manager. On the other hand, characteristics of both an ideal female and an ideal female manager were perceived to be dissimilar in all the other categories. There was not even a perceived compatibility between an ideal female and ideal female manager, pointing to a severe identity crisis for women in managerial positions.

As part of the conflicting roles of women professionals, the role of mother and wife conflicts with career roles. A 1992 study compared twenty female and twenty male Turkish white-collar workers and found that marriage had a negative effect on women's careers (Kabasakal, 1998, 1999). In this study, 50 per cent of women indicated that marriage had an adverse impact on their careers, while not a single man indicated so. Furthermore, 75 per cent of women indicated that being a mother affected their careers negatively, while only 5 per cent of men pointed to a negative influence of being a father on their work life. Similar findings were reported by Aycan's recent study (2002) which also suggested that men had more negative attitudes towards women in management (i.e., believing that they are not suitable for managerial jobs) due to women's family-related roles and responsibilities.

For Turkish women in managerial and highly prestigious professions, the conflicting roles of wife, mother, and career result in these women having different dynamics compared to women in unskilled or semi-skilled jobs or to other career women in more developed countries. Turkish women in high status jobs and who come from a privileged background, are in a more advantageous position in reconciling the conflicting demands of their career and home duties by delegating the housework and child-rearing responsibilities to low-paid domestics (Öncü, 1979). Given the fact that wages paid to domestics in developing countries are relatively low, professional women with a high socio-economic background can easily employ at least one domestic at home. In addition, Turkish society is characterized by high levels of family collectivism (Kabasakal and Bodur, 1998), where there is high interdependence between members of larger family members, and it is common practice that grandmothers and aunts take on part of the housework and child rearing responsibilities for career women in the family.

Studies on the characteristics of the few women who were able to move into senior managerial positions, show that senior women managers come from a privileged background (Kabasakal, 1998, 1999; Arbak, Kabasakal, Katrinli, Timurcanday and Zeytinoglu, 1998). It is likely that the elite background of women helps in overcoming the lower status associated with femaleness and provides the prestige that is required for execution of power and influence in executive positions (Kabasakal, 1998a, 1998b).

Women entrepreneurs

As can be seen in Table 18.7, in 1990 only 0.2 per cent of economically active women were in the position of employer and 7.3 per cent were self-employed. When the percentage of women among all entrepreneurs is considered, there are only 7 women employers per 100 men employers, and 13 self-employed women per 100 men in this category. These statistics show a negligible amount of women engage in entrepreneurial activities.

Table 18.7 Percentage of employed population by employment status, 1990

	Employee	Employer	Self-employed	Unpaid family worker
Male	50.1	2.0	30.7	17.3
Female	17.7	0.2	7.3	74.8
Women per 100 men	20	7	13	243

Given the fact that women are not able to find paid jobs as much as their male counterparts, it would be expected that they would engage more in starting a new venture, which would provide them the opportunity to work in exchange for economic gain. Studies conducted in the industrialized western countries show that a significant number of women have engaged in entrepreneurial activities as a reaction to the barriers they faced in organizations (Davidson and Cooper, 1993). On the other hand, entrepreneurship is a rare activity among Turkish women. Among all types of labour, entrepreneurship seems to be the category with the lowest representation among Turkish women.

The low levels of entrepreneurship among women may be related to the dominant patriarchal relationships in society and family. Because women's main role is perceived as being restricted to inside the house, many entrepreneurial activities that family members engage in are considered to be under the ownership of men. Berik's (1990) study on weaving activities show that women conduct the weaving operations at home and male members of the family engage in selling the carpets at market and receiving the money. Thus, even when women engage in entrepreneurial activities, they are restricted to production indoors, whereas men deal with outside relationships.

A study carried out on 220 women entrepreneurs in the capital city, Ankara, showed that entrepreneurship entails serious difficulties for women (Özgen and Ufuk , 2000). Although most of the women (88.6 per cent) perceived themselves as successful entrepreneurs, 87.7 per cent stated that they experienced stress related to work and family matters. Moreover, 71.4 per cent of women entrepreneurs in the sample experienced conflict between their entrepreneurial roles and family roles as wife, mother, and housewife; and faced difficulties in balancing their work and family lives. In another study on 463 dual-career family members with preschool children, Aycan and Eskin (2000) found that women experienced significantly more work-family conflict compared to men.

While the number of women entrepreneurs is negligible and pilot studies point to the difficulty of reconciling their entrepreneurial roles with family roles, some Turkish women entrepreneurs have achieved great success economically. As an example, the United Nations European Commission of Economics included nine Turkish women in their list of outstanding women entrepreneurs in the world (www.unece.org). A qualitative analysis of information that was released by the media about these women points to the fact that most of them come from an elite background, are highly educated and graduated from prestigious universities.

Country legislation supporting women in the workforce

One of the targets of the modernization and westernization project based on Kemalist principles and the new republic was offering free, widespread education at all levels for both girls and boys. Parallel with this mission, primary school education was made mandatory for both sexes in 1923. As a consequence of this application, the education level of both sexes, and particularly of females improved drastically. Another cornerstone of the reforms was related to family structure. The Swiss Civil Code, which included the Family Law, was adopted in 1926. The new Family Law abolished polygamy, granted women the right to choose their spouses and initiate divorce, and recognized women as equals of men in legal areas, such as witnesses in courts and maintaining property. To serve the purpose of improving women's place in the public arena, women were granted the right to vote and be elected in municipal elections in 1930 and in national elections in 1934.

In addition to the laws that influence the general status of women in society, there are two sets of laws that cover the employment-related issues of individuals in Turkish society (Zeytinoğlu et al., 2001): the Constitution and the Labour Law.

According to the latest Turkish Constitution, which was accepted in 1982, all individuals are equal before the law, irrespective of language, race, colour, sex, political opinion, belief, religion and sect, or any such consideration. It also states that state organizations and authorities shall act in compliance with the principle of equality in all proceedings. Under the Constitution, every individual has the right and duty to work and no one shall be required to perform work unsuitable for her/his age, sex or capacity. Minors, women, and persons with disabilities shall enjoy special protection with regard to working conditions. Every individual had the right to work in the public service and no criteria other than merit, shall be taken into consideration for employment in the public sector. The employment related laws are, in general, gender-neutral in their wordings in most articles, yet there are few articles that are discriminatory against women.

According to the Labour Law, there is a restriction to the employment of women in underground and underwater work, night work and dangerous or heavy work. This work in general is higher paid, and although it could be argued that this legislation discriminates against women, it has not been challenged in Turkish courts. With some exceptions, women are not allowed to work in industrial night work. The night work restriction limits women's employment in high paying jobs such as mineral exploration and extraction, manufacturing and processing, construction, energy and gas generation operations (Zeytinoğlu et al., 2001). Thus, although these articles in the Labour Law aim to protect women from adverse conditions, they lead to discriminatory practices.

The understanding of 'equal pay for equal work' has been accepted since 1950. However (as previously discussed), there is a big gap between men and women's pay in practice. The ratio of female to male earned income is estimated to be 0.45 (HDR, 2001), pointing to the fact that, in general, women's income is less than half of men's income. In addition to outright discrimination, other possible explanations of the wage gap are likely to be women's lower education, their concentration in lower paying sectors and their lower hierarchical level. Thus, it can be argued that laws have not been completely successful in promoting the status of women in employment.

Initiatives supporting women in the workforce

In order to understand if private and public organizations in Turkey apply any policies to enhance the status of their women employees, interviews with managers of two management consulting firms were conducted by the authors. These two consulting firms have a wide customer-base and provide services in human resources applications. As reported by the interviewed managers, no firm among their customers was identified as providing any initiatives to enhance the status of women in management.

On the other hand, there were some initiatives by public offices that were targeted at improving economic value of women's labour in the free market. In 1990, the Ministry of Labour and Social Security established the Directorate of Women's Status and Problems with the aim of coordinating and initiating research projects, training programmes, pilot projects, research, and publications that were likely to improve women's status in economic activities and society. In 1993, the Directorate of Women's Status and Problems, in collaboration with the United Nations Development Programme, started the National Programme for Supporting Women's Contribution to Economic Development. This programme included sixteen research projects, many training programmes, and a database about women's labour. Furthermore, among the pilot projects at local level, one included the establishment of a sales centre targeted at marketing the home-made food products produced by women at home and another, the establishment of a weaving workshop where women could use the weaving facilities to be later sold in the market.

Another example of support for women's labour and entrepreneurship by public organizations is the extension of a special bank credit targeted at women entrepreneurs. In 1993, Halkbank, which is a public bank, offered credit with relatively lower interest rates to women, with the purpose of motivating entrepreneurship.

In addition to the efforts of some public offices to support women's economic contribution, another area where there is a need to support women is politics. Like other organizations and companies, political parties do not engage in any organizational initiatives to promote women's representation in the national assembly, nor in municipality elections. On the other hand, KADER (Association for Training and Supporting Women Candidates) was established in the late 1990s as an NGO (non-governmental organization) by a few elite women with the purpose of increasing women's participation in politics. KADER's activities include training women candidates and voters, lobbying, and getting media coverage.

The future

The Turkish Republic, founded in 1923 by Kemal Atatürk, has a strong state ideology that promotes westernization and modernization of society. The new republic achieved a series of reforms, which has serious implications for modernization and the emancipation of Turkish women.

Kemalist principles have been successful to a significant degree, particularly among middle and upper income groups in urban areas, while their influence had been limited among lower socioeconomic groups and in rural areas.

The Turkish state achieved significant success in providing social and political rights, and widespread education for Turkish women. The laws of the republic recognize women as equal to men in major legal areas and women were granted the right to vote and be elected in the 1930s.

The employment related laws are, in general, gender-neutral in their wording in most articles, yet there are a few articles that are discriminatory against women. Primary education has been compulsory for both girls and boys, and as a result, the literacy rate of women has increased drastically, although there is still some gap between the education levels of women and men.

Despite significant reforms and improvements in their status, the participation of women in economic life seems to be concentrated in unpaid family work, including agriculture or home-based production. When paid work is considered, women seem to be heavily concentrated in low-paid, labour intensive sectors, such as the textile or food processing sectors. In addition, women seem to be frequently employed in the informal sector, such as domestics or cooks, where these jobs do not provide any social security. Women's lowest contribution yo economic life seems to be in entrepreneurship, as the number of women entrepreneurs in society is negligible. There is a big wage gap between men and women particularly in the private sector, while women's wages come close to the wages of their male counterparts in the public sector.

Contrary to the disadvantageous position of women in general, women with middle and upper socioeconomic backgrounds enjoy high levels of participation in high status professions, such pharmacology, medicine, law, and academia. The number of women in high status professions can be considered to be a high ratio even in comparison to many developed western societies. In addition, in line with the state principles, the public sector provides significant employment opportunities for women in both unskilled and skilled jobs. Furthermore, the wage gap seems narrower in the public sector compared to private organizations.

While the number of women in prestigious professions is relatively high, women's representation in executive and decision-making posts are scarce. The number of women in parliament, boards of chambers, and senior executive positions in both public offices and private companies is very low. The existence of the glass-ceiling phenomenon seems to be a reality for Turkish women.

Despite the attempts at modernization, Turkish society is characterized by masculine middle eastern values and practices (Kabasakal and Bodur, 2002). Modern and traditional roles are simultaneously present in Turkish society, even among middle and upper classes. Traditional values promote segregation of gender roles, the role of women as mothers and wives and traits that are considered to be feminine. The dominant sex-role stereotypes associate femininity with characteristics that are considered to be negative and passive, whereas masculinity is perceived to be more positive and active (Gürbüz, 1988). The attributes associated with femininity and managerial roles seem to be in conflict with each other, posing an identity crisis for women in management (Türk-Smith, 1991).

Those few women who are able to get promoted to decision-making and power positions as executives seem to come from privileged backgrounds (Kabasakal, 1998, 1999). Furthermore, the few women entrepreneurs who were elected as being outstanding in their performance, also come from an elite background. It can be argued that the prestigious background of these women provides them the necessary status needed to be accepted for powerful decision-making positions.

Looking into the future, in order to improve the status of women in all segments of society, there is a need to improve their education level and close the gap between the two sexes in terms of their education. While primary education is mandatory for both girls and boys, the Turkish state needs to strictly enforce this legislation on families, particularly in the case of girls. It is expected that the increase in primary education from 5 to 8 years will significantly improve the education level in society, yet there are discussions in society and among politicians about the possibility of further increasing primary education to 11 years.

In general, laws that influence the general status and employment related issues of women are gender-neural. On the other hand, there are a few articles in the Labour Law that lead to discriminatory practices and the Turkish parliament needs to remove these articles. Furthermore, CBOs (community based organizations) and NGOs (non-governmental organizations) can be more proactive in providing training to unskilled women that would help them in improving the market value of their labour. CBOs and NGOs can focus on training women in starting their small businesses, which would aid in improving the employment status of women as well as contribute to the growth rate in the economy in general.

References

Arat, Z. (1994), 'Liberation or Indoctrination: Women's Education in Turkey', *Boğaziçi Journal: Review of Social, Economic and Administrative Studies*, **8** (1-2), 83-105.

Arat, Z. (1999), *Deconstructing Images of the Turkish Woman*, New York: Palgrave.

Arat, N. (1986), *Kadın Sorunu (The Problem of Women)*, Istanbul: Say Publications.

Arbak, Y., Kabasakal, H., Katrinli A.E., Timurcanday, O. and Zeytinoglu, I.U. (1998), 'Women Managers in Turkey: The Impact of Leadership Styles and Personality', *The Journal of Management Systems*, **10** (1), 53-60.

Aycan, Z. (2002 – manuscript under review), 'Key success factors for women in management in Turkey', *Applied Psychology: An International Review*.

Aycan, Z. and Eskin, M. (2000), *A cultural perspective to work-family conflict in dual-career families with preschool children: The case of Turkey*, Paper presented at the Fifteenth International Congress of the International Association for Cross-Cultural Psychology, July 16-21, 2000, Pultusk, Poland.

Berik, G. (1987), 'Women Carpet Weavers in Turkey: Patterns of Employment, Earnings, and Status', *Women*, Work Development Series No. 15, Geneva: International Labour Office.

Davidson, M.J. and Cooper, C.L. (1993), *European Women in Business and Management*, London: Paul Chapman Publishing.

Eraydın, A. (1998), 'Dış Pazarlara Açılan Konfeksiyon Sanayinde Yeni Üretim Süreçleri ve Bu Sektörde Çalışan Kadınlar' (New Production Processes in the Ready made garments Industry and the Role of Women), *İktisat Dergisi*, **377**, 44-53.

Eyüboğlu, A., Özar Ş. and Tufan-Tanrıöver, H. (1998), 'Kentli Kadınların Çalışma Koşulları ve Çalışma Yaşamını Terk Nedenleri' (Working Conditions of Urban Women and the Reasons of Leaving Work), *İktisat Dergisi*, **377**, 37-43.

Gök, F. (1990), 'Türkiye'de Eğitim ve Kadınlar' (Women and Education in Turkey), in Tekeli, Ş. (ed.), *Kadın Bakış Açısından 1980'ler Türkiye'sinde Kadın*, Istanbul: İletişim, pp.165-183.

Güneş-Ayata, A. (1994), 'Women in the Legislature', *Boğaziçi Journal: Review of Social, Economic and Administrative Studies*, **8** (1-2), 107-120.

Gürbüz, E. (1988), 'A Measurement of Sex-Trait Stereotypes', Master's Thesis, Boğaziçi University.

Gürüz, K. (2001), 'Dünyada ve Türkiye'de Yükseköğretim: Tarihçe ve Bugünkü Sevk ve İdare Sistemleri' (Higher Education in Turkey and the World: History and Administration Systems), ÖSYM Publications.

Gümüşoğlu, F. (1998), 'Cumhuriyet Döneminde Ders Kitaplarında Cinsiyet Rolleri (1928-1988)' (Gender Roles in Textbooks), in *75 Yılda Kadınlar ve Erkekler*, Istanbul: Tarih Vakfı, pp.101-128.

İlkkaracan, İ. (1998), 'Kentli Kadınlar ve Çalışma Yaşamı', in *75 Yılda Kadınlar ve Erkekler*, Istanbul: Tarih Vakfı, pp. 285-302.

Kabasakal, H. (1998), 'Top Women Managers in Turkey', in *75 Yılda Kadınlar ve Erkekler*, Istanbul: Tarih Vakfı, pp. 303-312.

292   *Women in Management Worldwide*

Kabasakal, H. (1999), 'A Profile of Top Women Managers in Turkey', in Arat, Z.F. (ed.), *Deconstructing Images of the Turkish Women*, New York: Palgrave, pp. 225-240.

Kabasakal, H. and Bodur, M. (1998), Leadership and Culture in Turkey: A Multi-Faceted Phenomenon, Unpublished manuscript.

Kabasakal, H. and Bodur, M. (2002), 'Arabic Cluster: A Bridge Between East and West', *Journal of World Business*, 105, 1-25.

Kabasakal, H., Boyacigiller, N. and Erden, D. (1994), 'Organizational Characteristics as Correlates of Women in Middle and Top Management', *Boğaziçi Journal: Review of Social, Economic,and Administrative Studies*, 8 (1-2), 45-62.

Kabasakal, H. and Dastmalchian, A. (2001), 'Introduction to the Special Issue on Leadership and Culture in the Middle East', *Applied Psychology: An International Review*, 50 (4), 559-589.

'Kadınlar' (Women) (1990), *Cumhuriyet*, p.7, 15 September.

Kalaycıoğlu, S., Rittersberger, H. (1998), 'İş İlişkilerine Kadınca Bir Bakış: Ev Hizmetinde Çalışan Kadınlar', in *75 Yılda Kadınlar ve Erkekler*, Istanbul: Tarih Vakfı, pp. 225-236.

Koray, M. (1991), 'Günümüzdeki Yaklaşımlar Işığında Kadın ve Siyaset' (Women and Politics in the Light of Current Approaches), Türkiye Sosyal Ekonomik Araştırmalar Vakfı.

ÖSYM (2000), Higher Education Statistics 1999-2000.

ÖSYM (2001), Higher Education Statistics 2000-2001.

Öncü, A. (1979), 'Uzman Mesleklerde Türk Kadını' (Women in Specialized Professions), in Abadan-Unat, N. (ed.), *Türk Toplumunda Kadın*, Istanbul: Araştırma, Eğitim, Ekin Publications, pp. 253-267.

Özar, Ş. (1994), 'Some Observations on the Position of Women in the Labor Market in the Development Process of Turkey', *Boğaziçi Journal: Review of Social, Economic and Administrative Studies*, 8 (1-2), 21-43.

Özbay, F. (1982), 'Women's Education in Rural Turkey', in Kağıtçıbaşı, Ç. (ed.), *Sex Roles, Family and Community in Turkey*, Bloomington, Indiana University.

Özbay, F. (1990), *Küresel Pazar Açısından Kadın Emeği ve İstihdamındaki Değişiklikler: Türkiye Örneği (Changes in Women's Employment and Labor in the Global Market)*, İnsan Kaynağını Geliştirme Vakfı.

Özbay, F. (1994), 'Women's Labor in Rural and Urban Settings', *Boğaziçi Journal: Review of Social, Economic and Administrative Studies*, 8 (1-2), 5-19.

SIS (State Institute of Statistics), Census of Population Social and Economic Characteristics.

Tabak, F. 'Women Top Managers in Different Types and Sizes of Industry in Turkey', Master's Thesis, Boğaziçi University.

Tan, E.M. (1979), *Kadın Ekonomik Yaşamı ve Eğitimi (Women's Economic Life and Education)*, Türkiye İs Bankasi Kultur Publications.

Tekeli, Ş. (1990), *Kadın Bakış Açısından 1980'ler Türkiye'sinde Kadınlar (Women From the Perspective of Women in 1980s)*, Istanbul: İletisim.

Türk-Smith, Ş. (1990), 'Kadın Yöneticileri Bekleyen Sorunlar: Kadın Yönetici Zihinlerdeki İdeal Yönetici Olabilir mi?' (Problems of Women Managers: Can Female Managers Be Ideal Managers?), Unpublished manuscript.

Tan, M.G., Ecevit, Y. and Üşür, S.S. (2000), *'Kadın-Erkek Eşitliğine Doğru Yürüyüş: Eğitim, Çalışma Yaşamı ve Siyaset' (Approaching Gender Equality: Education, Work Life, and Politics)*, TÜSİAD Yayınları.

Ufuk, H. and Özgen, O. (2000), *'Kadın Girişimcilerin Sosyo-Kültürel ve Ekonomik Profili: Ankara Örneği' (Socio-Cultural and Economic Profiles of Women Entrepreneurs: The Example of Ankara)*, Ankara: KOSGEB Yayınları.

United Nations Development Programme (2001), 'Human Development Report: Making New Technologies Work for Human Development'.

Zeytinoglu, I.U., Özmen, Ö.T., Katrinli, A.E., Kabasakal, H. and Arbak, Y. (2001), 'Factors Affecting Female Managers' Careers in Turkey', in Çınar, M. (ed.), *The Economics of Women and Work in the Middle East and North Africa*, JAI, pp. 225-246.

Chapter 19

Women in Management in Israel

Dafna N. Izraeli

Introduction

This chapter provides a snapshot profile of women managers in Israel. On the assumption that women's careers need to be understood within the wider context, the chapter highlights the socio-political and cultural developments that shaped the extent and nature of women's participation in management. It begins with a description of recent trends in women's labour force participation, and education. It then proceeds to focus attention on three groups of women: managers, directors and entrepreneurs. The next section summarizes legislation and various initiatives directed to advancing women, including the provision of childcare. Given the current military conflict and economic downturn in the region, the chapter closes on a pessimistic note regarding the opportunities for women in management in the near future.

Labour force characteristics

The last two decades of the 20th century saw a significant increase in both the proportion of women in the civilian labour force (see Table 19.1) and in their commitment to the labour market.

Table 19.1 Women's labour force participation, 1980-2000

Women in labour force	1980	2000
% of all women in LF	36	48
% of married women in LF	39	56
% of 25-64 year old women in LF	50	60
% working part time (<35 hrs/wk)	47	42
Women as % of total labour force	37	46

Source: CBS, 2001, Table 12.1

Compared to 1980, women today are more likely to be employed, to stay employed over the life-time and to work full time. Surveys indicate that husbands increasingly expect their wives to contribute to the family income and women increasingly consider it their obligation to do so (Zemach, 2000). Work for pay has become an important aspect of women's self identity, alongside their strong commitment to family life. Women's employment is a major factor in keeping family incomes above the poverty line and families increasingly rely on women's employment to maintain their current standard of living (Stier and Levin, 1998).

Israel, by every measure – rate of marriage, number of births per woman and rate of divorce – is a family centred society. In this respect it more closely resembles the less advanced economies of traditional societies than to the advanced Western economies of which it is officially a part (Peres and Katz, 1991). The taken for granted primacy of the husband's career over that of his wife, however, is showing signs of giving way to new options. For example, in a study (Zameret, 1999) of gender identity among a random sample of the urban adult population, 84 per cent of the women and 69 per cent of the men agreed that a woman should be employed even if she doesn't need to do so for financial reasons, and two thirds of the women and some 61 per cent of the men agreed that: 'Even though the family may suffer as a consequence of women's employment, women should look after their careers'. Another survey (Zemach, 1999) based on a similar sample, found that 86 per cent of married women and 81 per cent of married men said that when both husband and wife are employed, there should be an equal division of responsibility for income and family responsibilities, but only 33 per cent of the women and 37 per cent of the men said that in fact such an equal division existed in their respective homes.

There are significant ethnic and national differences in women's labour force participation. In 2001, among Jewish women, 63 per cent of those born in Israel compared to 37.3 per cent of those born in the Muslim countries of North Africa and the Middle East (referred to as 'Easterners') and 46.4 per cent of those originating from Europe and North and South America (referred to as 'Westerners'), were in the labour force. Comparing nationalities, 53.4 per cent of the Jewish women were in the labour force compared to 42.6 per cent of Arab Christian women, 24.5 per cent of the Druze and only 17.5 per cent of Muslim women (CBS, 2001). Relative to their representation in the labour force, Christian women were over-represented among semi-professionals and Muslim women were over-represented among underpaid factory workers (Haberfeld and Izraeli, 2002). Labour force participation among Arab women is hindered by insufficient child-care facilities, poor educational facilities, limited employment opportunities, cultural norms that object to women working outside the home and discrimination (Bram and Avtiasam, 1997; Izraeli, 1999). Eastern women, but much more so Arab women face 'multiple jeopardy' (King 1988) – not only the simultaneous oppressions stemming from their being Eastern/Arab, female, and most likely lower class, but also the multiplicative relationships among these disadvantaged identities.

Education remains the best single predictor of women's labour force participation. For example, in 2001, among all mothers of children age 2-4, 79 per cent were in the labour force compared to 86.1 per cent among the same mothers with 13 years and more schooling. Similarly among mothers with 3 children under the age of 14, 71.9 per cent were in the labour force, compared to 85 per cent among the same mothers with 13 and more years of education (CBS, 2001). The growing number of women in higher education (discussed below) re-enforces their attachment to the labour market.

Approximately 43 per cent of employed women were employed in the state sector – a decline from 46 per cent in 1980. The decline is partially an artefact of the recent tendency for the state to hire 'temps' (mainly women) in response to pressure to show savings in government expenditures. The entitlements of temps to tenure and fringe benefits is currently a contested issue in Israeli labour relations. Women constitute over 62 per cent of those employed by the state, with the great majority employed in education, health and welfare and public administration. Although earnings for skilled workers and professionals are higher in the private than in the public (government and Histradrut – General Federation of Labour) sector, gender discrimination is also greater (Gabai, 1992) and the gender gap in hourly earnings is even greater today than it was in the 1970s, despite the increase in women's human capital and commitment to lifelong employment. In the private sector, individual employers have greater freedom to discriminate and the salary range between the bottom and the top is much greater than in the public sector where collective agreements and public scrutiny make it harder to discriminate and set a ceiling on salary levels. With the current government emphasis on privatization and the emerging ideology that grants entrepreneurs greater freedom from public control – the gender income gap may be expected to increase (Haberfeld and Izraeli, 2002).

Women pursuing education

The 1990s was a period of rapid expansion of degree granting academic institutions. The number of students studying for the first degree grew on average 8.2 per cent a year and the total number of students enrolled in academic degree programmes reached 206,689, more than double a decade earlier.[1] The expansion was absorbed primarily by the newly established colleges that specialize in fields closely related to the labour market such as computer sciences, management sciences and law. Women continued to increase their investments in formal education using the 'qualification leverage' (Crompton and Sanderson, 1989) for improving job prospects in the labour market and also for making inroads into traditionally male-dominated occupations. In 1968 women constituted 43 per cent of all university students, in 1990 they were 51 per cent and by the academic year 2000/1 women had surpassed men at all three academic levels and constituted 57 per cent of all students in academic institutions. They made significant inroads into traditionally male dominated professions such as law, medicine, architecture, accounting, and areas within business administration such as marketing and human resources, as well as relatively new fields in the media and computer sciences.

Table 19.2   Percentage of women in the student population by degree and field of study 2000/1

Field of study	Degree			Total
	First	Second	Third	
Total	58.5	58.1	52.1	57.0
Humanities	71.8	74.9	61.8	72.3
Social sciences	67.3	69.5	58.9	67.6
Business & Management	52.3	46.1	52.8	47.6
Law	54.0	49.6	44.6	52.9
Medicine	50.2	47.7	64.4	49.8
Math, Statistics & Computer Sciences	34.7	28.2	28.6	33.6
Physical sciences	35.6	39.8	34.9	36.2
Biological sciences	66.0	66.3	56.3	63.8
Engineering & architecture	24.9	23.2	26.6	24.7

Source: CBS 3/2001, Table 5, p.60

From Table 19.2 we observe that in the universities women are over-represented among students in the humanities, social sciences, and biological sciences. In 2000, women comprised almost half the students in business, management and law, occupations that lead to managerial positions. Women, however, remain under-represented among specializations associated with the new hi-tech industry which has gained such prominence in Israel in the last decade. The small proportion of women among engineering students is hidden by the combination of engineering with architecture. The majority of women are in architecture. Women constitute only some 15 per cent of engineering students.

The general interest in women's education stems from the widely accepted theory that human capital contributes to achievement and that increased formal education leads to enhanced opportunities for advancement. Research suggests, however, that women receive lower returns than men for their investment in education. Institutionalized discrimination in the form of gendered beliefs about the greater suitability of men for management, furthermore, puts the burden of proof on women that they are worthy of promotion. For example, a study of 712 graduates of business administration (Rachman-Mor and Danziger, 2000) found that from the beginning of their respective careers, a significantly higher proportion of men than women filled senior managerial positions and that with increased seniority and greater relevance of one's former job for one's present job – the gender gap in achievement of a senior managerial position increased. Men benefited from the interaction between seniority and relevance of previous job for present job. The interaction of these two variables had no effect for women. In other words, unlike men, women's human capital is less cumulative. At each stage in their career, women need to negotiate terms and prove their value in ways that men need not.

Women in management

Israeli women are relative latecomers to the field of management. In 1981 they constituted less than nine per cent of the managers but over 36 per cent of the labour force. By 2000 they constituted 26 per cent of the managers, 48 per cent of the professionals and 45.7 per cent of the labour force. The significant increase in women's representation among managers and administrators is best understood within the context of the major transformation of Israeli society from a collective, protectionist, and state-centred society, to a more individualist, open, neo-liberal one (Ezrahi, 1997; Shalev, 1992). Individualism was accompanied by an increased emphasis on material success as the mark of achievement. The term 'career', previously associated with selfishness and exploitation, lost its pejorative connotation and by the 1980s, became a legitimate object of aspiration – even for women (Izraeli, 1991). The cultural ascendancy of the market, the expanding economy of the last two decades and the accompanying growth in managerial positions – from 3.7 per cent of the labour force in 1981 to 7.3 per cent in 2000 – opened a window of opportunity for women. Women began moving up organizational and occupational ladders, encouraged and supported by women's organizations and feminists working in government.

The growth of the civil rights movement and civil rights litigation within the new liberal discourse, increased sensitivity to discrimination against women (Ziv, 1999). Whereas in the United States, justice for women followed the movement for racial justice, in Israel, women were the first major beneficiaries of this movement, followed later by other groups. From the mid-1980s claims for group equality were transformed into civil rights language as feminist organizations began to challenge group-based discrimination via political, grassroots, and legal means. The focus of this challenge was on women's under-representation in prestigious and influential positions. The Supreme Court supported women's claims for access to prestigious positions in a number of benchmark decisions that established the principle of gender equality and legitimated the use of affirmative action as a means for achieving it.

Personal profile

Women managers, like women generally, adhere to the family imperative and combine family and work life. From Table 19.3 we observe that the proportion of women managers who are married is not significantly different from the proportion among non-managers.

Table 19.3   Marital status by gender and managerial status, 2000*

	Married	Separated	Divorced	Widowed	Single	
Men managers	85.9	0.7	3.0	0.5	9.9	n/a
Women managers	71.9	1.0	9.8	2.2	14.8	2.04
Women non-managers	73.6	1.2	9.1	2.7	13.5	2.27

*Source: CBS, Labour Force Survey 2001
n/a not available

In 2000, among women age 25-64, 75 per cent of the managers were married, 8.8 per cent divorced 2.3 per cent widowed and 13.9 per cent never married compared to women in the labour force who were not managers where 78 per cent were married 8.1 per cent divorced. 2.8 per cent widowed and 11.1 per cent never married. The majority of those who were single in 2000 will probably marry at a later time. Women managers had on average 2.04 children and non managers 2.27 children. The small difference in number of children may be partly explained by the fact that in Israel, religiosity is the main predictor of number of children, not occupation. Women who become managers are less likely to be orthodox.

Table 19.4   Managers and non-managers by gender, age, schooling and hours worked*

	Mean age	Years of Schooling	Academic Institution #	Hours Weekly
Men managers	44.6 yrs	14.6 yrs	51.2	53.1
Women managers	41.1 yrs	15.1 yrs	59.6	44.6
Women non-managers	38.1 yrs	13.5 yrs	35.0	35.5

*Source: CBS, Labour Force Survey 2001
Proportion whose last school attended was an academic institution

Table 19.4 illustrates that women managers were on average slightly younger than men managers, reflecting their more recent entry, and older than women non-managers. They were also on average more educated and more likely to have attended an academic institution than either men managers or women non-managers. They worked on average 9.1 hours a week more than did women non-managers but 8.5 hours fewer than men managers. The most frequently cited explanation in surveys for the paucity of women in management is women's family responsibilities which limit the time they are able to devote to their careers.

Women managers are more likely to work in economic areas with shorter working hours, such as the public sector.

Distribution by specialization and economic branch

There is a definite gender structure to the distribution of managers among fields of specialization and economic areas.[2] For example, although in 2000, women comprised only 26 per cent of all managers and administrators, they constituted 55.5 per cent of the human resource managers, 41.4 per cent of financial and tax managers and 28.1 per cent of advertising and marketing managers. Forty-one per cent of all women managers were in these three fields. Women were also over-represented among managers of community services where they comprised 47 per cent of the managers. Women were most under-represented among managers at the top levels of government services (where they constituted 16.7 per cent of the managers) and among the more senior managers of business firms (9.8 per cent), among production managers (14.4 per cent) and security managers (16.4 per cent).

When we examine women's participation by economic areas, we find that they were most under-represented among the managerial ranks in extractive and transformative sectors – the productive sectors – and over-represented in the service sectors including producer services (banking insurance real estate) social services (health education welfare, government administration) and personal services. Women constituted 48.5 per cent of the managers employed in health, education and welfare, but only 17.5 per cent of the managers in industry. Among managers employed in industry, the highest proportion of women managers was found in the poor paying textile industry.

Women have made greatest gains in the public or government sector where they enjoy considerable visibility and positions of authority (Halperin-Kaddari, in press). Women constitute 44 per cent of the judges at all levels and 29 per cent of those of the Supreme Court. At the present time, the State Attorney is a woman. Women have recently acquired positions of authority in the ministry of finance which until the last decade was a bastion of male power. Similarly, at the time of writing, the Income Tax Commissioner, the Supervisor of State's Income, the Supervisor of the Financial Market and Insurance, the Head of the Israel Securities Authority are all women. Women served in positions of Chief Scientist in the Ministry of Education, Ministry of Health, The Ministry of Science and The Ministry of the Environment. Another precedent appointment was that of a former Commander of the Women's Corps of the Israel Defence Forces, as Chief Commander of Israel's Prison Service, in May 2000. In general, the importance of professional credentials for moving into senior positions in the public sector reduces the salience of gender, especially where women openly compete for jobs (Izraeli, 1999). Skill assets are less intrinsically gender based than are organization assets (Savage, 1992). The three ministries with the greatest proportion of women in senior positions - education, justice and health - are ministries with the highest proportion of professional employees. Political patronage and personal loyalties play a more important role in the most senior government positions. Given that in 2002 only three of the 27 ministers and none of the deputy ministers were women – the masculine advantage should be obvious.

Whereas women constituted 44.2 per cent of the managers in the government/public sector, they constituted only 22.7 per cent of the managers in the private/business sector which employs the great majority of managers – 88.2 per cent of all men managers and 73.4 per cent of all women managers.[3] In the private sector women were most likely to be in staff rather than line positions. They moved into positions of expertise, but rarely into positions of power and control over the organization and its resources. For example, among the 177 top paid executives for 2001 (Globes, 2002) – only three were women. Among the CEOs of 580 publicly traded companies, only 21 (3.6 per cent) were women And among the 100 leading companies in the country, only one was headed by a woman – the daughter of the founding family. Among the top 160 commercial and service firms only two were headed by women.

A survey conducted by MIDGAM (2000) of a representative sample of 384 industrial firms with more than 5 employees (using a broad definition of manager: 'a worker responsible for the work of others') found that 61 per cent of the firms surveyed had no women managers. Larger firms (50 employees and over) were more likely to have women managers than small firms but the larger the firm, the smaller the proportion of women managers. Women managers, furthermore, earned significantly less than their male counterparts. Only 23 per cent of the men earned under 10,000NIS a month gross (approximately US$2500 in 2000 exchange), compared to 44 per cent of the women. Women managers earned approximately 87.5 cents to a man's dollar and were less likely to be given a company car (67 per cent compared to 82 per cent). Only thirty five per cent of the firms surveyed had policies to facilitate women combining work and family – in most cases the policy was limited to flexible work hours. Seventy per cent of the women respondents and 57 per cent of the men respondents (mainly CEOs and Personnel Managers) said there was discrimination in favour of men at the managerial level. As one CEO of a hi-tech start-up observed (Rosen-Genut, 2001, p.24):

> Chauvinism still has free rein at senior levels. It is simply unbelievable. At meetings of senior levels and even at board meetings, executives accompany their words with chauvinist comments, without regard to whether a woman is present or not. Generally there are no women but it is not hard to understand how a woman would feel if she happened to be there.

Women directors

In March 1993, the Knesset (Israeli parliament) passed an affirmative action amendment requiring ministers to appoint qualified women to boards of the approximately 750 government companies in which women were not properly represented. Ministers initially did not comply with the amendment and in

December 1993, the cabinet approved the appointments of three male directors to two government-owned companies whose boards had no women directors. The Israel Women's Network – a feminist lobby, consequently filed two petitions in the Supreme Court demanding that the government and the relevant ministers explain why they did not appoint women directors as required by law. On November 1, 1994, the Supreme Court sitting as a High Court of Justice annulled the appointment of the men as directors and required the ministers to appoint women in their stead (High Court of Justice 1994). The judgment confirmed the legality of affirmative action and provided the moral justification for its use.

The strong position taken by the Court had an almost immediate impact on appointments to the boards of government-owned companies. Ministers sought women candidates and more women came to see themselves as potential candidates. For example, in response to a reporter's questioning, a newly appointed woman director asked why she had not thought of becoming a director before the judgment, the director replied: 'It was beyond my dreams as a woman; I am not one who does not put up a fight, but the board of directors was always outside the domain. For me, it was like thinking of [participating] in a beauty contest' (quoted in Lori, 1995, p.22). The Supreme Court judgment had made it possible to imagine what had previous been unimaginable.

Between 1993 and 2000, the proportion of women directors of government companies increased from approximately 7 per cent to 38 per cent,[4] and the proportion of companies with no women directors declined from 69 per cent in 1993 to 21.5 per cent in 1997 (Izraeli and Hillel, 2000). In only three per cent of the firms, however, did women serve as Chair of the Board. Arab men constituted four per cent of the directors and Arab women just over one per cent.

Whereas the use of affirmative action to promote women to positions of influence in the government sector was perceived as a legitimate practice given the public nature of ownership, the attempt by feminist organizations to introduce affirmative action in the private sector met with much greater opposition on the grounds that it was not legitimate to interfere in the market economy. In 2000 a survey of publicly traded industrial firms found that 51 per cent still had no women directors (MIDGAM, 2000).

Women entrepreneurs

Broad sweeping changes which took place in Israeli society during the 1980s and 1990s (referred to earlier) resulted in an accelerated increase in the number of new businesses and in a growing interest among wide segments of the population in becoming business owners (GEM, 1999). These changes include the push toward privatization of the large government-owned sector of the economy, and the growth of the private business sector popularly referred to locally as 'the new Israeli capitalism'.

In the 1990s – the decade of the hi-tech boom – 'the entrepreneur became Israel's newest culture hero and role model, a figure to be respected and emulated by large parts of the younger generation' (GEM, 1999, p.9). If the older generation valued security of tenure uppermost, for the new generation, especially of the more educated labour force, job opportunity became the ideal, and the growth of the private business sector was the arena of activity. Starting a business became a more respectable occupation than it had been in previous decades and there were new resources to make this possible. As an example, in 1990, only one venture capital fund was active in Israel. By 1998, 46 such funds (among 101 registered venture capital and investment firms) were operating.

The Government viewed entrepreneurship as an important vehicle for the economic integration of some half million immigrants from the former Soviet Union who arrived between 1988 and 1993 and encouraged these developments by the creation of technological incubators, the Small Business authority and a network of Centres for Promoting Entrepreneurship. Women were encouraged to take advantage of these opportunities and in a few cases special programmes for training would-be women entrepreneurs were sponsored with public funds.

Women's organizations, liberal feminists in cooperation with femocrats (feminists working in government bureaucracies), viewed these developments as opportunities for women and inserted a woman's agenda into the various government sponsored initiatives. For example, in 1996, the small business authority established a woman's committee for the purpose of encouraging entrepreneurship among women. Centres for Promoting Entrepreneurship ran special training programmes both for women generally and for women with special needs such as Arab women and ultra-orthodox women wishing to set up home-based businesses. Programmes were often run in cooperation with one of the big banks that realized the potential of women as a client base. In 1998, 31 per cent of the applications for assistance from the Centres for Promoting Entrepreneurship came from women, compared to 25 per cent in 1995. At the time of writing a legislative proposal 'to encourage women in business' that would require government tenders to give preference to businesses whose majority owner/s and active manager/s are women, passed the first reading in the Knesset.

In 2000, only 5.9 per cent of the female labour force could be classified as entrepreneurs, compared to 15.6 per cent among men. Of these 8.5 per cent of the men and 4.5 per cent of the women were self employed; 7.1 per cent and 1.4 per cent respectively were employers (CBS, 2001, pp.12-33). Women's businesses are concentrated in a small number of economic branches including services and retailing and are under represented in wholesaling, manufacturing and big business in general. Most women in manufacturing are family members of owners or founders and the number of women CEO's of manufacturing firms can be counted on one hand. In most cases of husband-wife partnerships it is the men who look after the financial affairs and make investment decisions.

The great majority of women's businesses are small, life-style ventures – rather than growth-oriented firms characterized by the centrality of the owner, and the small number of employees if any (Lerner et al., 1997). A study of women's life-style ventures in Israel (Lerner and Almor, 2002), found that 58 per cent of the firms were concentrated in the service sector (e.g. childcare, graphics, advertising), 23 per cent were in manufacturing (mainly fashion and cosmetics) and 19 per cent were retail businesses (mainly fashion and apparel stores), and they employed an average of 15.2 persons. Moreover, 29 per cent of the businesses did not employ any additional persons and 9 per cent employed 55 or more employees. Flexibility and the desire to give priority to family over work were important motivators for women to open their own business.

Among the thousands of hi-tech start-ups that mushroomed during the 1990s, only a very small proportion −less than two per cent were established by women alone or in consort with others (Rosen-Genut, 2001). The number of women managers in the hi-tech industry, however, grew from 900 in 1996 to approximately 2200 by the end of 1999. Most women managers in this new sector were in human resources or marketing and communications, fields particularly vulnerable to layoffs during the economic downturn that hit the hi-tech industry after 2000.

An in-depth survey of 25 women entrepreneurs of start-ups (MIDGAM, 2000a) revealed the following. The great majority were academic women with a second (22 per cent) or third (60 per cent) degree most often in a field related to the start up such as natural sciences, computers or engineering. Most had no previous experience in a hi-tech firm but about half had husbands in related fields who were instrumental in establishing the firm. Although the age ranged from 24 to 63, most women were 40 years and more. About a quarter were over 54. Apart from one women who was divorced and two who were single, all the others were married and had children. About half worked at least 16 hours a day, a third 12-15 hours and only about a sixth 11 hours or less. The three most cited reasons for establishing the start-up were firstly, the desire to realize their talent, knowledge and personal experience, secondly the desire to cooperate with spouse and finally, an invention by the entrepreneur. Most women reported that they received encouragement from their environment and did not experience special hardships as women, apart from the greater scepticism and the tendency (especially among investors), to have less confidence in women's ability to succeed. The three major concerns of these women were fear of failure, concern about neglecting the family and concern regarding difficulties in mobilizing capital (MIDGAM, 2000a). The latter is not because capital was in short supply, but rather that investors had more confidence in men and especially men who had been trained in the hi-tech units of the military where few women serve.

Country legislation supporting women in the workforce

Since the 1950s Israel was among the leading states in granting special protection to working women, and especially to working mothers. The issue of granting equal opportunity, beyond mere formal equality, however, is a more recent one that emerged only in the mid-1980s. It was not until the mid 1980s that women pressured for legislation that would accommodate protective measures to the concept of equal opportunity (Raday, 1995). Forced protections such as the prohibition on night work and the requirement of early retirement which damaged women's opportunities in the labour market, were made optional, but not eliminated. Maternal rights such as 12 weeks maternity leave with full pay covered by the National Security Institute, and up to one year leave without pay or paid leave of absence to care for a sick child, were transformed into parental rights while preserving the mother's privileged position. Only if the mother failed to use her sick leave does the right transfer to the father. Fathers were granted the right to take up to six of the 12 weeks maternity in place of their wives provided mothers returned to work during that time. However, only several hundred fathers have availed themselves of this right to date.

The 1988 Equal Opportunities in Employment Law for the first time combined the demand for formal equality with the recognition of the legitimacy of different provisions for men and women on the basis of biological differences and that such provisions do not constitute discrimination. Furthermore, the law put the onus of proof on the employer that s/he did not discriminate among employees or persons seeking employment on account of their sex or personal status in acceptance for employment, terms of employment, advancement, vocational training, and dismissal. The law also recognized sexual harassment as a form of prejudice.

The 2000 amendment to the Women's Equal Rights Law (1951) 'represents the most significant legislative development on the level of the principle of gender equality' (Halperin-Kaddari, in press).

> In a nutshell, the amendment starts with a declaration of the law's intention to ensure total gender equality and women's advancement in all areas of the state, the society the economy, and the family and goes on to prohibit all forms of discrimination against women, whether intentional or *de facto*. It then proceeds with the guarantee of substantive equality, including affirmative action, and explicitly relates to equality in human dignity, including the delineation of social rights (Ibid. p. 9).

The Knesset's readiness to promote equal rights for women, however, stops short of providing budgets required for their effective implementation. There are no effective agencies responsible for implementation and there have been relatively few cases of discrimination claims taken to court to date. In 1995 the Knesset passed the equal pay act which replaced earlier laws and requires equal pay and other remuneration for essentially equal, equivalent work or work of comparable worth performed for the same employer in the same workplace. While an improvement over earlier legislation, until 2002, the law had not been used to challenge pay inequities.

In recent decades, The Supreme Court sitting as a High Court of Justice in about a half dozen cases has had a powerful impact on establishing the principle of gender equality. All the cases dealt with women's entry into male dominated occupations and their right to representation in prestigious occupations (Ziv, 1999). The Supreme Court has been the major proponent of affirmative action and of the view that it is an integral part of the principle of equality. Its impact on the ground, however, has been curtailed by resistance to the principle of equality in favour of other interests. In 1998, despite the Supreme Court judgment advising the Minister of Work and Welfare to search for a suitable woman candidate for the position of Associate Director of the National Insurance Institute where all nine Associate Directors were men, the Minister gave the job to a man from his political party. Political interests prevailed.

Childcare

The availability and quality of alternative child care services and the determinants of access are universally issues of central importance to working women. Most employed mothers in Israel extend the 12 week paid maternity leave to 6 or 8 months. The law requires employers to hold jobs for up to one year of unpaid maternity leave. Upon return mothers face a number of alternative childcare options.

The state subsidizes a national network of childcare services run by three large women's organizations, where cost is graded to income. These daycare centres generally operate from 7am to 4 pm. In addition municipalities support childcare services and there are privately run kindergartens. In 2000, fifty two per cent of the children aged three and 71 per cent of children aged four attended some kindergarten. The rate was very different for Jews and Arabs: 64 per cent of Jewish children but only 20 per cent of Arab children aged 3 attended kindergarten and 87 per cent of Jewish children but only 29 per cent of Arab children aged 4 attended kindergarten (Saar, 2000).

Education is compulsory and free from the age of 5. It is free but not compulsory from the age of 4, since services are not everywhere available. The short school day which for grade one ends at noon, and increases slightly over the years of primary school is a major constraint for women pursuing managerial careers.

Initiatives supporting women in the workforce

We may distinguish between two kinds of initiatives to support the advancement of women – official initiatives sponsored by government and grass roots initiatives sponsored by individual feminists or women's organizations. At the government level, the Authority for the Advancement of the Status of Women established in 1998, replaced the narrower mechanism of the Prime Minister's Adviser on the

Status of Women operating since the early 1980s. Given its very small budget and limited advisory powers, the Authority has not been an effective mechanism for advancing women. The Department for the Advancement of Women within the Civil Service, established in 1996 serves to address complaints by women, sponsors educational programmes and regularly collects and disseminates statistics on women's representation in the civil service. The most significant government sponsored body is the Knesset Committee for the Advancement of the Status of Women established in 1992 and granted the status of a permanent Knesset Committee in 1996. It has been a vital force in promoting the advancement of women whether by sponsoring legislation, putting women's issues on the national agenda and monitoring the implementation of legislation.

The earliest private initiatives to promote the advancement of women include the establishment of the Senior Women Executive Forum within the Israel Management Centre (1986) and courses for training women in management (1988) and women wishing to become directors (1993). Toward the end of the 1980s a new genre of women's organizing emerged whose purpose was to expose aspiring women to the special knowledge required to become managers, entrepreneurs or company directors. These forums initially sponsored by women's organizations and women's magazines and later by municipalities, banks, and a variety of other organizations, emphasize personal transformation, skill acquisition and networking among women as means for achieving goals and independent, and economically successful women as the end product. While most would likely protest the label 'feminist' they may be described as promoting what Ferree and Hess (1985:42) classified as 'career feminism'. Women are encouraged to act in ways few women have acted before them: to take an interest in money, to negotiate terms, to assert themselves, and to take risks. The organizations use role models for forging a cultural and cognitive connection between femininity and economic or business achievement. While resisting the male monopoly of the business world, these women's organizations do not challenge the gender structure of power within it. They are engaged in what I call 'regulated resistance'. The resistance is to the male monopoly on the formal knowledge concerning the requirements for opening and running a business enterprise. The organizations also resist those elements of the traditional scripts for women that exclude them from managing money, taking loans, entering into financial negotiations. Women's presumed responsibility for managing the home and the normative priority of her family commitments over her work are not challenged.

Individual companies, with rare exception, have not initiated policies or programmes to advance women. At best they have permitted flexible starting and ending times to accommodate working parents. Two exceptions are Intel and Amdox, large hi-tech firms which sought to attract women and established in-house childcare services. Individual women (and a few men) have succeeded in negotiating shorter working hours to meet family obligations. There is usually a trade-off between shorter hours and promotion opportunities.

The future

A popular adage states that predictions are difficult, especially about the future. Israel operates in a turbulent environment politically, economically and militarily. Women's advancement into management and within management during the last two decades was largely the result of two factors: the opportunity structure of an expanding economy with a strong demand for educated workers and women's increased commitment to the labour market and career ambitions. Whereas the latter condition persists and results in the advancement of individual women, the former has changed radically.

The opportunity structure was hard hit with the onset of the Intifada in October of 2000. The collapse of the fragile peace process between Israel and the Palestinian Authority, and the intensification of military conflict deeply affected the economy over and above the global recession. Israel is currently in what is perhaps the deepest recession in its history. The amount of venture capital invested in 2000 was half that invested the year before. Hi-tech start-ups folded one after the other and then the bigger firms cut back on their labour supply with human resources, public relations, customer service, communications and marketing, the areas where women managers were concentrated, as the most expendable. Although individual women continue to excel and gain access to more senior positions, the near future for the majority of educated and aspiring women does not look promising. Historically, under conditions of strong competition for managerial jobs, the masculine bias privileges men.

References

Bram, I. and Avtisam, I. (1997), 'The Status of the Arab Women at Work', in Maor, A. (ed.), *Women: The Rising Power*, Sifriat Hapoalim Publisher. pp. 228-242.*

Central Bureau of Statistics (2001), *Statistical Abstract of Israel*, no. 52.

Central Bureau of Statistics (2002), *Students in Universities and Other Institutions of Higher Education*, 2001, http://www.cbs.gov.il/hodaot2002/06_02_23.htm.

Crompton, R. and Sanderson, K. (1989), *Gendered Jobs and Social Change*, London Unwin Hyman.

Ezrahi, Y. (1997), *Rubber Bullets: Power and Conscience in Modern Israel*, New York: Farrar, Straus & Giroux.

Ferree, M.M. and Hess, B.B. (1985), *Controversy and Coalition, Working Parents and the Revolution at Home*, New York: Penguin.

Gabai, Y. (1992), 'Wages, Taxes and Costs of Labour in Financial Institutions and Government', *Rivon Lekalkala*, **38**, 51-608.*

Globes, (2002).

Haberfeld Y. and Izraeli, D.N. (2002), 'Gender Inequality within Majority and Minority Groups in Israel', *Race, Gender & Class*, **9** (in press).

Halperin-Kaddari, R. (in press), *Women in Israel: A State of Their Own*. Philadelphia, PA.: Pennsylvania University Press.

High Court of Israel (1994), 453/94, 454/94, Israel Women's Network v. Government of Israel et al., PD (5) 501.*

Izraeli, D.N., 'Women and Work: From Collective to Career', in Swirski, B. and Safir, M.P., *Calling the Equality Bluff: Women in Israel*, New York: Pergamon Press, pp. 165-177.

Izraeli, D.N. (1999), 'Women in the Labor Force', in Izraeli, D.N., Friedman, A., Herzog, H., Bijaoui, S., Naveh, H., Dahan-Kalev, H. and M. Hassan, *Sex, Gender, Politics*, Tel Aviv: Hakibbutz Hameuchad. pp. 167-216.*

Izraeli, D.N. (2000), 'The Paradox of Affirmative Action for Women Directors in Israel', in Burke, R.J. and Mattis, M.C., *Women on Corporate Boards of Directors: International Challenges and Opportunities*, Boston/London: Kluwer Academic Publishers, pp. 97-110.

Izraeli, D.N., with Hillel, R. (2000), 'Women's Representation in Boards of Government-owned Companies: 1993-97', Unpublished Report, Bar-Ilan University, Israel.*

King, D.K. (1988), 'Multiple Jeopardy, Multiple Consciousness: The Context of a Black Feminist Ideology', *Signs*, **14** (1), 42-72.

Lerner, M. and Almor, T. (2002), 'Relationships among Strategic Capabilities and the Performance of Women-owned Small Ventures', *Journal of Small Business Management*, **40** (2), 109-225.

Lerner M. and Avrahami, Y. (1999), *Global Entrepreneurship Monitor*, Israel Executive Report, Tel Aviv University.

Lerner, M., Brush, C. and Hisrich, R. (1997), 'Israeli Women Entrepreneurs: An Examination of Factors Affecting Performance', *Journal of Business Venturing*, **12**, 315-339.

Lori, A. (1995), 'Everything You Can Do', *Ha'aretz*, September 1, Supplement, p. 18.*

MIDGAM Consulting and Research Inc. (2000), *Women Managers in Industry – Representation, Performance Evaluation and Conditions of Employment*, Ramat Gan, December.*

MIDGAM Consulting and Research Inc. (2000a), *Women Entrepreneurs of Start-Ups*, Ramat Gan, May.*

Peres, Y. and Katz, R. (1991), 'The Family in Israel: Change and Continuity', in Shamgar-Handelman, L. and Bar Yosef, R. (eds), *Families in Israel*, Jerusalem: Akadamon (in Hebrew), pp. 9-32.

Rachman-Mor, D. and Danziger, N. (2000), 'Early Career Gender Differences among Graduates of Business Administration', *Megamot* **30** (2), 262-279.*

Raday, F. (1995), 'Women in the Labour Market', in Raday, F., Shalev, C. and Liban-Kobi, M. (eds), *The Status of Women in Society and Law*, Jerusalem and Tel Aviv: Shoken.

Rosen-Genut, A. (2001), 'Difficult to be a Woman Manager', *Status*, Feb. pp. 24-26.*

Saar, R. (2000), 'The Proportion of 3-4 year Olds in Kindergartens is Low Compared to Europe', *Ha'aretz*, May 28.*

Savage, D., 'Women's Expertise, Men's Authority: Gendered Organization and the Contemporary Middle Classes', in Savage, M. and Witz, A. (eds), *Gender and Bureaucracy*, Oxford, England: Blackwell Publishers, pp. 124-154.

Shalev, M. (1992), *Labour and the Political Economy in Israel*, Oxford, England: Oxford University Press.

Stier, H. and Levine, A. (1998), 'Poor Women in Israel', Conference on *Women and Social Policy*, Tel Aviv University.*

Zameret, H. (1999), *A Profile of the Israeli Woman at the Dawn of the 3rd Millennium*, Tel Aviv: The Israel Institute for Economic and Social Research.*

Zemach, M. (2000), *Survey of Characteristics of Business Women* conducted for the Small and Medium-sized Business Authority in Israel, Tel Aviv.*

Ziv, N. (1999), 'The Disability Law in Israel and the United States: A Comparative Perspective', *Israel Yearbook of Human Rights*, **28**, 171-202, Tel Aviv: Tel Aviv University.

Notes

1   The population of Israel in 2001 was approximately 6, 300,000.
2   Unless otherwise indicated, the statistics are derived from the Central Bureau of Statistics, Labour Force Surveys for 2000-1 and the Census for 1995. I express my appreciation to Jasmine Alkalai for her assistance in analysing the data.
3   In 2000, the government sector employed approximately 25 per cent of the labour force but only about 16 per cent of the total managers.
4   The proportion declined to 34 per cent in 2002 according to the report of the Government-owned Companies authority.
*   Hebrew.

SECTION VI
WOMEN IN MANAGEMENT –
SOUTH AMERICA

Chapter 20

Women in Management in Argentina

Ana Kessler, Haydée Kravetz and Roberto Kertész

Introduction

The situation of women in Argentina with regard to their opportunities for development concerning their position in the workforce and as managers, has improved notably during the last decades, although we cannot yet proclaim a state of genre equality. Traditionally, women's assigned roles were those of mothers, homemakers, child-minders and mistresses. However, in agricultural communities, they worked shoulder to shoulder with their husbands, as well as tending to household and childcare roles. However, with the advent of the industrial revolution during the 19th and first half of the 20th Century, more and more Argentinian women joined the workforce, although this was predominantly blue collar workers.

Furthermore, the middle and upper classes, at least in Argentina and most countries of Latin America, considered women working outside the home and in higher education as 'inappropriate'. According to one of the author's (Kertész, 1981) experience as a psychiatrist and psychotherapist, in the decades between 1960 to 1980, around half of middle- to upper-class women accepted this standpoint, although many of them expressed their frustration, playing the Transactional Analysis 'game' of *If it weren't for you* ... (Berne, 1964) blaming their husbands, who reinforced the *status quo*. Only half of our female clients worked outside their homes in those days. Presently, practically all of them work and/or study in universities, sharing the education and care of their children with their husbands, mothers, nursemaids, or pre- and after-school care programmes. The increasing number of divorces, facilitated by changes in legislation, during the 1980s, added new variables to this setting, with greater degrees of freedom, but also loading extra stress on the separated and/or remarried couples. Due to financial pressures (fewer husbands being able to support their families with a single income) and changes in attitudes towards women's role in society during the second half of the 20th Century, more and more Argentinian women joined the workforce. Nevertheless, we must also consider that the main local immigration came from the south of Italy and the poorer Spanish provinces, dominated for hundreds of years by the Arabs, who left a lasting influence of their values regarding the roles and rights of women.

In Argentine history, the roots of justification for masculine predominance are based on historical and cultural roots, related to the processes of conquering by the Spaniards, intermarriage, colonization and integration of geographic regions. The great economical changes and the sexual revolution had a strong impact on the job market, provoking important modifications in the roles played by men and women compared to previous generations. However, we must take into account that in spite of these changes, the 'glass ceiling' which limits the entrance of women into higher management positions, has not yet disappeared.

To better analyse the situation of women in Argentina, in this chapter we have adopted the 'gender breach' concept, representing the proportional difference between different indicators, corresponding to the sexes, calculated as a quotient between the values assigned to women and men. If it is equal to 1, there is no difference; if it is below 1, the breach is negative for females; then if it is over 1, obviously the breach is positive. This differential regarding the gender breach sets up the Human Development Indicator, which has been developed by the United Nations through the UNPD programmes. Furthermore, the United Nations proposed that this indicator was better than the GNP (Gross National Product).

A comparison made in 1997 between 174 countries showed that Argentina was placed number 39 within the country categorization (which includes those with a high level of human development). There are 45 countries in the top level category and Argentina is included in this context. The other group is composed by 94 countries with medium development, and the last 35 are considered in the lower ranking.

Table 20.1   Analysis of the indicators: Human Development Index (HDI) and Gender Related Development (GRD)

Index	Longevity	Education	Decent level of living
HDI	Life expectation at birth	Adult literacy campaigns Combined matriculation	Adjusted by income per capita in Parity of Acquisitive Power (PAP) in dollars
GRD	Feminine and masculine expectation at birth	Feminine and masculine rate of literacy Feminine and masculine rate of combined matriculation	Adjusted by income per capita in PAP in dollars, based in feminine and masculine participation in income derived from remuneration

Source: United Nations Report on Human Development, 1999

In view of the advancement of worldwide welfare, accompanied by its inequitable distribution over the planet, we consider that this is a valid index which takes also into account the degree of achieved levels of education, life expectancy and participation of the population in income.

On the HD Index, Argentina is among the six countries whose position in the relationship between GRD and HDI is equal to zero, meaning that the participation of women's development is stable. This reveals that the mean achievement regarding human development is equal in proportion. In the report for 1999 produced by the Programme of United Nations for Development (PUND), coordinated by Richard Jolly, the methodology for the formulation of the index was modified, resulting in changes in the categorization of some countries. According to this adjusted and improved measurement, Argentina was still at the same level and showed a positive performance in all the series related to human development (see Table 20.2).

Table 20.2 Measurements in Argentina, 1997

Life expectation at birth	72. 90
Adults literacy rate	96. 50
Gross general matriculation rate	79.00
Real Gross National Product in US$	10,300.00
Index of life expectancy	0.80
Schooling index	0.91
IGP (internal gross product) index	0.77
HDI value	0.827
	(+ 0.800 : High)
GNP –HDI relationship	0.10

Source: United Nations Report on Human Development

Labour force characteristics

When examining the female employment rates by age, illustrated in Table 20.3, the majority of female employment in Argentina is concentrated in the 20-45 year age range, and diminishes after the female retirement age of 60 (this fall is observed in males after 65 years).

However, to interpret the statistic data of Table 20.4, we have to take into account that the census information refers to a period in which the unemployment levels were substantially lower than they are today: they remained at 6 per cent until 1993 and later began to increase, surpassing 20 per cent.

Table 20.3   Distribution of female population according to employment activities and ages

Conditions of economic activity

Age groups	Total	Economically active population			Economically non-active population			
		Total	Employed	Not Employed	Total	Pensioned	Students	Other Situations
Total	100	39.7	36.5	3.2	60.3	14.1	9.7	36.5
14	100	10.5	8.8	1.7	89.5	1.0	74.8	13.7
15-19	100	29.8	23.5	6.2	70.2	1.4	46.8	22.0
20-24	100	52.6	45.2	7.3	47.4	0.9	12.8	33.8
25-29	100	54.5	50.4	4.1	45.5	0.9	3.3	41.3
30-34	100	53.3	50.0	3.3	46.7	1.2	1.71	43.8
35-39	100	53.5	50.6	2.9	46.5	1.6	1.1	43.8
40-44	100	53.7	51.3	2.5	46.3	2.4	1.2	42.7
45-49	100	51.8	49.5	2.3	48.2	4.3	0.7	43.2
50-54	100	45.1	43.0	2.0	54.9	9.2	0.6	45.2
55-59	100	34.4	32.7	1.7	65.6	19.2	0.5	45.9
60-64	100	22.2	21.1	1.1	77.8	37.5	0.5	39.9
65-69	100	14.2	13.4	0.7	85.8	52.3	0.4	33.2
70-74	100	8.9	8.5	0.4	91.1	64.9	0.3	25.9
75 and more	100	4.6	4.4	0.2	95.4	76.3	0.3	18.9

Source: INDEC (National Institute of Statistics and Census), 2000

Table 20.4   Activity and unemployment of the female population by age groups, heads of household, level of occupation and gender breach. National totals, 1991 (over 14 years of age)

Age groups	% Rates of				Gender breaches Rates of	
	Active		Unemployed			
	Males	Females	Males	Females	Active	Unemployed
Total	75.1	39.6	5.3	8.1	0.5	1.5
14-19	42.9	26.1	15.9	20.6	0.6	1.3
20-29	87.8	53.3	6.7	10.8	0.6	1.6
30-39	95.2	53.2	3.0	5.8	0.6	1.9
40-49	93.9	52.7	2.8	4.5	0.6	1.6
50-59	85.9	39.8	3.7	4.7	0.5	1.3
60 and more	38.9	12.8	5.3	4.9	0.3	0.9
Conjugal situation						
Living together	83.7	37.7	3.1	6.2	0.5	2.0
Not living together	63.1	42.6	10.0	10.4	0.7	1.0

Heads of Household

Heads	82.0	45.0	3.1	5.5	0.5	1.8
Not Heads	64.6	38.8	10.3	8.8	0.6	0.9

Degree of education

Primary school, incomplete	69.1	29.0	3.1	11.3	0.5	3.6
Primary school, complete; high school, incomplete	74.3	34.4	4.3	12.1	0.5	2.8
High school, complete and college/university, incomplete	81.7	51.9	7.1	7.6	0.6	1.1
College/university complete	90.8	79.3	3.7	1.4	0.9	0.4

Sources: INDEC 2000: National Census of Population and Housing, 1991

Table 20.5 highlights the comparisons between the distribution of the female working population in 1991 versus 1997. Certainly, during this eight year period, there were substantial increases in the numbers of women entering the majority of the occupational categories. The highest increase in female employment between 1997 and 1991 occurred in self owned businesses (+14.1), followed by public administration (+8.1) and commerce, hotels and restaurants (+6.4), professionals (+5.5), followed by activities with lower growth rates. Interestingly, the participation of women in social and health services diminished by 14.4 per cent during that period despite significant growth in this area, due to the influx of more men taking jobs in this section. Female participation in Primary (−7.7) and Industrial (−3.1) activities was also reduced, and this was primarily as a consequence of the modernization of machinery and equipment.

Table 20.5 Distribution of female working population by categories, 1991 versus 1997

	1991			1997			Differ-ences
	Distribution, %		Females as	Distribution, %		Females as	
	Males	Females	% of all	Males	Females	% of all	
Occupational category						37.9	
Employers	8.7	4.1	20.5	5.9	2.8	22.6	+ 2.1
Employed	60.8	51.5	31.8	70.3	74.9	35.0	+ 3.2
Self-owned business	26.5	16.3	25.3	22.9	20.2	39.4	+ 14.1
Domestic help	0.2	19.8	97.9				
Workers without wages	3.8	8.4	55.0	1.0	2.1	53.7	- 1.3
	100	100		100	100	37.9	
Occupational classification							
Professional	6	5.2	32.9	9.4	9.5	38.4	+ 5.5

Technician	15.9	21.9	43.8	15.8	22.1	46.1	+ 2.3
Blue-collar worker	53.4	31.6	25.1	54.3	27.9	23.9	- 1.2
Unskilled	24.7	41.3	48.7	20.6	40.4	54.5	+ 5.8
Branch of activity						37.9	
Primary	15.0	5.2	16.0	1.4	0.2	8.3	- 7.7
Industrial	21.3	12.8	24.9	25.3	11.5	21.8	- 3.1
Building	10.4	0.4	2.1	12.8	0.4	1.8	- o.3
Commerce, hotels, restaurants	21.9	18.6	31.8	19.2	19.5	38.2	+ 6.4
Transportation, warehouses, communications	7.4	1.2	8.5	11.3	2.5	11.9	+ 3.4
Finance, insurance, real estate	5.5	5.1	34.01	9.7	9.0	36.3	+ 2.3
Public administration and defence	9.0	6.1	27.2	8.0	7.2	35.3	+ 8.1
Education	2.1	14.6	79.3	2.4	14.0	78.0	- 1.3
Social and health services	2.2	8.2	67.4	8.8	16.3	53.0	- 14.4
Domestic help	1.2	24.1	91.4	1.1	19.4	91.4	0
Other	4.0	3.7	33.8				

Sources: INDEC and data of authors

Women pursuing education

Argentina maintains a tradition of predominantly middle class educated women originating from the university reforms of 1918. In Table 20.6 we can see through the gender breach, the increase in women students, especially at the university level, with a final breach of 1.3, surpassing the male presence. By the 1960s, the numbers of women entering university began to increase substantially and by 2002, 52.4 per cent of all students were women. In Tables 20.7 and 20.8 this high female participation is confirmed, as the gender differences surpass the unit, except in rural zones. Moreover, one should note in particular the higher education data, with 1.3 gender breach scores for female participation at the three levels in Table 20.8. More recent surveys have shown that 52.4 per cent of all higher education/university students were female and women now constitute 40 per cent of all management/business degree courses (*La Nación*, 2002).

Table 20.6 **Distribution of women from 25 to 29 years of age, according to highest education level obtained and gender breach. National totals, 1960, 1970, 1980, 1990**

Year		Level of education and gender breach			
	Total	No education	Elementary	High school	College and university
1960	100	8.7	73.5	15.0	2.8
Breach		1.1	1.0	0.9	0.5
1970	100	4.1	65.2	24.6	6.1
Breach		1.1	1.0	1.1	0.7
1980	100	2.8	51.9	31.3	14.0
Breach		1.0	1.0	1.1	1.0
1990	100	1.5	39.4	33.7	25.5
Breach		0.9	0.9	0.9	1.3

Sources: INDEC and National Census of Population and Housing

Table 20.7 **Distribution of female population of 25 years and over, according to the highest education level obtained. Rural/urban and gender breach. National totals, 1991**

	Total	Rural	Urban	Rural/ urban	Gender breach
Total	100 %	100 %	100 %	0.1	1.1
Never attended	4.6	13	3.6	3.6	1.2
Primary, Incomplete	23.0	40.9	21.0	2.0	1.0
Primary, Complete	35.2	33.4	35.4	0.9	1.0
High school, Incomplete	11.0	4.7	11.7	0.4	0.8
High school, Complete	13.7	4.5	14.8	0.3	1.1
College/University, Incomplete	4.3	1.0	4.6	0.2	0.8
College/University Complete	8.3	2.7	8.9	0.3	1.2

Source: INDEC, 1998

Table 20.8   Gender breach in the achievement of higher education by urban and rural areas and in the age group 18-29 years. National totals, 1991

| | Geographical area | | | |
Educational level	Total	Urban	Rural	Age group, 18-29
Complete high school and over	1.1	1.1	1.3	1.3
Complete college	1.0	1.0	1.6	1.3
Complete university	0.7	0.7	0.5	1.3

Source: INDEC 2000
1=feminine presence is equal to masculine; less of 1=lower, over 1= superior

Women in management

Presently, Argentinian women have augmented their inclusion in positions of managerial responsibility and now constitute 28 per cent of all managers (INDEC, 1997). However, the number of women occupying senior executive positions and members of corporate boards of directors, are still a minority, not exceeding 10-15 per cent (according to a verbal survey performed by the authors in 2001). Unfortunately, to date there is not more precise data available.

Argentine history contains names of women who have excelled in many areas and professions, and lately some have also entered the military. During the last decade, women have increasingly joined branches of the army, air force, navy and the police force. However, despite 52.4 per cent of all university students being female (*La Nación*, 2002), only four of the Rectors in the 37 state universities are women, and presently only one in the 51 private ones.

In relation to the position of women in politics, women in Argentina secured the right to vote when Congress sanctioned the Female Vote Law in 1947. The first female representative entered Congress in 1952. However, it was not until the 1990s that women were taken seriously with the promulgation of the Law of Shires which enabled a minimum female participation rate of 30 per cent in the parliament, and seven years later, in the Senate. According to the United Nations in 1996, 5.6 per cent of Ministers were female. Table 20.9 illustrates that the percentage of females in parliamentary posts of the National Legislative Body in 1997 and 1999 has remained quite static with women constituting around 3 per cent of Senators and 28 per cent of Parliamentary Deputies. Nevertheless, the relatively high percentage of women at the latter level in the House of Deputies, places Argentina in third place for this type of category in the democratic world.

Table 20.9 Percentages of females in Parliamentary posts of the National Legislative Body

Benches	Year	Number	% Females
Senators	1997	2	2.9%
	1999	2	2.9%
Delegates (deputies)	1997	73	28.4%
	1999	72	28.0%

Source: National Council of the Woman for 1997 and House of Deputies and Senators for 1999

Woman entrepreneurs

What is evident, is that the number of women in Argentina setting up their own businesses is increasing rapidly. In 1991, 20.5 per cent of all employers were women and this had increased to 22.6 per cent by 1997. Furthermore, during the same period the proportion of women owning their own business increased to 39.4 per cent of all self-owned businesses from 25.3 per cent in 1991 (see Table 20.5).

Regarding micro-firms, presently only 20 per cent reach the second year and 10 per cent the third. Women take 2-3 times longer to initiate businesses, but indications are that they have greater success rates compared to their male counterparts. Unfortunately, to date, there is a scarcity of specific data or research on these Argentinian female entrepreneurs other than these basic statistics. However, there are a number of initiatives aimed at supporting these women. AHEFA (Association of Women in Family Businesses) for example, is a private organization offering advice and training for women who remain relegated in decision-making in firms. In addition, a programme entitled 'PyMe Mujer' (Medium and Small Business-Women), is financed by the InterAmerican Development Bank as part of the OP761 'Women in Development'. It fosters the starting of individual and co-operative businesses, facilitating the financing and training for women over 27 years of age. A Forum of Business Women and Entrepreneurs has also recently been created by Ana Kessler as Secretary of State.

Table 20.10   Distribution of the total female migrant population and index of femininity by country of birth, 1991

Country of birth	Total of migrants	Distribution % Migrant women	Index of femininity
Total	1.615.473 (100.0%)	844.797 (100.0%)	109.6
Italy	20.3	19.8	104.3
Paraguay	15.5	16.6	127.0
Chile	15.1	14.5	100.1
Spain	13.9	14.8	124.9
Bolivia	8.9	8.2	93.2
Uruguay	8.3	8.1	105.1
Brazil	2.1	2.2	129.3
Poland	1.8	1.8	107.1
Peru	1.0	0.8	68.5
Germany	1.0	1.0	112.6
Portugal	0.8	0.7	87.1
Ex Yugoslavia	0.8	0.8	103.9
Rest	10.6	10.8	114.7

Source: INDEC 1999, 1991 National Census

Country legislation supporting women in the workplace

Since The Reform of 1918 which was a paradigmatic model for higher education, there have been a number of legislative changes to attempting to address gender equality. The Federal Law of Education No. 24195, for example, established an educational policy of equal opportunities, rejecting all kinds of discrimination and eliminating any discriminatory stereotype in the teaching materials. Furthermore, The National Constitution of 1994 has had the most legislative impact in relation to equal opportunities and included:

- Maternity laws.
- A Women's Day.
- Antidiscriminatory Law.
- Law No. 24.467/ 95 and its Reform, the No. 25.300/ 01, called Small and Medium Business Statute (i.e. Labour Law Reform).
- Law No. 24.012/91, of Quota in the Legislative Power, showing a clear trend towards the progressive elimination of all forms of discrimination against women in Parliament and includes a 30 per cent quota of female candidates.
- Law No. 23.302/85, a National Law regarding aborigine policies and of support for these communities.

- Law No. 426/84, an Integral Law for aborigines in the Province of Salta. All Argentine provinces have a similar legislation.

Initiatives supporting women in the workforce

As previously mentioned, the initiatives to introduce strategies and policies to promote gender equality in participation and treatment in the workplace, in government and non-government sectors, public and private companies, independent and other professions, currently places Argentina in third place in the democratic world in the Chamber of Deputies and third in the Chamber of Senators.

The 'Tripartite Commission for Equality of Treatment and Opportunities between Males and Females', dependent on the Ministry of Labour, has as its objective the pursuit of the good practice for women in the work force. This has been instigated by the Consultative Forum, composed of a net of non-governmental organizations, distributed in different geographical areas. Its goals also include the implementation of initiatives for aboriginal women in the country.

The Law related to the Female Trade-union Quota, concerning the electoral processes in Trade Unions and Commissions of Collective Negotiations, also proposes a 30 per cent female quota, similar to the Law of Quotas linked to Representatives of the Legislative Power. Moreover, the ISPM (Social and Political Institute of Women) has launched the '50-50 Campaign for Decision Making' for 2005 aiming to exceed the 30 per cent quota for representation of females in the Chamber of Deputies (which is currently 28.1 per cent). Another initiative being pursued involves introducing the Law of Quotas for the Judicial Power.

A final important initiative in Argentina, is supported by the Interamerican Development Bank as part of POLID (Programme of Leadership for Women) and includes the following programmes:

- 'Support Programme for Production – Transformation Process' (816/OC-AR).
- 'Education Reform and Investment Programme' (850/OCAR).
- 'Technical Higher Education Reform Programme' (1060/OC-AR).
- 'Education System Improvement Programme' (1345/OC-AR).
- 'Programme for on-the Job Training' (ATN/MH-6026-AR).
- 'Worker Skill Certification Programme' (ATN/MH-6605-AR).
- 'Training for Retail Commerce' (ATN/ME-6718 AR).

The future

Clearly, the developments in Argentina reviewed in this chapter illustrate that many of the legal, gender, race or religious barriers facing women in the work force in the differing developed areas in this country, have begun to break down to varying degrees. Nevertheless, barriers in relation to cultural attitudes and beliefs towards working women and professional women still persist.

We believe that all future activities must point towards the improvement of education, life expectancy and the equality of opportunity in the workplace. In particular, we strongly support programmes such as those initiated by IDB are some of the most effective due to the energy invested in education, as a means of breaking down gender stereotyping and barriers.

Consequently, we would endorse the following actions:

- To recommend the Law of Quotas for the lists of election to Senators in the Legislative Power.
- To approve the Law of Quotas for the lists of Trade Union Representation.
- To increase the health budget.
- To increase the education budget.

Argentina is in the midst of a severe crisis affecting all areas of growth, but we trust that women will be a fundamental force to overcome these problems and as a consequence, gain the degree of respect from the society that they undoubtedly deserve.

References

Berne, E. (1964), 'Games People Play', New York: Grove Press.

Catalyst (1998), 'Advancing Women in Business', San Francisco: Jossey-Bass.

Driscoll, D. and Goldberg, C.R. (1993), 'Members of the Club: The Coming of Executive Women', New York: The Free Press, Macmillan.

Durrieu, M. (1999), 'Se Dice de Nosotras', *Catálogo*, Buenos Aires.

Estensoro, M.E. (ed.) (1995), 'La Ventaja de Ser Mujer', *Mujeres y Compañía*, Multimedios XX, **1** (1), 24-7, Buenos Aires.

INDEC (1997), National Institute of Statistics and Census.

INDEC (2000), National Institute of Statistics and Census.

Interamerican Development Bank (IDB) (1994), 'La Mujer en el Desarrollo', Washington, D.C.

IDB: La mujer en las Américas (1996), 'Cómo Cerrar la Brecha entre Géneros', Washington, D.C.

Kertész, R. (1981), Advanced Transactional Analysis Seminar, Instituto Privado de Psicología Medica (Ippem), Buenos Aires.

Kertész, R. and Kermsan, B. (1985), 'El Manejo del Stress', *Ippem*, Buenos Aires.

Kertész, R. (1996), 'El Rey León: Lucha por el Poder y la Sucesión en una Empresa Animal', *Empresa Familiar*, **2**, pp. 18-20, Uflo, Buenos Aires.

Kertész, R., Atalaya, C., Kertész, A. and Luege, A. (1996), 'Family Life Script and its Impact on the Business', *Proceedings of the 1995 Family Firm InstituteConference*, pp. 140-5.

Kessler, A. (1997-99), 'Programa PyMe Mujer', Institutional Report, Secretary of Small and Medium Businesses, Buenos Aires.

Kessler, A. (1999), 'Mujeres empresarias', Secretary of Small and Medium Businesses, Buenos Aires.

Kravetz, H. (1998), '*Por* qué Sociedades de Garantía Recíproca', and 'Financiamiento a Pymes', Interamerican Bank of Development publication.

Kravetz, H. (1999), 'Garantías Otorgadas y Préstamos a Emprendimientos de Mujeres', *Foro Hispanamericano de Microempresas*, Mexico.

La Nación Journal (2002), *Report on Universities*, May 11.

McCubbin, H.I. and Figley, Ch.R. (1983), 'Stress and the Family', Vol. I, New York: Brunner & Mazel.

Maslow, A., 'Toward a Psychology of Being', 2nd Edition, New York: D. Van Nostrand.

Rosen, R.J. and Berger, L. (1991), 'The Healthy Company', New York: Jeremy P. Tarcher /Perigee.

Pitchel, V. (1992), 'Mujeres Argentinas', *Planeta*, Buenos Aires.

UNICEF (1999), 'Manual de Entrenamiento en Género', United Nations, Washington.

UNICEF/INDEC (2000), 'Situación de la Mujer Argentina' Ministry of Economy, Argentina, Serie Social Ventura, A. (1996), 'Las que Mandan', *Planeta*, Buenos Aires.

SECTION VII
WOMEN IN MANAGEMENT –
AFRICA

Chapter 21

Women in Management in South Africa

Babita Mathur-Helm

Introduction

Until the early 1990s, South Africa was dominated by apartheid, which discriminated; segmented and segregated its society in many ways, more so in terms of gender and race. However, from 1990 onwards, and especially since 1994, when its new democratic government was elected, signifying the fall of apartheid, a major transformation has occurred in South Africa's political, social and economic environments. Equal opportunity and affirmative action legislation was implemented to redress the past imbalances created by apartheid and as a result issues of women's rights and empowerment, pay equity, and sexual discrimination came to the surface.

The aim of this chapter is to investigate and examine barriers hindering women's entry and advancement in management positions, across racial boundaries in South Africa. The chapter gives an overview of and an insight into the complexities experienced by the women managers' of South Africa by reviewing the factors prevailing across South Africa's various sectors.

Historically South Africa has been a traditional, hierarchical and 'white, male-dominated' society that exercised a bureaucratic and command and control style of management. Confronted with challenges to implement opportunities for its people, the country is determining that its multinational organizations, private and public sectors, rapidly change to meet the global needs. However, the glimpses of the past still appear in South Africa's current business environment and therefore impact on the culture of its multinational organizations (Mathur-Helm, 2002), as well as its public and private sectors.

Labour force characteristics

Women in South Africa, made up 36 per cent of the economically active population in 1985 which increased to 41 per cent of the workforce by 1991 (Erwee, 1994) and decreased to 39.4 per cent by 1996, even though women formed 54 per cent of the South Africa population. Analysing further, women constituted two-thirds of the service sector and more than half of the clerical and sales personnel jobs (Statistics South Africa, 1996). According to Naidoo (1997b) women are over-represented in 'pink-collar' jobs, for example, 96 per cent of registered nurses; 90 per cent of occupational therapists and radiotherapists; 86 per cent of social workers; 79 per cent of hairdressers; 67 per cent of teachers and 96 per cent of domestic workers. In contrast they are under-represented in jobs such as, artisans and apprentices (5.1 per cent); communication and related jobs (5.9 per cent); registered engineers (3.1 per cent); judges and magistrates (9.6 per cent); and metal and engineering industry workers (0.8 per cent) (Naidoo, 1997b). Thus, it is indisputable that if the *status quo* remains, and young women continue to be encouraged towards a 'pink-collar' career, the chances of women reaching the higher-level management positions in South Africa will be very slim and therefore demographically, management in South Africa will continue to be the converse of the demographics of the general South African population.

Some researchers argue that, South Africa's black women are the group, by race and by gender, that are moving upwards most rapidly on the occupational ladder (Prekel, 1995). However, evidence suggests that while they have successfully entered the lower levels of jobs (Naidoo, 1997b), they have not moved up to the higher levels due to cultural and social barriers, therefore their representation in management is lacking. Furthermore, preliminary findings of a 1999 private sector study by the South Africa Commission on Gender Equality reported that, women held fewer than one in four jobs, but most of these jobs were held by 'white women' (Jacobson, 1999). Therefore, according to the distribution of the general population in South Africa (Statistics South Africa, 1996), black people comprise 75 per cent, white people 13 per cent, coloured people 9 per cent and Asian people 3 per cent, and the majority of South African women are black. However, white women occupy 77.6 per cent of managerial, executive and administrative posts (Naidoo, 1997b), while black women occupy only 22.4 per cent of these posts and coloured and Asians hold virtually none.

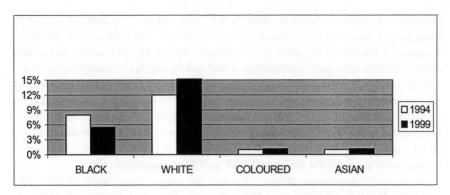

Figure 21.1 Percentage of South African women holding legislators, senior official and senior management positions between 1994-1999

Source: Adapted from Booysen (1999)

Figure 21.2 illustrates that, in 1994, of the total South African population in legislators, senior officials, and senior management positions, women represented only 22 per cent, of which 12 per cent were white, 8 per cent were black, 1 per cent coloured and 1 per cent Asian. In 1999, although women's representation went up to 23 per cent in legislators, senior officials, and senior management positions, coloured and Asian women remained constant at 1 per cent each respectively, while white women increased to 15 per cent, and black women decreased to 6 per cent.

Women pursuing education

While more and more women are entering into employment, companies claim that they lack suitably qualified women to promote to managerial positions (Erwee, 1994). Thus, according to Erasmus (1998) it is imperative to train and develop more women to meet the organizational requirements. Contrary to the rapid rate with which the socio-political environment in South Africa is changing, the rate of change in education, employment and training patterns is quite slow (Erwee, 1994).

While South Africa's women are trying to equip themselves, through education and qualification for workplace requirements, South Africa still has an over-representation of males (especially white males) and an under-representation of females (especially black females) in management as well as in management training programmes (Booysen, 1999). Masculine values and practices, including the 'White Western' values and practices have dominated the South African landscape for decades, and still prevail, allowing very restricted space for females to function effectively. Consequently decisions about women's general education, in-house managerial training curriculum and course content, along with management practices are affected. Similarly, educational achievement, including acquiring a Master of Business Administration degree (MBA) which, has proven quite helpful in advancing women into lower and middle level management (Adler, 1993) has only recently become a prerequisite in South Africa. Indeed, few women who have succeeded into senior executive positions have attained it without having an MBA. Therefore, while an MBA is a primary avenue to management careers, it has proven to be useful to women only for entrance into management positions and/or promotion into middle level management, since criteria for senior management is not reliant solely on MBA qualifications (Adler, 1993).

South African women at present comprise only 10 per cent of the MBA students. Traditionally, South African women have not pursued business or university degrees, due to lack of incentive. Until 1989, the University of Pretoria's Graduate School of Management was the only institution to offer an annual 'Women as Executives' for women managers who were climbing the corporate ladder (Erwee, 1994). But, as in Europe and the USA, a typical MBA student is a white, middle class male; similarly, 'MBA in South Africa is a man's world' (*Sunday Times*, 2001). Thus the type of person attending a school to take an MBA degree has hardly changed at all over the past decade (Bickerstaffe, 1994). Evidence suggests that until 1999, the percentage of women students on MBA programmes in the six South African university business schools averaged not more than 20 per cent of total student numbers, with white women representing approximately 16 per cent and black women approximately 2 per cent. Asians and coloured women made up the other 2 per cent (Booysen, 1999; Strasheim, 1998). However, more recently South Africa's Business Report (2001) states that South African women MBA student numbers have halved to only 10 per cent, while 60 per cent is white male representation, and 30 per cent is represented by black men.

Furthermore, the faculty and administration of business schools remain predominantly white and male (Booysen, 1999). Statistics suggests that the percentage of women on the full-time teaching staff of university business schools in South Africa averages 20 per cent (Booysen, 1999). This under-representation of women in business education and management training not only causes scarcity of female teachers, but also of women mentors and female role models (Booysen, 1999). Thus, due to the greater number of male students and male lecturers in management development in South Africa, the potential management talent pool from which organizations can draw, is also skewed in terms of its representation of the population and gender groups, favouring white males (Booysen, 1999).

Women in management

Recent research indicates that, since 1994, the influx of women into the work force is beginning to result in increasing numbers of women occupying positions of leadership in the country (Booysen, 1999). However, South African women of all races are still disadvantaged and are a wasted resource, and hardly hold any senior positions, especially in the corporate world (Naidoo, 1997a; Erasmus, 1998; Bennett, 1999; Jacobson, 1999). Evidence suggests that 'white males' constitute the decision making power of the private sector and thus dictate the importance placed on issues of development. This raises serious issues of how, when and, indeed if ever gender issues will be addressed (Fischer 1995) thus, making progress in this regard very slow (Mathur-Helm, 2002).

The latest statistics on management indicate that the white community *still* accounts for the largest percentage of management (57 per cent), and is over represented as a population group in comparison with the percentage that it forms of the general population (Booysen, 1999). Furthermore, according to Booysen (1999) white males hold 41 per cent of management positions, while white females hold only 16 per cent, however, the black community represents 27 per cent of management, with black males comprising 20 per cent and black females only 7 per cent, thus indicating that 'white males' are still over-represented in management, while females as a group, especially black females are under-represented (see Figure 21.1).

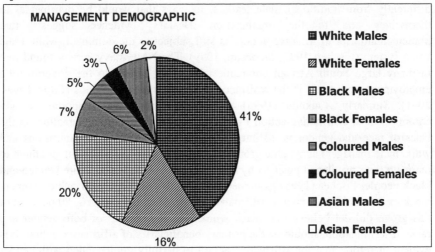

Figure 21.2 Distribution of South Africans in management positions by population groups and gender

Source: Adapted from Booysen (1999)

South African women in management face similar barriers to their progress and advancement, as their female counterparts world-wide, due to the dominant management practices which are, for historical reasons, Western (Binedell, 1992; Khoza, 1994; Christie, 1996; Manning, 1997; Booysen, 1999). Nevertheless, the post-apartheid government has passed a significant number of laws, which touch upon central gender issues (Budlender et al., 1999). However, according to the South African employment equity bill (1997), it is 5000 times more likely for a white male South African (the previously most advantaged group) than for a black female South African (the previously most disadvantaged group) to be in a top management position. Present day South Africa is thus still experiencing not only male dominance, but also white dominance in management (Booysen, 1999).

According to Mathur-Helm (2002) the 'Employment Equity Act, 55' of 1998, was passed, with the intention of encouraging the employment of more women, which resulted in greater equity in the workplace. However, to date, of the 6.2 million employed females, only 1.6 per cent are managers and the rest occupy lower level jobs (South Africa Population Census, 1996). Several individual, organizational and social barriers account in varying degrees for this under-representation of women in senior leadership positions (Govender and Bayat, 1993; Naidoo, 1997a; Erasmus, 1998). Erasmus's (1998) study on South African career women found that, in spite of being talented, educated and committed to their careers, barriers that keep these women from being promoted, relate to the misconceptions that women do not show leadership potential and behave differently from traditional male leaders, in ways that would be detrimental to themselves and to the organization. Besides, evidence suggests that implementation of affirmative action, is still subject to the dominant, white male value system (Fischer, 1995; Jacobson, 1999). The NMG-Levy survey found that in many large South African companies the major barrier to the government's employment equity act, is the resistance to change racial traditions (*Cape Times*, 2001). Similarly, Tsukudu (1996) suggests that it is very important to get commitment to affirmative action from top management, as discrimination on the basis of race and gender is institutionalized in South African organizations and white male managers as an elite group will, if there is no commitment, continue to maintain their privileged position by closing off opportunities to white women and black people. Fischer (1995) examined the attitudes of white men, white women, black men and black women to affirmative action. Her study reports, 80 per cent of this group did not believe that black women, as the victims of both gender and racial discrimination, should be the primary beneficiaries of affirmative action. It is evident therefore, that for affirmative action to be fully implemented with gender in mind, it would take decades for the effects of centuries old inequality and discrimination against women in terms of both gender and race, to be eliminated.

Furthermore, there is a vast difference between the representation of white and black females in management in South Africa. In a comparative study on the status of white and black women in the South African corporate world, Naidoo (1997b) found that white women are over-represented in managerial, executive and administrative posts, in contrast to black women occupying only manufacturing and production services and related jobs. This suggests that inequality within inequality still exists in management positions, between white and black women, with black women still being in the most disadvantaged position (Naidoo, 1997b).

Affirmative action raises expectations among all people of colour and among women as a group. Nevertheless, in South Africa, affirmative action is conceptualized as the advancement of blacks (African origin) only (predominantly black males) and excludes Asians (people of south Asian origin), coloureds (mixed race), and white females. Consequently the development of women may be neglected and seen as subordinate to the development of black people (Fischer, 1995). It is evident that issues of advancement of women have not been afforded the importance that they deserve, since affirmative action has focussed primarily on the need to address racial imbalances within organizations, with gender issues being marginalized or overlooked (Masango, 1994; Fischer, 1995). Thus, the barriers hindering progress and advancement of South Africa's women in management are typically patriarchy, 'white male domination' in management and decision-making, stereotyped gender roles and racism. All this is not only evident in South Africa's corporate world, private and public sectors, but is also prevailing in its education system, legislature and media.

Women in senior executive positions

Despite a report, which found that in South Africa, women's representation is more prevalent in the public sector (Business Report, 2000), the reality is that very few women are in senior level management positions, in either the public or corporate sectors in South Africa (Booysen, 1999; *Sunday Times*, 2001) and still, top executive positions in South African businesses are filled predominantly by white men (*Cape Times*, 2001). A recent annual survey by Deloitte and Touche's Human Capital Corporation reported that white men filled 93 per cent of chief executive positions (*Cape Times*, 2001). A previous study done in 1997 suggested that, 87 per cent of management in the public service (at the level of director and above) were men, and only 13 per cent were women, and over half of the male public sector managers were white (Booysen, 1999; South Africa Central Statistical Service, 1998). Naidoo's (1997b) study on senior positions in the corporate sector found that, within the 657 listed companies, women comprised only 1.3 per cent (49) of the 3773 directors. Of these directors, only 14 women were listed as executive directors, chairpersons, managing directors, and less than 1 per cent of women were listed as board members. An earlier study conducted in 1996, reported only 2 per cent women as board members on South African listed and non-listed companies, and according to *Fair Lady* Magazine (1996) in 1995 women made up a paltry 0.5 per cent of board members. Similarly another survey of listed and non-listed companies found 7 per cent women as non-executive directors (Jacobson, 1999).

According to the Business Report (2000), one major South African organization had the largest representation of women on its board, where 5 out of its 12 board directors were females. However, of the top 300 listed and government owned South African companies, only 37.7 per cent had female board directors and out of the total number of these board directorships, women still represent only 5.8

per cent. Similarly a report on 'Women board directors in South Africa's top private and public companies', commissioned by the CWDI (Corporate Women Directors International), found that 7 of the top 10 companies in South Africa, had no women on their boards at all (Business Report, 2000). The report also found that the board representation by women was more prevalent in the public sector, and that when government organizations were excluded from the listing, the figure dropped to 4.3 per cent representation of women in the boardrooms. Thus suggesting, that although the percentage of employed women in South Africa is rising over time, their representation at higher level positions is still disproportionately low.

Women in politics

Yet, when turning to the South African Parliament, it is clear that it has come a long way. During the apartheid era there was only one woman, Helen Suzman, in the 'whites-only' Parliament, who served from 1953 until the late 1970s. According to Rajab (1999), the current position of women in South African politics is improving rapidly, especially after a quota was introduced to increase the representation of women by 30 per cent, in government, by the year 2000. Furthermore, Rajab (1999) points out that of the 400 Parliamentarians, more than 100 were women, including the youngest cabinet member. The quota has nearly been reached with recent figures being 29.8 per cent representation of women in parliament, as opposed to 27 per cent of their representation after the 1994 elections and 2.7 per cent previous to that (Booysen, 1999).

In present day South Africa, many senior governmental positions are occupied by women, including the following nine ministerial positions: Agriculture and Land Affairs; Communications; Foreign Affairs; Health; Housing; Intelligence; Mineral and Energy Affairs; Public Service and Administration and Public Works. There are also six Deputy Ministers who are women: Arts, Culture, Science and Technology; Environmental Affairs and Tourism; Justice and Constitutional Development; Mineral and Energy Affairs; Defence; and Trade and Industry. The Director-General of the Department of Finance; Speaker and Deputy Speaker of Parliament; and finally, the Chairperson of the Portfolio Committee on Transport are all women, who are, widely considered to be highly talented and effective members of the cabinet (Rajab, 1999). Consequently, it would seem that initiatives aimed at enlarging the pools of talent from which leaders are drawn and more specifically at breaking down socialized patterns (Booysen, 1999; De Villiers, 1998; Patton, 1998; Cullinan, 1998; Naidoo, 1997b), have been implemented. However, according to Van der Westhuizen, (1999) parliament is still patriarchal, since it has a male representation of 70.2 per cent. Similarly, parliament has the unspoken incentive system, which awards 'male' ways of operating, e.g., the male mode is apparent in debates, which makes the parliament a gendered organization (Budlender, et al., 1999).

Women entrepreneurs

The results of a study on expatriate women managers in South Africa's multi-national corporations (Mathur-Helm, 2002) indicated that, South African culture does not recognize its professional women as 'Focussed Business Women', but rather encourages and glorifies the image of its women managers in their traditional roles. Thus suggesting, that those qualities which, make women 'acceptable' in traditional terms can undermine their self-confidence and make them unable to be assertive in ways needed to succeed in a managerial career (Erwee, 1994). Moreover, due to the implementation of equal opportunity legislation and affirmative action, more women are now entering the workforce and are attaining management positions (Booysen, 1999). However, more women are also considering non-corporate career paths, by pursuing other opportunities for self-development, such as entrepreneurship (Erwee, 1994). Research indicates that in 1984, women ran 80 per cent of small businesses owned by black people (Schomer, 1983; Erwee, 1994). According to Erwee, (1994) in 1990 the Small Business Development Corporation (SBDC) estimated that 25 per cent of its clients were women. Evidence suggests that more black women are running their own businesses and Asian women are working in their family businesses (Erwee, 1994). Furthermore, according to a previous study, South African women entrepreneurs are creating jobs for others as well (Erwee, 1994). They employ their family members, neighbours and friends to help them run the business. Currently, an increasing number of women in cities, townships and rural villages are taking initiatives to advance their work life by running their own enterprise/small businesses.

Country legislation supporting women in the workforce

Women have become legal equals in the workplace during the past few years (Erwee, 1994). The South African government has passed a number of laws, touching upon 'Central Gender Issues' - the 'Liberation of Abortion Act 1996', the 'Customary Marriage Act 1998' and the 'Domestic Violence Act 1998', the 'Maternity Provisions and Breast-feeding Code 1997', 'Basic Conditions of Employment Act 1996' and the 'Sexual Harassment Code in the Labor Relations Act 1996' (Haffajee, 1998). Current day South Africa considers gender equality as one of the core issues in building democracy for post apartheid South Africa (Budlender et al., 1999), expecting that democracy will create greater opportunities for women to participate in policy and decision making. The socio-economic profile of the female workforce shows that implementation of affirmative action and employment equity legislation has brought women to the forefront of the work environment. While women who have benefited from it are primarily those in government and legislative jobs, barriers continue to persist for South Africa's women in the private and corporate sectors in the form of recruitment and placement practices, salary, promotions and workplace treatment.

Erwee (1994) suggests that until 1988, South African women of all races fared reasonably well, in comparison to their male counterparts in supervisory and departmental positions, confirming that pay parity existed between women and men at all levels, but that the problem of achieving promotion into senior management and thus receiving the higher salaries, remained difficult. Presently in South Africa, women are not only under-represented in senior management positions, but there also exists a wage gap between men and women with the same education, training and credentials (Booysen, 1999).

Although, company's training policies, reward structures, and benefits (Erwee, 1994), determine growth and advancement of women into senior management positions, in the present day South Africa, women's under-representation in management training programmes is still continuing, as most South African companies still do not regard further training for women as necessary. Evidence suggests that, until 1982-1984, South African companies provided women with inadequate career planning, insufficient access to training programmes, and few promotional opportunities (Erwee, 1994). A survey of career development practice of 58 manufacturing, financial, and consulting companies found that only 34 per cent of the companies offered supervisory training, and fewer than that provided career management programmes for women (Erwee, 1994). A recent NMG-Levy survey of 8,250 Equity Reports found that 91 per cent of promotions in top and senior management positions in South Africa went to white managers, out of which only 17 per cent were women (*Cape Times*, 2001). Moreover, since racial issues in South Africa overshadow gender issues, affirmative action does not recognize women's empowerment training as an important issue. Hence, beneficiaries of 'black advancement' are primarily black men. Besides, gender itself is racially segmented, thus marginalizing all other forms of discriminations. Consequently, a chasm has been forged between white and non-white females, which is preventing them from uniting and acknowledging the existence of gender bias, which is common to both (Mathur-Helm, 2002). Furthermore, according to Mathur-Helm (2002), South African white females are more likely to side with their male counterparts and remain rather oblivious to gender discrimination, which is often raised by 'non-white' females. If gender discrimination is within the non-white community only, it is recognized as a 'non-white' domestic issue that is non-work related. Similarly, Booysen (1999) indicates that in the female management group, white females outnumber black females, which makes white females the second most over-represented group in management. Thus, black women managers in particular face greater hardships (Erwee, 1994) in South Africa with the extended family system and their traditional lifestyle, as compared to white women counterparts who have access both to relatively more crèches and to the possibility of employing black domestic workers (Erwee, 1994).

However, it is assumed that with more and more women entering politics and government organizations in the country, there is a hope that it will increase the economic and social well being of women. According to Budlender et al., *(*1999) women in parliament can influence the rules, by ensuring that structures and processes are less hierarchical and more participatory. Evidence suggests that the USA and other legislatures with higher proportions of women pass more laws benefiting children and dealing with women and families. Similarly, in Scandinavian countries increased representation of women has led to the introduction of women friendly social policies, indicating that having women in the parliament increases sensitivity to gender issues (Budlender, et al., 1999). To date, South Africa's women parliamentarians, have advocated for and managed to accrue visible dividends on issues such as reproductive health, nutrition, equality in education and in employment, child care and related policies (Budlender et al., 1999), which would otherwise have probably remained dormant.

Initiatives supporting women in the workforce

Historically, South Africa had no incentives to promote the job prospects of its women. Presently, South Africa's government has taken initiatives to support the advancement of women, including, a National Women's Empowerment Policy, the signing of a number of United Nations Conventions on Women, the Joint Standing Committee on the Improvement of the Quality of Life and Status of Women, and the Commission on Gender Equality (Booysen, 1999).

Not many studies have so far examined the ways in which management and executive jobs are advertised. The broadcasting and print media industry of South Africa is bringing mass awareness about the importance of valuing and utilizing the talents and capabilities of women, as well as the barriers they face to achieve success and advancement in their jobs, however, it is amazing the way in which the media advertises top executive and management positions. Advertisements for such positions persistently ask for those managerial traits, which are embedded in male styles and practices such as assertiveness and competitiveness, in contrast to recognizing female traits. Similarly, in most countries, job advertisements for top management positions in private sectors, imply the male style of management. For example, in Germany, 95 per cent of notices advertising top management positions in the private sector use the masculine noun form (Adler, 1993). Correspondingly, the *Fortune* Magazine (1990) suggests to women wanting to succeed in the workplace: 'Look like a lady; act like a man; work like a dog' (Booysen, 1999; Erwee, 1994; Govender and Bayat, 1993). Women applicants are naturally expected to learn, adopt and imitate the traits of effective white male managers (Booysen 1999), to succeed in management and top executive jobs. However, research indicates that, women tend to rely on co-operation to achieve goals and adopt an indirect style of communication (Tung, 1997). Furthermore, several studies have emphasized the emergence and the worth of feminine values and style in leadership and management (Booysen, 1999; Erasmus, 1998; Lawrence, 1998; Naidoo, 1997b; Rosener, 1995; Erwee, 1994). These studies suggest that worldwide and in South Africa, a second wave of women are moving into top management by adopting and drawing from the styles and traits that come naturally to them, by being interactive, supportive, collaborative, flexible and participative, that appear to be particularly effective in today's fast changing global environment (Rosener, 1995).

The future

The most important point to emerge from the evidence presented in this chapter, is that in South Africa, the marginalization of women's empowerment and gender equality persists. It seems that race will continue to remain the focus of equality, thus overlooking the need for gender equality. The future of South African women therefore remains uncertain.

With the change in the current emerging global climate, organizational practices in South Africa are struggling to change from being rigid, traditional and hierarchical, towards being more flexible and transparent. Private companies and corporations have started implementing employment equity and affirmative action policies, but barriers still persist, as men continue to resist enlarging the number of female executives.

Regardless of the new appreciation for the interactive style that women are equipped with and the increasing emphasis on the importance of human resource utilization (Rosener, 1995). South African organizations have yet to discover the talents and skills that women bring to management such as, resilience, ability to share power and information by being participative and interactive, ability to motivate without being aggressive and flexible to change. By realizing this, South African organizations will be fostering and utilizing their women workforce effectively. This will not only fulfil the structures and cultures of the new global work organizations, but will also allow them to transform towards decentralized and flexible systems by being at the forefront of workforce empowerment through information sharing, knowledge and skills and freedom to make decisions.

However, one can conclude that South African women in management irrespective of race, are becoming more aware of their work and personal lives, consequently their work attitudes and expectations are changing. As they are becoming aware of the global trends, they are learning to equip themselves with knowledge, skills and capabilities required to be successful in the global corporate world.

References

Adler, N.J. (1993a), 'Women Managers in a global economy', *HR Magazine*, **38**, 52-55.

Adler, N.J. (1993b), 'Competitive Frontiers: women managers in the triad', *International Studies of Management and Organization*, **23**, 3-23.

Bennett, J. (1999), 'How South Africa's leaders fit the cloth they helped cut', *Sunday Business Times*, 7 June.

Bickerstaffe, G. (1994), 'Which MBA? A Critical Guide to the World's Best' (6th edition), Menlo Park, CA: Addison-Wesley.

Binedell, N. (1992), 'New Approaches', *People Dynamics*, **10** (3), 1-11.

Booysen, L. (1999), 'A review of challenges facing black and white women managers in South Africa', *South African Business Review*, **13** (2), 15-26.

Budlender, D., Goldman, T., Samuels, T., Pigou, P. and Valji, N. (1999), 'Participation of Women in the Legislative Process', European Union Parliamentary Support, European Commission, South Africa, CT.

Cape Times (2001), 'More whites promoted', 13 November.

Christie, P. (1996), Stories from an Afman(ager)!, Pretoria: Sigma Press.

Cullinan, K. (1998), 'All new laws will pass through a "gender lens"', *Sunday Independent*, 9 August.

Davidson, M.J. (1997), 'Occupational Stress and the Black women managers', *Business and Contemporary world*, **9** (1), 229-247.

Davidson, M.J and Cooper, C.L. (1993), *European Women in Business and Management*, Paul Chapman, London.

De Villiers, C. (1998), 'Letter received on gender statistics', Cape Town Parliament, South Africa.

Erasmus, B. (1998), 'Women Power: aspects of working life in the late 1990s', *Management Today*, 25-28 June.

Erwee, R. (1994), 'South African Women: Changing career patterns', in Adler, N.J. and Izraeli, D.N. (eds), *Competitive Frontiers*, Cambridge, MA: Blackwell, pp. 325-342.

Fielden, S.L. and Davidson, M.J. (1996), 'Sources of Stress in Unemployed Female Managers - a pilot study', *International Review of Women and Leadership*, **2** (2), 73-97.

Fischer, S. (1995), 'Placing women on the affirmative action agenda', *People Dynamics*, **13** (5), 23-25.

Govender, D. and Bayat, S. (1993), 'Leadership Styles: The Gender Issues', *Journal of Industrial and Social Relations*, **13** (314), 139-144.

Haffajee, F. (1999), 'Who will cook for the women MP's', *Mail and Guardian*, 25 February.

Headbush, B. (2000), 'Women have only 5.8 per cent of board positions', Business Report, 6 October.

Izraeli, D.N. and Adler, N.J. (1994), 'Competitive Frontiers: Women Managers in a Global Economy', in Adler, N.J. and Israeli, D.N. (eds), *Competitive Frontiers: Women Managers in a Global Economy*, Cambridge, MA: Blackwell, pp. 3-21.

Jacobson, D. (1999), 'Women still on the road to nowhere', *Sunday Business Times*, 16 May.

Khoza, R. (1994), 'The need for an Afrocentric Management approach', in Christie, P. Lassem, R. and Mbigi, L. (eds), *African Management: Philosophies, Concepts and Applications*, Pretoria: Sigma Press, pp.117-124.

Lawrence, M.J. (1998), 'Gender and Leadership', Unpublished manuscript.

Manning, T. (1997), 'Radical Strategy: How South African Companies can win against Global Competition', Sandton: Zebra Press.

Masango, S. (1994), 'Black Economic Empowerment: Making much business sense', *Journal of Human Resource Management*, **10** (3), 12-13.

Mathur-Helm, B. (2002), 'Expatriate Women Managers: At the Crossroads of Success, Challenges and Career Goals', *Women in Management Review*, **17** (1), 18-28.

Naidoo, G. (1997a), 'Women must assert themselves in organizations that disregard them in formal structure', *People Dynamics*, **15** (2), 20-27.

Naidoo, G. (1997b), 'Empowerment of women in the corporate world', *People Dynamics*, **15** (5), 30-35.

Patton, C. (1998), 'Prejudices in the corridors of power: A woman's work is still not done in Parliament', *Sunday Times*, 2 August.

Prekel, T. (1995), 'Success Stories: Black Women Managers in South Africa', Workshop presentation at European Women Management Developing Network, Annual Conference, Philadelphia.

Rajab, D. (1999), Devi's Diary, 'Identity and culture of the rainbow nation: Women still in the corporate backscat', 1996, *Fair Lady*, 6 March.

Rosener, J.B.(1995), *America's Competitive Secret: Women Managers*, New York: Oxford University Press.

Schomer, H. (1983), 'South Africa: Beyond Fair Employment', *Harvard Business Review*, (June), 145-156.

Statistics South Africa (1996), South African Population Census.

Strasheim, C. (1998), 'Product and Service Quality in Management Education', unpublished MBA thesis, University of the Witwaterstrand Business School, South Africa..

Sunday Business Times (2001), 'It's a man's world', Survey: Universities and Business Schools, 21 October.

Thiel, G. (2001), 'Brain drain of South Africa executives could "devastate economy"', *Cape Times*, 15 August.

Tsukudu, T. (1996), 'Mentoring for career advancement in South Africa', *People Dynamics*, **14** (3), 13-18.

Tung, R.L. (1997), 'Canadian Expatriates in Asia-Pacific: An Analysis of their Attitudes toward and experience in International Assignments', Paper presented at the Society for Industrial and Organizational Psychology, Orlando, FL.

Van der Westhuizen, C. (1999), 'Battle of the Women MP's is not Easy', Naweek-Beeld, 17 June.

Van Wyk, M.W. (1998), 'A critical analysis of some popular objections to affirmative action', *SBL Review*, **2** (1), 1-8.

Index